THE GLORIOUS
REVOLUTION

THE GLORIOUS REVOLUTION

1688: Britain's Fight for Liberty

EDWARD VALLANCE

PEGASUS BOOKS
NEW YORK

THE GLORIOUS REVOLUTION

Pegasus Books LLC
45 Wall Street, Suite 1021
New York, NY 10005

First Pegasus Books edition 2008

Library of Congress Cataloging-in-Publication Data is available.

ISBN: 978-1-933648-24-8

10 9 8 7 8 6 5 4 3 2 1

Printed in the United States of America
Distributed by W. W. Norton & Company, Inc.

For Mum and Dad

CONTENTS

THE 'QUIET' REVOLUTION

[The Glorious Revolution] established the tradition that political change should be sought and achieved through Parliament. It was this which saved us from the violent revolutions which shook our continental neighbours and made the revolution of 1688 the first step on the road, which, through the successive Reform Acts, led to the establishment of universal suffrage and full parliamentary democracy.

MARGARET THATCHER[1]

The Glorious Revolution brought into power, along with William of Orange, the landlord and capitalist appropriators of surplus value. They inaugurated the new era by practising on a colossal scale thefts of State lands, thefts that had hitherto been managed more modestly. These estates were given away, sold at a ridiculous figure or even annexed to private estates by direct seizure. All this happened without the slightest observation of legal etiquette . . . The bourgeois capitalists favoured the operation with the view, among others, to promoting free trade in land, to extending the domain of modern agriculture on the large farm system, and to increasing their supply of agricultural proletarians ready to hand. Besides the new landed aristocracy was the natural ally of the new bankocracy, of the new-hatched *haute finance* and of the large manufacturer, then depending on protective duties.

KARL MARX[2]

O n 30 June 1688 seven English peers, opposed to the pro-Catholic policies of the reigning King James II, wrote to the Dutch Stadtholder, the Protestant William, Prince of Orange, requesting his assistance.[3] On 5 November 1688 William landed with a sizeable army and began a march upon London. James went out to meet him with a numerically larger force, but lost his nerve for the battle, partly as a result of defections to the other side from his officer ranks. Fearing for his own and his family's safety, James made an attempt to flee the country on 11 December but was captured. However, on the 22nd the King succeeded in escaping to France. With the throne vacant and unrest in the city, the government was temporarily placed in the hands of the Prince of Orange and a convention of peers and MPs was summoned to decide how to settle the kingdom. On 13 February 1689 William and his English wife Mary, the Protestant daughter of James II, were crowned joint monarchs, as well as being tendered a document called the 'Declaration of Rights' which listed the country's grievances against its former king. These events, which came to be known as the 'Glorious Revolution', form the subject of this book.

There was a large amount of common ground between Margaret Thatcher and Karl Marx in terms of their interpretation of the Revolution of 1688. The two agreed that this was not a popular revolution, but an event orchestrated by the English ruling class, through Parliament. They concurred in seeing 1688 as essentially bloodless, involving no violent uprisings, and both believed that the accession to the throne of William and Mary laid the foundations for Britain's rise to greatness as a commercial and imperial power in the eighteenth and nineteenth centuries. Above all, they were united in considering the events of 1688–9 as not really being revolutionary at all. For Thatcher, indebted to the ideas of eighteenth- and nineteenth-century Whig historians, the 'Glorious Revolution' marked the beginning of a 'tradition', the first step on the long *parliamentary* road by which Britain became a mass democracy. For Marx 1688 represented only the confirmation of an earlier revolution, the civil wars of the 1640s which had established the ascendancy of the emerging bourgeoisie.

The attitudes of Marx and Thatcher, from the late nineteenth and the late twentieth century respectively, reflected a wider public consensus about the 'unrevolutionary' nature of the Glorious Revolution. Thatcher's comments were made in a House of Commons debate about sending a humble address to the Queen celebrating the tercentenary of the events of 1688–9. These had, the address stated, 'established those constitutional freedoms under law which Your Majesty's Parliament and people have continued to enjoy for three hundred years'.[4] Conservative MPs, such as Sir Bernard Braine, eulogised over the fact that the Glorious Revolution had established parliamentary government and opened the way for 'the expansion of commerce, the extension of influence overseas, the building of empire and later that truly remarkable and peaceful transition from empire to a free Commonwealth'.[5]

The leader of the Labour opposition, Neil Kinnock, countered Thatcher's opening salvo by suggesting that the revolution had really been a 'fudge' and 'compromise' between Whigs and Tories designed to avoid a 'second revolutionary civil war'. The actions of the Prince of Orange were wholly motivated by self-interest reflecting a level of 'Dutch opportunism not now seen outside the realms of the European Nations Cup' (a reference to the Netherlands football team's trouncing of England in the tournament earlier that year – a trophy which the Dutch went on to win). However, despite the cynicism that Kinnock saw as motivating the actions of most of those involved in the events of 1688, he concurred with Thatcher (along with the historians Lord Macaulay, G. M. Trevelyan, A. J. P. Taylor and Christopher Hill) in seeing the revolution, in Taylor's words, as 'the foundation of our liberty'.[6]

Kinnock, along with other Labour frontbenchers, went on to abstain from voting on the motion, but a significant group on the left wing of the party voted against submitting the address to the Queen. The former cabinet minister Tony Benn complained that what happened in 1688 was not a revolution but a 'plot by some people . . . to replace a Catholic king with another king more acceptable to those who organised the plot'. Neither was it bloodless given the repression in Ireland of the supporters of James II. It certainly did not herald, Benn said, 'the birth of our democratic rights', the House of Commons representing only the richest 2 per cent of the population and excluding 'working people, or middle-class people and . . . women'. He begged members to vote against the address 'or, if they cannot do that, to abstain, so that at least we do not have to tell children that democracy had nothing to do with the franchise; it was all because William of Orange had to give an assurance to justify the fact that he landed an army in Torbay and took over, in order to repress the Catholics and the Irish'.[7]

The Liverpool Walton MP and former communist Eric Heffer (who had stormed off the Labour conference stage in response to Kinnock's attacks on Liverpool's Militant-led city council), echoed Benn's comments. Heffer stated that 1688 was 'neither glorious nor a revolution'. This was because the 'real revolution had already taken place when, the day after the king's head was cut off in 1649, the House of Lords was abolished'.[8] Jeremy Corbyn, MP for Islington North, paraphrased Marx in stating that the accession of William and Mary effectively guaranteed 'the powers of the landowning classes as well as bringing them the Protestant religion and the discrimination against Catholics that followed.' Adopting an increasingly strident tone, Corbyn alleged that the 'so-called glorious revolution of 1688 paved the way for the processes of imperialism and colonialism. Implicit in the wording of the Bill of Rights is the domination of colonies throughout the world and all the disgusting and degrading events that followed from that, such as slavery and the domination of subject peoples.'[9] (Corbyn was right to view the Glorious Revolution as a significant chapter in the growth of both the British Empire and the role of slave labour within it, but he was on much shakier ground in his reading of the Bill of Rights.) Bob Cryer, MP for Bradford South, complained that the motion had suggested that 'some sort of millennium was established [in 1688] and that our people have enjoyed constitutional freedoms under law for 300 years'. This was 'patently offensive' when the lives of those workers who 'lost limbs and lives in the factories during the industrial revolution' and whose 'average life expectation was less than 30 years' were recalled.[10]

Beneath the partisan rhetoric, this debate displayed the consensus that existed between those poles apart on the political spectrum over the events of 1688–9. Conservatives like Thatcher applauded the Glorious Revolution because it was a revolution by Parliament, not the people. Left-wingers dismissed its historical significance for exactly the same reason (preferring 1649 instead). For Tories, the lack of popular agitation had saved Britain from experiencing the anarchy and terror of the French revolution. For socialists, this represented no revolution at all, but merely a putsch by the political and financial elite in order to consolidate the establishment's power. Sir Bernard Braine and Jeremy Corbyn could agree that the Glorious Revolution was a turning point in Britain's history as a colonial power, but while the Tory Braine saw the birth of empire (with the happy ending of the commonwealth) as a cause for celebration, the anti-imperialist Corbyn viewed it as the beginning of a shameful and reprehensible epoch in our national history.

The debate on this tercentenary address, with its surprisingly literate references to historians such as Trevelyan, Hill and E. P. Thompson, rested upon a broad agreement among historians of a variety of ideological and methodological hues about the Glorious

Revolution. This historiographical consensus had been effectively established by the late eighteenth century. The early eighteenth-century debate on the subject was dominated by the issue of what had actually happened in 1688: had James effectively abdicated the throne by fleeing the kingdom or had he broken an original contract with the people and forfeited his crown? Whigs, if not endorsing the radical, natural-rights-based theories of the philosopher John Locke, argued that James had broken the trust invested in him by the people, by attacking the subject's liberties, property and religion, and the people had consequently been absolved from their duty of allegiance to the King. However, unlike Locke's *Two Treatises of Government*, most pamphlets utilising contract theory issued after 1688 tended to locate this agreement in England's 'ancient constitution', its supposed repository of Anglo-Saxon customary laws that guaranteed the rights and privileges of the people and Parliament, making it a restorative revolution rather than a progressive one.

The Revolution settlement, in England at least, consciously fudged the issue of whether James had broken his original contract with the people and instead opted for stating that he had 'abdicated' by fleeing the kingdom and thereby left the throne vacant. This version of events was designed to satisfy Tory opinion and avoid a clear breach with their core beliefs of non-resistance and passive obedience, just as the institution of a joint monarchy was meant to provide wriggle-room for Tories attached to the principle of indefeasible hereditary right. Like moderate Whigs, conformist Tory opinion agreed that the Revolution had been made to defend the 'ancient constitution' but saw this as embodying the values of loyalty to lawfully (and therefore divinely) constituted authority. Under Queen Anne, Tory writers became increasingly vigorous in condemning the notion that any resistance had been offered to James II in 1688. The Anglican minister and Tory polemicist Henry Sacheverell put forward this position in the starkest and most controversial terms in a sermon delivered on the auspicious date of 5 November 1709. He stated that they were the greatest enemies of the Revolution and 'his late Majesty, and the most ungrateful for the deliverance, who endeavour to cast such black, and odious colours upon both. How often must they be told, that the King himself solemnly disclaim'd the least imputation of resistance in his Declaration; and that the Parliament declar'd, that they set the crown on his head, upon no other title, but that of the vacancy of the throne?'[11]

Sacheverell's sermon, and works supporting it from other Tory propagandists, appeared to threaten both the Whigs' political revival since 1688 and, with its attacks on the Toleration Act, the concessions won for dissenters as a result of the Revolution settlement. Such an assault could not go unanswered, and Whig writers and politicians upheld the right of resistance. However, now as a party of government, they did so with a number of reservations about the highly exceptional circumstances which made that exercise of resistance permissible. Robert Walpole argued that resistance to monarchical authority 'ought never to be thought of, but when an utter subversion of the laws of the realm threaten the whole frame of a constitution, and no redress can otherwise be hoped for'.[12] Only one of the Whig managers of the charges against Sacheverell, Nicholas Lechmere, actually made any mention of a contract between the crown and the people. The rhetorical weakness of this position, in that it actually seemed to confirm much of Sacheverell's own arguments about the general illegality of resistance, was picked up on by Simon Harcourt, one of his defenders. By reinterpreting the supreme power as constituting King, Lords and Commons, and not just the monarch alone, Harcourt was able to argue that Sacheverell was correct to suggest that in 1688 there had been no resistance of public authority. Sacheverell was nonetheless found guilty, but his sentence was so light that it was generally viewed as a victory for the Tory party. The electorate appeared to agree with Harcourt and Sacheverell and delivered the Tories a healthy majority in the new Parliament.

The Jacobite rebellion of 1715, and the association of the Tory party with it, put an end to the party's revival in fortunes in the last years of the reign of Queen Anne. Instead, it ushered in the long rule of a Whig oligarchy, institutionalised via the Septennial Act, which effectively neutered the Revolution settlement's commitment to frequent elections. For the government Whigs, advocating Revolution principles of active resistance and contractual government now looked like little more than an invitation to Jacobite insurrection. The supporters of Walpole and the 'Robinocracy' (as the ruling clique was called by its 'Patriot' opponents) now contended that those who talked up the right of resistance were as much enemies to the constitution as those that had sought to increase the royal prerogative beyond its legal bounds. Whig writers still maintained that the Revolution had preserved England's 'ancient constitution' from the absolutist designs of James II, but this had not been achieved by an act of public resistance to the monarch, but through the cowardly flight of the King in the wake of the providential arrival of William of Orange. The English Parliament, meanwhile, had acted quickly to avoid a descent into anarchy and mob rule. It was in the speedy restoration of political and social stability, rather than in any affirmation of rights of resistance, that the Revolution's glory lay.

The debate over the Revolution continued to undergo various permutations throughout the eighteenth century. The one-time Tory Secretary of State and former Jacobite Henry St John, 1st Viscount Bolingbroke, in seeking to create a new country alliance against the Whig ministry in the 1730s, came up with a new version of the events of 1688. Bolingbroke's interpretation followed that of the establishment Whigs in seeing the Glorious Revolution as preserving the 'ancient constitution', rather than in ushering in new governmental forms. However, Bolingbroke differed from Walpole's supporters in stressing (quite correctly) the extent to which the Revolution was a bipartisan achievement. In his words, 'The revolution was a fire, which purged off the dross of both parties; and the dross being purged off, they appeared to be the same metal, and answered the same standard.'[13] It was now necessary, he argued, for Tories and non-government Whigs to join forces again, to resist the encroachment on English liberties of a state which had undergone exponential growth since the 1690s. In response, Walpole and his allies shifted tack by rejecting the traditional Whig interpretation of the Revolution, now appropriated by Bolingbroke, that it was effected to defend the 'ancient constitution' and instead suggested that before 1688 the English people had frequently lived under arbitrary rule. It was the Glorious Revolution which was the founding moment of a new epoch of freedom for the English. In the words of the *London Journal*, 'our Modern Constitution is infinitely better than the Ancient Constitution: and that New England, or England since the Revolution, is vastly preferable to Old England, take it in any point of time, from the Saxons down to that glorious period'.[14]

The interpretation of the Revolution as a sort of constitutional year zero was persuasive. A minority of radical Whigs, such as Catherine Macaulay, effectively conceded the conservative interpretation of 1688 by now pointing to the shortcomings of the Revolution, particularly as regards its limited impact on political representation. However, the idea of the Revolution as a break from England's constitutional past proved problematic towards the end of the century, as far more radical revolutionary movements emerged, first in the American colonies and then in France. In this cauldron of international political upheaval, it seemed for moderates and conservatives wiser to stress the continuity of 1688, rather than its novelty.

What emerged, most influentially in the writings of Edmund Burke, was a counter-revolutionary revolution, an interpretation which reaffirmed the importance of 1688 in preserving the 'ancient constitution', one which had never endorsed giving resistance to public authority. This constitution was not shaped by sudden or abrupt upheavals, like that experienced in America or the one looming in France, but rather, like the action of water on rock, was moulded by subtle, slow and almost imperceptible changes. The Glorious Revolution, in Burke's vision, had seen no violent tumult, but only a 'small and temporary deviation from the strict order of a regular hereditary succession'. The revolutionaries, he argued, 'regenerated the deficient part of the old constitution through the parts which were not impaired. They kept these old parts exactly as they were, that the part recovered might be suited to them. They acted by the ancient organised states in the shape of their old organisation, and not by the organic *moleculae* of a disbanded people.'[15]

Moreover, it was a revolution effected by the English political elite in Parliament, not through the invocation of popular sovereignty. George Chalmers, writing in 1796, stated that he considered the

> *Revolution* as *glorious*; not because much was done; but because little was done; because none of the *old foundations* of our government were weakened, and none of the land-marks of the law were removed ... because it was achieved by the good sense of Englishmen; because the Parliament sat quietly and voted independently, what necessity demanded, and wisdom approved; because, when a mob presumed to interpose with premature tumult, King William signified to the mobbish chiefs, that he would not accept a sceptre from such mean hands.[16]

Burke's radical opponents, most notably Thomas Paine, were not interested in challenging his version of history. Instead, Paine and others began to argue that the past was not a suitable guide to the present generation in their political difficulties; indeed, they must free themselves from the weight of history and make their world anew:

Every age must be free to act for itself, *in all cases,* as the ages and generations which preceded it. The vanity and presumption of governing beyond the grave, is the most ridiculous and insolent of all tyrannies . . . The parliament or the people of 1688, or of any other period, has no more right to dispose of the people of the present day, or to bind or control them in *any shape whatever,* than the parliament or the people of the present day have to dispose of, bind or control those who are to live a hundred or a thousand years hence.[17]

With radicals implicitly conceding the conservative interpretation of the Revolution most ably articulated by Burke, the remembrance of 1688 ceased to arouse English political passions to the same degree it had previously. *The Times* reported that the centenary of the Glorious Revolution was celebrated at King's Lynn on 17 November 1788 at the town hall

by a numerous and respectable party of ladies and gentlemen of this place and neighbourhood; a subscription was raised for that purpose, and the gentlemen who were appointed to conduct the entertainment, displayed their taste and abilities in the most elegant and sumptuous manner. We are happy to add on this occasion, that all party animosity and political differences seemed to be entirely forgotten, and everyone used a laudable emulation to commemorate the glorious preservation of our civil and religious liberties. The only anxiety which seemed to dwell on the minds of the company was a heart-felt concern for the dangerous indisposition under which our most gracious Sovereign now labours [a reference to George III's mental illness].[18]

This view of the Revolution as a sensible, bipartisan affair, ensuring parliamentary government and creating a constitutional monarchy, became a staple of the English history textbook from the early nineteenth century up to the middle of the twentieth century. Edward Baldwin's *The History of England for the Use of*

Schools (1840) stated that the Revolution constituted 'the final settlement of the government of England'. It was the culmination of
the struggle 'between power and liberty' under the Stuarts.[19] Mrs
Cyril Ransome's *Elementary History of England* (1897) instructed
the reader that the Revolution marked 'the beginning of a new
period in English history. Since that date no one has been able to
pretend that the kings of England reign by any other than a
Parliamentary title, or that Parliament is not the supreme authority in the government of the country.'[20]

    School histories downplayed any military elements in this rev-
olution. Bertha Meriton Gardiner, the wife of the great Whig
historian of the civil wars Samuel Rawson Gardiner, wrote that
'William landed at Torbay in November, 1688, with a small army
of Dutch and English troops', thereby turning what was actually
an armada into a mere lifeguard for the Prince of Orange.[21] There
was, the textbooks assured children, virtually no loss of life as a
result of William's landing. Ross's *Outlines of English History for
Junior Classes in Schools* (1860) taught students that in 'all this great
movement there was no fighting', nor was 'a revolution so quietly
effected, and rarely has there been so clear a case for resistance
to the constituted authorities'.[22] Houghton's *A Summary of the
Principal Events in English History* (1875) informed pupils that 'this
great change was effected without bloodshed; by the mere
strength of the hatred the English bore to tyranny'.[23] Such authors
stressed instead the conditional nature of the English Parliament's
offer of the Crown to William and Mary, emphasising the
importance of the Declaration of Rights and its statutory equivalent, the Bill of Rights. According to Gardiner, by taking the
crown upon the terms of the Declaration of Rights, William
acknowledged that he 'must give way to the wishes of the House
of Commons'.[24] G. T. Warner and C. H. K. Marten's *The Groundwork of British History* (1936) followed the same line, claiming that
the Bill of Rights 'completed the work which Magna Charta had
begun'.[25]

The views present in these school textbooks and primers were distilled and refined in the great liberal historian George Macaulay Trevelyan's single-volume *History of England* (1926), the first work of its kind for over fifty years and the dominant historical narrative of the nation in the interwar period. Trevelyan stated that the glory of the events of 1688–9 'did not consist in any deed of arms, in any signal acts of heroism on the part of Englishmen ... The true "glory" of the British Revolution lay in the fact that it was bloodless, that there was no civil war, no massacre, no proscription, and above all that a settlement by consent was reached of the religious and political differences that had so long and fiercely divided men and parties.'[26] The Revolution did more than simply arbitrate 'successfully between the two great parties whose feuds bade fair to destroy the State. It decided the balance between Parliamentary and regal power in favour of Parliament, and thereby gave England an executive in harmony with a sovereign legislative.'[27]

The version of the Glorious Revolution encapsulated in Trevelyan's work survived the emergence of the group of British Marxist historians linked to the Communist Party of Great Britain (CPGB), whose populist works aimed to offer the public an alternative to the traditionalist, nationalist and imperialist histories generally dished up in schools. Indeed, Marxist historians of the seventeenth century such as Christopher Hill and A. L. Morton borrowed much of the Whig/Liberal analysis of 1688–9, though they grafted it on to a narrative of class struggle. Morton's *A People's History of England* (1938), the CPGB's quasi-official national history, concurred with earlier works in seeing the offer of the Crown to William and Mary as being conditional. The Bill of Rights, according to Morton, laid down 'the conditions upon which the Whig bourgeoisie was pleased to allow the monarchy to continue to exist'.[28] Hill's *The Century of Revolution* (1961) argued, like earlier school histories, that the Revolution was necessary to maintain social order. James II's policies had led to anarchy and rioting in London, so the elite saw that the restoration of some government was necessary to maintain 'social subordination'.[29] After the turmoil of James's rule, the Glorious Revolution saw 'a restoration of power to the traditional ruling class, the shire gentry and town merchants'. Although the Declaration of Rights was rather vague as a 'statement of political principles', it established that any 'future ruler would at his peril defy those whom Parliament represented'.[30]

In a work designed for a more scholarly audience, Hill would go on to elaborate on how Britain in the seventeenth century had undergone two bourgeois revolutions, one 'unwilled', the civil wars of the 1640s, and one consciously 'willed' by the social elite, the Revolution of 1688.[31] However, though the aim of the Revolution was to consolidate the power of the bourgeoisie, the fruits of these events in legal and constitutional terms were very similar to those described by Whig and Liberal historians: 'effective parliamentary control over the executive, the rule of law and the political independence of judges, restored traditional local government and greater freedom of the press. It ended rule by royal favourites and ideological sycophants, most of whom were recent converts to the rulers' religion.'[32]

The Revolution was the cornerstone of the Whig interpretation of British history, and much of this account, describing it as a bloodless political coup which established constitutional monarchy and religious toleration in Britain, was successfully incorporated into later Marxist accounts. However, from the 1970s onwards a historiographical movement known broadly as 'revisionism' began to attack the key shibboleths of the Whig reading of early modern British history. The post-war retreat from Empire, economic decline and a growing lack of confidence in social scientific models of historical change (in particular, those informed by Marxism) undermined the optimistic teleology of the Whig account, with its description of a steady movement towards parliamentary democracy. Revisionist scholars such as J. P. Kenyon and J. C. D. Clark attacked the 'shallowness', 'superficiality' and 'glibness' of Trevelyan's account of Britain's 'sensible revolution'.[33] Instead, the revisionists presented the Revolution as little more than a dynastic usurpation that changed virtually nothing beyond the line of succession. Kenyon's *Dictionary of British History* described the Glorious Revolution as simply the 'events that brought about the removal of James II from the throne and his replacement by his daughter Mary and her husband William of Orange'.[34] These historians emphasised the importance of the role of William III himself in shaping events, rather than English MPs. The 'Revolution of 1688 was a dynastic revolution,' affirmed the historian Robert Beddard, 'one that came from above, from inside the royal family, not from below.'[35] Revisionist scholars, in particular Jonathan Israel, emphasised the importance of the military dimension. They agreed with earlier historiography in seeing the Revolution as bloodless, but stressed the extent to which 1688 represented an invasion by a foreign power, driven by the commercial and political interests of the Dutch Republic. Equally, the settlement of 1688–9 was shaped not only by the desires of William III but also by the presence of an occupying army in the capital.[36]

Revisionist historians pointed to the vagaries of the Revolution settlement and scotched the idea that either the Declaration of Rights or the Bill of Rights placed conditions upon the acceptance of the crown. 'The Revolution monarchy,' according to Beddard, like its Restoration predecessor, 'depended upon trust, not upon contract.'[37] The politicians who enacted the Revolution settlement, were not, in this reading, constitutional innovators. They preferred seeing their actions as restorative, returning England to its 'ancient constitution', which had been threatened by the novel and dangerous policies of an absolutist papist, James II. The contractual theories of government of John Locke represented an isolated voice in a political discourse that was dominated by the discussion of the power of divine providence to confer a title, and the duty of giving obedience to a monarch de facto (in possession of the throne), rather than *de jure* (holding the title by hereditary or legal right). These revisionist historians, most notably J. C. D. Clark, also stressed the limited and contested nature of the religious settlement embodied in the 1689 Toleration Act. According to them, the Anglican Church-State remained a powerful and resilient entity well beyond the Revolution settlement. That settlement itself was less than secure given the continued military threat from the supporters of the Catholic Stuart pretenders to the throne, the Jacobites, a threat that did not finally diminish into insignificance until the late eighteenth century. This revisionist interpretation of the Glorious Revolution has filtered down into schoolbooks. The most successful recent textbook on Britain's seventeenth-century history, Barry Coward's *The Stuart Age* (1980 and many subsequent editions), states bluntly that the 'most striking feature of the Glorious Revolution was its failure to effect any fundamental changes in the English Church or constitution'.[38]

There is much to be said for the revisionist interpretation of the Glorious Revolution, particularly in its emphasis upon the dynastic struggle, the role of Dutch military power and the continued importance of confessional conflict after 1688. Yet it should also be noted that there is much in this new picture of the Revolution that will be familiar from the older Whig and Marxist reading. The idea that this was a revolution that was not really a revolution at all reiterated those older interpretations of events. The revisionist picture, though it did take note of the military aspects of the Revolution, also stressed the extent to which it unfolded with little bloodshed. Like previous historians, revisionists also assumed that this was a revolution engineered by the political elite with very little involvement from the mass of the people. In the revisionists' version of events the Glorious Revolution remained Britain's quiet revolution.

This book challenges both Whiggish and revisionist interpretations of the Glorious Revolution in a number of important ways. First, it argues that the Revolution was very far from being bloodless. Revisionist historians, as well as their Whig, liberal and Marxist predecessors, have tended to focus predominantly on events in England. However, a cursory survey of how events unfolded after 1688 in Ireland and Scotland reveals that, as a British revolution, it was marred by horrific violence. The Revolution settlement in Ireland was enforced by military conquest and in Scotland too the issue of the succession was contested by arms and sealed by the bloody massacre of Glencoe.

Even in England itself, this Revolution represented much less a peaceful transfer of power from one dynasty to another than one important stage in a protracted and messy struggle over the royal succession. Most recent accounts of the Revolution tend to begin their narrative in 1685, with the accession to the throne of James II. However, if the issue of the succession is important, and it is the contention of this book that this was the central issue at stake in 1688–9, then the story of the Glorious Revolution should really begin in the 1670s, when James's conversion to Roman Catholicism became public knowledge. This event raised English fears concerning the prospect of being ruled by a popish monarch prone, it was believed, to arbitrary government and bent on the destruction of the Protestant religion. These anxieties led to the turmoil of the so-called 'Exclusion Crisis', when Whig politicians, spurred on by rumours of a 'Popish Plot' to assassinate King Charles II and place his brother on the throne, attempted to bar James from succeeding to the crown by legislative means. The plot itself was completely fictitious, but the paranoia aroused by the threat of Catholic insurrection led to the deaths of many innocent suspected 'plotters'.

The failure of exclusion to prevent James from inheriting the throne prompted some to take more desperate measures. A rising led by Charles's eldest illegitimate son, the Duke of Monmouth, attempted to seize the crown by force, but Monmouth's followers, mainly poor labourers and farmhands, were cut down in their thousands by the royal army at the battle of Sedgemoor, and hundreds more rebels were hung, drawn and quartered after the

'Bloody Assizes' which followed. Even during the Revolution in England, skirmishes between James's and William's forces occurred in which soldiers were killed and there were mass panics and riots in December 1688, owing to rumours of an impending massacre of English Protestant civilians by the King's disbanded Irish soldiers. The political changes that followed the dynastic revolution were, then, achieved at a high cost in human lives.

Moreover, this book also challenges the revisionists' claim that the constitutional changes wrought by the Revolution were insignificant. Whig historiography portrayed the Glorious Revolution as a battle between the forces of liberty (represented by William III) and the forces of tyranny (headed by James II). Whig historians were right to see the Revolution as a fight for liberty, but what that liberty meant was highly contested. There was the liberty that James II wanted for his Catholic and nonconformists subjects, far more extensive than that granted by the Toleration Act, but which he attempted to secure through sometimes illegal means. There were the liberties secured by the 'ancient constitution' (entrenched, it was felt, by Protestant hegemony in church and state) that many of James's Protestant subjects wanted to see preserved from the perceived threat of Catholic absolutism. There was the liberty that the Catholic Irish sought from English interference, denied by William's army at the cost of thousands of lives. There was the liberty that English merchants sought post-revolution to trade without the restrictions of royal monopolies, a freedom which, once secured, led to a massive increase in the slave trade. In the seventeenth century, many thought of 'liberty' as 'the privileges, immunities or rights enjoyed by prescription or grant' (OED), for example, the rights of members of Parliament to freedom of debate. Both before and after the Revolution, very few people conceived of liberty in the terms of the philosopher John Locke, as 'the idea of a power in any agent to do or forbear any particular action', that modern, liberal understanding of liberty as entailing a broad freedom from state or church interference in

matters of private belief. Yet, through the establishment of legal toleration for most Protestants and the lapsing of controls on the press,
both changes wrought as much by expediency and contingency
as by principle, the state had taken an important step back from
making windows into men's souls, and an important step towards
permitting the free discussion of public affairs. An important move,
however unintended, towards the freedoms enjoyed by modern
liberal democracies had been made.

Again, chronology is important. There is much to support the
idea that the immediate settlement of 1688–9 was a fudge designed
to satisfy all parties and the Declaration of Rights did not place significant conditions upon the crown. However, by extending the
discussion of political changes to incorporate the whole of William
III's reign, it is possible to look at the longer-term impact of the
change of dynasty upon the British constitution. If the Bill of Rights
does not represent a prototype of a written constitution, William's
need for parliamentary taxes to pay for war with France between
1690 and 1697 led to greater and greater concessions to the legislature: regular sessions, scrutiny of executive spending, even approval
of royal appointments. By 1695 Parliament's transformation from an
early-seventeenth-century 'event', infrequently called at the whim of
the monarch, into a permanent institution had also led to changes
in the conduct of politics. Frequent Parliaments meant frequent and
contested elections, participated in by an electorate that was at the
largest it would be until the Great Reform Act in 1832. Party poli-
ticking out of doors was mirrored by partisan voting in the House,
with only a minority of MPs voting across party lines. Government
office, too, increasingly became a way to reward electoral success. A
more recognisably modern era of party politics had begun.

Finally, this book demonstrates that though this cannot be called
a revolution by the people, in that the most significant figures in
driving events forward were a European princeling, a British king
and a small gaggle of politicians and clerics, it can be described as a
popular revolution. Whig historians of the Glorious Revolution

used to cite the lapsing of the Licensing Act of 1695 as the point at which Britain gained a free political press. However, before this date it was already clear that a sophisticated news network of printed news-sheets, manuscript newsletters and word of mouth was keying ordinary people into current events. Both William of Orange and James II recognised the importance of courting public opinion in winning their struggle over the British crown. Arguably, it was James's failure in this battle for popular support that cost him control of his capital, as it descended into anti-Catholic rioting, unrest that also contributed to the King's decision to flee the country. Through evidence gathered from depositions for uttering seditious words, loyal addresses and subscription to oaths of loyalty, this book also uncovers how ordinary people reacted to these events and demonstrates that they were anything but uninterested in the outcome of this British Revolution.

A POPISH PLOT?

On 17 October 1678 two men, a baker and a farmer, were passing some waste ground on the south side of Primrose Hill, then just north of London, when they noticed a pair of gloves and a stick lying in a hedge. On reaching the nearby White Horse tavern they alerted the landlord, who accompanied them to the spot. There, behind the bushes, lay the body of Sir Edmund Godfrey, a Middlesex magistrate who had gone missing five days earlier. Godfrey was fully clothed, his body lying face downward, a sword run through his chest, its point protruding some six inches from his back. His money had not been taken but there was no sign of his wallet.

The verdict of the coroner's jury was wilful murder. The inquest had revealed that Godfrey had suffered two sword wounds, a superficial one to his chest and then the one on his left breast, which had passed right through his body. However, these seemed to have been inflicted post-mortem. Contusions round his neck indicated to the jury that he had been strangled to death. In reaching this conclusion the jury glossed over some confusing details about the state of Godfrey's body. His shoes were clean, though the ground was muddy, indicating that his body had been carried to the scene. The sword he was impaled upon was his own and his neck appeared to have been broken.

In other circumstances Edmund Godfrey's strange death might have been the occasion of mild curiosity, perhaps even a lurid murder pamphlet or two. However, a few weeks earlier, two men, Titus Oates and Israel Tonge, had requested that Godfrey take their depositions on oath as to the truth of their accusations of a 'Popish Plot' to kill the King. Oates and Tonge were remarkable characters, and it says something of the atmosphere of the times that the words of these two oddballs were ever given any credence. According to contemporary descriptions, Oates's physical appearance alone would have a left a permanent impression on whoever met him. He had, it was said, 'the speech of the gutter, and a strident and sing-song voice, so that he seemed to wail rather than to speak. His brow was low, his eyes small and sunk deep in his head; his face was flat compressed in the middle so as to look like a dish or discus; on each side were prominent ruddy cheeks, his nose was snub, his mouth in the very centre of his face, for his chin was almost equal in size to the rest of his face. His head scarcely protruded from his body and was bowed towards his chest.'[1]

Oates's life up until this point had been as colourful as his appearance. His father, Samuel Oates, had been a Baptist chaplain in the New Model Army and, through the patronage of Sir Richard Barker, had acquired the clerical living of All Saints', Hastings. He was probably related to the 'Captain Oates' who was executed at York in 1664 for his part in the 'Presbyterian Plot' of that year. Titus was educated at Merchant Taylors' school and Gonville and Caius College, Cambridge, although his academic career was cut short at both institutions by expulsions. He transferred from Gonville to St John's but was sent down without a degree in 1669 after a dispute with his tutor about a tailor's bill. He was not, in any case, academically able, his tutor dismissing him as a 'great dunce'. Despite his lack of academic qualifications and his separatist religious beliefs, he took holy orders in the Anglican Church and was presented to a curacy at Sandhurst in Surrey, with the help, it seems, of Lord Howard, a Roman Catholic. He acquired another living, Bobbing in Kent, in March 1673, but was ejected after complaints from parishioners about his drunkenness and heterodox religious opinions.

He returned home to Hastings, but was soon in hot water again, after accusing an enemy of his father's, William Parker, of sodomy. The case went up to the Privy Council, which exonerated Parker, who at once brought a case for £1000 in damages. Oates hastily left the country in May 1675 as a ship's chaplain but was dismissed from this post, again under a cloud, in early 1676, when the frigate returned from Tangiers. His connections with the London Roman Catholic community, which may in part have been a result of sexual proclivities as heterodox as his religious beliefs, led to his being appointed chaplain to the Earl of Norwich's household. He again succeeded in infuriating his employers and was out of a job within three months. On 3 March 1677 his career took a new turn, as he converted to Roman Catholicism.

Oates was admitted into the Church by a lunatic priest named Berry, who had converted between Protestantism and Catholicism innumerable times himself. Again, Oates's social connections made up for his lack of intellect, tact or self-discipline. Richard Strange, the head of the Jesuit Order in England, arranged for him to attend the English College at Valladolid in Spain. Strange's decision to fund Oates's education was remarkable since Oates knew no Latin or Spanish, in which languages all instruction at the College was given. As soon as this was discovered Oates was forced to return to England, where he met 'Captain' William Bedloe and his brother James. The two were master con-men and James quickly relieved Oates of ten pieces of eight. Broke, Oates turned again to his patron Strange, who provided the money and letters of introduction necessary for him to be enrolled at the college of

St Omer in northern France. Here he presented himself under the name Sampson Lucy on 10 December 1677 and remained until June 1678, when, having lost the support of Strange, who had been replaced as Jesuit provincial by Thomas Whitebread, he was yet again expelled.

It was at this point that Oates struck up his partnership with Israel Tonge. He had met Tonge on a number of occasions before, but it was only now, armed as Oates was with his knowledge of the Society of Jesus, that Tonge became really interested in him. Tonge was obsessed to the point of insanity with the idea that there was a Jesuit plot afoot to overturn Protestantism in England. Like Oates, he seems to have come from a family of plotters and plot hunters. His relative Thomas Tonge was executed in 1662 for his part in Venner's Rising, an insurrection by members of the radical Fifth Monarchist sect, a group who believed that violent revolution was necessary to overturn earthly government and make way for the rule of Christ and his saints. Tonge had begun his professional career during the civil wars. He had been made a Fellow of University College, Oxford, during the Parliamentarian Visitation in 1649. Having secured the title of Doctor of Divinity, he was then appointed to a fellowship at the newly established Durham College. The closure of the college in 1659 and the Restoration of Charles II in 1660 made pickings lean for this Puritan clergyman and for a while he settled in the small country living of Leintwardine in Herefordshire. However, in June 1666 he was appointed to the living of St Mary Stayning in the City of London but his enjoyment of this prestigious new post was short-lived. Less than three months later the church and most of the parish were reduced to ashes in the Great Fire. The experience seems to have driven Tonge to a mental breakdown.

He spent two years as chaplain to the army garrison at Tangier but through the influence of Sir Richard Barker, a City physician, he acquired the living of St Michael's, Wood Street, on his return. With the addition of the rectory of Aston in Herefordshire in

1672, Tonge was out of financial difficulties and he settled down to live the life of a comfortably off widower in Barker's household in the Barbican. Material comfort did not, though, bring mental ease. Tonge remained obsessed by the cataclysmic destruction of his London parish in the Great Fire. He became convinced that the Jesuits had been responsible for it, and not only this event but also the civil wars and the execution of Charles I. In 1671 he undertook a translation of French attacks on Jesuit casuistry under the title *Jesuits' Morals* but sales of the pamphlet were disastrous, a reminder that the reading public did not have a limitless appetite for tales of Jesuit intrigue. Undaunted, he settled down to compose his *History of the Jesuits*, a work which did not find a publisher until 1679. Around 1675 he appears to have heard the first rumours of a Catholic assassination plot to kill Charles II, from a man called Richard Greene.

Tonge was in a desperate state when he and Oates crossed paths again in August 1678. He had just failed to convince Parliament of the dangers of a Popish Plot and was frantic that his story was not being believed. The elaborate story that Oates constructed from his recent encounters with the Jesuits gave Tonge exactly the validation he needed at this point. On 1 August Tonge sat spellbound as Oates wove his elaborate tale of a Popish Plot in which, he claimed, the conspirators had also planned to kill off their Protestant bloodhound, Tonge. He further whetted Tonge's appetite by refusing to let him read the manuscript himself. On 10 August, after the penniless Oates apparently had tried to sell his story to the Jesuits themselves, he finally left Tonge a written account of his story set out in forty-three numbered paragraphs, 'under the wainscot at the farther end of Sir Richard Barker's gallery in his house at the Barbican, near to the Doctor's chamber door'.[2] Tonge was now convinced that he must take Oates's story to the King. His friend Christopher Kirkby, a chemist who had had contact with Charles II, himself an amateur scientist, handed the King a letter detailing the plot. Charles asked to know more about it, and on the King's return from his morning walk in St James's Park, Kirkby regaled him with the full colourful story.

Pope Innocent IX, Kirkby claimed, had provided funds for two Jesuits, Thomas Pickering and John Grove, to shoot Charles II, four Irishmen to stab him and Sir George Wakeman, the Queen's doctor, to poison him. The King then requested to speak with both Kirkby and Tonge later that evening. At this meeting Tonge told Charles that the Catholics planned to follow the assassination by raising the three kingdoms of England, Scotland and Ireland against his brother, after which they were to be subjugated piecemeal by the French. The King questioned some aspects of the story, namely the involvement of the French and of persons of quality like Wakeman. He was, though, sufficiently concerned about Tonge's evidence to turn the matter over to his chief minister, the Earl of Danby, for further investigation.

The following day Tonge and Kirkby were interviewed by Danby and Tonge appears to have given the minister the same forty-three-article narrative originally supplied to him by Oates. Danby's first move was to have the named assassins shadowed and the Jesuits' correspondence intercepted at the Post Office. This prompted Oates or Tonge, in desperation at having their fabrication uncovered, to forge incriminating letters which were sent to Thomas Bedingfield, the Duke of York's Jesuit confessor. However, the cover-up backfired and instead led to Charles's brother James hearing of the plot (about which he had previously been kept in the dark) via Bedingfield. James now pressed his brother to reveal the matter to the Privy Council in order that they could get to the bottom of things. Oates himself, possibly in fear of his life at the hands of old Jesuit acquaintances, came out of hiding and on 6 September took the momentous decision (almost certainly prompted by Tonge, who wanted to cover his back by having his 'source' swear to the truthfulness of his story) to give evidence on the plot before a Justice of the Peace, Sir Edmund Berry Godfrey.

At this stage, however, there was no sign that the plot would prove anything less than simply one of the many still-born rumours of diabolic schemes to assassinate the King. Charles, previously open-minded about Tonge's information, had had his suspicions raised by the forged letters sent to Bedingfield. Tonge was once again in a state of desperation, sensing that the frustration he had encountered in getting his story heard in 1677 would be repeated. However, James remained determined that the matter should come before the Privy Council and on 27 September Oates's testimony was heard by the Committee of Foreign Affairs, a committee comprising the King, the Lord Chancellor, the Lord Privy seal, the Lord Treasurer and two Secretaries of State. The plot was deemed serious enough to warrant a special meeting of the full Privy Council the next day, to which Oates was summoned to give evidence in person. He delivered a bravura performance, reciting his now well-rehearsed story, deftly sidestepping questions about the forged letters by stating that Jesuits always wrote in a 'disguised hand'.

The following day, the 29 September, another session was held, in which the King momentarily caught Oates off guard with questions on the topography of Paris and the physical appearance of Don John of Austria, whom Oates had claimed to have met. However, Oates also had a stroke of luck in his readiness to elaborate on the involvement of Edward Coleman, the Duke of York's secretary, a man Oates had never actually encountered. Without the evidence that was found in Coleman's papers, the material seized from the other Jesuit suspects looked remarkably thin. As the Lord Chancellor commented a few days after the Council had heard the evidence of the suspects named by Oates, 'amongst the many bags of papers that have been seized there doth not appear one line relating to this matter'.[3] Coleman's letters, however, were a different case entirely. His correspondence with Louis XIV's confessor, La Chaise, contained derogatory references to Charles and, more importantly, Coleman's own ill-considered thoughts on altering the religion and government of England. On 16 October the

King was informed of the content of the letters and Coleman was taken into custody at Newgate. The Council was concerned to appear to be prosecuting the plot rigorously as Parliament was due to meet in three days, and the King ordered Sir William Jones to draw up indictments against the Jesuits in prison by Christmas, but as yet there was no mood of panic. However, the discovery of Godfrey's body, and the testimony of Oates at the bar of the House of Commons, would change the atmosphere completely.

Sergeant Maynard, in a speech before the House of Commons, captured the impact of Godfrey's 'murder' on the revelations of a Popish Plot: 'What ground was there for Godfrey's death? Nothing but in relation to Mr Oates' information. How many lies and stories were made to persuade the world about it? But when the murder was discovered the world was awakened.'[4]

Oates and Tonge's story, which had been treated with some scepticism by the King and court, now gripped the capital. Parliament quickly moved to put in place measures to secure the King from the popish threat and on 30 October Charles issued a proclamation banishing all Catholics from within twenty miles of London. The impact of Oates's testimony before the Commons was to lead to the drafting of a bill to exclude Catholics from both Houses. The momentum behind the bill was increased by Oates's testimony that leading Catholic peers, including the Duke of Norfolk and the Earl of Berkshire, were secretly commissioned by the Pope to act as officers to lead a massive popish army. (Another name included on Oates's list of officers in this army was that of John Lambert, the Cromwellian general who had been in prison since 1660 and was now quite insane; the Commons skimmed over this slip-up).

On 28 October there were rumours of another Gunpowder Plot and the cellars were searched for explosives. The celebrations of 5 November themselves were marked by the burning of many effigies of the Pope and the delivering of countless sermons on the dangers of popery. The governor of the East India Company wondered whether he should send his wife and children out of town for fear of a papist massacre of Protestants.

Further weight was added to the news of the plot by the evidence of William Bedloe, a fantasist in the mould of Oates and Tonge, whose imagination was fired by the £500 reward for the discovery of Godfrey's murderers. His career as a professional criminal, robber, highwayman and confidence trickster hardly made him a watertight witness but Bedloe cunningly turned his ill repute to his advantage. He had indeed, he said, been 'a great rogue, but had I not been so I could not have known these things'.[5] Bedloe claimed that Godfrey had been murdered in Somerset House as part of plan involving the Catholic Lords Powis and Belasyse to restore popery by force. He had heard that the Jesuits intended to depose Charles II and put him in a convent where he would be offered the throne again if he would acknowledge Catholicism as England's national religion. If he refused, the government would then be left in the hands of the Catholic lords. However, according to Bedloe, the rather bizarre idea of getting the King to a nunnery (akin to putting a fox in a hen house) was dropped in the summer of 1678 in favour of a straightforward assassination by the Jesuits Keynes and Conyers at Newmarket, while the King took his early-morning walk. The opposition Lords Shaftesbury, Ormonde, Monmouth and Buckingham would be killed with him. However, Oates's revelations had scuppered this plot and so Bedloe claimed he had fled to Bristol.

The motive that Bedloe gave for Godfrey's murder, that the Jesuits wanted to gain access to Oates's original depositions so that they could trip him up in court, made no sense, as in English common law sworn depositions could not be brought in as evidence by either side. Similarly the inclusion of Shaftesbury and other opposition peers as targets for Jesuit assassins was fairly obviously a sop to Whig opinion. It was equally unlikely that the Catholic lords named would have been able to raise the huge numbers of men, forty thousand in the London area, that Bedloe claimed would be armed in the plot. Nonetheless, Bedloe's story was soon corroborated by the evidence of a Catholic silversmith, Miles Prance, who had worked at the Queen's Chapel in Somerset House. Prance had been taken into custody on the information of a lodger in his house, who, tellingly, was in arrears on his rent. Identified by Bedloe as one of those present at Somerset House at the murder of Godfrey, Prance made a confession that an Irish priest named Fitzgerald had commissioned him, along with three other men, Hill, Berry and Green, to kill the magistrate, as one of the Queen's enemies. Prance recanted this story before the King as 'a thing invented by him and a perfect lie' but a spell in the condemned cell in Newgate changed his mind.[6] Denied heat or light in his cell, Prance was found by the Anglican clergyman William Lloyd, who had been harassing him day and night to confess, almost frozen to death on the morning of 11 January 1679. In exchange for his life, Prance admitted he was one of the murderers and gave evidence on oath as to the complicity of the others. On the strength of his testimony, Green, Berry and Hill were hanged for murder in February 1679.

(However, the assassins named in Bedloe's original testimony, Ireland, Grove and Pickering, were not exonerated. New evidence from Stephen Dugdale, a former land steward to the Catholic Lord Aston and by far the most reputable of the elaborators of the Popish Plot, condemned them, as well as Lord Strafford, and to a lesser extent Lords Belasyse and Arundel. Mobs gathered at Newgate and the Recorder of London's house demanding that 'justice' be done and on 24 January Ireland and Grove were executed.)

There is almost unanimous agreement among historians that the men who went to the gallows for Godfrey's murder were innocent. There were no regicidal Jesuits lurking in corners to kill the King, the Queen was not concocting potions with her doctor to poison her husband and there was no secret Catholic army that could be used to return England to popery. Speculation on who did kill Godfrey began almost immediately after his body was discovered and has continued to the present day. As in any good murder mystery, almost all of the dramatis personnae have been viewed as potential suspects. It has been suggested that Oates and Tonge killed Godfrey to lend weight to their story of a Popish Plot. Sir Edmund's work as a magistrate has also raised the possibility that he was slain by someone who had previously appeared before him in the dock. The prime candidate in this respect is the notoriously violent Philip Herbert, 7th Earl of Pembroke, whom Godfrey had found guilty of murder. Another suggestion has been that the magistrate was simply the victim of a random killing by persons unknown, though the fact that he still had cash on his person makes a bungled mugging unlikely.

By far the most plausible explanation is that the magistrate was not murdered at all but took his own life. The bruising on his neck was most likely made not by the hands of his killer but by a noose around his throat, which explains why his neck was broken. The discovery of Godfrey's private correspondence has revealed a perplexing character who was prone to bouts of severe depression. Doubtless Oates and Tonge's revelations weighed heavily on his mind and the burden may have been made greater by the threat of blackmail by Oates. Godfrey was unmarried and it is possible that both he and Oates were part of a clandestine homosexual community in London. Oates had been dismissed from his previous position as ship's chaplain on the frigate the *Adventurer* for homosexual practices. He was known to frequent a club in Fullers' Rent, Holborn, which seems to have been a meeting place for both gay men and Roman Catholics. It has been suggested that it was this gay Catholic community that funded Oates's education at the Jesuit College in Valladolid. Oates could have demanded that the magistrate investigate their claims about a Popish Plot or face having his sexual proclivities made public. Equally, Godfrey may have been having second thoughts about the wisdom of conveying Oates and Tonge's allegations to Edward

Coleman, a convert to Roman Catholicism and secretary to the Duchess of York.

It appears that Godfrey's brother, Michael, a man with connections to City Whig politicians, decided to kill two birds with one stone, at once rubbing out the stain on his family's honour brought by a suicide (and thereby the loss of his brother's estate to the Crown, as required by law in all cases of self-murder) and making considerable political capital out of Edmund's death for his Whig allies. He, or some of his accomplices, stabbed the magistrate's corpse with his own sword and transported his body to Primrose Hill to make it look like he had been murdered. There are other signs that Godfrey's death was manipulated for political ends. His will asked only for a pauper's burial, reflecting his rather austere character, but he was given what amounted to an unofficial state funeral, attended by hundreds of thousands of mourners, including leading Whig peers and MPs. William Lloyd preached his funeral sermon on the text of 2 Samuel 3:33–4, 'Died Abner as a fool dieth?' and was guarded in the pulpit from further Jesuit subterfuge by two burly curates. Commemorative daggers were fashioned with the legend 'Memento Godfrey, 12 October 1678' for Protestants' self-defence. Despite his apparently poor qualifications – he was a friend of Catholics like Coleman and the Irish healer and 'stroker' Valentine Greatrakes – Godfrey had been transformed into a Protestant martyr to rival Cranmer, Latimer and Ridley. The funeral and the pamphlets and sermons that commemorated his death were excellent propaganda for those whose real aim was less to investigate the Plot than to exclude the Catholic James, Duke of York, from succeeding to the throne.[7]

Until November 1678 the Popish Plot had not been linked to the problem of the Duke of York's religion. Oates himself had attempted to keep James out of the plot (probably out of fears for his own safety had he implicated him) and he insisted that the Jesuits had forged the Duke's signature and seal on Coleman's letters. However, the testimony of Coleman was too damning for this damage-limitation exercise to work. Excerpts from the letters of the kind, 'We have here a mighty work upon our hands . . . no less than the conversion of three Kingdoms . . . There were never such hopes of success since the death of Queen Mary, as now in our days'[8] were hardly ambiguous, and Coleman's verdict on James that he was 'converted to such a degree of zeal and piety as not to regard anything in the world in comparison of God Almighty's glory, the salvation of his own soul and the conversion of our poor Kingdom' effectively condemned his royal master.[9] The Earl of Shaftesbury moved on 2 November that the Duke be removed from the King's presence and the motion received a considerable amount of support, even from figures linked to the court. The next day it was agreed that James should cease to attend the Privy Council, its Committees 'and all places where any affairs of the nation were agitated'. The Commons also moved to produce a new test act that would exclude Catholics, including James, from the court as well as Parliament unless they had sworn the oaths of allegiance and supremacy and taken a new anti-Catholic declaration, more impervious to Jesuitical equivocation than that included in the original Test Act of 1673. However, opposition from the Lords and pressure from the King and James himself meant that when the bill was finally sent down, on 21 November, it contained a proviso exempting the Duke from its provisions. In this form the bill was passed in the Commons by a mere two votes.

The opposition's disappointment at losing this vote was reflected when members belatedly discussed the King's Speech the following day. Some MPs urged that it was pointless to talk about securing the King's person unless the succession was also discussed. The speaker, Edward Seymour, probably prompted by the Council, responded by suggesting that the Commons draw up an act limiting the powers of a Catholic monarch, denying him control of the army, the revenue and all appointments in Church and State, and another to ensure that Parliament continued to exist on the King's death instead of being automatically dissolved. The opposition remained dissatisfied, producing a bill which would take the radical step, not tried since 1642, of putting the militia in Parliament's hands. The King would not permit this contravention of the Militia Act of 1661, which had reversed the Civil War ordinance, and vetoed the bill on 30 November.

The boundaries of debate had now been set. The Parliaments of 1679, 1680 and 1681 would all be dominated on the one hand by proposals from the crown for measures to 'limit' the power of a Catholic successor and on the other by proposals from the Whigs to exclude the Duke of York from succeeding to the throne. Titus Oates's incredible story of a Popish Plot, probably manufactured for no greater reason than to earn himself some food and lodging at Parliament's expense, had been co-opted into a wider political struggle over the religious affiliations of the heir to the throne and the prerogative powers of the King. Charles's first minister, the Earl of Danby, was impeached on 19 December after revelations from Ralph Montagu, the former ambassador to Paris, showed that Danby had been negotiating with Louis XIV for a secret treaty and financial subsidy.

This news again put the Commons into a state of near hysteria. William Harbord believed that Montagu had more to tell but would 'not press it upon him, because poisoning and stabbing are in use'. He was afraid, he said, 'that the King will be murdered every night. A peer, and an intimate of the Earl of Danby said, "There would be a change in the government in a year." He has poison both liquid and in powders.' Danby was impeached for high treason and the articles alleged that he had concealed evidence about the plot and 'reproachfully discountenanced the King's witnesses in the discovery of it, in favour of popery'.[10] The Lords, however, refused to commit Danby to prison, and on 30 December 1678 Charles prorogued Parliament, complaining of how he had been ill used. On 24 January he announced to his councillors that the Cavalier Parliament, which had sat since 1661, had been rendered impotent by faction fighting and that he was to

call for fresh elections for a Parliament that would meet in March
1679.

The elections saw any candidate associated with the government, or with the Duke of York, struggle to get a seat. Sir John
Werden lost the Reigate election, 'not that they [the electorate]
had any dislike to him, but they said he was secretary to the Duke
and because he voted in the last Parliament for his master's continuance in the Lord's house'.[11] A petition from a group of
Middlesex freeholders to their newly elected members reflected
what the public expected from Parliament: measures to promote
the safety of the King, the maintenance of the Protestant religion,
liberty and property and the strengthening of habeas corpus.
When Parliament did meet at the beginning of March, the
Commons pressed on with Danby's impeachment, despite the
King's attempts to pardon him, and then when this failed, send
him into hiding. Finally, realising the situation was helpless,
Danby gave himself up to Black Rod on 15 April and the following day was incarcerated in the Tower.

In addition to pursuing the King's ministers, Parliament continued to investigate the Popish Plot and Sir Robert Southwell
expressed the hope that 'popery be laid fast for one age'. Oates
published his history of the plot in April and continued to give
depositions for new MPs who had not yet heard the full story.
However, in trying again to embellish his tale, Oates suffered some
setbacks. On 25 April he called a man named Lane before the
Lords' Committee on Examinations to support his claim that
Danby had tried to suppress his evidence, tying in neatly with the
Commons proceedings. However, Lane denied all knowledge of
the matter, instead haranguing Oates himself and, much worse,
the King, whom he described as an associate of 'whores, rogues,
pimps and panders, and that the King never went sober to bed'.[12]
Significant new witnesses proved in short supply and the Lords
were sluggish in their prosecution of the Catholic peers.

The lack of new evidence did not prevent MPs from raising the issue of the succession. On 27 April the Commons debated the preservation of the King but this soon turned into a discussion of the Duke of York. It was resolved unanimously that James's Catholicism and his position as heir to the throne were a red rag to would-be popish plotters. (The vote, of course, was impossible to challenge as it accused the Duke of nothing.) The Commons was then instructed to draw up an abstract of 'such matters as concern the Duke of York, relating to the plot'. The King intervened via Lord Chancellor Finch to tell the House that, while he would never consent to the alteration of the succession, he was prepared to accept legislation to differentiate between a Protestant and a papist successor; to provide for Parliament's automatic sitting on his own death; to transfer powers of ecclesiastical, judicial and military appointment to Parliament during the reign of a Catholic monarch; and to recognise that Parliament enjoyed the sole right to raise money.

Southwell noted three types of response in the Commons to the King's offer. One group responded favourably and were ready to draw up these measures; another group doubted the effectiveness of limitation measures in restraining a popish successor and wanted instead the Princess of Orange, Mary Stuart, to succeed. The most interesting response, however, came from those who muttered that 'his majesty is so backward in agreeing to the execution of Pickering and the priests who have been condemned . . . that they are for present laws of defence against popery, and that the model laid down in the speech should even presently be put in practice'.[13]

On 11 May the Commons voted a motion to bring in a bill to exclude James from the throne but before the House broke up, MPs resolved *nem. con.* to stand by Charles with their lives and fortunes in defence of the King's person and Protestant religion, adding, 'if his majesty shall come by any violent death (which God forbid!) that they will revenge it to the utmost upon the papists'.[14] Here MPs were recalling the 'association' made in 1584 in defence of Elizabeth I, again from the threat of a Catholic assassination plot. Despite these protestations of loyalty, the Exclusion bill passed its second reading on 21 May. The King was sufficiently alarmed to take the advice of Sir William Temple and Danby (still counselling Charles from the Tower) to prorogue Parliament.

Rumours of Catholic plotting continued while Parliament was no longer in session. In the provinces, the veneer of legal due process barely concealed a pogrom against Catholic priests. Philip Henry reported that two priests were hung, drawn and quartered, one at Denbigh and one at Chester, 'as were several others in other counties'.[15] Catholics were accused by the Earl of Burlington of starting fires 'almost every second night'. Although the prosecution of the plot suffered some setbacks, especially the acquittal of Sir George Wakeman on 18 July, the lapsing of the Licensing Act added fuel to the fire as press censorship, always a difficult task at the best of times, became nigh impossible. Seditious libels upon court figures abounded, some even targeting the King. One balladeer called on Charles to cease 'thus to pollute our isle;/ Return, return to thy long-wished exile'.[16] Tracts such as Charles Blount's *An Appeal to the Country from the City* played on public fears by suggesting that, should James succeed to the throne, the result would be a massacre of Protestants such as the French Huguenots had suffered on St Bartholomew's Day in 1572.

The King hoped that a new Parliament might serve him better than the last one, and in July it was announced that Parliament was dissolved and elections would be called for another, which would meet on 7 October. Many elections for this Parliament were contested (an unusual enough fact in the seventeenth century when many 'contests' were in fact 'selections' cooked up between local grandees) and again the cry of the electorate was 'no courtier'. Fears about the succession were raised anew, as Charles suffered from a severe fever in August, leading James to return from exile in Brussels in case his brother should die. This illness brought the Duke back into English politics and allowed him to face down his main rival for the succession, the Duke of Monmouth, who was himself forced into exile on 24 September. Shaftesbury, meanwhile, left the Privy Council to return to open opposition.

Charles, under pressure from James, agreed to prorogue the meeting of Parliament for another eight days. In the meantime fears about a Popish Plot were reinvigorated by a new piece of Catholic subterfuge, 'the Meal Tub Plot'. On 20 October Thomas Dangerfield, alias Whilloughby, was arrested. He led the authorities to papers that seemed to show that Sir Robert Peyton and various Green Ribbon Club members (who were predominantly sympathetic to the Whig party) and Presbyterians had planned mass armed resistance to York's succession. But this 'Presbyterian Plot' hindered rather than helped the Catholic cause when it was revealed that Dangerfield was the stooge of a Catholic midwife, Elizabeth Cellier. Evidence was found hidden in her meal tub that this was in fact a Catholic plot to throw the Protestants into confusion and the idea of a popish conspiracy was given a new lease of life. Mass 'pope-burning' processions were organised on 5 and 17 November (the second to tie in with Elizabeth I's accession day). The procession on the 17th was particularly elaborate, with a figure representing 'Sir Edmund Godfrey, on horseback, murdered, in a black wig and pale-faced, and behind him rode one of the murders'.[17] The event was said to have been witnessed by over a hundred thousand spectators, including the King himself, and, in disguise, the French ambassador.

Popular pressure, however, did little to persuade the King to recall Parliament. When Shaftesbury and fifteen other peers stopped the King on his way to chapel and presented him with a petition for the sitting of Parliament his response was to postpone it until November 1680 and issue a proclamation against petitioning which immediately became the talk of the town. The petitioning campaign in the winter of 1679–80 did not manage to get Parliament recalled, but it did have the effect of convincing some that Charles, and not his brother, was the real problem, and others that the populist tactics of the Whigs were going too far and order needed to be restored.

In the spring of 1680 Charles was taking steps to crush opposition to him. JPs and other officers were purged and the Corporation Act (aimed at keeping Protestant dissenters out of public office) was rigorously enforced. Local authorities were encouraged to prosecute both nonconformity and Catholic recusancy. The Duke of York was recalled from Scotland and the King made a show of filial affection by attending with him an entertainment at the house of the Lord Mayor of London, Sir Robert Clayton. Bishop Carleton of Chichester was impressed by the change in the state of affairs: 'the dissenting party in all parts of this country are more crestfallen since his majesty began to act like himself, like a King and to let people know they are but subjects'. The Popish Plot, too, was running out of steam. By May 1680 it was alleged that even in London it was thought 'only a piece of state pageantry, and no real thing, and that mischief, if true, was full satisfied in the death of those few miscreant martyrs'.[18] Tory propagandists such as Sir Roger L'Estrange were now successfully arguing that it was in fact the nonconformists and their political allies the Whigs who were the real plotters, bent on reviving the upheaval and misery of the Civil War era.

Shaftesbury and his allies now had to rely on rather desperate tactics to keep the issue of the succession before the public. In June a Middlesex grand jury was persuaded not only to petition the King for Parliament to sit but also to indict the Duke of York as a popish recusant and the Duchess of Portsmouth, the King's French mistress, as a common whore, though the attempt was thwarted by Sir William Scroggs. In midsummer Henry Cornish and Slingsby Bethel, radical exclusionists (and in Bethel's case, a republican), were elected as London's sheriffs but were disqualified because they had not taken the Anglican sacrament, as required by the test act. They quickly qualified themselves and were elected again at a disorderly meeting in July at which one of the sheriffs was 'taken by the throat and punched in the breast'.[19] The Duke of Monmouth paraded in the West Country, drawing well-wishers wherever he went and styling himself as a rightful prince and claimant to the succession (the baton-sinister, denoting his illegitimacy, was erased from his coat of arms on his coach.)

Charles issued a proclamation on 26 August that Parliament would finally meet in October. There was a widespread belief that the King might still accept the idea of exclusion, if it was tied to a generous financial package from Parliament. When Parliament sat it immediately displayed its independent spirit by electing its own speaker in William Williams, rather than waiting for royal guidance, and taking the then revolutionary step of printing each day's votes. The plot was again dragged back into the political limelight, as Dangerfield alleged that James had urged him to kill the King. This provided the pretext for the revival of the discussion of exclusion.

On 4 November a new Exclusion bill was brought in, to which a proviso was added that James would be treated as if he were dead and the Crown would pass to Mary and William of Orange as heirs, disappointing Monmouth's ambitions. Now the King brought his pressure to bear. In a debate in the Lords on 15 November, with Charles standing by the fire, the peers voted down the bill by sixty-three votes to thirty. Frustrated at this attempt, the Commons tried to bring in exclusion by the back door by adopting the suggestion of an Association modelled on the Elizabethan precedent, but with the proviso that all who refused it would be excluded from office (a move again aimed at the Duke of York). MPs attempted to sweeten the pill by offering the King money for the garrison at Tangier, the fleet and the maintenance of alliances if he would accept the bills to exclude the Duke of York, create an Association and guarantee frequent Parliaments, but Charles officially refused this offer on 4 January 1681. Again the King used his prerogative to prorogue Parliament on 10 January; it was scheduled to meet again on the 20th.

However, on the 18th he dissolved his troublesome Parliament and called a new one, to meet in Oxford in March.

New elections again saw opponents of the court harping on the dangers of popery, and Shaftesbury finally managed to get James presented as a popish recusant to the Middlesex Grand Jury. However, there was also a growing public feeling that the last two Parliaments had been too obstructive and had achieved little. At the Bristol election candidates sympathetic to dissent were defeated and members loyal to Church and State returned in their place. Moreover, behind the scenes, precisely the sort of secret diplomacy that in Montagu's revelations had sealed the fate of Danby, was again taking place. Charles was offered £385,000 over three years by the French ambassador if he would give up his alliance with Spain and keep England's Gallophobic Parliament from sitting.

When the Oxford Parliament met it quickly got back to the themes of the Popish Plot and Exclusion. The Commons tried to bring in another witness, Edward Fitzharris, who claimed to have evidence against York, the Queen and the Duchess of Portsmouth, but the Lords refused to agree to this. The King presented his proposals for a regency – Princess Mary was to govern during the reign of her father – but this too failed to satisfy MPs, who again voted to bring in an Exclusion bill. On Monday morning, as MPs gave the bill its first reading, they were interrupted by a summons to Christ Church hall, where the King dissolved Parliament so suddenly that only Charles, but none of the Lords, was in his robes. The King departed for Windsor after lunch, leaving MPs to pack their bags and go home. There would never be another Parliament called in his reign.

How do we explain the atmosphere of panic that followed Godfrey's death and yet the relative ease with which Charles eventually dismissed the Exclusion Parliaments? It is important first of all to understand why the fantastic allegations of Oates, Tonge,

Bedloe and Prance were so easily believed and went so unchallenged (even though some individuals, especially the King, were aware that they were, at least in part, false). The reaction of Parliament and the general public to news of a Popish Plot should not be dismissed as mass hysteria. Since the Elizabethan era antipopery had emerged as a potent force in English politics. The notion of a Catholic conspiracy to subvert Protestantism and suppress English liberties was given credence by the real threat from the Spanish Armada and the discovery of the Gunpowder Plot in 1605. Later in the seventeenth century the threat of popery was located closer to the Crown, as Charles I's evil counsellors and Catholic Queen were seen as encouraging him to raise an Irish army to crush Parliament and bring in Romanism by the back door via the introduction of 'Arminian' ceremony and liturgy in the Church of England. When a real Catholic rebellion broke out in November 1641 in Ireland, with the rebels claiming to be acting on the King's behalf, it was widely believed that they had slaughtered two hundred thousand Protestant settlers, many times the number of Protestants in Ireland at that time. Fear of popery played a major part in leading England into civil war and was an important recruiting slogan for Parliament's army.

Charles II well understood that questioning Oates and Tonge's story too seriously would not discredit them but rather leave him open to accusation that he was soft on popery. The atmosphere of fear and paranoia was exacerbated by the fact that Oates's revelations did not become public knowledge until April 1679. Before that date only the council and Parliament (whose debates remained officially secret) knew the precise details, while the wider population was left only with rumour and speculation. In the meantime London's Catholics were viewed with intense suspicion. One William Staley, the son of wealthy Catholic banker, was hung, drawn and quartered on 26 November 1678 for apparently stating (in French) that the King was a great heretic and that he, Staley, was ready to kill him himself. Charles showed some compassion and allowed Staley's body to be handed over to his family. The Privy Council, however, contradicted the King's order and insisted that Staley's corpse be given the usual treatment reserved for traitors. His body was exhumed from his family grave, the head impaled on London bridge and the four quarters on the gates of the City.

The localities were also in a state of panic. There were reports of armed Catholics riding at night from Yorkshire in the north to Gloucestershire in the south-west. Those who questioned the official version of Godfrey's death were punished by the courts. In June 1682 two men were fined and pilloried for printing and publishing letters which implied that Godfrey had committed suicide. The magistrate's reputation as a martyr for the Protestant cause was not to be besmirched. During the Exclusion Crisis all claims to truthfulness were viewed through the distorting lens of anti-popery. The nonconformist Roger North summed up the atmosphere of the time: 'It was not safe for anyone to show scepticism. For upon the least occasion of that sort, What, replied they, don't you believe in the Plot? (As if the plot were turned into a creed) . . . And this sort was the reasoning at that time even amongst the better sort of people who should have known better.'[20]

This should not lead us to the mistaken conclusion that the politics of 1678–85 were all about popish plots and the succession of a Catholic to the throne. Many other issues contributed to the turbulence of these years: fears about what uses the King's army would be put to (as in 1641) and whether it would become a permanent or standing force; suspicions about the secret diplomacy Charles was conducting with Louis XIV and the extent to which he had simply become a pensionary of the French monarch; and concerns about the need to limit the powers of the present King as much as those of a popish successor. This heated political environment led to the development of the first proper party system in Parliament, with the emergence of Whig and Tory groupings.

The differences between Whig and Tory groupings used to be characterised almost wholly in constitutional terms, with the Tories seen as advocates of divine-right royal absolutism and the Whigs as supporters of parliamentary constitutionalism and even, in the case of some radicals, republicanism. These distinctions are misleading as many Tories believed as firmly in legal monarchy and the rule of law as some moderate Whigs did, a fact which helps explain how so many Anglican Tories came to oppose their rightful King during the Glorious Revolution. The key divide between the two groups came over the Church, with the Whigs more sympathetic to dissent and the Tories supporting an intolerant Anglicanism, though it should be stressed that both groups were violently anti-Catholic. The splits that emerged in the later 1680s can largely be explained in terms of what individuals saw as the greater threat to Church and State: Protestant nonconformity or Roman Catholicism.

The idea of excluding James from inheriting the throne had been around since the mid-1670s, so the term 'Exclusion Crisis' is a poor way of describing the politics of this period. Many other options were discussed for dealing with the problem of succession; the placing of limitations on the powers of a Catholic King, such as removing his control over the appointment of ecclesiastical and civil officers; the prospect of a regency, with James's daughter Mary, the Princess of Orange, reigning in his place; the legitimation of the Duke of Monmouth, the King's oldest bastard son, or a royal divorce so that Charles could remarry and beget a Protestant heir. Nonetheless, once Whigs had successfully implicated the Duke of York in the Popish Plot, as certified by a Commons vote on 27 April 1679, subsequent Parliaments in 1680 and 1681 came to be dominated by the discussion of Exclusion bills. Whig propaganda revived the horrors of Mary Tudor's reign as an example of what life under a Catholic monarch would be like, but they also pointed to Louis XIV's France and his persecution of the Huguenots as a model that James would doubtless follow in England. Tied in with this was the problem of standing armies, which the Whigs urged would be maintained by a Catholic King in order to pursue his religious policies. That army would have to be supported by a heavy burden of taxation, reducing the English people to a dreadful poverty.

The Whigs' support for exclusion reverses the old historical notion that they were advocates of mixed-monarchy or parliamentary constitutionalism. As they readily admitted, 'limitation' proposals offered by the court actually encroached on royal prerogative far more than exclusion would have. Radical Whigs, such as the ex-Leveller John Wildman and the classical republican Henry Neville, tended to distance themselves from exclusion proposals. However, in one very fundamental way Whigs did display the belief that government derived its authority from the people. By arguing that Parliament and King could together alter the line of succession, they were suggesting that the people's representatives could choose whom they wished to have as their head of state. Whig support for Exclusion was combined with their defence of Protestant nonconformists. They blamed the bishops in the House of Lords for the failure of the second Exclusion bill in November 1680 and accused Tories of being more ready to set up a mass 'than shake hands with a Presbyterian'.

Tories, on the other hand, argued that monarchs ruled by divine right and therefore the hereditary succession could not be broken. They revived the political theory of Sir Robert Filmer, whose most famous work, *Patriarcha*, published in 1680 but written during the civil wars, argued that God had given the world to Adam and his heirs in succession, exclusive of the rest of posterity. However, Tories did not rely solely on these absolutist arguments but urged that a popish successor was due obedience according the law. James was the next rightful heir according to English law and, indeed, the law would protect the English people from the possible dangers of having a popish monarch. He could not, they urged, make laws, or alter the constitution of the government without the consent of a Parliament. In fact, it was the Whigs, not James, they claimed, who wanted to destroy the constitution. While admitting the reality of the Popish Plot, the Tories stated that the Whigs were using it to alter and ruin the government both in Church and State. They linked Whiggery to the Puritans/parliamentarians of the 1640s who had killed their King and set up a republic in his place. Whig support for toleration would only help the growth of popery in England and the internal divisions that their policies would provoke would weaken the country and make it vulnerable to French attack. The mental connections made in English minds between popery and arbitrary government allowed Tories to argue that the real Popish Plot was being fostered by Puritan 'commonwealthsmen' (radical Whigs).

From 1679 to 1681 the opposition to the Crown appeared to be very strong and the Whigs secured majorities in the Commons for Exclusion bills in October 1680, January 1681 and March 1681. Momentum was sustained by mass petitioning for the early recall of Parliament. In January 1680 Charles was presented with two petitions from London and Wiltshire signed by a total of ninety thousand people. However, loyalty to the crown and the Anglican Church could also inspire popular support. The Tories responded with their own counter-petitioning campaign, abhorring the positions of their Whig rivals. Charles II's Declaration of April 1681 explaining why he had dissolved the last Parliament of his reign prompted 210 loyal addresses from the localities. Further addresses followed in the wake of the Earl of Shaftesbury's alleged plans to form an armed Protestant Association to resist the Duke of York and more petitions, abhorring the Whigs' regicidal plan known as the Rye House Plot, followed in 1683.

However, it was not simply the case that Charles II was able to rule without Parliament for the rest of his reign as public opinion came increasingly to view the greatest threat to public order to come from the Whigs, not from any Popish Plot. The ferocity of the debates in the Parliaments of 1679, 1680 and 1681 obscures the extent to which Charles's authority remained relatively secure. He exercised his right to dissolve and prorogue Parliaments with little direct opposition. His personal presence in the Lords in November 1680 probably played a major part in the defeat of the second Exclusion bill. He purged with ease leading Whigs like the Earls of Suffolk, Manchester and Essex from the lieutenancy and commissions of the peace. The judiciary was fully behind the Crown and most importantly, Charles's financial strength enabled him to live off his own means after 1681. The severe challenges to royal authority laid down by the Whigs can give the impression that England teetered on the brink of another civil war in the 1680s. The truth was, however, that Charles II was in a far more powerful position than his father, thanks in part to French 'gifts', and once he had decided finally to decisively employ his prerogative powers to dissolve Parliament and reshape civic corporations in a more loyal mode, there was no stopping him by legal means. Attempts to reverse the 'Tory reaction' by force only revealed the weakness of domestic rebellion as a threat to the State by the 1680s and simply made the smears that the Whigs were old fanatical parliamentarians in sheep's clothing stick. A popish successor would inherit the throne and the English Parliament would be in no shape to impose limitations upon his authority. It was James's opponents, not the King himself, who wished to postpone the recall of Parliament in November 1688.

By 1685 the Whigs were in disarray. Shaftesbury had died in exile. William Lord Russell and Algernon Sidney had been executed for their alleged part in the Rye House Plot, a desperate attempt to assassinate Charles II. A third conspirator, the Earl of Essex committed suicide in the Tower. The Duke of Monmouth was also forced to flee the country, tainted by involvement in attempts to murder his father. The Duke of York's return from exile in 1682 was met with rapturous celebration. Political opponents had been purged from the boroughs through extensive use of *quo warranto* writs compelling them to substantiate the legality of their charters, which were frequently found forfeit in court. New charters were consequently drawn up, giving the King approval for the appointment of civic officers. Tax revenue had soared to £1.3 million. Finally the King had abandoned his pursuit of a policy of accommodation with Protestant dissenters and put his support behind a campaign for a rigid Anglican uniformity in worship. Magistrates persecuted Protestant nonconformists and Catholics, driven on by the Privy Council.

The Stuart dynasty looked as secure as it had ever done upon the British throne. Yet this security had been bought at the price of leaving the King in thrall to his 'natural' supporters, the alliance of Tories and Anglicans. The games of Charles II's early years, of playing off one faction against another, had been abandoned. The danger was, as has been stated earlier, that these Anglican Tories were not mere Stuart sycophants or advocates of unrestrained royal power. They believed in a hereditary monarchy that was legally bound to defend the Church of England. James II would discover what would happen when he tested the political allegiances of Tories against their religious convictions.

2

The Protestant Duke and the Popish Prince

Now were the hearts of the people of God gladdened, and their hopes and expectations raised that this man might be a deliverer for the nation, and the interest of Christ in it, who had been even harassed out with trouble and persecution, and even broken with the weight of oppression under which they had long groaned. Now also they hoped that the day was come in which the good old cause of God and religion that had lain as dead and buried for a long time would revive again; and now was the sounding of trumpets and alarm for wars heard.

EXCERPT FROM THE RECORDS OF THE AXMINSTER
CONGREGATIONAL CHURCH ON THE LANDING OF
THE DUKE OF MONMOUTH[1]

Jeffreys made all the West an Aceldama [field of blood]: some places quite depopulated and nothing seen in 'em but foresaken walls, unlucky gibbets and ghostly carcasses. The trees were loaden almost as thick with quarters as leaves; the houses and the steeples covered as close with heads as at other times with crows or ravens. Nothing could be [more] like Hell than all those parts; nothing so like the devil as he. Caldrons hissing, carcasses boiling, pitch and tar sparking and glowing, blood and limbs boiling and tearing and mangling, and he the great director of it all.

J. TUTCHIN

THE WESTERN MARTYROLOGY OR BLOODY ASSIZES (1689)[2]

In the summer of 1684 Thomas Dangerfield, professional perjurer and discoverer of the 'Meal Tub Plot', toured Cornwall impersonating James Scott, the Duke of Monmouth, Charles II's eldest illegitimate son. Like the real Monmouth, Dangerfield aped royal progresses by touring the countryside, touching for 'the King's evil' (scrofula – the form of tuberculosis which the monarchs were held to be able cure by the laying-on of hands). In dispensing his less than royal touch, Dangerfield fleeced his followers by tying counterfeit half-guineas about the necks of his dupes, while they, in return, gave him two genuine guineas. The Duke of York's attempt to indict Dangerfield for *scandalum magnatum* forced him to lie low but in March 1685 he was captured by Crown officers and imprisoned in Newgate. The following May he was tried and convicted of perjury for writing his narrative of the Popish Plot. Dangerfield was sentenced to stand in the pillory for two days and to be whipped from Aldgate to Newgate and from there to Tyburn. Although he survived this brutal punishment, on his return journey from Tyburn he was accosted by a Tory barrister, Robert Frances. Frances asked Dangerfield '"how he liked his race, and how did after his heats [meaning his whipping];" to whome Daingerfeild replyed, "You are the sonn of a whore."'[3] Dangerfield's foul-mouthed reply to Frances's insults earnt him a blow from the lawyer's small bamboo cane which pierced his eye, fatally wounding him. He died between two hours and two days later, according to different accounts.[4]

The fate of the real Duke of Monmouth was even worse than

that of the pretender's pretender. Already convicted by bill of attainder through Parliament as a traitor for raising a rebellion against the new king, his uncle James II, Monmouth was executed on 15 July 1685 without standing trial. James had thought to save his nephew from the slow strangulation of a short-drop hanging by ordering that he be beheaded instead. However, the words of the Norfolk victualler convicted of seditious talk in 1684 for stating that 'The Duke [of Monmouth]'s neck is so thick that they could not cut off his head' proved to be horribly prescient. It took some five blows from the executioner's axe to sever Monmouth's head from his body.[5] Indeed, the axeman threw down his weapon after the third blow and was only convinced to finish the job after threats from Bishops of Ely and Bath and Wells, who were in attendance.

Just over a month earlier, on 11 June, Monmouth had landed at Lyme Regis in Dorset to begin his ill-fated insurrection.[6] The rebels who had sailed from the Netherlands to the West Country were very poorly equipped: they came in two small ships, had only four small cannons, insufficient guns, no horses or wagons and very little food or cash. In these circumstances it was remarkable that a rebellion should be undertaken at all, and the decision to do so was made as a result of three main issues. First, the Earl of Argyll, a leading opponent of the King's policies in Scotland who had escaped from that kingdom with a sentence of death hanging over his head, had already secured money, men and supplies for a rising against James's regime in the north, and clearly the Duke had to act now if he wished to benefit from making a two-pronged attack. Second, Monmouth's own immediate options were severely limited. His breach with his uncle, the new king, was now irreparable. Once close, they had been pushed apart as Monmouth emerged as the figurehead for the exclusionists and as the Duke's patron, Shaftesbury, pushed him towards adopting more openly 'royal' behaviour. In letters James was now exerting greater pressure on his son-in-law, William of Orange, to monitor the behaviour of Monmouth and other Whig exiles. The other possibility for Monmouth, of working as a military commander for hire – he had once been captain-general of the King's forces in Scotland and had defeated the Covenanter rebels at the battle of Bothwell Bridge in 1679 – had not prompted any job offers from European princes. In fact, orders for his arrest had already been issued, at the instigation of King James, by Carlos II of Spain. Aside from taking part in the rising against his uncle, Monmouth's alternatives appeared to consist of attempting an unlikely rapprochement with James or waiting either, at best, for his expulsion from the Netherlands or, at worst, for the assassin's blade. Finally, Monmouth's own overinflated sense of honour and personal dignity, probably aggravated by constant Tory jibes concerning his mother Lucy Walter's low birth and loose morals, would be impugned if he allowed Argyll to begin a rebellion, while he, the son of the dead king, sat on his hands.

Monmouth's childhood had been traumatic as his mother moved him from the home of one of her lovers to another (her relationship with Charles was over by the early 1650s). Having already escaped one kidnap attempt in 1650 (possibly orchestrated by agents of the Commonwealth), Monmouth was seized from his mother in 1658 by Thomas Ross, one of Charles II's spies. Although by 1662 Monmouth had joined his father's court in England, he lacked the education of a gentleman and struggled with reading and writing. His oversensitivity to perceived assaults on his name (or that of his family) had a violent side, as when he ordered soldiers to mutilate an MP, Sir John Coventry, who he felt had insulted the King. His personal integrity was already heavily compromised by the activities of individuals like the inveterate plotter Robert Ferguson (later to turn Jacobite in the 1690s), who had promised to London republicans that Monmouth was ready to lead a rising in England. Could the Duke hope to emerge as anything other than a coward if he went back on these promises made by his supporters? Moreover, Ferguson had also issued false promises to his fellow rebels concerning the level of support Monmouth could expect in the capital if he made a landing in England.

For Monmouth, the expedition represented the last of throw of the dice in his political and military career, but the success of this all-or-nothing gamble was not dependent on his actions alone – for three reasons. First, it was vital that Argyll's operation in Scotland and planned risings prompted by Whig earls in northern England should prove enough of a distraction that James would be forced to split his army to fight on two fronts. Secondly, the seizure of control of the capital from the court by anti-Catholic mobs, as had almost occurred during the Exclusion Crisis, was necessary if James was to be deprived of the human and financial resources of London. Finally, Monmouth was also relying on the appeal of his cause being sufficient to gather enough men and supplies in the West Country to mount a serious challenge to his uncle's authority. In the first two instances the Duke would be bitterly disappointed, but in the third he met with surprising success. Argyll's expedition, despite being better equipped and organised than Monmouth's, and despite taking place in a nation with a recent history of resistance to the Stuart monarchy, proved a dismal failure. His troops, garrisoned at Eilean Dearg, fled at the sight of English naval ships and even his standard, proclaiming opposition to 'Popery, Tyranny and Arbitrary Government', fell into enemy hands. On 14 June the Earl himself, who had fled in disguise, armed with three pistols, was captured by a lowly weaver, John Riddell. Argyll was executed on 30 June 1685. When his head was cleaved from his shoulders, it was reported, his body jerked violently upwards and was thrown back on its feet as blood spouted from his severed neck, needing the executioners to pin it back on the ground.[7] Despite forecasts by a local astrologer, Hollwell, that a great battle between the Duke and the King would take place in Yorkshire, in which the Crown party would be routed, the hoped-for rising in the north did not take place either.[8]

The capital likewise remained loyal to the Crown and the mood of the crowd pro-Church and King.[9]

However, in the West Country and especially in Somerset, Monmouth managed to gather about him thousands of supporters willing to give their arms, money and lives for his cause. Between three and four thousand men joined his rebellion. The Duke had specifically chosen his landing site of Lyme Regis in the correct belief that it was an area where his cause would be warmly received. Some historians have portrayed Monmouth's support as coming mainly from Puritan agricultural labourers with sympathy for the parliamentarian 'good old cause', terrified by the prospect of living under a popish monarch. Certainly Somerset had a strong tradition of religious nonconformity, with a recorded eleven thousand dissenters attending 'conventicles' (nonconformist religious meetings) in 1669. During the civil wars areas of Somerset had demonstrated spontaneous support for the parliamentarian cause, and into the Restoration period the relief of the royalist siege of Taunton by Roundhead troops was still being celebrated with bonfires and feasting. During the 1660s and 1670s convictions for speaking seditious words revealed an undercurrent of sympathy for republican and/or parliamentarian ideals. John Diches, a labourer from Hatch Beauchamp, attacked a drinker in a tavern for having been a royalist soldier and for speaking against dissenters. Several leading figures in promoting the Popish Plot also resided in or near the county, such as the Earl of Shaftesbury, Thomas Thynne of Longleat, Edmund Prideaux, exclusionist MP for Taunton, and George Speke of Ilminster. Popular support for Monmouth was evident in Somerset even after the discovery of the Rye House Plot, with one Taunton serge weaver accused of spreading the rumour that the Duke had been found guilty of involvement in it simply 'because he was a Protestant Prince'. Support for the Duke was particularly strong in the county's cloth-working areas, among formerly prosperous artisans whose trade had suffered as a result of war and foreign competition.[10]

Yet Monmouth's appeal was not restricted to nonconformists or old republicans. If it had been, we could not expect him to have accumulated as many followers as he did. Rather, though the Duke initially avoided making any explicit claims upon the Crown (preferring, as William of Orange would later, to assert that all he wished to do was to secure a free Parliament),[11] it was the appeal of Monmouth as a royal pretender, as the 'true king', that attracted most popular support to him. These popular aspirations for Monmouth as a 'royal' deliverer fed upon rumours that had begun to circulate in the immediate aftermath of Charles II's death. It had been alleged, as with Charles I and his father James I, that James had murdered his brother. Anonymous papers found in March 1685 repeated the frenzied accusations made of James during the Popish Plot: that he had started the Fire of London, murdered Justice Godfrey and poisoned his brother to get his crown. One Mary Kemp of Waltham was said to have claimed that Charles II appeared to his brother as a ghostly apparition and accused James of murdering him. (The local authorities examined Kemp, only sixteen and very sickly, and took her into custody. They reported that if she was not given bail it was likely that she would die in gaol.)[12] Indictments for uttering seditious words reached a peak in 1684–5, with seventy-three of the eighty charges brought for public declarations of support for Monmouth or contempt for James. Interestingly, the greatest number of indictments occurred outside the counties directly involved in the rebellion. James's legitimacy was frequently questioned, despite the fact that it was legally sound. He was described as a 'rogue and a bastard'. Often his Catholicism alone was deemed enough to disinherit him. Thomas James, a clergyman of Sedgley in Staffordshire, was reported to have said, 'itt is not fitt a Popish king should reigne over us'.[13] Edward Swannell of Buckinghamshire was indicted in Easter 1685 for stating that the 'King of England was not King until he was crowned'.[14] In contrast, it was popularly affirmed that Charles had married Monmouth's mother and had a copy of their marriage certificate which he kept hidden in a secret 'black box'. Monmouth's popularity extended beyond the British Isles, as in the West Indian and American colonies colonists drank his health and acclaimed him as the rightful king. Bermuda had its own revolt against royal authority, the rebels claiming that the 'Duke was rightful king and no Papist'.[15]

Monmouth's image as a king-in-waiting had been carefully cultivated by his patron, the Earl of Shaftesbury, in the 1680s, as the popularity of the mock progresses, when the Duke had toured the West Country and the north-west greeting supporters, had demonstrated. Monmouth's own personality better fitted him for the role of a popular pretender than that of a godly national deliverer. He had never quite left behind the rakish behaviour of his youth, when he had courted almost as many mistresses as his own father (and produced almost as many bastards), spent vast amounts on wigs, balls and clothes and had had to be pardoned in 1671 for murdering a beadle who had attempted to break up a drunken brawl in a brothel in which the Duke was involved. Even when he finally met his fate on the scaffold, Monmouth refused to acknowledge the unlawfulness or immorality of his most long-lasting love affair with the married Henrietta Wentworth.[16] His personal behaviour (and indeed his rather lukewarm attachment to Protestantism) made him a poor candidate as a godly prince. However, what Monmouth's progresses had demonstrated was his easy conviviality when in conversation with ordinary people and his ability to show courtesy and kindness to marginalised groups and individuals. An example of this is his treatment of dissenters. As a group the Society of Friends refused to give hat honour – taking off one's hat in front of someone of higher social standing – viewing it as a prideful human affectation. While on his way to the south-west in 1683, it was reported that Monmouth had doffed his hat to a Quaker in Chichester (while allowing the man to keep his hat on his head).[17]

On his landing at Lyme the crowds that mobbed him, trying to kiss his hand and shouting, 'A Monmouth! A Monmouth!', were, then, in many cases attaching themselves to the image of a popular hero, a 'true king' who would champion the cause of the poor. The relative youth of most of Monmouth's followers indicates that for some this may have been seen as a romantic adventure. Monmouth's declaration, which was read aloud after he made landfall in Dorset, might have alienated gentry opinion in giving credence to outlandish claims that the Duke of York had started the Fire of London, instigated the Popish Plot and poisoned Charles. However, when it is borne in mind that William of Orange's declaration paid heed to the equally spurious rumour that James II's son was not his own but had been brought into the birthing room in a warming pan, the claims made in Monmouth's declaration appear less ridiculous.[18] What really counted was that in 1688 the political elite had become almost completely alienated from the King, whereas in 1685 the country's leadership was mostly satisfied with James's government. Given the demoralised state of the Whig party in 1685, all Monmouth really had to play upon at this point was popular rumours and fears.

As Monmouth marched northwards through Axminster to Chard, Ilminster and Taunton, he attracted increasing numbers of volunteers, some brought over to his side by the efforts of self-appointed recruiting agents like John Kid, the former gamekeeper of Longleat, who played on fears of a French invasion to gather supporters in Frome, Warminster and Westbury. Others joined the cause because they saw a chance to settle old scores. Several servants of Lord Weymouth who had either recently been dismissed or gone unpaid joined the cause and encouraged Monmouth's forces to take part in a raiding party on Weymouth's estate. Reports claimed that up to half of the Somerset militia had deserted to the rebels' cause. The success of Monmouth in attracting support began to decline only as the reality of the consequences of taking up arms against the Crown were brought home.

Having reached Taunton, Monmouth was faced with the choice of where to lead the rebels next and had decided to attempt to take Bristol, then Britain's second largest city, as the best alternative to what would have been an extremely risky direct assault on London (in that it would have forced his inexperienced, mainly infantry-based army across open fields where they could easily be cut down by James's professional army). He planned a surprise attack on the city from its eastern side, by crossing the River Avon at Keynsham. However, the King was one step ahead of him and had urged his commanders, the Earl of Feversham, John Churchill and Lieutenant-Colonel Oglethorpe, to actively prepare for the city's defence and to send out scouting parties to ascertain the exact whereabouts of the rebel army. On one such reconnaissance mission, Oglethorpe found the main rebel forces at Keynsham and engaged them with his cavalry, losing six of his men but inflicting a dozen casualties on his opponents.

The skirmish at Keynsham was a minor one, but it had a dev-astating effect on Monmouth's morale. Prisoners captured during the fighting alleged that the King's army was four thousand strong, thereby misleading the rebels into believing that an assault on Bristol would impossible, particularly now that Oglethorpe had discovered where the main body of the rebels would attack. Demonstrating an astonishing lack of confidence, Monmouth, rather than press on northwards to the Midlands in the slim hope of raising Whig peers such as Macclesfield, Brandon and Delamere into rising, effectively accepted defeat by choosing to retreat to Wiltshire, where there were reports that men and supplies would be provided for the rebel cause. Now the Duke's hopes were lim-ited to making a clean getaway before the King's army caught up with them. Even an attempt to raise his troops' spirits by urging the occupants of Bath to surrender as the rebels marched past its walls backfired as a lucky shot from a militiaman killed his herald. Disconsolate, Monmouth led his men to the village of Norton St Philip to camp for the night.

Meanwhile Feversham set off in pursuit of the Duke, already embarrassed by his gaffes in initially defending the wrong side of Bristol and fearful of the security of his position after his failure to take seriously the King's advice that Monmouth had his sights on the city. When an initial cavalry foray from Bath failed to find the rebels, the Earl ordered Percy Kirke, a hardened professional soldier whose Tangier garrison had experienced brutal combat with North African Arabs, and the Duke of Grafton, Monmouth's half-brother, to take a force of five hundred men to Norton St Philip to see if the rebels were still camped there. Monmouth, however, had barricaded the entrance to the village and had been alerted to the royal army's presence by the activities of Feversham's cavalry. Grafton, against the advice of the experienced Kirke, rushed down the barricaded lane in the hope of making a surprise attack but immediately came under fire and suffered heavy losses. It was only after an hour's shooting that his men were able to escape. There followed a long and fruitless artillery engagement between Feversham's forces and Monmouth's. In the end, with heavy rain turning the fields into a quagmire, there was no chance of the rebels pressing their advantage in a direct attack and the royal troops were able to retreat to dry quarters. In contrast, Monmouth's men stayed in the field until late at night, fearful of being cut down by cavalry if they left their defensive positions. Eventually they left Norton St Philip, leaving fires burning to deceive enemy scouts, and marched through the night to Frome.

The battle had proved a stalemate. Feversham had lost perhaps a hundred men, either killed or wounded by the rebels. He had again demonstrated his incompetence to the King, though he shifted the blame to Grafton. The engagement at Norton St Philip did, however, provoke a change of strategy. Feversham was now resolved not to engage the enemy directly, at least not until the army had received tents that would allow them to camp in the open, and would instead shadow Monmouth's army and billet his men in nearby villages at night. Monmouth and his men were filled with despair. Already forced into a retreat, the Duke was facing the fact that in the north there would be no rebellion inspired by Whig earls and in London the crowd remained loyal to the King. Even the promised men and supplies in Wiltshire had not materialised. The members of the Axminster Independent church, whose Old Testament rhetoric had espoused the justness of the Duke's cause, now found their eulogies turning into jeremiads, and deserted the rebellion. Furthermore, Norton St Philip, though scarcely a defeat for the rebels, had demonstrated the willingness of the King's army to fire on their own countrymen. In a pitched battle Monmouth knew that the superior training and equipment of James's forces would always win the day. At this point he was ready to throw in the towel and encourage his men to seek the benefit of the King's pardon, while he and other officers fled from the nearest seaport. Monmouth was only turned from this course of action by Lord Grey, who urged that to desert the cause now would be to the utter discredit of his honour and reputation.

The inadequacy of the county militias as a defence force nonetheless allowed Monmouth to retreat to Bridgwater by 3 July. The failure of the Devonshire militia to hold the town convinced Feversham that he needed the King to send regiments of professional soldiers over from Holland to crush the rebels. However, on the same day that the rebels reached Bridgwater, the King's army had arrived in Somerton, now equipped with tents and light artillery. Monmouth now planned to turn north again in the hope that he could reach the West Midlands and the north-west and raise men there. Meanwhile he hoped to mislead the royal army tracking him, and instructed his troops to bring soldiers, corn and cattle into Bridgwater, as if he planned to fortify it. At the last minute the plan was abandoned as the Duke was brought news that Feversham had pitched camp at the village of Weston Zoyland, just three miles away. Only open moorland lay between the royal army and the rebels and it seemed as if Feversham might have committed his final blunder in leaving his men open to a surprise attack.

However, what Monmouth was not told, and what he could not see, even when he viewed the prospective battlefield from Bridgwater church, was that Feversham's forces were not as open to attack as at first it had seemed. On the Bridgwater side of the village of Middlezoy, they were protected from a direct assault by a deep ditch, the Bussex rhine, which offered a real obstacle to an infantry advance and limited cavalry operations to two crossings at northern and southern ends of the village. Feversham, though, still had no inkling of what the Duke was planning, believing that he was bent on retreat, and consequently he had posted few scouts or patrols to cover the village from assault. Monmouth's plan required a great deal of discipline from his army of volunteers. They would have to march over five miles at night in complete silence, in either single or double file, to get to the battlefield. Once there they would have to reorganise themselves into deeper columns in the dark before advancing on the royal camp. Monmouth's cavalry, led by Lord Grey, would attack first from the north, driving the royalist troops out of their tents, while Monmouth's infantry would push forward and engage them in hand-to-hand fighting, where the superior training and discipline of the King's army would count for less.

The plan was still just about executable, even with Monmouth still unaware of the obstacle of the Bussex rhine awaiting them. However, two incidents lost the rebels the element of surprise. First, Lieutenant-Colonel Oglethorpe, again demonstrating a presence of mind that his superior officer clearly lacked, had chosen to take his cavalry troop to Bridgwater to check whether the rebels were still camped there. Pretending to be followers of Monmouth, they gleaned from the few remaining sentries in the town that the Duke and his army had left to attack Feversham's forces at Sedgemoor. Even so, Oglethorpe would still have taken time to rouse the King's army to the danger approaching them. But a more direct warning came from a loose shot fired by a nervous rebel trooper, alerting the royalists to the presence of Monmouth's army so close to them. The Duke was now forced to change his plan. He decided to deploy his forces so as to attack the royalists as quickly as possible, before, he hoped, they would have time to organise themselves. Grey was ordered to strike with his cavalry, which would be followed up by the three small cannons, offering them raking fire. The Duke then attempted to bring up his foot battalions, even though it was too late for them to be effectively organised into a concentrated battle formation.

Grey's men managed to find one of the crossing points across the rhine, but were held back by a royalist cavalry troop led by Sir Francis Compton that had been stationed to watch the Bridgwater–Glastonbury road. The rebel cavalry was split into two and in the dark failed to regroup. The portion that remained under Grey's control fatefully made a wrong turn and found themselves running across the main royal encampment, where they came under heavy musket fire. Monmouth's infantry, having been deployed in such haste, was now strung out and lines of communication between the different battalions broke down. Finally, as they approached the enemy's tents and soldiers, the discipline of the rebel soldiers slipped and they began firing at the royal camp from a distance at which their shots were highly unlikely to find a target. Reports of the battle recorded that many of the rebel infantry stood and fired like this for two hours, but without crossing the rhine they could do little real harm to their opponents. The majority of royalist casualties from the battle were the result of shots from the three small cannons fired by Monmouth's Dutch gunner, one of the few professional soldiers in his army. The pieces were too small, however, to do significant damage and by dawn the royalist troops had regrouped and were ready for a counter-attack. Seeing no sign of the rebel cavalry, Feversham ordered his horse, led by Oglethorpe, to attack and pushed his infantry forward to engage Monmouth's infantry. When Oglethorpe broke the rebel line, the forward battalions of the rebel forces disintegrated into a disorganised retreat, leaving the rear of the Duke's forces exposed. Caught unawares in open moorland in full sunlight, they proved easy meat for the royalist troops and cavalry and about a thousand of them (just under a third of Monmouth's army) were cut down. Those who escaped did not get far, caught by a boggy ditch which separated the moor from Chedzoy cornfield. As they tried to scramble up its banks, away from their pursuers, it became a turkey shoot for the royalist dragoons and cavalry. The rout of the rebels was complete within one hour of the royalists' counter-attack. Monmouth managed to escape but was discovered three days after the battle, on 8 July, hiding in a ditch, exhausted and half-starved, with nothing more to live on than some green peas in his pocket. He was sent to the tower on 12 July.[19] Three days later he was executed on Tower Hill. Monmouth gave no speech on the scaffold but submitted a written paper in which he disclaimed all title to the throne, denied that Charles and his mother had ever been married and asked the King to show kindness to his wife and children.

So ended the Duke of Monmouth's challenge to the English throne. What followed, in the summary executions of the rebels, the mass hanging and quartering of Monmouth's followers, tried at the Bloody Assizes, and the transportation of hundreds of others to the West Indies to work as indentured servants, soon entered the mythology of the arbitrary rule of James II manufactured by Whig polemicists and historians. The truth of what happened after Sedgemoor was only slightly less grisly than the image of the south-west turned into a field of blood perpetuated by writers like John Tutchin in the 1680s.

Debate has raged as to how many of the rebels were dispatched without trial after the battle but there can be little doubt that such summary executions did take place and that they were ordered by the Crown. Before the battle itself, the Earl of Sutherland had written to the Duke of Albemarle on the King's behalf that 'having consulted the most able in the law they say that such rogues as those of Kerton [Kenton] who proclaimed the late Duke of Monmouth King may be hanged without bringing them to formal trial'. He went on to state that the King left it to Albemarle's discretion as to how to proceed 'but would have some of them made an example for terror to the rest'.[20] After the battle Monmouth's Dutch gunner was hanged without trial, along with a royalist soldier who had deserted to Monmouth. On 6 July six rebels were executed outside the White Hart inn at Glastonbury.[21] On 7 July Feversham ordered Colonel Kirke to hang 'twenty of the most notorious rebels' at Weston Zoyland, of whom four were to be hanged in chains (so that their bodies could not be taken down by relatives and would instead serve as a reminder of the penalties for treason). Ten more were ordered to be hanged at Bridgwater and another twenty at Taunton. Here it appears some mercy prevailed, for through the intervention of Peter Mews, the Bishop of Winchester, Kirke's hand was stayed. Mews protested that this was 'murder in the Law . . . Now the Battel is over, these poor Rogues must be tried before they can be put to death.' Kirke and his troops, given the ironic label 'Kirke's lambs', had a well-deserved reputation for brutality. During the toasts following a raucous dinner party to celebrate the regiment's recall to London on 31 August, Kirke or his officers shot three rebels as part of the entertainment. However, commanders other than Kirke ordered or permitted the summary execution of prisoners or captured rebels. John Churchill, who would rise to become Duke of Marlborough under William III, had a Yeovil man executed on 26 June because he had acted 'obstinately and impertinately'. Overall, it has been estimated, about fifty rebels were killed without trial in Somerset.[22]

The man in charge of the judicial proceedings against the rebels, Lord Chief Justice George Jeffreys, has entered into popular memory as the epitome of the hanging judge. Appointed Lord Chief Justice by Charles II, he demonstrated his worth as legal bully-boy for the monarchy in the trials of the Rye House Plotters. At the succession of James II his influence grew, the new King raising him to the peerage.[23] The records of the Axminster Congregational church described Jeffreys as a 'man of violence and blood'.[24] Later martyrologies of the rebels attributed to him long-winded and vituperative speeches which he was said to have directed at condemned men and women but which he almost certainly, given the pressures of prosecuting so many cases, would not have had an opportunity to deliver. That said, the Bloody Assizes hardly represented a triumph for judicial fairness and, as in most treason trials of this period, Jeffreys saw his task as being to defend the person and authority of the monarch rather than worry too much about legal due process. James's comment to William of Orange that Jeffreys was 'making his campaign in the west' and the judge's own words to his royal master that he would pawn his 'life and loyalty that Taunton and Bristol and the county of Somerset too shall know their duty before I leave them' hardly give the impression that maintaining impartiality was a central concern for the Lord Chief Justice.[25] Jeffreys's temper was not cooled by the fact that he was suffering from acutely painful kidney stones at the time of the trials.

The government faced the problem of how to convict the many rebels who had not been caught in arms at Sedgemoor. The narrative of Henry Pitman, a doctor who had attended Monmouth's army, reveals the tactics employed by the authorities to gain confessions from prisoners. According to Pitman, agents of the king would call the prisoners forward one by one and tell them that 'the King was very gracious and merciful and would cause none to be executed but such as had been Officers or capital offenders: and therefore if we would render ourselves fit objects of the King's grace and favour, our only way was to give them an account where we went into the Duke's army and in what capacity we served him'. If they did not do this, they were told that they would certainly be punished as 'wilful and obstinate offenders'. This was enough to bring a bill against them at Grand Jury but not enough to secure a conviction on its own, so Jeffreys called up first twenty-eight that he had most evidence against and ordered them to be executed the same afternoon. The agents of the King then approached the remaining prisoners, again making grand promises concerning James's mercy if they would plead guilty – 'For the Lord Chief Justice told us that "if we would acknowledge our crimes, by pleading Guilty to our Indictment, the King, who was almost all mercy, would be as ready to forgive us as we were to rebel against him."' Instead, those who confessed were condemned to be hung, drawn and quartered.[26]

The judge's net caught both the old and the young. Dame Alice Lisle, seventy years old and the widow of a regicide, was accused of sheltering two fugitives after Sedgemoor: John Hickes, a nonconformist minister, and Richard Nelthorpe, a London lawyer. There was no evidence that Lisle had known that either of them was a rebel but a clear ruling from Jeffreys drove the jury to find her guilty. Her sentence – she was ordered to be burnt at the stake – was commuted to beheading after petitioning to the King. It was reported that she made no comments on the scaffold as 'she was old and dozy and died without much concern'.[27] At the other end of the age scale were the 'maids of Taunton', girls who had presented Monmouth with colours on his entry into the town and were indicted for misdemeanour. Albemarle made calculations of the wealth of their parents and forced them to sue for pardon at the price of £7000.[29] By the time the suit had been concluded, at the cost of £50–100 a girl, one of the 'maids' had already died in prison. There was little trace of sympathy from the royalist press, which portrayed the 'maids' as round-heeled yokels who had surrendered their petticoats to the Duke's cause and their bodies to Monmouth's lascivious embraces.[29]

The practice of milking the accused and their families for bribes in return for a royal pardon was commonplace, and 'pardon-mongers' like the Dorset attorney Andrew Loder made small fortunes out of the assizes. More often than not, Loder's customers found that their money had been completely wasted as in the end their relatives were saved not by his efforts (which were negligible) but by the general pardon issued by the Crown in March 1686. Samuel Bishop, the uncle of fourteen-year old Thomas Bishop, who had joined Monmouth's army, paid Loder £100 to secure a pardon for the boy. However, Loder, though asking for another £100 for his 'services', had not bothered to request a pardon and Thomas was saved only by the proclamation of March 1686. Samuel unsuccessfully sued Loder to try to recover his money.[30]

Those who were not pardoned were subject to the full punishment for treason: they were to be hanged until almost dead, then to be eviscerated while still alive, and finally their corpses were to be divided into quarters which would be boiled in salt water and tarred to better preserve them for public display. It is estimated that around 250 people were executed as a result of the bloody assizes, but the process of hanging, drawing and quartering was so lengthy that only about a dozen of the condemned could be dispatched a day. Edward Hobbes, Sheriff of Somerset, ordered the authorities in Bath to make preparations for the executions, first by erecting

> a gallows in the most public place of yor said cittie to hang the said traytors and a furnace or cauldron to boyle their heads and quarters, and salt to boyle therewith, halfe a bushel to each traytor, and tarr to tarr ym with and a sufficient number of spears and poles to fix and place their heads and quarters, and that you warne the owners of fower oxen to bee rady with a dray or wayne and the said fower oxen at the time herafter mencioned for the execution.

The list of requirements was so long that Hobbes had almost forgotten to mention a couple of crucial items: 'PS. You are also to provide an axe and cleaver for the quartering of the said rebels.'[31] All of these preparations had to be paid for, and parish registers, such as those of Axminster, recorded in emotionless, banal detail the costs of paying gaolers, executioners and gallows builders: 'Laid out about the execution of John Rose £2 18s and 10d. Paid for the building of the gallowse 16s.

'Paid Thomas Whitty for taking rebels 1s 6d. Paid for taking and carrying to prison Caleb Bragg, John Beere, Richard Samson £8.'[32]

Northmore, Sheriff of Devon, complained of the 'extraordinary charge of whippinge and executinge the prisoners', but reported that, having ridden to Wells, he had managed get some 'mitigation' for the county in this respect.[33] Boiled in salted water and tarred to preserve them from decay, the quarters and heads of the executed rebels were parcelled out across the south-west like so many Christmas hams. The executions carried on into late autumn, and a newsletter of October 1685 reported that three rebels were executed at Honiton: 'They were quartered and boiled and one of them sent to be hung up at Plymouth, another at Dartmouth and the other to be hung up there, his head on the top of the shambles and his quarters at the four quarters of the borough. They made no confession but died seemingly unconcerned.'[34]

The ongoing butchery of so many rebels so long after the defeat of the rebellion began to revolt even those close to the court. Sir Charles Lyttleton, who witnessed the execution of eight rebels at Taunton felt that more would be heard of this when the Parliament met: 'of the execution of so many traitors here . . . and all quarted, and more every day in other parts of ye country . . . near three hundred; and most of theyr quarters are, and will be, set up in ye towns and highways so that ye country looks already like a shambles'.[35] By the end of 1685 James II and his agents had turned the south-west into 'a vast anatomical museum'.[36]

However, death was not the sole punishment reserved for Monmouth's rebels. A further 850 men were sentenced to transportation, mainly to the West Indies, as indentured servants forced to give ten years' service before they were free to leave. (Those transported were finally pardoned by William III in February 1690, but through the petitioning of West Indies governors it was announced that, though the servants were free, they would not be able to leave the islands without the governor's permission.) Those who benefited from the sale of these servants were overwhelmingly courtiers and included some Catholics, such as the Queen and the West Countryman Jeremiah Nipho. This was despite the complaint of Jeffreys to the King (with no small hint of self-interest) that 'if your Majesty orders them [the prisoners] as you have already designed, persons that have not suffered in your service will run away with the booty, and I am sure sir, your Majesty will be continually perplexed with petitions for recompences for sufferers as well as rewards for servants'. The prisoners were after all, he said, 'worth 10l [pounds], if not 15l, a piece'.[37]

One of those sentenced to transportation was Henry Pitman, who, with his brother William, was sold first to Nipho and then by him to 'George Penne, a needy Papist'. Penne attempted to maximise his investment by suggesting that if a sufficient bribe were forthcoming from Pitman's family he would be prepared to free them. Consequently the family paid Penne £60 on the understanding that Henry and his brother would be sold to a nominal 'master' who would require no actual service from them. But Penne did not keep his bargain and sold the Pitmans to Robert Bishop, who, Henry claimed, once beat him so fiercely for refusing to work unless they were better fed that he broke the cane upon his back. After this beating Henry Pitman was placed in the stocks for twelve hours.[38] William Pitman died in service and Henry resolved to escape before he met the same fate. Through money sent by his relatives in England, he was able to purchase a boat and, along with seven other men (including six other former rebels), used the cover of a reception for the Governor of Nevis to escape from Barbados on 9 May 1687. A week later the party landed on the island of Saltatudos (so named because of its large, natural salt pans, from which the mineral was collected). The island, however, was already occupied by some privateers who claimed to be supporters of Monmouth and urged Pitman and his companions to join them on their ship. Persuasion having failed, they burnt Pitman's boat but he managed to persuade four of his party to remain on the island. The Crusoesque nature of Pitman's escapade was completed by his purchase of his own Friday from the privateers: he bought from them for thirty pieces of eight an Indian 'who I expected would be serviceable unto us in catching fish etc'.[39] With no boat to take them off the island, those who remained lived off turtle meat and eggs supplemented by fish caught with bow and arrow by the Indian and seabird chicks 'but they did eat extremely fishy'. Pitman relaxed by smoking wild sage in a pipe fashioned from a hollowed-out crab's claw.[40]

After three months on the island they finally saw an English ship, again of privateers, but they would take only Pitman, whose skill as a surgeon made him a useful addition to the crew, though they left some stores and fresh provisions for those who remained on the island. Travelling via the Bahamas and New York, Pitman finally secured in 1688 passage back to England, where he 'returned in disguise to my relations: who, before this time, unknown to me, had procured my Pardon; and joyfully received me, as one risen from the dead. For having received no account from me since I left Barbadoes; they did almost despair of seeing me any more.'[41]

The fate of those left behind on the island was less happy. John Nuthall and Thomas Waker, who had not been part of Monmouth's rebellion, attempted to re-rig a dilapidated boat left on the island by the privateers. They set sail in it but were never heard from again, presumed drowned. The remainder managed to seize a ship from another gang of privateers who landed on the island, but were later captured by a Spanish vessel that had deceived them by flying the British Jack. The Spaniards took them to St Jago, where they were kept as slaves for six months. John

Wicker, who wrote up their account, detailed the harsh conditions they faced there:

> When they went to sea, we were carried as their slaves, to pump ship, wash their clothes, and beat corn in great wooden mortars, with Negroes, with naked swords, always standing by as overseers: so that our hands have been bladdered [blistered], and so sore that we could hardly hold anything. When at home, our business was to row the canoe up two leagues into the country; full of jars, to fetch water, which we were forced to carry upon our naked backs a great way, to fill them.

One of their party, Jeremiah Atkins, another Monmouth rebel, died from fever aboard the Spanish ship. His body was dumped, without ceremony, into the sea. Wicker was finally freed from this harsh service by an order of the Governor of St Jago that all English prisoners were to be released.[42] By 1715 only 2 per cent of the rebels who had been deported to Barbados could be traced in that year's census. Most had by then escaped or bought their freedom, and a few, like William Pitman, had found the hot climate, poor diet and hard labour too much to bear.[43]

Given the gruesome punishment meted out to the Monmouth rebels, and the public distaste registered at their treatment, even by individuals close to the court such as Lyttleton, it might be expected that the rebellion represented a turning point in public opinion towards King James. However, although the continuation of execution of rebels into October and November of 1685 was unquestionably counter-productive, eliciting sympathy for Monmouth's followers and unease at the practices of the government, it did not lead to a fundamental breach between the Crown and the public. First, it is important to set the aftermath of the Monmouth rebellion in the context of the generally harsh treatment meted out to rebels in the Tudor and Stuart period. An estimated four thousand rebels were killed in the field during the western rebellion of 1549. Up to three hundred more may have been executed afterwards, though there is clear evidence of only forty-nine paying the ultimate penalty for treason. Following the northern rebellion of 1572, Elizabeth I demanded that seven hundred of the rank-and-file rebels should be executed according to martial law, although in all probability only 450 were put to death.[44] Nonetheless, this is still significantly more than the number estimated to have suffered after Monmouth's rebellion. Transportation was also a common punishment used by the Cromwellian regime against prisoners of war. So, in terms of the punishment of previous rebellions against the Crown, the treatment of the Duke's followers was not unprecedented. However, it was (with the obvious exception of the civil wars) the only major, popular rebellion in the seventeenth century and the last of this kind of popular uprising in English history, and the memory of the earlier, Tudor experiences may have dimmed somewhat.

More important in terms of shaping public reaction to Sedgemoor and its aftermath were James II's own strenuous efforts to stress that the Church of England was safe in his hands. In his speech to the Privy Council after his brother's death, which he wisely ordered to be printed for public consumption, James stated that he would make it his duty 'to preserve this government both in church and state as it is by law established'. He went on to say that he knew that the 'principles of the Church of England' were 'for monarchy and the members of it have shown themselves good and loyal subjects; therefore I shall always take care to defend and support it'. Moreover, he promised to rule according to law as 'the laws of England are sufficient to make the king as great a monarch as I can wish'.[45] These assurances were repeated before the Anglican clergy and the members of his first Parliament and they would only be undermined later on as James made clearer his intention to have the Test and Corporation Acts repealed.

Added to these public assurances about his commitment to the status quo in Church and State was James's clear attachment to the principle of hereditary succession and his equally clear lack of a legitimate heir. His wife, Mary of Modena, had not been able to bear him a child who had survived beyond infancy and James was resigned to the fact that the crown would fall on his death to his Protestant daughter, Mary, and her Protestant husband, William of Orange. At this stage, then, rule by a Popish Prince looked to be a short-term phenomenon and one which, if the King's guarantees concerning the Anglican Church were kept, was preferable to the war and anarchy that might follow support for a Protestant candidate like Monmouth.

Importantly, too, there was little sign that the crowd in London sympathised with Monmouth's cause. Most crowd activity in the 1680s was instigated by the Tories, not the Whigs, and until 1686 there was very little sign of public disaffection with James's rule.[46] The capital, then, remained secure. Equally there were no risings in the north, and in Scotland, the most unruly of the Stuart kingdoms in the later seventeenth century, Argyll's revolt represented the last, feeble assault on James's authority. The Tory reaction seemed to have effectively broken the strength of the Whig party both in London and in the provinces, with civic corporations and Parliament itself overwhelmingly occupied by those whose core intellectual attachments were to the established Church and the hereditary succession.

The legacy of Monmouth's rebellion was in the short term actually to strengthen James's hand. The failure of the militia to act as an effective domestic security force, and the length of time which it had taken for his professional army to assemble in numbers significant enough to subdue the rebel army, convinced James that he needed to increase the British military establishment. In the wake of the rebellion Parliament voted James his ordinary revenue for life, followed by additional customs duties to refurbish the fleet and extra duties on linen, silk and spirits to meet the cost of suppressing Monmouth's rebellion. The size of James's army was now almost doubled to nineteen thousand men. Without Parliament's approval James also redirected funds away from the ineffectual militia to maintaining his professional forces.

The ease with which this was achieved misled James into thinking that Parliament's and the nation's feelings of loyalty towards him were unconditional. He saw also the hand of God in the victory which had been presented to him, a providential blessing on his reign. His confidence boosted, the King pressed on with policies that would soon antagonise the many in Parliament who were opposed to any sort of toleration of Roman Catholicism beyond mere freedom of conscience. Aside from increasing the size of his army (which itself began to cause unease in a nation that had not too long ago endured military rule), James appointed some one hundred Catholic officers in the first year of his reign. Furthermore, he clamped down on discussions in Parliament that urged the enforcement of penal laws against nonconformists, both Protestant and Catholic, and dismissed the Earl of Halifax from the Privy Council when it became clear that he would not support relaxing the test acts. James prorogued his first Parliament, which had been sitting for less than two weeks, after both the Commons and the Lords insisted upon discussing the issue of Catholic officers before voting the King further money. This Parliament was never summoned again.

Moreover, although there was no more overt opposition to the King after the failure of Monmouth's rebellion, beneath the surface there is clear evidence of much residual loyalty to his cause. John Birch, a worsted comber of Combe Raleigh, Devon, when discussing the King's general pardon to the rebels in March 1686, was reported to have said that he knew of 'noe Rebellion there hath beene in this case; a Gratious King! I know not where I have any king, or noe, for I have not seen him [meaning Monmouth] this tenne days'.[47] Some of the Duke's followers were sustained by the belief that Monmouth was not dead at all but an impostor had taken his place on the scaffold. In Dorset two men claimed that Monmouth had not been taken and would 'come againe' and in Lyme Regis a man was arrested for saying that the Duke lived because 'an old man with a beard' had taken his place on the scaffold. In March 1686 a carrier proclaimed that the 'right King of England is alive' from Bolton's market cross, adding as a rider, 'I hate all Papists.' Neither was Thomas Dangerfield the last man to be whipped for impersonating the Duke. Charles Floyd was charged at the New Sarum Assize with 'Pretending himself to be the Duke of Monmouth', and in October 1686 John Smith was whipped from Newgate to Tyburn for the same offence.

Other rumours alleged that five men had been chosen to impersonate the Duke, dressed alike and each sworn to total secrecy. One had died on Tower Hill, thus tricking the government, for the 'Duke of Monmouth is not really dead, but only withdrawn until the harvest is over, and then his friends shall see him again in a much better condition than ever they did yet'.[48] The government censor Muddiman, writing on 23 March 1686, complained that there had 'been lately indicted at the Assizes at York, [some] who have endeavoured to maintain (I cannot say believed) that the late rebel duke of Monmouth was yet alive'. These false reports continued to spread, reaching France, where it was even rumoured that the 'Man in the Iron Mask' was, in fact, Monmouth. (The people of Provence were in the habit, at the time that the Man in the Iron Mask was a prisoner in the Ile Marguerite, of calling him 'Macmouth', in all probability a corruption of Monmouth).[49]

Unease at James's rule was, then, growing, but it was very far from being a threat to his authority. However, three events soon turned grumbling discontent into direct opposition. First, James's cousin, Louis XIV of France, revoked the Edict of Nantes (1598), which had given limited toleration to French Protestants (Huguenots). The persecution that followed was popular within France, but in England it raised fears that James, an admirer and, like his brother, a pensionary of the French king, would attempt something similar in his own kingdom. In fact, James's hopes for Catholicism in England extended no further than gaining them freedom of worship and the right to occupy public office. This, however, was more than enough to arouse new fears of a Popish Plot, as James attempted to fulfil these aims via prerogative means and the issuing of two Declarations of Indulgence. Finally, the prospect of a long line of Catholic Stuart monarchs was raised as Mary of Modena gave birth to a healthy male heir. No longer could it be hoped that the reign of a popish monarch would be a temporary aberration.

The poem 'Monmouth Worsted in the West', probably published in 1688, had the Duke returning to English shores to right the injustices done to his dead soldiers:

> Brittain's Rights I am renewing,
> can this give just offence?
> Those that glory in my Ruine,
> I in time may recompense:
> For I'll have a stronger Army,
> And of Amunition more,
> I'll have Drums and Trumpets charming
> When up I come on England's shore.

Whatever the delusions of popular rumour, Monmouth was dead, but in 1688 another pretender to the crown of less than impeccable heredity would land on English shores. His armada would contain far more than three ships and his soldiers were trained professionals, not cloth-workers and farmhands armed with scythes.

3

THE ANGLICAN REVOLT

A strange and astonishing providence the people of God passed
under at this time. Now the broken, scattered congregations were
gathered again, and such who a while ago were constrained to
skulk up and down in the solitary darksome night seasons in secret
corners and caves of the earth to worship God, that did gather
bread for their souls with the peril of their lives because of the terrible persecution, could now go in flocks and droves and assemble
by hundreds in the streets in open public places, and in the view
and sight of their enemies to wait upon the Lord in His pure insti-
tuted worship, and none that durst make them afraid . . . now a
popish prince was instrumental for easing the burdens of many
that did truly fear the Lord. Surely the hearts of kings are in the
hands of the Lord, and as the rivers of waters He can turn them
whithersoever He will.[1]

On 20 November Samuel Johnson, Protestant minister and
Whig polemicist, was degraded of his ecclesiastical status for

writing two seditious libels: 'An humble and hartie Address to all the Protestants in the present Army' and 'The Opinion is this, that Resistance may be used in case our Religion and Rights should be invaded'. Before the Bishops of Durham, Rochester and Peterborough and gathered London clergy, a Bible was put into his hand and then taken from him; his gown and cassock were taken off and he was pronounced and declared to be a mere layman. After his public degradation he was handed over to receive the secular punishments for his crime: he was to stand in the pillory two times, to be whipped from Newgate to Tyburn and fined five hundred marks. At the pronouncing of the sentence in the court of King's Bench, Johnson was reported to have uttered the following words:

'You whip upon my back Acts of Parliament and the Church of England . . . It is strange that I must be whipt for manteininge the laws, and the Protestant religion, when dayly are printed and published books conteininge treason.' And the Court sayinge that was more then they knew, he produced Slaughter's book of the reasons of his turning Papists, and being reconciled to the Church of Rome, which is treason by the law; and he called on the Atturney Genereal to use his office against him.

He then produced from his pocket several sets of rosary beads, which he hurled at the Attorney-General.[2] He was flogged with a cat-o'-nine-tails 317 times, but it was said that he never winced. His bravery so impressed the watching public that it was reported that when Johnson stood in the pillory, the crowd would throw nothing at him and gave three cheers when he was taken down.[3]

Johnson's punishment, and the public response to it, fit neatly into the classic Whig interpretation of the Glorious Revolution. Here James II was presented as a brutal, intolerant Catholic demagogue, whose arbitrary rule disgusted the English people and united Protestant opinion against him. However, Johnson, a staunch defender of the idea of an original contract between king and people, would find his opinions no more welcome after the Revolution. In 1692 he was beaten within an inch of his life by an angry mob for attacking the claims of those who argued that William III owed his title to divine providence and/or conquest. Moreover, in the last two years of James II's reign, English Protestants were anything but united. In pursuing a long-standing plan to establish religious toleration, James II came to reject his brother's alliance with Anglican Tories and instead attempted, with some success, to create a new politico-religious power base founded on a coalition of English Catholics and Protestant dissenters. The times made for strange political bedfellows, as the Earl of Halifax noted in his *Letter to a Dissenter* (1687):

> Popery is now the only friend to liberty, and the known enemy to persecution; the men of Taunton and Tiverton are above all other eminent for loyalty. The Quakers, from being declared by the Papists not to be Christians, are now made favourites and taken into their particular protection; they are on a sudden grown the most accomplished men of the kingdom in good breeding, and give thanks with the best grace, in double refined language.[4]

The letter itself was an impassioned plea for Protestants not to support James's policy of repealing the Test and Corporation Acts. Famously, Halifax warned that they were 'to be hugged now, only that you may be the better squeezed at another time'.[5] Yet, though some did express unease at cooperating with the King, many others, including former Monmouth rebels such as Edward Strode and Nathaniel Wade and Quakers such as Sir William Penn, worked to secure a 'packed' Parliament that would remove the penal laws and tests and free up civic, public and religious office for Catholics and dissenters. On the other hand, those who offered stoutest resistance to the Crown were not radical Whig commonwealthsmen like Samuel Johnson but those Anglican Tories who had been the greatest defenders of the hereditary succession in the late 1670s and early 1680s.

Most historians now accept that James did not, in fact, hope to convert England back to Catholicism by force. Although he became a very committed Catholic follower, his conversion had been a lengthy process. He had resisted overtures from his Catholic mother, Henrietta Maria, to convert in the 1650s, and throughout the 1660s he continued to take Anglican communion. Two events resolved this long struggle for his own soul: the secret conversion of his wife, Anne, in 1670 (James prevented Anglican clergy from ministering to her on her deathbed in 1671 so that she could receive Catholic last rites) and his subsequent belief that only the Roman church could offer assurance of salvation. By 1673 James's religious inclinations had become public knowledge, as he resigned his public office as Lord High Admiral so as not to be in breach of the Test Act and the same year married a Catholic Portuguese princess, Mary of Modena. The Pope placed the official stamp on James's conversion in 1676. Nonetheless, when James spoke of wishing to see Catholicism 'established' he meant that he wanted to see Catholics afforded the same political and religious freedoms as members of the Church of England, rather than to see Roman Catholicism immediately replace Anglicanism as the national church. (Of course, he hoped and believed that by allowing Catholics to worship openly and publish freely, many conversions would follow.)

As far back as 1674 James, then Duke of York, had been making overtures to English Presbyterians, offering them religious toleration via a royal indulgence in return for their political support.[6] His reasons for advocating such a policy were based as much on expediency as principle (he saw this as the best way to protect and advance Catholicism in England while dividing the strength of the Protestants) but in this regard he was no different from the majority of people in the seventeenth century. At this time toleration was often spoken of as being good for trade or for stability but very rarely as being a good thing in itself. However, in his treatment of dissenters, James, like his brother Charles, was able to make a distinction between 'peaceable' nonconformists, such as the Quakers, and rebellious 'fanaticks', such as the Monmouth rebels. The former were, in James's view, due the same degree of tolerance as he wished for his fellow Catholics; the latter, for their affront to royal authority, were due severe punishment.

The King's readiness to brutally repress his rebellious subjects betrayed a deeply authoritarian streak in his character that sat paradoxically with his genuine commitment to toleration. Contemporaries noted that in the last years of Charles II's reign it had been James who had urged him to exert himself more forcefully, telling him that 'monarchie must be either more absolute or quite abolished'.[7] These traits to James's character were a legacy of his earlier military career, the experience of which appears never to have left him. As an impoverished exile in France in the 1650s, he had turned to military service under General Turenne as a means of supporting himself, actively taking part in a number of campaigns, including the siege of Arras in 1654. When peace between France and the English protectorate forced James to leave the country, he entered the service of the Spanish monarchy and even fought against English forces at the battle of the Dunes in 1658. At the Restoration he was appointed Lord High Admiral, and despite his brother's protestations took an active part in military engagements at Lowestoft in 1665 (probably James's greatest military victory) and less gloriously, Southwold Bay in 1672, when he had to jump ship as his vessel was sunk. That was James's last naval engagement, as Charles finally lost patience with the heir to the throne repeatedly throwing himself into the firing line. However, James seems to have retained a martial sensibility throughout his life, and his response to disloyalty and insubordination were those of a military commander applying martial law.

Unfortunately for James, his piecemeal attempts to increase the freedoms of his Catholic subjects were already beginning to meet with strong opposition. He had had to prorogue his first Parliament, in part as a result of opposition to the appointment of Catholic officers in the army in contravention of the Test Acts. In January 1686 he issued a royal warrant licensing the printing of Catholic books for use in the royal chapel.[8] Obediah Walker, the Master of University College, Oxford, was given royal dispensation to withdraw from Anglican worship and hear mass in his lodgings.[9] Catholics were encouraged to worship openly, in the face of legal prohibition, and in the precincts of the Savoy in London the Jesuits established a new academy incorporating a church and a school.[10] The Anglican establishment responded to these royal initiatives by organising a rigorous campaign against 'popery' through the pulpit and the press.

James tackled his Anglican critics by issuing directions to preachers in March 1686 which ordered the clergy not to discuss the authority or power of the King (particularly his right to dispense with the strictures of penal legislation) but that instead they should stick to reminding subjects of the duties of obedience and subjection according to the homilies.[11] Here he was following the example of his father and grandfather, who had both issued similar orders to the clergy against factious preaching (and indeed the debt to the orders of James I and Charles I was revealed in the directions' prohibition against discussing predestination, a hot topic in the 1620s and 1630s but a dead issue in the 1680s). However, the directions failed to stifle the clergy or subdue the King's subjects. The Bishop of London, Henry Compton, ignored royal orders to discipline John Sharp, Dean of Norwich and Rector of St Giles in the Fields, for an anti-Catholic sermon. Again James's reaction to this show of Anglican passive disobedience seemed to share similarities with the actions of earlier Stuart monarchs. The King set up a Commission for Ecclesiastical Causes which used its authority over ecclesiastical persons to suspend Compton from his bishopric. This revived memories of the suspension of Bishop Williams by High Commission during the reign of Charles I. The court of High Commission had been abolished and its powers outlawed by the Long Parliament, and unlike other parts of the Anglican establishment it was not legally restored after the Restoration. There were very good reasons, then, for arguing that the commission was illegal.[12] At his appearance before the court in August, Compton contested its authority and demanded to see a copy of its commission, a request which was peremptorily refused by the commission's president, Lord Chancellor Jeffreys (formerly Judge Jeffreys).[13]

In London the Anglican-Tory crowds, who had remained largely loyal during the Monmouth rebellion, demonstrated their opposition to the increasingly public nature of Catholic worship in the capital. Here the catalyst was the opening of a Catholic chapel in Lime Street in April 1686. This was supposedly for the private use of a foreign dignitary, the Elector Palatine, but was clearly part of James's plan to reintroduce public Catholic worship into England. Under prompting from Compton, the Lord Mayor of London had already complained about the plans for the chapel, and its opening provoked rioting in the city. Priests were attacked and a crucifix was taken from the building and placed on the parish pump. The city militia, the trained bands, refused to subdue the rioters, arguing that, as they were only engaged in 'pulling down Popery' they could not 'in conscience hinder' them. In Bristol the Tory Lord Mayor arrested Catholics found celebrating mass, brazenly telling some who threatened to inform the King of his activities that he would save them the bother and do it himself.[14]

The hostility of both the clergy and the Tory magistracy to his designs led James to reactivate the proposals made in the 1670s for an alliance between Catholicism and Protestant dissent grounded on the offer of religious toleration. In March 1686 he issued warrants releasing a number of Quakers from prison and exempted William Penn from the obligation to take the oaths of allegiance and supremacy, opening the way for him to occupy public office.[15]

In June 1686 the King's use of his dispensing power to free individuals from the provisions of the Test Acts and penal laws was upheld in the courts in the test case of Godden v Hales. At the same time the King issued pardons to a number of Monmouth rebels who had been exempted from provisions of the general pardon. This activity caused consternation in Somerset, where it was said that some former rebels behaved 'very insolently to the fear of his Majesty's loyal subjects by threatening to sue them for pretended trespasses during the said rebellion and otherwise molesting them'.[16]

While increasing his overtures to the nonconformists, James stepped up his efforts to break the Anglican monopoly on university education. The dispensations given to Obediah Walker aroused relatively little opposition in Oxford, but in July 1686 the King nominated John Massey as Dean of Christ Church even though he was a mere MA who had progressed no further than deacon's orders. In addition to his lack of academic qualifications, the royal dispensations from taking all oaths and the sacramental test clearly signalled that he was a Catholic. Once installed, however, the new Dean was given scant respect by either Fellows or students. Massey was jeered by students and his attempts to set up a Catholic chapel in the college disrupted.[17] At Cambridge Edward Spence of Jesus College was compelled to make a public recantation for delivering a speech before the university satirising the Roman Catholic Church.[18] As in Church and State more generally, the King's aim was not to replace Protestant personnel at both universities en masse with Catholic placemen. Gilbert Burnet, one of William of Orange's chief propagandists and later made Bishop of Salisbury, reported that James's aim was that by frightening the universities into submission they might be encouraged to set up one or two Catholic colleges 'and then as the king sometimes said in the circle, they who taught best would be most followed'.[19] In the winter of 1686–7 the King eventually dismissed his brothers-in-law, the Protestant Earls of Clarendon and

Rochester, after extensive efforts to secure the conversion of Rochester to Catholicism had failed and as time passed the government fell further under the control of Catholics at court, such as Father Petre and the Catholic sympathiser the Earl of Sunderland.

By the beginning of 1687 there were two clear aims to royal policy: first, to solidify the King's developing alliance with dissenters and secondly to produce a Parliament that would pass the repeal of the Test Acts and penal laws. To achieve the second objective, James undertook an intensive programme of 'closeting' as many members of the Lords and Commons as he could, in order to ascertain how they stood on the subject of removing the laws. The Hydes had been the first and most prominent victims of this process and they were shortly followed into the political wilderness by Lord Maynard, controller of the Royal Household, and Lord Yarmouth, its treasurer. Others were promoted through royal patronage, such as the Catholic Lord Arundel, granted the Privy Seal, and the King's bastard son James Fitzjames, created Duke of Berwick, Earl of Tinmouth and Baron Bosworth. Despite these changes, James's royal household remained predominantly Protestant in make-up.[20] Nonetheless, the interviews of some with the monarch gave them the impression that he might resort to extraordinary measures. Sir Thomas Dyke had told him that his conscience would not allow him to consent to the repeal of the tests or the penal laws, to which James replied that there was nothing of conscience in the question as he had promised to defend and maintain the Church of England 'and so I will if they will gratifie me in this thinge, and trust to me; but otherwise, this beinge the only thinge they cann gratifie me in, I will take other courses'.[21]

Statutory repeal was necessary to safeguard the political and religious emancipation of Catholics and dissenters affected by the issuing of a new royal declaration of indulgence on 4 April 1687. At this stage James still anticipated that his Protestant daughter,

Mary, Princess of Orange, would succeed him and reverse any toleration gifted only by royal prerogative. Similarly, the indulgence (along with the judgement in Godden v Hales which upheld the royal power to give dispensations from the Test Acts) freed Catholics and dissenters to occupy public office and thereby, it was hoped, would allow the King to 'pack' Parliament with members likely to assent to the removal of the tests and penal laws. James's expressed wish in the declaration that 'all the people in our dominions were members of the Catholic Church' sent a collective shiver down the spine of most Anglicans, even if it was undercut with the later statement that 'conscience ought not to be constrained, nor people forced in matters of mere religion'.[22] Some nonconformists as well as Anglicans expressed reservations. The Presbyterian minister Daniel Williams managed to persuade fellow dissenting divines in London not to send an address of thanks to the King, arguing, like Halifax, that 'it was better for them to be reduced to their former hardships, than declare for measures destructive of the liberties of their country'.[23] However, as the Axminster book of remembrance noted, many others 'were too much ensnared and entangled by endeavouring to ingratiate themselves into the favour of this popish prince, professing such faithfulness and loyalty to him and presenting several addresses which savoured too much of a temporising spirit'.[24] Overall, more than eighty loyal addresses were received from dissenting groups and their effusive praise of James's grant of toleration filled the pages of the government's official organ, the *London Gazette*. The Independents and Baptists of Gloucester renamed their monarch 'King James the Just' for his offer of indulgence.[25] Suffolk Congregationalists waxed lyrical, stating that God had made James 'a Covering Cherub to us, under whose refreshing Shadow we promise our selves Rest'.[26] For Essex dissenters the King was a paragon of 'Princely love', making himself a 'Universal conqueror, beloved at home, and formidable abroad, You have poured Shame upon Tyranny, and are become a Pattern of the sweetest Goodness and safest Policies'.[27] Dissenting tradesmen and merchants chimed in with the arguments of the declaration of indulgence by extolling the benefits that toleration had had for their businesses.[28]

However, as critics noted, the loyalty of some of those who sent in addresses was scarcely unimpeachable. One of the first addresses to be received was from former Monmouth rebels, thanking the King for his clemency.[29] In some cases the protestations of loyalty offered seemed almost too strident; for example, that given by the Norwich Congregationalists: 'however we may have been misrepresented, we are for Monarchy: And do not only acknowledge that Monarchy is the Onely Ancient, Legal and Rightful Government of this Nation: but that it is also the best Government'.

As the Tory magistrate Sir John Bramston noted in his autobiography, 'These are, and euer haue been, loyall subiects (wee all know), in a wronge sence.'[30] It was harder to know what might have been the political allegiances of the 'Orphans whose portions are owing to them from the Chamber of the City of London', who sent in an address on 7 August 1687.[31] The broadsheet satire *The Humble Address of the Atheists, or the Sect of Epicureans* (1688) parodied the self-serving nature of many of the addresses. The King's 'unlimited toleration' had, it said, freed 'the nation from the troublesome Bygottries of Religion, and has taught men to conclude, That there is nothing, sacred or Divine but Trade and Empire, and nothing of eternal Moment as secular Interest'. Thanks to James many had now 'given over that Troublesome enquiry after Truth, and set down that easie Inference, That all Religion is a Cheat'. Yet there was a sting in the tail of this pastiche, for now that the King had freed them from 'the solemn Superstition of Oaths, and especially from those slavish Ceremonious ones of Supremacy and Allegiance' and declared that he expected 'no more from your People, than what they are obliged to by the Ancient Law of Nature', he must have given them leave 'to preserve and defend themselves, according the First Chapter of Nature's *Magna Charta*'.

But the gathering of loyal addresses and their publication in the *London Gazette* was less an exercise in seeking public approval for the royal indulgence than a means of manufacturing consent. It should be noted that only one address from Roman Catholics was printed: the overall aim was to present the image of Protestant gratitude for this toleration gifted by the King's prerogative.[32] Moreover, in some cases the revision of charters that many towns and boroughs had undergone in the reign of Charles II allowed the court to remodel corporations and grand juries in order to produce sufficiently effusive addresses. The address received from Droitwich in Worcestershire was clearly issued after the purge, as it thanked James not only for his grant of liberty of conscience but for 'the bringing of a Quo Warranto against the Bayliffs and Burgesses of this place, in order to relieve us from the unreasonable and insufferable Oppressions which we lay under'.[33] The address from the Grand Jury of Hereford also appeared to be the product of a recent reshuffle, as the magistracy promised to elect to Parliament only those members who would repeal the Test Acts and penal laws.[34] Edward Strode, former Monmouth rebel and now royal appointee as High Sheriff of Somerset, informed the court of his confrontation with existing members of the county magistracy. Retiring to an inn for dinner after the quarter sessions, Strode was accosted by Lord Fitzharding, who told him that he 'had return'd a grand Jury of purpose to addresse, and yt ye King had not made me sheriff for nought, and more to this purpose'.[35] Addresses that were deemed inadequate in their expressions of loyalty were sent back for further revision, as in the case of the corporation of Hull.[36]

Yet, despite the obvious massaging of some corporations to produce sufficiently supportive replies, a large number of addresses made it into print which, upon closer examination, did no more than confirm the widening gulf between the King on the one hand and the Tory magistracy and Anglican clergy on the other. These addresses focused on the King's promise in his Declaration of

Indulgence to 'protect and maintain our archbishops, bishops and clergy, and all other subjects of the Church of England in the free exercise of their religion as by law established, and in the quiet and full enjoyment of all their possessions, without any molestation or disturbance whatsoever'.[37] The addresses returned by the Anglican clergy overwhelmingly thanked James for this promise, while making no mention of the benefits of his grant of religious toleration.[38] At Oxford Professor William Jane succeeded in stopping the Anglican clergy of the county from sending any vote of thanks to the King.[39] The clergy were further dissuaded from signing addresses of thanks for it by the Archbishop of Canterbury, William Sancroft, who composed a lengthy list of 'Reasons against Subscription' condemning the Indulgence for 'endeavouring to abrogate laws for their [the dissenters'] sake'. The Tory magistracy also refrained from applauding James's royal indulgence. The humble address from the town of Ludlow stated that as others had been effusive in thanking the King for his indulgence, they would be as generous in their praise of his promise to secure the Church.[40] Other towns and boroughs gave implicit criticisms of the King's policies in their addresses. That from Richmond, near London, hinted at the spectre of 'fanatick' government prompted by James's intrusion of Whigs and dissenters into civic government. They were, they said, 'infinitely sensible of the Blessings of our Deliverance from a Republican Tyranny of near Twenty years continuance, where the Church of England, as the pillar of this Imperial Monarchy, was still the burden, and the mark of all their Envy and Malice' and so thanked the King for his assurances concerning his care for the Church of England in the Declaration.[41] The address from the city of Bath reflected on James's pardoning and employing former rebels. They referred to their loyalty in defending the city from

> James Scot and his Abettors; and our resolutions at that time were
> so Loyally fixt, that we resolved to die at our Gates, rather than

suffer them to come within the Walls of this your Majesties City; which plainly appeared by killing the first to that Party that summoned the City to surrender. And now Great Sir, we again return your Majesty our due and hearty Thanks, not only for your Gracious Favour to us for the enjoying our Religion, but for your Mercy, Clemency and Goodness in pardoning your greatest Enemies; hoping that may cure their distracted Minds. If not, we your majesties loyal subjects of this City, will be always ready to hazard our Lives, in defence of your Majesties most Sacred Person; which that God may always preserve, shall be the Prayers of us.[42]

The division that was now opening up between the Crown and its former Anglican-Tory allies was not only reflected in these less than loyal addresses but also in the culmination of the King's struggles with the University of Oxford in the Magdalen College affair. The College had ignored a royal order to elect Anthony Farmer, a nominee of Obediah Walker, as its President, complaining that Farmer was 'debauched and lewd' (the Fellows claimed that Farmer had paid someone to procure a naked woman for him and that when the King's letter appointing him President arrived at the College, he had been at a boozy knees-up at the Lobster tavern in Abingdon, where he caused uproar by trying to French-kiss a young woman in public).[43] Instead, the Fellows voted in their own candidate, John Hough.[44] The College continued to flout the King's will when it took no notice of a further order deposing Hough and putting in his place Samuel Parker, Bishop of Oxford. James resolved to settle the matter, visiting the university in person in September of 1687. The Fellows tendered a petition to James in which they affirmed that it was not in their power to obey the royal mandate, which was in contravention of the College's oaths and statutes. The King responded furiously:

is this your Church of England's loyalty? One would wonder to find so many Church of England men in such a business. Go back and shew yourselves good members of the Church of England. Get ye gone; know I am your King and I command you to be gone. Go and admit the Bishop of Oxon Head, Principal (what do ye call it of your College) . . . I mean President of the College. Let him know that refuses it, – Look to't, they shall find the weight of their sovereign's displeasure.

After James's outburst the Fellows were ordered to retire to the College's chapel and elect Parker President, but despite the threat that they could otherwise 'expect to feele the heauie hand of an angrie King', they continued to disobey. In November 1688 the ecclesiastical commission expelled twenty-five Fellows, and by March 1688 their places had been taken by Roman Catholics and Bonaventura Gifford, Parker's successor as Bishop of Oxford, had been appointed as their President.[45] Oxford's sister university, Cambridge, was similarly unwilling to bend to royal demands, refusing to confer the degree of MA on Alban Francis, for which the vice chancellor, John Peachall, was deprived of his post.[46]

The stance of Magdalen College has been cited as a classic example of Anglican 'passive resistance' to James's romanising policies: it offered no direct challenge to the King's authority or dispensing power, but steadfastly refused to follow his commands, falling back on the obligations of the college statutes and oaths. In the spring and summer of 1687, however, a number of leading figures, including Danby, Halifax and Compton, were actively courted by the Prince of Orange, who sent over two envoys, Dijkvelt and Zuylestein, to improve his contacts with English politicians.[47] At this stage William and his allies limited themselves to frustrating James's attempts to secure approval for his indulgence and for the repeal of the tests and penal laws. William resisted pressure from James to publicly endorse taking off the tests and instead had a letter distributed in England detailing his support for religious toleration but his opposition to allowing Catholics to occupy places of public trust.[48] The King's agents reported the effectiveness of this letter and other pamphlets in galvanising public opinion against submitting to the repeal of the tests.[49] Although armed intervention was not discussed at this stage, the building of these contacts between William and leading figures in England clearly paved the way for the Dutch invasion.

Royal declarations of indulgence had been defeated by Parliament in 1662 and 1673 and, given the equivocal response presented in the loyal addresses, we might deem James's declaration likewise a failure. Yet, viewed in the terms of his earlier schemes, it was arguably a success. As he had hoped it would in the 1670s, the offer of religious toleration had driven a wedge between the Church of England and Protestant nonconformity and helped cement an alliance between Whiggery and dissent, and Catholicism and the Crown. Whig propagandists like the Presbyterian Henry Care, once the author of the leading exclusionist news-sheet the *Weekly Pacquet of Advice from Rome*, turned their literary efforts towards promoting the cause of religious toleration. Presbyterian ministers Vincent Alsop and Stephen Lobb delivered eulogies on the King's munificence. Former Cromwellians and Fifth Monarchists took up places as magistrates.[50] A number of the associates of the philosopher John Locke (now in exile as a result of his links to the Earl of Shaftesbury and the Rye House Plot) encouraged him to return home and plead for a royal pardon.[51] The collaboration of so many Whigs and dissenters with the Crown's policies raised Anglican-Tory fears, not only of popish absolutism but also of republican 'fanaticism'. The memories evoked were not only those familiar episodes of popish cruelty and treachery, the reign of 'Bloody' Mary and the Gunpowder Plot, but also more recent experiences of rule by sectaries, major generals and commonwealthsmen in the 1650s.

In July 1687 James formally dissolved his first Parliament and began engineering a new one that would confirm the freedoms granted by his indulgence through the repeal of the tests and penal laws. To achieve this, the King adopted two strategies. First, he went on a royal progress through the west and north-west of England (the two areas that had seemed the likeliest sources of insurrection in the first year of his reign). Secondly, he instructed royal agents to survey the opinions of JPs, Deputy Lieutenants and other county and civic officers concerning the repeal of the tests and penal laws through the tendering of three questions. James's progress was not a resounding success. In September the Prince of Orange received reports that 'few of the gentry waited on his Majesty' during his progress.[52] Some of those who did attend appear to have had deep misgivings. The Cheshire Presbyterian minister Henry Newcome recalled how he and other ministers had arranged to meet the King on Rowton Heath: 'It being thought fit that something should have been said to the king, and it fell to me as the senior etc., but I was utterly averse unto it. Mr Jolly accepted it. The brethren were greatly unsatisfied, so that I should have had blame.' The potential embarrassment was averted as 'his majesty came by us and stayed not; but put off his hat, and passed on. And so there was nothing said, and all was well.' (Newcome's ambivalence towards James is further revealed by the fact that he had a new loyal address to the King suppressed.)[53] The King himself appears to have enjoyed the exercise little, avoiding the dubious pleasure of a fish supper laid on in his honour by the mayor and corporation of Holywell by escaping through a back door.[54] The miserable tour culminated in Oxford, with James's verbal assault on the recalcitrant Fellows of Magdalen.

Following the royal progress, in October 1687 the Lord Lieutenants were instructed to gather replies from their deputies, sheriffs and magistrates to three questions: first, would they, if elected to Parliament, vote for the repeal of the Test Acts and penal laws? Secondly, would they assist in the election of candidates who would assent to removal of the tests and laws? Thirdly, would they support the Declaration of Indulgence 'by living friendly with those of all persuasions, as subjects of the same Prince, and good Christians ought to do'. The third question received an

overwhelmingly positive response, with only one individual reply-
ing negatively. Thomas Waite, a magistrate of York, complained
that 'as a Justice' he had 'sworne to observe Law and Justice, the
neglect whereof is fineable and punishable, and by the 20th of K.
Ed. 3.1, noe justice is to neglect or defer it for the King's letters,
writs commands, which if he doe, he is to be at the King's Will for
body, lands and goods'. He reminded the royal agents that, according to the 1670 Conventicle Act, he was obliged to act against
nonconformist meetings, on pain of a fine of £100 for failure, and
was likewise bound by the Test Act of 1678, and therefore could
not 'with safety publickly declaire to support any Declaration out
of Parliament, that is contrary to these laws'.[55]

It has been suggested that the returns reveal the growing tolerance of the political nation, given that only one negative response
was received to the third question. Certainly some of those interviewed appeared willing to consider the repeal of the penal laws if
they could not countenance the removal of the tests.[56] Yet, when
most of the respondents replied positively to the third question, all
that they were really agreeing to was to keep the peace and not
make windows into men's souls. This was made clear by the
number of replies which hedged in their assent with the words 'as
far as the law allowed', which, as Waite had pointed out, included
the Test Acts and the penal laws, directly contrary to the King's
indulgence.[57] The responses of some were risibly evasive: the
Bedfordshire JP Samuel Rhodes answered:

> affirmitavely that he will reedily and willingly confirm [sic] to it
> [the Declaration of Indulgence], But wth all declares it is not for
> want of inclination if he complys not wth what the King desires.
> This answer being not intended for a fixed opinion or resolution,
> for if he be resolved of any thing it is, that he will be convinced of
> anything, where ye argument to ye contrary shall be more forcible.

Like the loyal addresses received from Anglican clergy and Tory magistrates, these were hollow promises. What James sought was not merely the public's assent to granting 'liberty of conscience', if that meant merely tolerating private opinion, but also its consent to the full religious and political emancipation of Catholics and dissenters. Indeed, it has to be wondered why the crown bothered tendering this question, couched as it was in such generous terms. Perhaps it was intended, like the loyal addresses, to give at face value the impression of broad public approval for James's policy of toleration.

The two key questions, whether respondents would repeal the tests if they stood in Parliament or would support the election of MPs that would, received overwhelmingly negative replies. Only just under a quarter of those canvassed replied positively to the proposal that the tests should be repealed.[58] Even this number is probably an exaggeration of support, as the process of purging the bench and the corporations went on at the same time as officers were being tendered the three questions (the canvassing itself taking place from the autumn of 1687 to the summer of 1688). Consequently the ratio of nonconformists, Anglicans and Catholics in place was not constant.[59] It was alleged by the Bishop of Carlisle that set answers had been developed to the King's three questions: 'it is believed most of our Gentlemen will agree upon one and the same answer though given in severally indistinct papers, as they have lately done in other counties.'[60] Certainly many of the replies received are remarkably similar and this uniformity may also have been a result of answers not being recorded verbatim.[61]

The dismal response James received to the first two questions casts doubt on the likely success of his project of producing a Parliament pliable enough to consent to the removal of the tests. We can never have a definite answer as James abandoned the plan before it ever came to the polls. However, there are very good reasons for thinking that, had William not intervened when he did, James might have achieved his goals. First, it is a mistake to see the tendering of the three questions as a means by which the King could test public opinion. This was not the primary intent of the exercise: it was to identify, rather than quantify, those who would comply with repeal and those who would not. Those who objected were to be removed from their places and more pliable individuals put in their stead. The secret instructions given to the King's agents make it clear that this was part of the machinery of a political purge, not a form of seventeenth-century opinion poll. They were ordered 'to inspect the present state of each Corporation, with respect to the Magistrates in being, whether there be any in, that are not fitt and proper, or whether any are omitted to be put into the Government, which if placed therein, may be useful and serviceable for promoting and securing good Elections, as also any methods and expedients that have a tendency thereunto'.[62] By the side of names of judges and civic officers, agents would place their comments as to the reliability or otherwise of these individuals. Beside the name of one Lincolnshire magistrate was the comment: 'This is one of the worst of them, fitt to be turned out.'[63] Particular notice was taken of how many Catholics and wealthy dissenters lived in each area.[64]

By the spring of 1688 over twelve hundred members of town corporations had been turned out. Those put in their places were, in the words of Sir John Bramston, 'Papists, and where not Papists, Fanaticks'.[65] The intruded were widely reviled: in Somerset the new sheriff, Edward Strode, was threatened with physical violence by former grand jury members, refused the gaol rolls by the former sheriff, Edward Hobbes, had one of his bailiffs indicted on a misdemeanour and was burnt in effigy in local towns.[66] Dr Robert Grey, rector of Bishop Wearmouth and prebendary of Durham cathedral, was accosted by John Lamb, a newly appointed Catholic justice of the peace, 'a busy, active and fierce man for that party' while he was riding from his rectory to the city. Lamb 'overtook the Doctor, sneered at him and told him he wondered he would ride upon so fine a palfrey when his Saviour was content to ride upon a colt, the foal of an ass; the doctor replied "'tis true, Sir, but the king has made so many asses justices of the peace, he has not left me one to ride upon.'" Sir John Reresby was disdainful of the social standing of the new appointees, observing that of two Justices put in the West Riding commission one could not read or write and the other was a bailiff for rents, while 'neither of them have one foot of freehold land in England'.[67]

Yet, as a result of the nature of seventeenth-century elections, the obvious hostility towards the new incumbents in the magistracy and corporations was less important than the intruded individuals' support for repeal. Most elections at this time were not contested and candidates were instead 'selected' through discussions amongst local bigwigs. For example, in the 1685 elections, out of 270 seats in Parliament, only in seventy-four were contests recorded. Hence it was far more important, and a far more realistic objective, to try to secure a loyal bench and common council than to try to win over the majority of the estimated two hundred thousand voters in England at this time.[68] The crown's relative lack of interest in the electorate itself can be seen in the new charter issued for the corporation of Hull, which left the franchise completely unchanged, knowing that what mattered was to secure the loyalty of the magistracy.[69]

Precedent might suggest that James's scheme would fail, given the hostility of his first Parliament to the introduction of Catholic officers into the army, despite the extensive *quo warranto* campaign undertaken by Charles II to remodel the bench and corporations between 1681 and 1685. However, the goals of the two kings in revising town charters were quite different, for whereas Charles wished to break the power of urban Whiggery and dissent, arguably to help prevent his having to call another Parliament, James wished to promote just these elements, precisely so that he could assemble a Parliament which would consent to taking off the laws. In fact, in some ways, rather than representing the intrusion of new elements into local government, James's purges represented something like the restoration of the 'natural' order in urban government: kicking out the Tory squirearchy imposed by Charles and reintroducing merchants and tradesmen who represented the genuine elite in towns and cities.[70]

Finally, James's opponents appear to have been less than certain that he would fail in his design. Sir Patrick Hume, a former associate of the Earl of Argyll, wrote to William of Orange that, if the dissenters could be brought to favour repeal, 'no doubt the King and they will carry the Corporations or Towns and some Counties. I am confident that hopes of the contrary are ill founded and will prove vain.'[71] Another correspondent wrote to the Prince that, despite James's unpopularity, 'yet the King is still assured that by his power in the Corporations he shall have a House of Commons to his liking, and doubts not of getting such a Party in the House of Lords as will do what he seems to desire.'[72] The King's agents also expressed confidence in securing MPs who would consent to the repeal of the tests: 'The Roman Catholiques, Independants, Anabaptists, and Quaquers, that are numerous in many places, are generally in your Ma[jes]ties interest, notwithstanding the many rumours, and suggestions to divide and create jealousies among them. These are unanimously agred to elect such members of Parliament, as will abolish these Tests and Lawes.'[73] Indeed, one of James's officers, John Eston, complained that it was to 'the misery of this Kingdom, that so much Democrasie is mixed in the Government, that thereby the exercise of ye Souvraign power should be in any manner limited by ye suffrages of the common people, whose humours are allwayes fluctuating, and ye most part of them guided, not by reason, but deliberation like mere animals'. Thankfully, Eston said, the King now had an opportunity to alter the democratic element of the constitution to better serve his needs, 'for otherwise wee may be destroyed by that which was before our preservation. And I hope this will be considered of next Parliam't, whether I have ye honour to sit there or not.'

The circumstances of the previous reign were now reversed: it was the King's opponents, and not the crown, who most feared the summoning of a new Parliament. It was the likely prospect of a 'packed' Parliament removing the legal barriers to Catholics occupying high office, combined with two other events, the issuing of a second Declaration of Indulgence and the birth of a legitimate male heir, which led some English politicians to take the extraordinary step of inviting a foreign head of state to invade their country.

The announcement of Mary of Modena's pregnancy in January 1688 touched off a crisis over succession that had been brewing for years between James II and his Protestant subjects. Mary had suffered from a number of miscarriages and it was commonly assumed that the Queen was now barren. The news that she was now with child came as a profound shock to the many who had taken comfort from the fact that James was not in good health, and that on his death the crown would fall to his Protestant daughters. The possibility that the Queen would give birth to a healthy male heir, who, it was assumed, would be raised as a Catholic, dealt a severe blow to the hope that the romanising policies of the King's reign would be short-lived. Rumours about the pregnancy began to circulate almost immediately. Henry Hyde, the Earl of Clarendon, noted on 15 January that 'the queen's great belly is everywhere ridiculed, as if scarce anybody believed it to be true'. Satirical lampoons on the pregnancy began to appear as the beginning of March. *Mr Partridge's wonderful predictions, pro anno 1688* predicted that 'there is some bawdy project on foot either about buying, selling or procuring a child, or children, for some pious use' and that 'some child [is to be] put upon a lawful heir to cheat them out of their right and estate'.

The issue of the Prince of Wales's paternity was part of the discussions between Protestant politicians in England and William of Orange. The Earl of Devonshire, writing to William on 13 March, reported ominously that 'the Roman Catholics incline absolutely that it should be a son' and that 'it is certain, that we expect great extremities'. Princess Anne, embittered at the threat the child posed to her inheriting her father's throne, actively encouraged the belief that it was a fraudulent pregnancy, writing to her sister Mary that there was 'much reason to believe it a false belly. For methinks, if it were not, there having been so many stories and jests made about it, she should, to convince the world make either me, or some of my friends, feel her belly.' The birth of the prince was officially accompanied with much celebration in newsletters and gazettes, with fireworks set off and bonfires lit. At the same time, however, discussion continued as to whether he was really the King's son. Narcissus Luttrell reported that 'People give themselves a great liberty in discoursing about the young Prince, with strange reflections on him, not fit to insert here.' In a mock dialogue, the Prince of Wales's nurse told the papal nuncio, 'O Lord sir, now the whole kingdom laughs at the sham; and there's never a joiner in town but has a patter of the bedstead; nay, the next Bartholomew Fair they intend to have a droll called "The Tragedy of Perkin Warbeck".' Other pamphlets claimed that though the Queen had indeed been pregnant, the father was the papal nuncio himself, the aptly named Ferdinand d'Adda, not James.

Meanwhile, on 27 April 1688 James issued a second Declaration of Indulgence, this time with instructions that it was to be read from the pulpit by all Anglican clergy. The issuing of a second Declaration was in part a response to continued Anglican persecution of nonconformists in the face of the first royal indulgence.[74] If the Anglican clergy would not conform to the King's policy of toleration, it was also hoped that the issuing of a second Declaration would provoke some members of the Church of England into actions that would effectively end any prospect of an alliance between nonconformity and Anglicanism. However, the second Declaration in fact prompted a crucial change of tack by the Anglican hierarchy. Seven bishops, Sancroft, Trelawny of Bristol, Lloyd of St Asaph, Turner of Ely, White of Peterborough,

Ken of Bath and Wells and Lake of Chichester, sent forth a petition asking to be excused from reading the Declaration. However, whereas in the reasons against subscription drafted by Sancroft a year earlier there had been obvious digs at the toleration being afforded to nonconformists, here the bishops claimed that their actions stemmed not 'from any want of due tenderness to Dissenters'. They went on to affirm their support for toleration for fellow Protestants, provided that it was settled by Parliament, not royal prerogative.

James responded to the petition by having the bishops indicted for seditious libel and placed in the Tower. However, his confrontation with the episcopacy backfired. The bishops' plight elicited considerable public sympathy, and the Anglican pamphleteers were now winning nonconformist converts by raising the possibility of religious toleration (for Protestants) secured by statute. The Anglican prelates even received a visitation from ten dissenting ministers who claimed that they 'could not but adhear to them as men constant in the Protestant faith'. Furthermore, Whig lawyers, such as Treby and Somers, provided the bishops' defence counsel. This unusual and, as it would turn out, short-lived alliance between the Whigs, the bishops and the dissenters, was further hastened by the birth of the King's son on 10 June.

The bishops were acquitted of the charges against them on 30 June, and as the news of the not guilty verdict was spread, a great huzzah erupted 'and it passed through the Hall extreame loud; so into the yards and to the water side, and along the river, as far as the bridge'.[75] The same day Henry Compton, the suspended Bishop of London, and six peers, the Earl of Danby, Richard, Viscount Lumley, Edward Russell, Earl of Orford, Henry Sidney, Earl of Romney, William Cavendish, Duke of Devonshire and Charles Talbot, Earl of Shrewsbury, issued an invitation to William of Orange pledging their support if he brought a force into England against James. The seven promised the Prince that almost all of England was behind him: 'your Highness may be assured there are nineteen parts of twenty of the people through-out the Kingdom who are desirous of change; and who, we believe, would willingly contribute to it if they had such a protection to countenance their rising as could secure them from being destroyed before they could get to be in a posture able to defend themselves.'

They also predicted that there would be great numbers of deserters to the Prince's cause from the King's army. However, this optimism was undercut by the fact that they insisted that William needed to act now in case of the further changes 'not only to be expected from a packed Parliament, but what the meeting of any Parliament (in our present circumstances) may produce against those, who will be looked upon as principal obstructors of their proceedings there; it being taken for granted that if things cannot then be carried to their wishes in a parliamentary way, other measures will be put in execution by more violent means'.[76]

The 'invitation' also chided William for having sent his congratulations to James II on the birth of his son: 'The false imposing of that [child] upon the princess and the nation, being not only an infinite exasperation of the people's minds here, but being certainly one of the chief causes upon which the declaration of your entering the kingdom in a hostile manner must be founded on your part, although many other reasons are to be given on ours.' William's agent James Johnstone also encouraged him to air suspicions about the Prince of Wales's authenticity by sponsoring secretly the publication of pamphlets to this effect. In addition, the allegedly supposititious nature of James's son formed a large part of the public justification offered for inviting William of Orange to intervene in English affairs.[77] Some Jacobites later claimed that this had been a long-standing strategy, to use a royal birth as the pretext of invasion on the grounds that the child was not the King's. Anne's absence from her stepmother's lying-in may also have been a planned attempt to cast doubt on the authenticity of the pregnancy: Williamite literature claimed that Anne had been sent away 'on purpose to keep her at a sufficient distance till the scene was over'.[78]

Given, as we have seen, that James did not seek the forcible reversion of England back to Catholicism and that his aims were limited to securing the political and religious emancipation of Catholics and dissenters, we need to understand why leading English politicians were prepared to commit treason, and risk plunging their country into another civil war, by inviting foreign military intervention. Fundamentally, though James was not bent on establishing himself as absolute monarch of a Catholic state, a number of features of his rule succeeded in giving the impression to others that this was the case.

First, England was experiencing an unprecedented level of militarisation domestically. A large royal standing army was camped on Hounslow Heath, west of London, and in garrison towns like York and Hull the brutality of martial law was imposed on the civilian population. In York ringleaders of a violent clash between the citizens and soldiers were punished by martial law, being made to ride a wooden horse until blood came out of their mouths. Forced labour was conscripted in Hull in the crisis of 1688 to fortify the city's defences. The rule of martial law effectively indemnified the army from being brought to account for offences against the civilian population. In September 1688, when the mayor of Scarborough complained that he had been 'tossed in a blanket by the command of Captain Waseley who quarters in that town', the case was dismissed when the Captain pleaded the royal pardon.[79] This increasing militarisation of English society was accompanied by a royal campaign against the carrying of arms by private individuals, driven by James's well-grounded suspicion of the Whig peerage after the Rye House Plot and Monmouth rebellion. The King instructed Lord Lieutenants in December 1686 to search and seize 'muskets or guns' under the terms of the Game Act of 1671. As its name implied, this act had been originally designed to prevent the poaching of game within royal parks and forests by the poor. However, James employed it in a novel way, using an alleged threat to national security to legitimate a far more sweeping and wide-ranging confiscation of firearms in private hands. The general disarmament the King wanted was never properly enforced, but it gave a clear signal about the monarch's intentions.[80]

Secondly, the King's brusque and authoritarian personality did not inspire the confidence that he was a monarch who was intent on ruling according to law. He seems to have transferred from his earlier career as a naval commander the same method of dealing with subordinates, but what might have been an appropriate way to address a naval ranking was less apposite for a bishop or peer of the realm. James lacked his brother's ability to negotiate and to conceal his own intentions. His belief that a lack of conviction had cost his father his life led James to feel that if his policies were being criticised the correct response was to press harder and crush his opponents rather than concede ground. This intransigence was exacerbated by the King's sense that he was the providential instrument of a Catholic God's will, a belief confirmed, it seemed, by the many occasions when James had avoided dire calamity: in the 1640s to escape Parliament's clutches, in the 1660s in naval engagements with the Dutch and in the 1680s from the threat of plot and insurrection. Added to these personality traits was the fact that a number of James's actions as king were of dubious legality: the commission for ecclesiastical causes appeared to be an infringement of the act of 1661, the judgement in Godden v Hales was only secured after James had dismissed half of the original judges, the issuing of royal indulgences had been declared illegal by Parliament on numerous occasions[81] and the actions against the Fellows of Magdalen seemed to be an attack, not only on the Anglican monopoly on education but also on private property, invading the legal freehold of the fellowships.

Thirdly, and perhaps most importantly, James's actions in England were viewed in the context of his rule in Ireland,

Scotland and the American colonies, and against the background of events occurring in France. In Ireland James had replaced the Protestant Earl of Clarendon as Lord Lieutenant with the Old English Catholic Richard Talbot, Earl of Tyrconnel. Tyrconnel set about filling the ranks of James's army in Ireland with Catholics, who by September 1686 constituted 67 per cent of its privates and 40 per cent of its officers. Catholic judges were also appointed, and these romanising policies accelerated after January 1687, when Tyrconnel became Lord Deputy. *Quo warranto* writs were used to give Catholics a two-thirds majority in most corporations, ensuring that a future Irish Parliament would be overwhelmingly Catholic. Revenues of the Church of Ireland were redirected to fund Catholics. Similar policies were adopted in Scotland, where Catholics were again placed within the army. The King dissolved the Scottish Parliament for failing to agree to religious toleration and instead in February 1687 issued a proclamation granting freedom of worship to Catholics and Quakers but not Presbyterians, whom James saw as his main political opponents. This was followed in June by a Declaration of Indulgence issued, the document said, by the King's 'absolute power, which all our subjects are to obey without reserve' that allowed complete toleration and admission to office for Catholics and rights of private worship and a relaxation of the penal laws for Presbyterian conventiclers.

In the American colonies James planned to do away with charter government and colonial legislative assemblies, and to carve up British North America into three or four vice-royalties, based on the Spanish model of government in Central and South America. The first step in this project was the creation of the new dominion of New England, under the direct control of the Crown through its governor, Sir Edmund Andros. The new dominion did away with representative assemblies, taxed without the colonists' consent and enforced the Navigation Acts.[82]

Fears of arbitrary government were heightened further by the revocation of the Edict of Nantes in 1685 by Louis XIV, which brought about the loss of religious freedom and legal equality for France's one million Huguenots (Calvinist Protestants). Fifteen hundred were sent to serve as galley slaves, while between fifty thousand and eighty thousand fled to England with horrific stories of their sufferings. James was ambivalent towards these refugees, permitting them to set up their own French churches but only if worship was conducted according to Anglican rite, a measure that, it was widely reported, was designed to encourage the Huguenots to leave England and seek sanctuary elsewhere.[83] James, like his brother, favoured a pro-French alliance for commercial as well as politico-religious reasons. James was director of the Royal African Company and believed that England's future lay in colonial expansion, seeing the Dutch as a threat to British trade and empire-building. Combined, these factors created the very strong impression, if not the reality, of an attempt to erect an absolute Catholic monarchy on the French model in England.

The situation that James faced in the summer of 1688 bore considerable similarities to the circumstances that his father, Charles I, faced in the summer of 1640. Then, as now, unpopular royal policies had led to an almost complete breakdown in the functioning of government at a local level. Then, as now, the opponents of royal policy nonetheless lacked the independent military power to resist the government. In 1640 Charles's critics had resorted to colluding with the Scots, urging them to invade and force the King to call Parliament. In 1688 James's critics entered discussions with William of Orange to intervene militarily in England and force the King to reverse his policies. However, even by the summer of 1688, when his alliance with dissent was breaking down, James still possessed a far stronger hand than his father had done. Increased trade meant that James was by far the most financially independent Stuart monarch and the power of Parliament over the royal purse strings had been considerably weakened. Moreover, unlike Charles, James had a large, well-trained and well-paid standing army with which to defend himself. Thirdly, the King's programme of political management was likely to prove so successful that there would have to be significant revisions in electoral procedures for a 'free' Parliament to be produced. The English crown was, then, James's to lose, rather than William's to win.

4

THE DUTCH INVASION

On the 5th day of the 9th Month, the land was invaded by a vast body of men of a strange language, having for their General the Prince of Orange, who in a few days marched through the land with vast preparations for war.[1]

On 28 April 1688 William Coward wrote to the Earl of Sunderland from Wells with news from the Somerset quarter sessions. He reported that 'one Elias Bragge alias Clarke' had been committed to the gaol there for speaking treasonable and seditious words, having referred to 'a design of an intended invasion from Holland and other foreign parts upon the account of the late Duke of Monmouth'. Coward thought it his duty 'with some other Justices of the Peace to take Bragg's examination' and transmit it to Sunderland, 'for though it be but a strange sort of account that Bragg gives and very incoherent and improbable in itself, yet the country being filled with a general discourse of it,' he presumed to send the King's minister a copy.[2]

Bragg's rumour would soon turn out to be correct, though the actual reasons for the Dutch invasion had nothing to do with Monmouth's rebellion. For the Dutch Stadtholder, William of Orange, military intervention was necessary to secure his wife's patrimony from a legitimate Catholic heir and gain an anti-French Parliament which would bring Britain into a European alliance against his greatest enemy, Louis XIV. For the merchants of Amsterdam, who held the real political and economic power in the United Provinces, bringing Britain into an anti-French alliance would help break the economic stranglehold Louis had placed on Dutch trade. Dutch propaganda produced for British consumption presented William's expedition as a crusade to liberate the isles from popery and arbitrary government. Similar literature produced for Europe-wide consumption stressed the need for the Dutch intervention to check the seemingly limitless ambitions of the Sun King. However, as with more recent conflicts, a war sold as a mercy mission was really instigated for reasons of geopolitical and economic self-interest.

For his part, James appeared remarkably unconcerned by rumours of the kind sent to the Earl of Sunderland. Even when more concrete information filtered through, he appeared unwilling to treat it with much seriousness. Partly this was a result of poor intelligence. The French had a good inkling that the Dutch were preparing an armada to invade England as early as May 1688. However, James's ambassador at The Hague, the Marquis D'Albeville, did not become aware of the preparations until the third week in September. Moreover, the ambassador's dispatches were not, in any case, coming directly to the King but were going first to Sunderland instead. Nonetheless, James had already been warned of the danger by the French diplomat Usson de Bonrepos on 25 August and by Ferdinand d'Adda, the papal envoy, on 31 August.[3] Yet, late into the summer of 1688, his correspondence with his son-in-law presented the image of a monarch in blissful ignorance of the preparations being made against him. Writing from Windsor on 31 August, the King told William, 'this place itself affords little news', adding, 'What news from your side of the water?'[4]

What William didn't tell his father-in-law was that he was assembling an invasion force approximately four times the size of the armada sent by the Spanish in 1588. Aside from the massive logistical effort required, William was also engaged in a frenetic round of diplomacy, designed to secure troops both for the invasion force and to guard the borders of the Dutch Republic from French forces, should they launch an attack on the United Provinces while the majority of its army was in England. A key figure in this diplomatic alliance was the young Frederick, Elector of Brandenburg, heir to William's estates and personal fortune. By September William had secured Frederick's agreement to secure the Republic's frontiers along the Rhine, as well as some of the Elector's troops for the invasion of England. Other German princes quickly came on side in reaction to the election of Louis's nominee, Cardinal Wilhelm von Fürstenberg, Bishop of Strasburg, as Archbishop-Elector of Cologne. In response, the Dukes of Zell and Wolfenbüttel promised to furnish William with four thousand men and the Duke of Hesse-Cassel offered three thousand. The contest over the archbishopric of Cologne represented one part of the French king's schemes for increasing his power in the Holy Roman Empire. Louis now saw himself as presented with a small window of opportunity to extend his territories in Germany. The Habsburg Emperor Leopold, on 6 September, had recaptured Belgrade from the Ottoman Turks (who had not so secretly been supported by the French king) and Louis feared that, if he delayed acting, the Emperor might be able to conclude a swift peace, allowing Leopold to turn his attention westwards. If, as Louis anticipated, William was going to get bogged down in a new civil war in England, this would also remove one of the French King's most formidable enemies from obstructing his plans. Without Dutch support, it would be easier to coerce German states into accepting French claims to parts of the Palatinate and other lands which Louis had annexed since 1678. Louis's preoccupation with Germany significantly weakened James's position. There would be no immediate military assistance from France in the form of either men and arms sent to England or a diversionary attack on the Netherlands.

Aside from winning over other European states and principalities, William also had to convince the Dutch elite, through their federal Parliament, the States General, that his proposed invasion of England was in the United Provinces' best interests. For them the war was more about saving Dutch trade, particularly the herring industry, than rescuing the English people from popery and tyranny. As Admiral General, William could decide on the strength of the Dutch fleet without their approval and raise customs duties without consent to pay for any enlargement. However, he could not go to war without the approval of the States General, which was dominated by the rich bankers, merchants and traders of Amsterdam. This obstacle encapsulated the conundrum at the heart of the Dutch state: it was a federal republic, dominated by a commercial elite, rather than a landed aristocracy, but it had a territorial princeling as its head of state. These two political forces, the burgomasters of Amsterdam and the Princes of Orange, were often at loggerheads. The few occasions when they acted in concert were those when the whole survival of an independent Dutch state appeared to be in jeopardy. The States General were suspicious of the Prince of Orange's motives in intervening in English affairs. The prominent burgomaster Nicolaas Witsen wondered whether 'considering the proximity of the Princess [Mary] to the crown, he thought some higher reward than labour might be in store for him'.[5]

However, the Amsterdam elite were increasingly open to the need for some sort of military action as a result of the growing damage the rivalry between the Dutch and the French was doing to trade. Commerce between the two countries was now even worse than it had been during the crisis of 1672, when the Dutch had been forced to breach their dykes and flood the land, in order to halt the advance of French forces. Louis XIV's aggressive actions pushed the States General further into accepting William's policy. A ban on the import into France of herrings from the Netherlands crippled the Dutch fishing industry. In late September Louis ordered the general arrest of all Dutch ships in French ports. With support from the former English ambassador at The Hague, Bevil Skelton, on 30 August, the French ambassador, D'Avaux, also warned that any act of aggression against England would be deemed a breach of the peace between Holland and France. The implicit threat of military retaliation was a hollow one (and Skelton was sent to the Tower by the King for his presumption), but it encouraged the belief in Holland that the Dutch were now seriously in danger from an Anglo-French alliance.

The States General was finally convinced to support the war after appeals were made by the ailing Grand Pensionary Gaspar Fagel on William's behalf. He acknowledged that William did have a personal interest in the invasion, but urged that he was motivated not by a desire for personal aggrandisement but by a wish to keep the English Crown in the hands of Protestants. The dangers of not intervening in English affairs were grave, Fagel said. Domestic rebellion against the King's policies was inevitable, and, if James won, the country would fall to Catholicism and into an even deeper alliance with France. If James lost, England would become a republic again – and he reminded them what an enemy to Dutch trade the Commonwealth and Protectorate had been in the 1650s.

Final consultations with other European heads of state to seek their consent or at least acquiescence in William's design revealed that the deposition of James was already being discussed, at least by the Prince of Orange's ministers. The Holy Roman Emperor Leopold had already been persuaded that the Prince was only intervening on behalf of the people of England, but William's *chef de cabinet*, Simon van Pettekum, put the issue in a nutshell. 'Would it not,' he said, 'be very advantageous for the Emperor to have a King of England completely in agreement with the House of Austria about France', to which the Imperial envoy Kramrich replied that this was certainly the case but that the 'Emperor would not wish the price of so great an advantage to be such a black action as that of a prince dethroning his uncle and his father-in-law'. 'Oh really,' said Pettekum bluntly, 'what does it matter to the Emperor if the King of England is called James or William?'[6]

The scale of the Dutch invasion force meant that it was impossible to keep the preparation completely secret, although it was widely rumoured in Europe that the massive armada was being built for an attack on France. The fleet consisted of forty-three men of war, four light frigates and ten fireships, as well as seven light yachts to act as messenger. However, the gunships were designed to protect the troop transports, made up of over four hundred flyboats, for fifteen thousand soldiers, eighteen battalions of infantry and 4092 cavalry, rather than to directly engage James's fleet. The armada carried arms for twenty thousand soldiers, three hundred tons of hay, tin pontoons for crossing rivers, wagons, corn, flour biscuits, medicines and hospital stores, bridges to embark cavalry, four tons of tobacco, one thousand pairs of boots, fifty hogsheads of brandy, six hundred hogsheads of beer and six thousand guilders' worth of salted herring.

In addition to stores for the troops and sailors, the ships carried vast amounts of propaganda to be distributed in England, to convince the English population of the good intentions of the Dutch forces. Around sixty thousand copies of William's Declaration were printed in English amid great secrecy by specially commissioned printers working simultaneously in The Hague, Rotterdam and Amsterdam. Portable printing presses were carried as well, to produce further pro-Williamite literature after the fleet had landed. William had already used the English press to his advantage in the 1670s when he had sponsored pamphlets against

Charles II's pro-French foreign policy. Before William landed his advisers had given him extensive guidance on the content and distribution of tracts and he had established contacts with printers and publishers in England.

Key elements of this Williamite propaganda initiative were the Prince's two declarations, issued on 10 and 24 October (the first of which had been drafted as early as August 1688). The first declaration made reference to two rumours which would later assume great importance in public debate: first, that James's baby son was not his own and secondly that the King's government in Ireland was a model for his government in England. Copies were posted through the penny post and additional copies were produced by English printers. Staged ritual endorsements of the declaration rammed home the way in which it was a test of support for the Prince. In Plymouth the garrison came over to William when the governor of the town read out his manifesto and asked individual officers and battalions to declare for it. This propaganda was also relatively cheap. Some tracts sold for as little as a penny, and many were read aloud or passed around to those who had not bought them. Visual as well as written propaganda was important to the Orange cause. Playing cards were manufactured with images depicting key events in the Revolution, and forty-nine prints and thirty-one medals made in support of William's cause have been found. Fourteen of these prints referred to the rumour that the Prince of Wales was illegitimate, sired by a Jesuit priest or a miller, by showing fake coats of arms for James's son featuring a windmill (for the miller) and a lobster (symbol of the Society of Jesus).

When the penny finally dropped, James's ambassador, D'Albeville, was taken aback by the scope of the Dutch scheme: 'An absolute conquest is intended under the specious and ordinary pretences of religion, liberty, property and a free parliament and a religious, exact, observation of the laws; this and a war against France, they make account, will be but a work of a month's time.'[7] It was not until 10 September that James began to be persuaded that something was afoot and only on 24 September that he was finally convinced that the Dutch were really going to invade. On 28 September news of the Dutch invasion plans was relayed to the public via royal proclamation. Fundamentally, the King appears to have been unwilling to accept that his daughter and son-in-law could be plotting against him. The betrayal was probably made worse by the evasive replies that James and Queen Mary had received from the Prince and Princess, which, if not outright lies, were certainly economical with the truth. In July Mary Beatrice had reproached the Princess of Orange for her lack of affection towards the newly born Prince of Wales: 'since I have been brought to be, you have never once in your Letters to me taken the least notice of my son, no more than if he had never been born.' The Princess's reply was a neat piece of casuistry: 'all the King's children shall ever find as much affection and kindness from me as can be expected from children of the same Father.'[8] Her choice of words was deeply loaded, given that by now Mary Stuart, through correspondence with her sister Anne, had become deeply suspicious about the paternity of James's reputed heir. Her measured response to the Queen's letter, and the cessation of prayers for the Prince of Wales in the Princess's chapel, also hinted at deeper intrigues. William meanwhile responded with half-truths to James's questions concerning rumours of a military build-up in the Netherlands, stating that 'the States-General hath not the least thought of being the aggressors at this juncture and would only act defensively'.[9] This was correct in the sense that William had, at the time of writing, yet fully to convince the States General of the case for war. However, the Prince's own intentions were clearly more belligerent.

Despite the poor intelligence the King was receiving and his own unwillingness to believe his family capable of such a betrayal, Britain was not caught unawares by the Dutch invasion plans. As a precautionary measure, James had in August already ordered the navy to patrol the North Sea on the watch for any suspicious movements and cancelled all leave for the army. The permanent military establishment in England was now larger than it had been under any previous Stuart monarch and there were further permanent forces in Ireland and Scotland which could be recalled should the Dutch succeed in making a landing. The King, however, was now caught between two schools of thought. The Catholic hardliners at his court, such as his Jesuit confessor, Father Petre, attempted to convince him that he could beat the Dutch in the field and that he should make preparations for a military confrontation with William. The Earl of Sunderland, however, urged James to attempt to win back support in England by making a number of concessions to Anglican-Tory opinion. Sunderland himself was now gripped by panic and despair: the need to disown the debacle instigated by Skelton had cost him the confidence of the French and he was reviled by English politicians for his politic conversion to Catholicism. If he lost the King's support he would be left defenceless. However, as he conceded to the French ambassador in private, Sunderland felt James's situation was hopeless and that 'the King could do nothing in his present state but escape the best way he could, for he had no hope of outside aid and he might well be driven from England in a week'.[10]

Initially James fell in with his chief ministers' advice to make concessions to Anglican-Tory opinion. This represented an uncharacteristic move for the King. He had been convinced that it was his father, Charles I's, lack of resolution which had cost him his life. If he was not the most loved monarch that had ever sat on the British throne, James did at least enjoy a reputation for plain dealing which neither Charles I nor Charles II had enjoyed. At this moment of crisis, however, he backed away from his opponents. The writs for his new Parliament, issued on 21 September, were cancelled four days later. On 22 September James agreed to consult the bishops and peers on what further measures to take to answer their grievances. On 24 September he invited nine bishops, including the Archbishop of Canterbury, William Sancroft, and three

others who had been prosecuted for seditious libel, to meet him
and offer some recommendations as to what should be done in the
situation. Meanwhile Sunderland dissuaded James from issuing an
order for a general arrest, similar to that sent out during the
Monmouth rebellion, of those suspected of complicity in the
Orangist conspiracy. Instead, he convinced the King to issue a
general pardon to his opponents.

Sunderland's advice here was seriously mistaken. In contrast to
1685, when the gentry and lords had conspicuously stayed at
home, the Dutch invasion was accompanied by a serious domestic insurrection in the north that was being planned by a
combination of Whig and Tory Lords. In September 1688 the Earl
of Danby wrote to the Earl of Chesterfield with news of the
planned Dutch armada, which he wrongly anticipated would land
that month in the north-east. Danby appeared certain that the
issue would now come to blows but expressed his determination to
'rather lose my life in the field than live under an arbitrary power,
and see our laws and religion changed, which is now visibly the
King's intention'.[11] It was clear that the Earl was preparing for
the worst, making his will in the first week of October.[12] With
Danby leading the rebels in Yorkshire, the Whig peers the Earl of
Devonshire and Lord Delamere coordinated risings in Cheshire,
Derbyshire and Nottinghamshire.[13] The issuing of a royal proclamation on 28 September ordering all subjects to arm for the
defence of their country provided a convenient pretext for many
conspirators to equip themselves. The Catholic Lord Fairfax
raised some suspicions in early October concerning the activities
of Danby, but these were dismissed by the governor of York,
Sir John Reresby. The one attempt made by the government to
arrest a conspirator, Lord Lumley, ended in farce as the agent
sent out to apprehend him, John D'Arcy, was one of Lumley's
co-conspirators.[14]

On 3 October the bishops offered their list of recommendations
to the King. The first urged that the government should be put in

the hands of Anglicans and the charters restored in the corporations, a recommendation which led to the restoring of borough
charters surrendered on *quo warranto* writs since 1679, an order for
the dismissal of all officers who had been put in post after that
date – which caused chaos and consternation in the localities –
and finally the dismissal of Sunderland on 27 October. The recommendations also demanded the suspension of the ecclesiastical
commission, which had already been adjourned since August on
Sunderland's advice. The King agreed to this and also reinstated
Henry Compton to his ecclesiastical functions. It was further
requested that the King should not employ his dispensing power
and that he should restore the Fellows and President of Magdalen
College, to which James again consented. In the Church, the
Anglicans petitioned the King 'to call a Parliament where the Act
of Uniformity might be settled and provision made for a due liberty of conscience', to stop the four foreign bishops from invading
the spiritual jurisdiction of the Anglican hierarchy, and to fill the
vacant bishopric of York. The bishops also pleaded with James to
convert to Protestantism, a request which the King stated was out
of the question.

Contemporaries doubted the sincerity of these concessions and
with good reason. On 4 October James summoned a meeting of
his Catholic courtiers and reassured them that he would not agree
to anything that would be to their disadvantage. As he saw it, the
main aim of these concessions was to undercut the justifications
for the Prince of Orange's intervention and consequently point up
the ulterior motives for the Dutch invasion, conquest of England
and seizure by force of his throne. The bishops themselves gave a
lukewarm response to the King's request that they produce public
prayers on the subject of the invasion. The wording of the prayer
offered urged God to 'preserve that holy Religion we profess,
together with our Laws and ancient Government', 'and unite us all
in . . . one and the same Holy Worship and Communion'.[15] It did
not escape James's notice that this appeared more to be a prayer for

the success of William's design than for its failure. On 16 October he earnestly pressed the bishops to 'declare an abhorrence of the invasion itself' but they refused.

Meanwhile the King continued in his attempt to rebut the charges made in the Prince's declaration. On 22 October he launched what amounted to an extraordinary public enquiry into the circumstances of his son's birth. Forty witnesses swore on oath that they had witnessed the birth of the Prince of Wales and their depositions were published for public consumption. James told those summoned that he had called them, as he expected to meet the Prince of Orange on the field of battle and that he did not wish there to be any uncertainty about the succession in the event of his death. Such public testimonies to the legitimacy of James's heir were too late to shift the opinion of the King's eldest daughter, Mary, who by October had ceased to reply to either her father's or her stepmother's letters.

James himself appears to have been worried to the point of paranoia about the potential impact of William's propaganda, burning all copies of the Prince's declaration that he could find. At meetings to respond to the declaration selected portions were read but the King would not allow anyone to see his full copy. The Earl of Clarendon had to borrow Princess Anne's copy in order to get a full sight of it, only to find out that this was actually James's one and only copy, which he had lent to his daughter. However, the King's own propaganda initiative was not without its own success. James increased the circulation of the *London Gazette*, encouraging its editors to highlight stories favourable to his cause and playing down William's successes and ordering the devotion of the first columns of each issue to royal declarations. Added to this, James's royal proclamations (particularly those publicising the concessions which undercut the grievances in the Prince's declaration) were printed and heavily circulated and he sponsored special prayers condemning the sin of rebellion. His propaganda frequently raised the spectre of civil war that the Dutch invasion might bring in.

There is evidence that the fear of political anarchy was bringing some people to the King's side. A correspondent of John Ellis recorded that many of the 'richer' and 'soberer' sort of people, were afraid that the current events were 'like to entail war upon the nation'.[16]

James persisted in his attempts to get the bishops to condemn William's invasion plans and in particular to refute the claim that the Prince had been invited to intervene by some of the English nobility. On 1 November the King had asked Henry Compton whether he had been involved in calling the Prince over, to which question the Bishop of London offered a flat lie by denying he had anything to do with the letter. The following day Compton and four other bishops were again questioned about their involvement and again protested their innocence, with Sancroft stating that he could not believe any prelates were involved in the design. Nonetheless, they continued to refuse to issue a statement making clear their abhorrence of the Dutch invasion. At one final meeting on 6 November, the day after William's forces had landed in the south-west, James asked them if they had prepared a paper condemning the Prince of Orange but again they offered nothing, Sancroft first complaining that it was not certain that the declaration was authentic. More pointedly, the Archbishop stated that the clergy had got into trouble before for involving themselves in political matters and were not keen to do so again. Despite further pressure from James, the prelates were unmoved. Losing his patience, James attempted to assert himself: 'I am your King. I am Judge of what is best for me. I will go my own way. I desire your assistance in it.' The bishops, however, would only go so far as agreeing to issue a public statement of their innocence, printed under the King's authority. However, James insisted that it should be published by the bishops as this would have more credibility, the public, he said, now being ready to believe the very worst of him, even that he would impose a fraudulent son upon them as his heir. Again, however, the bishops demurred, stating that they would only comply with his demands in a free Parliament. Seeing that further argument was fruitless, the King drew the audience to a close: 'I will argue no further. If you will not assist me as I desire I must stand upon my own legs, and trust to my self and my own arms.'[17]

To this end James had been making strenuous efforts to increase the strength of both his army and navy. By the end of October the fleet numbered thirty-seven men-of-war and eleven fireships, but there were reported problems in getting men to serve. In the summer the King had already had to visit the fleet to quell a near mutiny over the open celebration of mass by some Catholic officers.[18] In the meantime James and his admiral, Lord Dartmouth, waited on the wind; if it blew easterly, Dartmouth would be pinned down in the mouth of the Thames, while William could set sail. To monitor the prevailing breeze, James had an enormous weathercock mounted on the roof of the Banqueting Hall, where he could see it from his apartments.

To strengthen the English army, troops from Ireland and Scotland were drawn back to England and orders were given for fresh forces to be raised. However, the new men were raw recruits and the raising of Irish troops was counter-productive, heightening fears among the English population about the threat of massacre of Protestants at the hands of armed 'papists'. On 11 October a newsletter reported that in Portsmouth, where most of the Irish soldiers were based, there were complaints that the 'rude Irish have caused many families to leave that place, having committed many robberies'.[19] In another incident it was reported that Irish soldiers had assaulted some English officers after an argument in an alehouse, killing a number of them.

Efforts to raise the militia as a second line of defence revealed the near-complete erosion of trust between local and central government that James's attempts to 'pack' Parliament had effected. The new Lord Lieutenants and Deputy Lieutenants who had been appointed were often individuals with insufficient local clout to raise any men. James had not called a muster since the outbreak of the Monmouth rebellion, and the militia's performance had been so dismal, with several units defecting to the rebels, that the King could be forgiven for seeing it as more of a liability than a help. However, the militia's long abeyance caused problems. Demands for the militia to be raised anew often met with negative responses. The Earl of Lindsey, one of the northern conspirators, stated pointedly that as 'musters are not pleasing to your majesty, they have met but once since your coronation'.[20] The situation was not helped by James's diversion of the funds for it into his professional army. The Earl of Bristol informed Sunderland that 'the Militia having beene for some time laid aside, the people charged are unprovided of Armes & Coates . . . the souldiers must all be new listed and sworne, and . . . it will take up two or three months to make a new regulation'.

Some of the King's supporters made bullish assessments of the impending conflict. Nathaniel Molyneux wrote to Roger Kenyon that the King now had a 'great army' which was 'in good equipage . . . that such an ocasione requires for carryinge all war-like instruments to destroy theis fooles, forraingers and strangers that cannot be soe wyse as to stay in their own countrye'. He ended his letter promising to give further news when 'theis madmen invade us, and then . . . [I] will tell you both of their landinge and sending home again (if not well mannered).'[21] The Imperial envoy, on the other hand, gave a far more pessimistic assessment of James's position: 'the King of England has against him all the clergy, all the nobility, all the people, all the army and navy, with few exceptions.'[22]

These preparations left James with around forty thousand men in arms. Though the field army camped at Hounslow Heath numbered only around twenty-five thousand men, as many others remained stationed in ports and garrisons as a result of the uncertainty as to where Prince William's armada would land and the desire to protect royal magazines and fortresses from the threat of domestic insurrection. There has been some debate among historians as to the size of the opposing force led by William of Orange. The long-accepted view was that the Prince had an army of around fifteen thousand, but it has recently been suggested that his forces may have numbered more than twenty-one thousand, placing them at only a slight numerical disadvantage to the King's army. Contemporary estimates are also at variance. John Whittle, an English chaplain with the Dutch forces, wrote that when the troops disembarked at Brixham, 'The number of all his [William's] Forces and Souldiers [was] about fifteen thousand four hundred and odd men.'[23] The intelligence that the crown was receiving from the west placed the Dutch forces at sixteen thousand infantry and five thousand horses (the 'horse pretty good, but the foot very ordinary, and much inferior to ours').[24]

To some extent this debate over numbers is academic as the two armies never met on the field of battle. What is clear, however, is the degree of confidence that William had in the ability of his army to carry off his plan. The units selected constituted the crack battalions of the Dutch army and were far more battle-hardened than those that James had to deploy. Unlike the Duke of Monmouth, for whom domestic support was an absolute necessity, the Prince had little need of or interest in securing military aid from English rebels once he had landed. As William made clear in his rather disgruntled speech to the south-western gentry when they finally publicly came out in support of him, what the Dutch required was not their 'military assistance' but their 'countenance and presence'. Public support from the English for his intervention was valuable in that it validated the claims made in William's propaganda that he had only landed on British shores at the invitation of the English people, to secure them from tyranny and popery. However, as we will see later, William was less than willing to arm or otherwise support the English rebels in the north for fear that this might later create a challenge to the total military hegemony of the Dutch.

This lack of interest in English military support for the invasion was reflected in the process of determining where the best landing site for William's fleet might be. Both the King's and William's supporters in England appear to have been uncertain as to where the Dutch armada would attempt to land. As we have seen, the Earl of Danby thought they might make landfall at Hull, and the same harbour was targeted as a potential embarkation point by the government. A number of English reports in October carried the news that the Dutch were at sea and preparing to land at Sole Bay in Suffolk. However, at this stage the Dutch fleet remained in dock, while Admiral Herbert, the Englishman nominally placed in charge of William's invasion armada, counselled against making a landing in the north-east on the grounds that first, its coastline was extremely treacherous in the winter, secondly that it was sparsely populated and would afford less support for an invading army and thirdly that it contained a number of royal garrisons, such as those at Hull and Scarborough, which might slow the progress of the Prince's forces. Although Herbert's reasoning was sound, he was little more than a figurehead, designed to give a British face to what was a Dutch naval operation, and his advice held little sway. In fact, it appears that no firm decision was made on where to land the fleet, with the matter largely being left to which direction the wind was blowing in. This reveals again the extent to which the Dutch were relatively uninterested in factors such as the level of support for William's intervention in different parts of England.

The invasion force first left the Netherlands on 30 October but was beaten back to harbour by a fierce storm in which several ships and five hundred horses were lost. Dutch news-sheets deliberately exaggerated the level of damage caused in order to lure the English into believing that lengthy repairs would be required before the armada could set out again. Such news was greeted with glee in Whitehall, where it appeared to the King that the special prayers he had ordered for the safety of the kingdom had brought the blessings of divine providence down upon him. The King's reaction to the storm also revealed how far the concessions he had made in September were, in his view, no more than temporary expediencies. James immediately issued orders to stop the process of restoring borough charters. The dissenter Roger Morrice saw this as 'very instructive to let us know that the Restauration proceeds not from inclination but from necessity and that the Court will change their Councils if the present distresses were over'.[25]

However, the damage that the Dutch fleet had incurred was quickly repaired and by 2 November the armada was under sail again, the famous 'Protestant Wind' blowing it along England's south coast. For those who caught a glimpse of it, it was an awesome sight, one spectator at Dover recording that the flotilla was so large that while he had seen the first ship at ten in the morning, it was not until five in the afternoon that the last one went past. At this point the Prince ordered the fleet to stretch out in a line across the Channel between Dover and Calais, so that, according to Gilbert Burnet, 'our Fleet reached within a league of each place . . . This sight would have ravish'd the most curious Eyes of *Europe*. When our Fleet was in its greatest splendour, the Trumpets and Drums playing various Tunes to rejoyce our hearts.'[26] Lord Dartmouth had been given clear orders by James to 'burn, take and otherwise destroy and disable' the Prince of Orange's boats, but instead the King's Admiral chose to hang back and await further orders. While he waited the wind shifted direction, blowing south-westerly, leading the Dutch to make a landing at Brixham in Devon, whilst James's ships were blown north and had to take shelter in the Downs (the stretch of water between Deal and the Woolwich Sands developed as an anchorage by Henry VIII).

The Dutch army disembarked on the auspicious date of 5 November (old style), the anniversary of England's last deliverance from the threat of popery. An apocryphal local tradition holds that when William landed at Brixham and was asked what his business was he replied in a strong Dutch accent, 'Mine goot people, mine goot people, I am only come for your goots, for all your goots', to which, it was reported, a local wit replied, 'Yes and for our chattels too.'[27]

It was not only the English who enjoyed poking fun at foreigners. While, over several days, the whole invasion force was gradually landed, William's secretary and childhood tutor, Sir Constantijn Huygens, used his spare time to record the unusual habits of the local people. He was particularly struck by the fact that Englishwomen seemed to be habitual pipe smokers: 'At one spot,' Huygens recorded in his journal, 'there were five women saluting [the Prince], each with a pipe of tobacco in her mouth, as we very often saw, smoking quite shamelessly, even young children of 13 or 14. We enjoyed studying the way these island people lived, and how addicted to tobacco they all were, men, women, even children.' Huygens couldn't stop laughing when his hostess, 'young and pretty', breastfed her baby while she smoked a pipe, which she handed to the child when he stopped sucking. The astonished Dutch politician recorded that the baby 'took it and put in his mouth and tried hard to smoke'.[28]

On 9 November the Prince's forces approached the city of Exeter, Burnet having already ascertained the day before that the mayor, Sir Christopher Broderick, would not attempt to resist William's coming and that the bishop, deans and chapters of the cathedral had already fled. The Prince of Orange's entrance into the city had all the hallmarks of a royal progress. The invasion force entered in full regalia, led by the Earl of Macclesfield and the other English cavalry. The arrival of the Prince's troops also provided the people of Exeter with what was probably their first glimpse of black people, the English troops being swiftly followed by two hundred West African attendants, clad with 'Imbroyder'd Caps lined with Fur, and Plumes of white Feathers'.[29] After them came another two hundred Finnish troops dressed even more exotically than the Africans, wearing 'Bear Skins taken from the Wild Beasts they had slain . . . with black Armour, and broad Flaming

Swords'. William himself came in riding on a white horse, clad in armour and with forty-two footmen following behind him.[30]

News of William's landing in the south-west on 5 November had reached James within twenty-eight hours, the messenger apparently killing seven horses (and almost himself) in making his frenetic ride to London. The capital and other towns and cities in England were now gripped by anti-Catholic rioting. The Catholic chapel in St James's was set upon on 11 November by the mob, who were dispersed only by the promise from 'Lord Craven and guards' that they would blow it up the next day. However, as the priests came the following day to remove their possessions, their goods were seized by the crowd, who took two cartloads 'and burnt them on Holborn Hill and in Smithfield; whereupon the guards were sent to suppress them, with orders to fire with bullet, which they did, and killed 4 or 5, and forced the rest to retreat'.[31] On 14 November there were similar anti-Catholic riots in Norwich as a crowd of around a thousand people surrounded the Catholic chapel in the city.[32] The rioting in London forced James to reconsider his initial plan to remain in the capital and wait for the Prince to come to him. Instead, he now prepared to go out to meet William's forces at Salisbury and made arrangements, given the clear hostility of the populace, for the Queen and Prince of Wales to be taken out of the country to the safety of France.

The King left for the west of England on 17 November. Meanwhile the plans for a rebellion against his government led by Whig and Tory peers in the north came to fruition. The northern lords had delayed taking action owing to their confusion as to where William would land his invasion force, which turned to disappointment when news reached them that the Prince's armada had arrived in the south-west. There had already been one failed pro-Williamite insurrection. A rising in Gloucestershire in support of the Prince had been rapidly put down by the loyal Lord Lieutenant, the Duke of Beaufort. Lord Lovelace, a radical Whig peer and former associate of the notorious John Wilmot, Earl of

Rochester, had attempted to join up with William's forces, taking seventy armed men to Exeter, but several of them were killed in a bloody skirmish with Beaufort's militia and Lovelace himself was captured. However, the concentration of the King's forces in the south and the natural preoccupation of the government with William's army in the west gave the northern conspirators greater opportunity to organise their resistance unabated. The first to publicly come out in support of the Prince was the hot-headed Whig peer Lord Delamere, who had earlier been implicated in the Monmouth rebellion. On 15 November Delamere urged his tenants and supporters in Cheshire and Lancashire to join him in taking up arms against the King. His declaration put the case for supporting the Prince of Orange in simple terms of choosing between doing nothing and accepting the onward march of Catholicism and slavery or taking up arms and striking a blow for Protestantism and traditional English liberties. 'No man,' he said, 'can love fighting for its own sake, nor find any pleasure in Danger; And you may imagine I would be very glad to spend the rest of my days in peace, I having so great a share of Troubles. But I see All lies at stake, I am to chuse whether I will be a Slave and a Papist, or a Protestant and a Freeman: and the case being thus, I should think my self false to my Country, if I sate still at this time.'[33]

Delamere had chosen to break ranks with his co-conspirators and, rather than wait for assistance from William, take action independently. The lack of caution expressed in his words and actions contrasted with the more moderate position adopted by the Earl of Devonshire. He had entered Derby on 17 November with a sizeable force of cavalry drawn from his large household at Chatsworth and his tenantry. However, the declaration Devonshire issued in a bid to gather more support in order to seize control of Nottingham avoided any direct statement of support for the Prince of Orange and instead pressed only for a free Parliament which 'the Army now on foot may not give any Interruption to'.[34]

Delamere joined Devonshire in Nottingham on 21 November. Having ascertained that the populace were loyal to the rebels (through raising a false alarm that a royal army was approaching, which led the public to hastily barricade the Trent bridge), the two issued a joint declaration which represented a middle-ground position between the demand for a free Parliament made in Derby and the unqualified call to arms issued in Cheshire. The conspirators acknowledged that it was 'rebellion to resist a King that Governs by Law; but he was always accounted a Tyrant that made his Will the Law; and to resist such an one, we justly esteem no Rebellion, but a necessary Defence'. The King's concessions, they said, were 'like plums to children, by deceiving them for [a] while . . . till this present storm that threatens the Papists, be past, as soon as they shall be resettled, the former Oppression will be put on with greater vigour'. The only way that the constitution and church could be preserved from the threat of Catholic double-dealing was via the resolutions of a free Parliament.[35]

Delamere then moved south, where he met little opposition, the small force of loyal militia commanded by the Duke of Beaufort having melted away after the Duke chose to drop out of sight as William's forces marched east. Delamere was able to free Lord Lovelace from Gloucester gaol without difficulty. In Yorkshire the appointment of the loyal Anglican the Duke of Newcastle as Lord Lieutenant in place of the Catholic Lord Fairfax did little to strengthen the Crown's position in the county. Newcastle had had limited success in fulfilling royal orders to raise a regiment of eight hundred men and, as the invasion force had landed in the south-west, he saw little military value in keeping the regiment together. Newcastle also appeared to be completely unaware of who was involved in pro-Williamite plotting, appointing the conspirators John Darcy and Sir Henry Goodricke to the lieutenancy. The conspiracy in Yorkshire came to a head on 22 November, as the Earl of Danby used the militia to gain control of York. The Deputy Lieutenants had been assembled on the pretext of writing a loyal address to the King but actually so that they could put forward a declaration for a free Parliament and the Prince of Orange. At the meeting itself the signal was given that they were under attack from Catholics with a cry that the 'papists were risen and had fired at the militia troops'. At this call Danby and his fellow conspirators 'made a party with their servants of 100 hors, wel armed and well mounted, and rode up to the four militia troops drawn out for another purpas, and cryed for a free Parlament and the Protestant religion and noe poperie'.[36] Having taken control of the militia, they then placed the loyalist governor, Sir John Reresby, under effective house arrest. The Yorkshire conspirators quickly moved on to take control of the magazine at Scarborough and then Hull, which was heavily defended and would have been much harder to take. However, a mutiny by the Protestant officers and men led to their taking over the town and placing Catholic officers and men in the gaol.

The closeness that the revolution came to outright war was revealed in Danby's *Thoughts of a private person about the justice of the gentleman's undertaking at York* (1689), in which he insisted upon the limited powers of kings of England and argued that if they acted arbitrarily they could be resisted 'or else we might not resist the Devil should he creep into the Court in a Jesuits habit and get a comission to cut all our throats'. Danby rehearsed the argument, familiar from the Civil War, that it was not an attack on the sanctity of the King's person to resist James's unlawful commands. However, this was armed resistance and 'if any thing befall his [James's] person by their hands, it is but a chance and accidental thing, which may happen also in peaceable times'. The agreement made between the northern conspirators formally acknowledged that they were at war with the King, the lords signing an agreement to 'oblige themselves upon their respective honours and faith to abide by and acquiesce in such expedients as shall be resolved the said subscribers to be sufficient *during this time of war*'.[37]

James himself now travelled westwards, accompanied by the French ambassador Barillon, preparing to meet the Prince of Orange's forces in a pitched battle. Barillon commented on the poor morale of the King's officers: 'Even if they aren't capable of treason it's still obvious that they won't fight with a good heart, and the army is perfectly aware of this.'[38] James's intelligence concerning William's movements was poor, his spies were defecting to the Prince and the Dutch had effectively cut off lines of communication. It was also becoming increasingly difficult for him to know which of his officers he could trust. The regiments sent to make first contact with William's army contained a number of leading conspirators, Lord Cornbury, the King's nephew, Thomas Langston, in charge of the Duke of St Albans' Horse, and Sir Francis Compton, of the Royal Horse Guards. On 16 November Cornbury and Langston went over to the Prince of Orange, Langston taking his whole regiment with him. Compton, however, lost his nerve and returned to the royal camp at Salisbury.

Cornbury's desertion also brought over to William the Tory Sir Edward Seymour. It was Seymour who suggested that the Prince's supporters at Exeter should bind themselves together via an association, like those used by the northern conspirators, otherwise 'we were as a rope of sand: men might leave us when they pleased'.[39] In pragmatic terms, the bond of association to the Prince of Orange signed at Exeter was a means of binding together the Prince's heterogeneous band of adherents while avoiding explicitly stating that William's supporters were resisting the king.[40] Yet it was, in fact, an astoundingly bold political statement. As Burnet commented, the model for it was a document known as 'Shaftesbury's association', used as evidence in the trial of the Whig earl for high treason in 1682 but probably written by the 'plotter' Robert Ferguson, who was part of the English contingent in the expedition of 1688. That association had also been drafted to deal with the possible problem of a popish monarch occupying the throne, by urging Protestants to arm and combine themselves

against his romanising policies. Here in 1688 was an association
made by English subjects to a foreign head of state while the actual
sovereign was still alive. The takers promised that they would
pursue not only those who attempted to kill or injure William,
'but all their Adherents, and all that we find in Arms against us'.
Even a successful assassination attempt would not divert them
'from prosecuting this cause . . . but that it shall engage us to carry
it on with all the vigour that so barbarous a Practice shall
deserve'.[41] Nowhere in this association was there mention of the
subject's duty of allegiance to James II and it seems probable that
the King was meant to be included in the clause discussing the
punishments to be handed out to the adherents of papists in arms.
The oath was also tendered to the public as William made his
progress east. Later the Assembly of Commoners also subscribed
to the association, with, according to the dissenter Roger Morrice,
fewer than twenty of 220 members refusing it. It was even
rumoured that no one would be allowed to hold public office
without joining the Exeter Association.[42]

The King arrived at Salisbury on 19 November in the middle of
a blizzard. He attempted to rally his remaining commanders to
him by announcing that he would call a free Parliament. However,
if they wished to join the Prince of Orange, he would give them a
pass. None of his officers took up this offer. At this crucial time
James's health began to deteriorate. He suffered severe nosebleeds
that laid him up for hours and for which he was prescribed opium-
based drugs by his physicians. It has been suggested that this
affliction was psychosomatic, a symptom of the extreme stress that
the King was under. However, at the time it was believed by some
that it was the result of a brain tumour 'which is inward from his
nose and up into his head'.[43] News of the King's illness was later
spread by defectors from his army and reported in Williamite
news-sheets. The story of James's nosebleeds was much discussed
in the Prince's camp. For Gilbert Burnet they were a physical,
bodily manifestation of the disordered nature of James's

government. 'Much purulent matter comes out,' Burnet wrote to
Herbert, 'so much it is generally thought his person is in as ill a
state as his affairs are.' Huygens had heard the same lurid account:
'a dirty stinking mess comes out of his nose'.[44]

A dose of 'sympathetic ash', prescribed by a local apothecary,
stopped the King's bleeding, and sensing the need for a clear plan
of action, James summoned a council of war on 22 November. His
commander in chief, the Earl of Feversham, argued that the army
should withdraw back to London. Yet James's second in command, Lord Churchill, stated that it would be madness to turn
back. Churchill, whose wife Sarah (a close confidante of Princess
Anne) was staunchly Whiggish in her political opinions and an
implacable enemy of popery, had already resolved to defect to
William when the time was right. James, probably now fixed on
fleeing the country, supported Feversham's reasoning and the foot
and artillery prepared to make an immediate retreat.

The next day, 23 November, the King found that both
Churchill and the Duke of Grafton had gone. Once Churchill's
defection was known, it was widely suggested in Catholic circles
that the King's illness was providential in source, in that, had he
not been incapacitated, James might have been delivered into the
Prince's hands by his own commanders. Churchill, for his part,
always insisted that he had wished that the King might have come
to a negotiated settlement with William, a stance that seemed
strangely at odds with his public advice to James. For the King the
news of the desertions was a bitter blow. 'If my enemies only had
cursed me,' he said, 'I could have borne it.' Yet, the flow of defectors to the Prince continued apace. News soon came that Colonel
Percy Kirke, renowned for his brutality in the wake of the
Monmouth rebellion, was now refusing to follow orders. Later the
same evening Princess Anne's husband, the Prince of Denmark,
and the Duke of Ormonde absconded. At the news of the former's
departure, James wryly replied with the same phrase that Denmark
had used on hearing of every previous defection: 'Est-il possible?'

The King left for London with his camp falling into chaos, as the rank and file also began to desert and local people started to panic about the looting and worse that the AWOL troops might commit. However, when he arrived in Whitehall he was to find that not only his commanders had betrayed him but his youngest daughter as well.

As King, James had a reputation as a resolute and authoritarian character. However, his confidence now appeared to disintegrate in the face of betrayal by his people, but more crushingly, by his family. Even had James decided to meet William in combat, it is questionable whether the outcome in 1688 would have been much different. The almost complete breakdown of communication between central and local government created by the campaign to 'pack' Parliament meant that the King's control over the localities was seriously diminished. This was reflected in the ease with which a serious rebellion in the north, led by a combination of Whig and Tory peers, was able to be planned and raised, effectively cutting off the option of bringing back royal troops from Ireland to help suppress the Dutch invasion force. The strength of William's own forces was reflected in his clear confidence in the ability of this smaller force to overcome James's numerically superior army. The Dutch leader also knew the full extent of the Orangist conspiracy against the King, which reached not only Parliament and the army but also the royal family itself.

Here there was a clear contrast with the behaviour of the Stuart dynasty during the Civil War. Then the royal family had remained united, resisting attempts by parliamentarians to install one of Charles's sons as a puppet monarch. In 1688, however, the family split along confessional lines, with the Catholic members continuing to support James and the Protestants siding with William. Public opinion seemed to have swung decisively towards James's opponents, with serious anti-Catholic rioting in London and other cities. In contrast, Williamite propaganda succeeded in drawing over thousands of people to the Prince's cause. James still had cards that he could play, William had yet to announce publicly a desire to take the British throne and most English politicians were unwilling to consider actually deposing their lawful King. However, though James would retain his belief in his own absolute authority, his shattered nerves and disintegrating army would mean that he had neither the will nor the means to shape events to his benefit.

5

PANIC AND FLIGHT

One thing I must say of the Queen, which is that she is the most hated in the world of all sorts of people; for everybody believes that she pressed the King to be more violent than he would be of himself; which is not unlikely, for she is a very great bigot in her way, and one may see by her that she hates all Protestants.

PRINCESS ANNE TO THE PRINCESS OF ORANGE, 9 MAY 1687

I am fully persuaded that the Prince of Orange designs the King's safety and preservation, and hope all things may be composed without more bloodshed, by calling a Parliament.

God grant a happy end to these troubles, that the King's reign may be prosperous, and that I may shortly meet you in perfect peace and safety; till when, let me beg of you to continue the same favourable opinion that you have hitherto had of your most obedient daughter and servant.

LETTER LEFT BY PRINCESS ANNE TO THE QUEEN ON
25 NOVEMBER 1688, EXPLAINING HER FLIGHT FROM
WHITEHALL[1]

The King had been betrayed by his bishops, his lords and his leading officers. On the desperate return march to the capital he learnt that his youngest daughter, Anne, had deserted him too. Anne's husband, the stolid George, Prince of Denmark, had already absconded from James's army, and on the night of 25 November, the Princess herself slipped out from her apartments in Whitehall. Anne had already given a clear indication of her approval of the Prince of Orange's intervention in a letter sent to her sister a week earlier. However, her antipathy to her father's romanising policies, and especially to her Catholic stepmother, had been evident much earlier. A rift had already opened up between James and Anne, in part as a result of his attempts to secure her conversion to the Catholic faith. However, this growing divide was also a result of the political realignment of the court after James's second marriage. The Anglican Princess Anne, with her Lutheran husband Prince George, had become the main focus for Protestant courtiers in England, with the King's second wife, Mary of Modena, seen as presiding over the Catholic faction at court.

By 1687 Anne was convinced that the King's advisers, if not her father himself, were intent on returning England to popery. She wrote to her sister Mary that Sunderland was 'working with all his might to bring in popery. He is perpetually with the priests and stirs up the King to do things further than I believe he would of himself.' Things had, she told Mary, come 'to that pass now, that, if they go on much longer, I believe in a little while no Protestant will be able to live here'.[2] It had been Anne who had first sown the seeds of doubt in Mary's mind concerning the paternity of the Prince of Wales. Moreover, though the influence upon Anne of her brilliant, staunchly Whig, favourite, Sarah Churchill, was considerable, it is worth noting that Anne's comments concerning Mary Beatrice were always far more vituperative than those expressed by Sarah.[3] For Anne the driving factors behind her decision to abandon her father were her hatred of popery and, most importantly,

her desire to protect her own and her children's claims to the succession which had been threatened by the birth of the Prince of
Wales.

Henry Compton, the Bishop of London, had already been in
contact with Lady Churchill concerning plans for the Princess's
escape, should it prove necessary, giving her details of his secret
address in Suffolk Street, just north of Whitehall. In the early
hours of 26 November these plans came into effect as Anne and
Sarah, using a recently installed back staircase to leave Whitehall
unnoticed, met up with Compton and his nephew, Lord Dorset,
who had a hackney coach ready to take them across London to a
safe house in Aldersgate Street. The timing of their departure was
fortuitous. Soldiers had already been placed outside Sarah
Churchill's lodgings (though these were rendered ineffective by the
back staircase, which communicated directly with the Princess's
quarters) and at three in the morning an order came from the
King that Anne was to be placed under guard. However, the
Princess's lodgings were not checked until ten. When news of
Anne's disappearance reached her, Mary Beatrice reportedly cried
'as if she had been mad'.

With the return of the King imminent, the capital could not
provide a safe haven for long and immediate preparations were
made to leave. The next morning the party left London through
Epping Forest (Compton wearing the distinctly unecclesiastical
garb of buff coat and jackboots topped off with a sword and
pistol), stopping off at the village of Loughton and then proceed-
ing to Dorset's mansion at Copt Hall. After a short stay they went
on (without Lord Dorset) through the countryside, reputedly
stopping at an inn to take refreshment, where, according to local
custom, they 'sat in a cart saying that but for their flight it [i.e. to
sit in a hangman's cart] might have been their lot'. The roads west
of London were now clogged with the King's soldiers making their
bedraggled way back from the camp at Salisbury, so the only way
for Anne to effect a reunion with her husband was to follow a

roundabout route, first heading north to join up with Compton's Orangist co-conspirators in Nottingham. At Castle Ashby they were joined by a force of cavalry recruited by the Earl of Northampton, and with this added protection their journey northwards began to take on the character of a royal progress. On reaching Market Harborough the Princess, who had now made her identity public, was greeted by a full civic entertainment as the mayor and alderman laid on two banquets for their unexpected royal guest.[4]

Anne's flight revealed the increasingly complex nature of political alliances during the revolution. Her presence in the Midlands attracted loyalists who were not prepared to actively support William but were drawn to the Princess simply to safeguard her person: men such as the Earl of Chesterfield, Sir Henry Every, Sir Gilbert Clarke, John Dalton of Derby, Robert Burdett of Foremark and Gilbert Thacker of Repton, a number of whom refused to take the Association to the Prince of Orange, regarding it as an act of treachery. Chesterfield made it clear that he attended Anne only out of concern for her personal safety, not because he supported William's intervention in English affairs, stating that he was 'come a purpose (if there were occasion) to defend her person with my life against any that would dare to attack her; but as to my being of her council, I did beg pardon for desiring to be excused because I had the honour to be a privy councillor to the King her father: and therefore I would not be of any council for regulating troops that I perceived were intended to serve against him'.

By 3 December they had reached Nottingham, now safely in Orangist hands, and Compton wrote to Danby seeking further military protection for the Princess and advice as to what course of action to take next. In a letter to the Bishop, Danby expressed the hope that Anne might come to York 'both for her security and the great addition it would give to our interest in these parts'. For the Earl the presence of the Princess in Yorkshire would considerably strengthen his political influence and ability to operate (as he hoped) as a powerful negotiator between the King and the Prince of Orange. However, Compton refused to act without the approval of William, and the Prince was clearly unwilling to allow Danby the opportunity to create an independent power base in the north. On 8 December he issued instructions to Compton for he and the Princess to return south to Oxford.

James arrived back in London on the night of 26 November to find that his daughter had disappeared. Though the desertion of her husband had already alerted the King to her potential disloyalty, the King was nonetheless shattered by the news. 'God help me!' he was said to have exclaimed. 'My own children have forsaken me.' The following day he invited all the peers to London to advise him how to proceed, with forty in total attending the meeting. The Earl of Rochester urged James to call Parliament as 'the only remedy in our present circumstances'. The peers advised James that he should enter into a treaty with the Prince of Orange and make such concessions as offering free elections, promising to desist from exercising the dispensing power, and giving a general pardon to 'all the Lords who are now with the Prince of Orange and who are up in the other counties and all the gentlemen who are engaged might have free liberty to be chosen and to come to parliament as if these stirs had never been'. To the last concession the King was resistant, demanding that Churchill at least should be made an example of: 'Churchill whom I raised so high, He and he alone has done all this. He has corrupted my army. He has corrupted my child. He would have put me into the hands of the Prince of Orange but for God's special providence.' Reminded by the lords that, having lost the opportunity to defeat William militarily, he now had to rely on the goodwill of the people, James was brought to reconsider. The following day instructions were issued for a new Parliament to meet on 15 January. James further agreed to send three peers, Halifax, Nottingham and Godolphin, as emissaries to the Prince of Orange, and sent out a proclamation not only giving pardon to those in arms against him but also rendering them eligible to stand in the new elections. William's supporters were not even required to lay down their weapons to gain the benefit of these concessions. However, some members of the Orangist conspiracy were now in an aggressively triumphalist mood. Clarendon remarked that James's offer of a royal amnesty to the rebels was met with mirth among the Prince's supporters. 'They wanted no pardon, they said, They would make the King ask pardon before they had done with him.'[5]

Yet the King now little expected that such overtures would win back the people's trust and affection. He had already made clear before the peers that he felt that flight was perhaps his only option: 'he saw he must either retreat or fly beyond seas, but he hoped if he was forced to ye last, God would restore him as he had once his brother.' He was now preoccupied by the belief that William sought his throne, 'that it would appear that the Prince of Orange came for the crown, whatever he pretended: but that he would not see himself deposed: that he had read the story of Richard II'.[6] Privately James told the French ambassador that he had agreed to the peers' suggestions simply to buy time in which to organise the escape of his wife, son and finally himself to France. The King said to Barillon that he could no longer expect any loyalty from his troops, except those from Ireland, and they were too small in number to resist the enemy. Were he to place himself at the mercy of a free Parliament, James expected they would seek to make him no more than the shadow of a king, 'which I could not endure, I should be forced to undo all that I have done for the Catholics and to break with the King of France'.

As a further preparation for his imminent exit, James also moved Lord Chancellor Jeffreys into Father Petre's apartments in Whitehall (Petre having already fled to France) in order to have the Great Seal close to him. Instruments affixed with this carried the force of law and could only be repealed by act of Parliament. Having the seal so close to him would, James hoped, allow him to dispose of it in the event of the crisis coming to a head and thereby throw the country into administrative confusion. The issuing of writs for a new Parliament had the additional benefit that it removed the main justification for the Dutch invasion, thereby adding weight to the Jacobite charge that William was no more than a foreign usurper.

The Prince of Orange was now keen to reach London as soon as possible in order to exert maximum influence over any political settlement. Apart from a couple of minor skirmishes, there was no resistance to the Dutch army's eastward march. As James had correctly surmised, only his Irish soldiers appeared to show any willingness to stand their ground. An advance troop of William's army entering the town of Wincanton encountered 120 Irish soldiers under Captain Sarsfield. Outnumbered, the troops under the command of Lieutenant Campbell were only saved by news that the whole of the Prince's army was shortly approaching.

Elsewhere towns fell to pro-Orangist forces. In December Newcastle was taken by Lord Lumley, proclaiming for the Protestant religion and a free Parliament, while the Duke of Norfolk secured Norwich with some three hundred armed men and declared for the Prince. In Gloucester the dashing Lord Lovelace, freed from gaol by the city's inhabitants, hastily organised a cavalry force which he led to Oxford. Meanwhile at Berwick William was approached about a treaty with the King and also received the news that James had called for a new Parliament to meet in January. Clarendon, at this point a visitor to the Prince's camp, was assured by William that he would keep to the terms of his declaration, and the same message was repeated by his Dutch favourite, Hans Willem Bentinck, and Churchill. However, Gilbert Burnet's response to the same news revealed some of the difficulties James's concessions gave to the Orangist camp. Burnet now used the same argument earlier employed by the King, that no Parliament could meet while the country was in such confusion, to demonstrate that it was necessary to forestall sending out writs until the nation was secured. On 4 December William entered Salisbury to a semi-regal welcome, but he could no longer afford to waste his time enjoying English civic hospitality.

Events in Europe had made the need for a resolution of affairs in England even more urgent. Louis XIV had a fortnight before formally declared war on the United Provinces, while the death of Caspar Fagel had also robbed the Prince of his main supporter among the powerful urban elite of Holland. As his army pressed on they encountered further resistance from James's Irish soldiers. On 7 December there was a bloody skirmish at Reading as an advance guard of the Prince's army some 250 strong ran into a troop of six hundred Irish dragoons, with William's soldiers getting the best of it (which perhaps shows that the Prince was correct to feel confident in the ability of his numerically inferior forces to overcome the royal army). The following day James's commissioners, Halifax, Nottingham and Godolphin, attended William. Halifax later reported a conversation with Burnet in which Burnet enthusiastically endorsed the idea of James taking flight as the best solution to the complicated political situation.

On 10 December James's commissioners handed him the reply that William had drafted with his English supporters: the scheduled elections would go ahead (despite the protests of some of the English exiles), papists were to be dismissed from office and all proclamations against the Prince were to be recalled and his supporters set free. The commander of Portsmouth, the Duke of Berwick, was to be replaced by an individual that William could trust not to surrender the port to the French. The Prince of Orange's army was to be paid for out of the Treasury and both the King's and the Prince's troops were to remain thirty miles outside London. Both men would preside over the opening of the new Parliament, either unarmed or each accompanied by the same number of guards. However, by now the King's wife and son were safely in France (after one abortive attempt at escape had failed) and James was resolved to follow them. He told Feversham that 'if I could have relied upon all my troops, I might not have been put to this extremity I am in, and would at least have had one blow for it'. Ailesbury, James's gentleman of the bedchamber, begged the King not to leave and urged him to think of other options: he could go to Nottingham and confront Anne or, failing that, go to York and challenge Danby 'with his broomsticks and wishtail militia . . . who will all run away. And then, Sir, secure Berwick and march into Scotland, and . . . that Kingdom will be entirely yours.'[7] It is a moot point whether any of these alternatives was in any way realistic by this time. The King had in any case been pondering his escape for over a fortnight. 'What would you have me do?' he said to Ailesbury. 'My children hath abandoned me . . . my army hath deserted me, those that I raised from nothing hath done the same, what can I expecte from those I have done little or nothing for?'[8]

His resolution to leave was confirmed by renewed bouts of anti-Catholic rioting in the capital and elsewhere which increased his fears for his own personal safety and that of his family. By the beginning of December rumours of a massacre of Protestants at the hands of armed papists had reached new heights. On 4 December the people of Southwark rushed to arms fearing they would be butchered by armed papists. On the 7th the Lord Mayor reacted to increasing hysteria by ordering that Catholics should be disarmed. The following day, at news of a reported massacre by fifty thousand Frenchmen, the city's male inhabitants remained in arms all night. On the 9th, hearing rumours of six barrels of gunpowder being stored in a Catholic house, a crowd demolished it before the magistrate could establish the truth.[9] Anti-Catholic rioting was not limited to London. On 7 December mobs in Norwich burnt and pillaged houses of Catholics and demolished the Catholic chapel. An entire regiment of troops was needed to quell the rioters. As the Tory magistrate Sir John Reresby noted of James's last days in England, 'ther was scarce an hour but his Majesty received, like Job, some message of some revolt or misfortune or other'.[10]

On the night of the 11th, James prepared to leave his kingdom, burning the writs which had only recently been issued for the calling of a new Parliament. With Sir Edward Hales, he took a small skiff down the Thames, throwing the Great Seal into the river on the way, before joining the larger vessel that had been arranged to take him to France. (Legend has it that the Great Seal was found in a fisherman's nets at Lambeth and returned to the Council of Peers, providing further evidence of God's providential blessing upon the Revolution.)[11] However, the King's attempt to flee was foiled when his boat had to take in sand for ballast at Faversham. Hales, a much-despised local figure (his house and deer park were at this point being ransacked by an angry mob), was recognised by some sailors. The King's identity was not immediately discovered, the seamen instead taking him for an 'ugly, lean-jawed hatchet faced popish dog'. James was searched for valuables 'so indecently as even to the discovery of his nudities'.[12]

The pair were taken to the Queen's Arms inn, where the King was finally recognised. However, this did not lead to an improvement in his treatment. The sailors returned James's sword but kept the three hundred guineas in cash that they had seized from him.[13] The pub was soon surrounded by a curious mob, while inside the seamen kept the King under close guard, even following him to the toilet when he had to relieve himself. One of the crowd, a man named Moon, apparently cursed the King to his face. When James found out the man's name, he remarked that he 'ought to be called Shimei, for Shimei cursed the Lord's anointed'. As news of his presence in the inn spread, the gentry of the area also came to James, not to pay their respects but instead to read the Prince of Orange's Declaration, to which one witness claimed the crowd roared their approval. They told the King that the Governor of Sheerness intended to surrender the fortress and the ships there to the Prince of Orange, 'which seemed to afflict him'. Rallying himself with an effort, James said piteously that he would agree to anything to avoid bloodshed.[14]

Having managed to get a message out, James was finally rescued by the still loyal Earl of Winchelsea but by this point he had clearly sunk into a deep despair. His mind dwelt on martyrdom and he combed the Bible that his captors had allowed him for suitable texts, settling on Maccabees 1:10: 'For I repent that I gave my daughter unto him, for he sought to slay me . . .' Winchelsea remarked that at this time James 'thought there was but one step between his prison & his grave'. Even if he escaped actual martyrdom 'he would forsake Sceptre & Crowne, & all the world's glory for Christ's sake; & he had that inward peace & comfort which he would not exchange for all the interest of the earth'. These words seemed to parallel the words of James's father, Charles, expressed upon the scaffold. The comparison was noted by the Earl of Ailesbury, too, when he finally arrived on 14 December to take the King back to London. He found James 'sitting in a great chair, his hat on and his beard being much grown'. Ailesbury was struck by the King's resemblance to his father, Charles I, in a painting made at his trial.[15]

James never forgot the rough treatment handed out to him by the inhabitants of Faversham. In a proclamation issued in 1692 he explicitly excluded his captors from the benefit of a royal pardon. It is revealing that the King continued to be dealt with harshly even once his identity was known. The failure of his first attempt to flee the country laid bare the low ebb to which public respect for the monarch had sunk. This was arguably the culmination of a long-term erosion of the sacral aura surrounding the Stuart dynasty. Perversely, the execution of Charles I had gone some way to restoring the religious mystique around the King, witnessed in the fervent cult of martyrdom that his death inspired. This sanctified image of kingship was quickly tarnished by the reign of Charles II. The notorious excesses of his court, and of the King himself, made public knowledge by Restoration poets and wits, were hard to reconcile with the notion of the monarch as God's deputy on earth. James was a more devout figure than his brother, but he was as sexually incontinent as his sibling (though he felt far more guilt for his infidelities). Most importantly, the King was a Catholic, married to a Catholic wife and increasingly surrounded by Catholic advisers. In prints and pamphlets poor devout Mary Beatrice was transformed into the archetypal Catholic succubus, draining the King of his virility while, cuckoo-like, attempting to present the offspring of an illicit liaison with the papal envoy as actually James's natural son, the heir to the throne. In the crisis of 1688 the English rebels had been noticeably unconcerned about the potential threat their activity posed to the King's person. Though, as we will see, there remained a sizeable body of the people who felt a continued duty of loyalty to him, public hostility to the King was sometimes expressed in the frankest terms. In May 1689 rioters in Newcastle, egged on by garrison soldiers, tore down a marble statue of James, erected only a few years earlier by the city's monomaniacally loyal mayor, Sir Henry Brabant, and hurled it into the Tyne.[16]

In the King's absence London slipped into near anarchy. Anti-Catholic riots continued to rage, with attacks on the residences of the representatives of foreign Catholic powers, including Spain, Florence, Venice, Tuscany and the Palatine. The *London Mercury* reported that 'Tuesday Night last and all Wednesday the Apprentices were busie in pulling down the Chappels and spoiling the houses of Papists; they crying out the Fire should not go out till the prince of orange came to Town'.[17] After they had torched the houses the rioters went in a mock procession carrying oranges on the top of swords and staves to demonstrate their support for William. As order disintegrated, key servants of the crown were seized as they attempted to make their escape. William Penn was taken in Whitehall, along with Father Ellis, one of the Catholic bishops. The crowd took greatest pleasure in the capture of James's hated Lord Chancellor, George Jeffreys, on 12 December in Wapping. Jeffreys had attempted to disguise himself by shaving off his distinctive beetle brows, blackening his face and dressing as a sailor. It was reported, however, that he was recognised by a former solicitor in the Chancery Court who had had his case for repayment of debts bawled out of court by the notoriously ill-tempered Lord Chancellor. An angry crowd surrounded the alehouse in which Jeffreys was waiting to board a ship to France. He was captured by the mob, who 'threatened to dissect him, saying "now we have the greatest rogue of all"'.[18] He was saved from being pulled apart only by the intervention of the trained bands, who carried him to court, still pursued by a mob seeking vengeance. The sight of the angry crowd was enough to cause the Mayor of London, to whom Jeffreys had been sent before, to pass out. (The Mayor died, it was said at the time, from fright a day later.) At the Lord Chancellor's own request, he was taken to the Tower, where he would be safe from the hostile public that gathered outside, some holding up nooses in front of his window. Jeffreys was later one of the few of James's servants to be exempted from indemnity for his action on behalf of his royal master, but he died in prison before being brought to trial.

The day after the Lord Chancellor's capture, the tension that had been increasing over the threat of a massacre by armed Catholics exploded into full-blown mass hysteria. On the morning of 13 December London was gripped by the rumour that the King's disbanded Irish soldiers would cast off law and discipline and begin a general slaughter of the Protestant population (although the actual number of armed Irish Catholic troops in James's army was small). News writers reported that an 'alarm was spread through City and suburbs of "Rise, arm, arm! The Irish are cutting throats"'. Within half an hour more than a hundred thousand men had turned out to resist the anticipated attack and inhabitants lit torches to illuminate their houses. One report claimed that the citizens were up until 5 a.m. waiting for the anticipated massacre. White Kennett described the panic as having been sparked off by word of mouth, by 'country fellows, arriving before Midnight at Westminster [who] caused a sudden uproar, by

Reporting that the Irish in a desperate Rage were advancing to London, and putting all before 'em to Fire and Sword'. Terriesi, the Catholic representative of the Duke of Tuscany, reported that the Londoners were 'discharging firearms, drums beating rapidly, and women, for greater noise were beating warming-pans, pots and frying pans, and such things'.[19]

The panic seems to have been sparked off by the disbanding of James's Irish troops by the Earl of Feversham on the 11th. The nonconformist Philip Musgrave reported that these troops were collecting around Uxbridge ready to 'burn, kill and destroy all they meet with'.[20] Ailesbury, on his way to fetch James from Faversham, found that at Rochester Bridge men were trying to hack down its central arch 'to hinder the Irish Papists from cutting their throats and of their wives and children, for all that Dartford was on fire and the streets ran with blood'. At the next stop, a post-house in Rochester, he went on to call on an old friend and found him 'half dead with fear, in a night gown and night cap. He told me he had not been in bed for three nights for fear of having his throat cut by Irish papists.' Through Chatham and Sittingbourne they saw crowds of people 'crying at their doors on each side, with their children by them, choosing rather to be murdered there than in their beds'.[21]

Rumours of Irish risings broke out in Norfolk on the 13th and 14th of the month and in Surrey on the 14th and 15th. In Kingston upon Thames inhabitants cut down trees to block a road against the phantom marauding Irishmen. The news quickly spread to the rest of the country. On 14 December the Mayor of Chesterfield wrote to Danby that seven thousand Catholics and Irish had burnt Birmingham and were marching on Derby. A Leicestershire minister, Theophilius Brookes, heard that the 'Irish were cutting off throats, Lichfield on fire and Burton attempted upon' and, steeled with this news, set off with a group of armed men to head the 'enemy' off.[22] On the 15th the news had reached Yorkshire with reports in Wakefield that Doncaster was on fire. Meanwhile the inhabitants of Doncaster, who had survived their fictitious immolation heard news that Birmingham and Stafford had been looted by the Irish. The Yorkshire antiquary Ralph Thoresby reported that in Leeds the city raised some seven thousand foot and horse soldiers for the defence of their lives and liberties. There were reports that nearby Beeston was burning, which led to a panicked flight from the city, with men and women seeking refuge in fields and barns. However, Thoresby's pregnant wife kept her head and climbed to the attic to see that Beeston was untouched. Yet another alarm was raised the same night, this time about an attack on Halifax. Thoresby remarked that he could see 'nothing but paleness and horror in the countenance of all men'. He went to sleep with his clothes on, in case the Irish should come while he was in bed.[23]

Alarms were reported across the Pennines in Lancashire and in Cheshire too. Warrington Bridge was barricaded and guarded against the anticipated Irish assault. Overall, there were reports of alarms in nineteen counties. The panic was encouraged by the publication of the spurious Third Declaration of the Prince of Orange, allegedly written by the spy and plotter Hugh Speke. This stated that there were many armed papists in and around London bent on fire and massacre and ordered officials to disarm and secure all papists.

Although the imagined massacre of Protestants never materialised, anti-Catholic mobs dished out very real violence to the property and persons of 'papists'. Ailesbury noted that the Catholic soldiers amounted to no more than twelve hundred men and these mainly hid for fear of reprisals from Protestants. King James's biographer Clark said of the Irish troops that they did not know where 'to get a meels meat or a nights lodging and [were] liable themselves to be knocked on the head in every town they came to . . .'.[24] Abraham de la Pryme recalled that the Protestants 'made most miserable of all the papists' houses they came near; for, under pretence of seeking for armes, they did many thousands of pounds worth of hurt, cutting down rich hangings, breaking through walls, pulling pieces of excellent ceilings . . . then they secured all the papists they could get, intending to carry them all away to prison'.[25]

The violence meted out to Catholics during the 'Irish Fright' of December 1688 was a continuation of crowd behaviour in the autumn. In October of that year Catholic chapels were sacked in London and similar attacks were made on Catholic 'mass-houses' and the homes of prominent 'papists' across England. Occasionally violence was used against Catholics themselves. In Cambridge in December 1688 a Catholic priest was attacked by an angry mob.[26] This violence was to some degree given sanction by William's Declaration of 10 October in which he said that the setting up of 'severall Churches and Chappells, for the exercise of Popish Religion' was against 'many expresse Lawes'. The activities of the crowd were further legitimated both by the decision of London juries that those shot at by troops in October 1688 while ransacking Catholic chapels were in fact 'loyal persons' and by James's own backtracking: on 11 November 1688 he had ordered all Catholic chapels to be closed.[27]

It has been suggested that the Irish Fright was the product of an orchestrated plan to spread disinformation by post. Certainly the rumour helped William's cause as individuals looked to the Prince to protect the nation in the wake of James's flight on 11 December (itself, as we have seen, prompted by his fears for his own and his family's safety, given the ferocity of anti-Catholic feeling in the capital). Hugh Speke claimed that during the Popish Plot he had familiarised himself with Whig sympathisers in the Post Office and the times at which the post arrived in various localities. This information enabled him in December 1688 to send out letters detailing the threat of an Irish massacre to sympathetic post-masters in the country so that they would reach offices at exactly the same time.

There are a number of reasons, though, for believing that the

rumour was not spread in this way and may not have been deliberately manufactured at all. First, the evidence of Abraham de la
Pryme contradicts Speke's story that the panic was spread by post,
stating that news of the Irish massacre came first by word of
mouth: 'This newse or report ran . . . quite through the country,
and for all it was some weeks a running northward, yet no one
letter appear'd out of the south concerning any such thing there till
it was always gone past those places where these letters were to go.'
Pryme believed nonetheless that it was an orchestrated plan 'set on
foot by the king and council to see how the nation stood affected
to their new king'.[28]

Yet the vision of an Irish massacre of English Protestants was
something of a recurring nightmare in the seventeenth century.
Rumours of this kind circulated during the Exclusion Crisis. In
early January 1681 the Lords declared that they were 'fully satisfied'
that 'for divers years . . . there hath been a horrid and treasonable
Plot and Conspiracy, contrived and carried on by those of the
Popish Religion in Ireland, for massacring the English, and sub-
verting the Protestant Religion, and the ancient established
Government of that Kingdom'. In the lower house Sir Henry
Capel said that although some people 'smiled at' the Popish Plot
in England, 'it is plain there was a Plot in Ireland' and 'the hopes
of a Popish Successor' were 'the Grounds of all this'.

It was not only the Catholic Irish who were seen as a threat to
the lives of English Protestants. There were frequent rumours
during James II's reign that he was entering into secret negotiations with the French. Court gossips circulated stories of a 'league
offensive and defensive', insisting always that James was keeping
'close to the French'. One illegally printed pamphlet warned that
the King's eyes were fast closed 'with the enchanted slumbers of
the French Delilah'. James's own ambassador in Paris, Sir William
Trumball, became convinced of a secret league between the two
kings. By the summer of 1688 these fears had reached a feverous
pitch. In August the Anglican minister Dr William Denton was

convinced that 'the King expects a squadron of French ships to be at his command', while in September, the Londoner William Westby averred that 'everybody speaks of a holy league' between James II and Louis XIV. So pervasive were the fears of an Anglo-French alliance that Dr William Sherlock thought 'this did more to drive the King out of the nation, than the Prince's army'. In addition to conducting secret diplomacy, James was suspected of seeking to replace English national political culture with that of France and to replace an English with a French style of government. One pamphleteer explained that the nation had looked to William of Orange because 'the three kingdoms of England, Scotland and Ireland [were] being reduced into the pattern of the French King in government and religion'. James's standing army was thought to turn 'the civil government into a military; and that is not the government of England'.[29]

In 1688 English Protestants were certainly being told to expect to be butchered by Irish Catholics or even by their own King's army any day. Broadsheets were issued warning of the threat of a popish massacre. *A true relation of the horrid and bloody massacre in Scotland, by the Irish papists*, printed at Berwick on 23 December 1688, reported that

> about 20000 Irish were landed in Scotland, about sixty miles from Edinburgh, putting all to Fire and Sword: to whom tis said the Apostate Chancellour of that Kingdom, will joyn with the rest of the Bloody Papists there. And truly . . . that Kingdom being un-arm'd, and un-disciplined those Massacres will in short space run a great length. I desire you may dispense this News abroad, if it be not in Town, before your Receipt of this; for that Country, and the North of England, without speedy relief, is in great danger of depopulation: And the Duke of Gordon hath in his possession the Castle of Edinburgh, whereby he can at pleasure level that City with the Ground . . . God defend England from the French, and his Highness the Prince of Orange from Bloody Popish attempts.

Material detailing the supposed horrors of the 1641 Irish Rebellion was reissued at this time. *A Relation of the bloody massacre in Ireland* (1689) related how in Kilkenny an 'English woman was beaten into a Ditch, where she died, her Child about six years old, they ript up her Belly and let out her guts'. Other atrocities against pregnant women were recounted in the same pamphlet: 'one Joan Alder they stabbed, and then put her child of a quarter [year] old to her Breast, and bid it suck English Bastard, and so left it to perish.'[30] *A Full and True Account of the Inhumane and Bloudy Cruelties of the Papists to the Poor Protestants in Ireland in the Year 1641* (1689) told how the rebels 'cut off Mens Privy Members and stopt their Mouths with them'.[31] Again the cruelty of the rebels to women was recounted: a gentlewoman was stripped naked 'and turned . . . out of doors, as if they would make all savages like themselves'.[32] Instances of cruelty to children were also highlighted: the rebels were alleged to have dashed out the brains of Protestant children 'crying these are the pigs of the English sows'.[33] In these pamphlets we can also see a growing identification of Protestantism with Englishness and Catholicism with Irishness. The victims of Catholic violence were described as English or Scottish, their attackers as simply 'Irish', with no distinction being made between the Old English (Catholic families of English descent) and the Gaelic Irish. The same pamphlet stated bluntly, that the 'Irish Nation is well known to be a people both proud and envious. For the commonality (they are for the most part) ignorant and illiterate, poor and lazy, and will rather beg or starve rather than work.'[34] *An Abstract of the Unnatural Rebellion and Barbarous Massacre of the Protestants in the Kingdom of Ireland in the Year 1641* (1689) concurred, stating that the Irish, before the Angevin conquest of the kingdom by Henry II in 1172, were 'generally void of all manner of civility, governed by no settled Laws, but living like beasts of Prey, biting and devouring one another; without any reasonable Constitution for determining of their properties'.[35] The author reported that some two hundred thousand had died as a result of the 1641 massacre, a figure widely accepted at the time, despite being several times the entire Protestant population of Ireland in the seventeenth century.[36]

Reviving memories of the 1641 rebellion not only heightened fears of a new Irish massacre but also reflected badly on the Stuart dynasty, owing to the widespread belief that Charles I had colluded with the Irish rebels in their uprising. Thomas Long reported that the myth of the 'Antrim Plot' (Charles I's alleged plan to use an army raised by the Catholic Earl of Antrim against his English subjects) was 'beginning to pass as Common Discourse in Cabals and Coffee-Houses'.[37] (This discussion of the Irish 'massacre' of 1641, and the raising of the possibility of another, was also a good way of distracting people from the actual rebellion against the lawful monarch that had already occurred in 1688, while encouraging the population to seek order and stability at the hands of the usurper, William.)

These tracts on the Irish Rebellion appeared around the same time as accounts of the gruesome deaths of Monmouth's rebels, written by the Whig writers John Dunton, himself a former Monmouth rebel, and John Tutchin. Tutchin recorded Monmouth rebels as prophesying the reign of William of Orange. Colonel Abraham Ansely told listeners on the scaffold that 'though it pleased God to block our designs, but he will deliver his people by ways we know not nor think not'. Another rebel was said to have told a bystander that 'before the year 88 be over, you will see all things turned upside down, and King James for what he had done would be turned out and another come in'. Tutchin portrayed Lord Chancellor Jeffreys, the chief prosecutor of the rebels, as perpetrating atrocities as great as those committed by the Irish rebels of 1641. Not only were Tutchin and Dunton creating a history of Whig martyrdom with which to justify their new political ascendancy as the result of providential justice but they were also creating an image of an English atrocity, perpetrated by James and Jeffreys, to match that committed by the Irish: the conversion of the West Country into a field of blood following the Monmouth rebellion. Again the implication, as with the material on the Irish rebellion, was that the same violence could be repeated in the England of 1688.[38]

By 1689, then, there was a host of works in print detailing the horrible crimes of Irish Catholics as well as the atrocities perpetrated by James's ministers. Englishmen and women were fully prepared for the visitation of such horrors upon them should they prove less than vigilant. In such a poisoned atmosphere a fully coordinated 'plot' was not needed to sow the rumour of an Irish rising, any more than it had been needed in 1641 to encourage Englishmen to believe that Irish Catholics had butchered their co-religionists in their hundreds of thousands.

Presiding over this chaotic scene was an *ad hoc* government constituted from peers summoned by the Earl of Rochester and the Bishop of Ely, along with the Lord Mayor of London and aldermen at the Guildhall. Ely and Rochester both hoped to make a last-ditch attempt to use their provisional government to negotiate a reconciliation between the King and the Prince of Orange. The first draft of a declaration made by Ely and Rochester sought William's help to secure 'Our Religion and Laws in a Free Parliamt', but stated that this Parliament should be called by James II. However, James's flight had wrested the initiative away from these loyalists, and instead the final version of the declaration issued from the Guildhall said that the peers sought security for their laws and freedoms in a free Parliament to be presided over by the Prince of Orange, but stopped short of inviting William into the capital. The Lord Mayor and aldermen were not so reticent and issued an open invitation to the Prince. These preparations were interrupted by the startling news that the King had been captured and the agreement among the peers was that James must be brought back to London.

When Ailesbury finally reached the King on 15 December, he found him in low spirits, full of bitterness, even towards his trusted courtier, concerning his treatment. However, James's mood was improved by getting his first change of clothes for four days, and finally being able to shave off his new beard. His confidence was further boosted by the reception he received on his return to London. He was cheered by his escort of 120 Life Guards and by the vast numbers of people who had gathered to see the King as he approached. An even warmer reception was given to James as he reached the city itself: 'The balconies and windows beside were thronged, with loud acclamations beyond whatever was heard of . . . in fine the joy was so great and general, that if there had been any foreigners in the streets and subjects of a despotic King or commonwealth . . . they would imagine that they had been all mad.' However, other reports commented that crowds looked on in silence and Barillon concluded that 'at heart, most of the people were for the Prince of Orange'.[39] Much of the happiness expressed at the King's return was really relief that the days of near-absolute anarchy in London were over, and hope that stable government would be restored. Indeed, very briefly it seemed as if the regular operation of government had returned as James presided over a meeting of the Privy Council which attempted to deal with the crisis in public order that had swept the nation.

Yet by this stage, if it had not happened sooner, William was clear that he wanted the crown of England for himself. The initial news that the King had taken flight had been received with barely concealed joy in his camp, immediately resolving all the thorny issues as to what the Prince was to do with his father-in-law once he reached London. Hearing that James had been taken at Faversham, William attempted to get him brought back only to Rochester rather than to the capital, but his messenger did not get through. The Prince demonstrated his anger at the turn of events when he arrested James's own messenger, Feversham, reporting the King's return, on the thin grounds that he had acted without authority in disbanding the royal troops. James quickly realised that his son-in-law did not intend to allow him to retain his grip on the reins of government. The King's own guards at St James's, Somerset House and Whitehall were swiftly replaced with Dutch soldiers.

In the early hours of 17 December Lords Delamere, Halifax and Shrewsbury woke the King from his now opiate-induced slumbers to inform him that William wished him to retire from London to Ham House, a residence up the Thames at Richmond. James asked if he might be allowed to move out to Rochester instead, a request to which William quickly agreed. Later that morning James was taken by barge to Gravesend and from there to his new, and very temporary, residence at Rochester. Contemporaries were aware that this second flight from the capital was less of James's choosing. Reresby spoke of James 'being forced to withdraw himselfe a second time'.[40] Clarendon noted the new mood of sympathy felt for the King among the crowds that gathered to watch him make his exit: 'It is not to be imagined what a damp there was upon all sorts of men throughout the town. The treatment the King had met from the Prince of Orange, and the manner of his being driven, as it were from Whitehall . . . moved compassion even in those who were not very fond of him.'[41]

It is clear that William intended James's stay at Rochester to be merely a staging post on his way out of the kingdom. The Dutch troopers guarding the King had clear instructions not to intervene should he attempt to escape. James himself remarked how well they treated him, and the fact that they were almost all Catholics was perhaps not accidental either. Letters from Mary Beatrice asking him to come and join her were intercepted but then passed on to him anyway, his request for passports was eagerly met and he was passed on a letter which alleged that the Prince of Orange felt that it was no longer safe for him to reside in England. James appeared to concur, telling Ailesbury that if he did not retire, 'I shall certainly be sent to the Tower, and no king ever went out of that place but to his grave.'[42] If we cannot say that James was pushed out of his kingdom, it is nonetheless true that he was shown an open door and invited to walk through it.

The same day that James left his capital for the last time, 18 December, William entered London. Huygens reported that crowds of people gathered to watch the Prince's entry, some with orange ribbons in their hair or carrying oranges on sticks. Throngs of people awaited William along the road to St James's, some standing knee deep in mud to get a sight of the Prince, but he disappointed them by taking the route through the park. It would not be the last time that he would attempt to distance himself from his new people. The diarist John Evelyn's first impressions of William, taken as he held audience at court for the first time, were, revealingly, of a 'very stately, serious and reserved' individual.[43] London was already under the control of English and Scottish regiments in the Dutch service, complemented by William's own Blue Guards. On 20 December the Prince agreed to cede civil administration of the country to the Lords for the time being but, crucially, retained control of the armed forces. To attempt to create some semblance of the return of normal government, the surviving members of Charles II's last Parliament were recalled, together with members of the City of London's common council, in order to constitute a House of Commons.

Meanwhile William's advisers were expressing some exasperation that James was failing to take the hint: 'he doesn't want to go,' Huygens reported. However, receipt of the letter warning the King of the threat to his safety (which may have been sent by Halifax) appears to have worked its intended effect. On the evening of 22 December James summoned his bastard son the Duke of Berwick, along with Ailesbury and Secretary of State Middleton, to his rooms and informed them of his decision to leave the kingdom. Before he departed James prepared a formal statement explaining his reasons for his second flight. He asserted that he was forced to leave his country by the obvious threats to his own person, evidenced by the arrest of Feversham, the changing of his guards and the Prince's demand that he retire to Rochester. William's duplicity was already clear from his declaration in which he had dared to cast aspersions on the legitimacy of the King's son. What could James now expect from 'one who by all arts hath taken such pains to make me appear as black as hell to my own people as well as to the world besides?' He would not remain in England and let the Prince make him his prisoner: 'I was born free and desire to continue to do so.' James would fly the country but only so that he should be free 'to redeem it from the slavery it is like to fall under' whenever the nation would open its eyes to who was its true protector.[44] Leaving the house by its garden (which backed on to the Thames and was curiously unguarded), he took a rowing boat with Berwick and his servants, reaching the mouth of the Medway by the early hours of the following morning, where he joined the *Henrietta*, the ship which would take him to France.

The King's second flight from the country had exactly the effect on English politicians that William hoped it might. Like James's first abortive attempt to flee, it forced the peers to look to the Prince to provide security and leadership. On 24 December they agreed to hand the civil administration of the kingdom over to William for the time being, leaving him temporarily in control of both civil and military government in Britain. There would now be no repeat of the situation in 1648 when Charles I, as a captive king, had attempted to play the army, Parliament and the Scots off against one another in round after round of fruitless negotiations. Neither would England be plunged into another civil war. James's formidable army had been disbanded with hardly a shot fired in anger. His navy had failed even to engage the Dutch armada. Danby's rebellion in the north could not hope to operate as a counter-balance to the Prince's military power, particularly once it was clear that Princess Anne would not become a figurehead for the aristocratic revolt in Yorkshire. When he received orders from William on 12 December to disperse his troops and attend the court in London, Danby had no alternative but to follow the Prince's commands with all possible haste.

Yet, though James's flight considerably simplified matters for William, the question of how to settle the government of England on a more permanent basis remained highly problematic. Could the King be said to have formally abdicated the throne? If so, should the crown pass to Mary, his daughter, or should William act as regent, with his wife only as nominal monarch, or should William rule alone, or both William and Mary as dual monarchs? It was a situation of unprecedented complexity and one which fashioned the deep political divides that dominated English society from the Glorious Revolution to the late eighteenth century. The sympathy that many felt for James's plight led some towards a conscientious abstention from participating in civil and ecclesiastical government under William. For others, their residual loyalty to the 'King over the water' led them to take part in armed conspiracy to recover his crown. The inclusive nature of the Revolution, with both Whigs like Delamere and Tories like Danby supporting William's intervention, made it almost impossible for the Prince to satisfy all the claimants for patronage after 1688. In many cases the new alliances forged between Whigs and Tories lasted little beyond the Christmas festivities. No one could dispute the fact of the King's absence (though there was much debate over whether James had jumped or been given a hefty push); nor was it easy to ignore the Dutch troops who policed the capital or William's own determination to take the English throne. Yet this was more than a usurpation or a palace coup, it was a revolution that was fought over in pubs and coffee-houses as much as in Parliament. It was the verdict of the people, as well as the peers and commons in Westminster, which would settle the crown on William's head.

6

SELLING THE REVOLUTION

Political language is designed to make lies sound truthful and murder respectable, and to give an appearance of solidity to pure wind.

GEORGE ORWELL

King James the second, having endeavoured to subvert the constitution of the kingdom, by breaking the original contract, between king and people, and by the advice of Jesuits and other wicked persons, having violated the fundamental laws, and having withdrawn himself out of this kingdom, has abdicated the government; and that the throne is thereby vacant.

RESOLUTION OF THE COMMONS IN THE CONVENTION,

28 JANUARY 1688[1]

King William is no king, I'll justify it, he is an outlandish Curr, a Sone of a Whore, he eats the bread out of his fathers mouth.

HENRY ELLYOTT, RESIDENT OF ST PAUL'S, COVENT GARDEN,

LONDON, 1690[2]

Islanders in the Shetlands had had no account of the events of the Glorious Revolution until a fisherman happened to land on their shores in May 1689. However, his story of the Dutch invasion, James's flight and the coronation of William and Mary was received as a seditious fantasy and instead he was indicted for high treason.[3] Yet by 1689 it was only in such far outreaches of the British Isles as the Shetlands that not even the barest outline of the tumultuous events that had taken place in Westminster had been received. In fact, news had more quickly reached the North American colonies, which received confirmed stories of James's flight in April 1689, leading to revolts against the current colonial administration in Boston, Maryland and New York.[4] Elsewhere the debates and deliberations of the Convention were quickly relayed to the public through news-sheets, illicit (and often inaccurate) pamphlet copies of speeches and via the heated gossip exchanged in coffee-houses and taverns. In this sense the Glorious Revolution was far from merely a 'swift aristocratic coup' and, as we shall see, in the capital in particular, popular interventions in the political process had a real impact. In other ways, though, the Revolution was really effected by a very small number of individuals, namely the Protestant wing of the Stuart royal family. In contrast, the Convention acted as little more than a talking shop which rubber-stamped a dynastic usurpation.

The debates in the Convention on the state of the nation, the declaration of rights and the coronation of William and Mary represented the constitutional climax of the old Whig interpretation of the crisis of 1688–9. Here the Convention formed the crucible for the founding of a new (and yet old) form of government: parliamentary monarchy. Yet to modern eyes the debates in the Convention seem archaic, tautological and confused. They focused not on the question of what sort of monarchy should be established in England but on who should be the effective monarch, William or Mary. The issue of whether James's eldest daughter, or her husband, should come to the throne had serious implications for the established rules of hereditary succession. For Tories like the Earl of Nottingham, it also raised a genuine dilemma of conscience: how could they accept William as king without breaking their oath of allegiance to James? It was fear for their souls, as well as for their political futures, which led many Tories to refuse to countenance the notion that the Prince of Orange should inherit the crown. As we will see, in comparison to the question of the succession, the idea of outlining the extent of the new monarch's powers, through a document such as the Declaration of Right, came almost as an afterthought. Even once enshrined in law, the Bill of Rights placed little in the way of fetters on William's freedom of action. Far from being a product of political consensus, the lack of agreement between Williamites and loyalists, Whigs and Tories, had left the settlement of 1689 open-ended and deeply ambiguous. From the 1690s to the era of Walpole, politics would largely be dominated by a contest over the precise meaning of the Glorious Revolution.

The last days of 1688 saw a dramatic resurgence in the fortunes of the Whig party, which only three years before had been effectively decimated through its association with popular insurrection and assassination plots. William's summoning of an assembly of commoners to assist the assembly of peers was more than an attempt to return to normal modes of governance. In picking a body composed of MPs largely drawn from the Oxford Parliament of 1681 (thereby overlooking James's legally legitimate first Parliament), the Prince virtually guaranteed that the body would be dominated by Whig members. With the addition of members from London's common council (who had been freed by William from the obligations of oaths and sacramental tests – allowing Protestant dissenters to take up office), it was a body designed to counter-balance the majority of Tories in the assembly of peers. Other events also pointed to the rapid revival of Whiggery. On 28 December came the release of two of the greatest martyrs for the Whig cause, Samuel Johnson and Titus Oates.

Oates's rehabilitation was the most dramatic of all. After his second conviction for perjury in May 1685, he had been fined, defrocked and imprisoned and ordered to be whipped from Newgate to Tyburn, and made to stand in the pillory as an annual punishment. During the anti-Catholic rioting in the capital from 11 to 13 December it was rumoured that Oates had been murdered in his cell, a victim, of course, of Jesuit poisoners. On his release 'the Doctor of Salamanca' was granted an audience with William at St James's Palace and restored as a pensionary of the state. Oates continued to peddle his stories of popish plots well into the 1690s.[5]

In this atmosphere of Whig triumphalism, some of William's more militant supporters suggested that it was unnecessary for the Prince, having been granted the title of *custos regni*, to seek any further public approval before taking the throne.[6] The Whig lawyers Serjeant Maynard, Recorder Treby and Henry Pollexfen urged William and Mary to order a proclamation declaring themselves king and queen. They cited legal precedents such as the so-called 'de facto law' of Henry VII of 1495, which, it was believed, made it lawful to obey those in possession of the throne as if they were the monarch by right.[7] Gilbert Burnet argued in his *Pastoral Letter* that William had a right by conquest to the English throne, having defeated James in a just war fought on behalf of the people.[8] By this stage William was unquestionably eager to have the crown settled upon him as soon as possible. However, exploiting arguments such as these was problematic. They seemed in blatant contradiction to the promise in his Declaration to leave the political settlement to a free Parliament. To take such action would also completely alienate the vast majority of Tory politicians. Moreover, arguments based on conquest drew further attention to the Dutch troops occupying the capital and raised additional questions about how free any new Parliament would be.

Instead, a new body, the Convention, was summoned to meet on 22 January 1689 to forge a settlement. The elections for the

Convention did display evidence of bipartisan cooperation, with several counties electing one Whig member and one Tory member without contest. Elsewhere, however, party feeling was present. William Sacheverell was defeated in Derbyshire for 'his not appearing for the prince'. In Newcastle there were complaints that no legal choice could be made without the King's writ.[9] From the beginning William made it clear that he expected no unnecessary delays to hold up the Convention's task, stating that 'next to the danger of unseasonable divisions amongst yourselves, nothing can be so fatal as too great delay in your consultations'.[10]

It was also clear from the opening of the Convention that the majority of members, Whigs as well as Tories, did not wish to see the return of James II as king. In the Lords several bishops omitted the prayer for the King when saying prayers in the House.[11] John Sharp, the Dean of St Paul's, who had raised James's ire by preaching an anti-Catholic sermon in 1686, now found himself in hot water with the Convention for preaching a sermon on 30 January (the anniversary of Charles I's execution) which denounced the killing or deposing of kings as a popish doctrine and was prefaced by prayers for King James and Queen Mary Beatrice.[12] Francis Gwyn remarked that it was 'now all over; neither he [James], nor his . . . [wife and children] are like ever to set foot here again'. Lord Dartmouth's wife felt that the Commons and Lords had acted 'as if he [the King] had never been'. When, on 4 February, James sent a letter to the Convention via his Scottish Secretary of State, the Earl of Melfort, a hated Catholic convert who had joined his master in exile, the Lords refused to read it, rejecting it out of hand as 'the letter of a private man; for he was no longer King'.[13]

Whigs appeared in the ascendant in the Convention, as they had done in the assembly of commoners. The speakers of both houses were Williamites, with the Whig Henry Powle speaker of the Commons (whose opponent for the position, the Tory Sir Edward Seymour, was profoundly shocked at not being appointed) and the Earl of Halifax (who defeated Clarendon) taking the equivalent post in the Lords. Members of the Convention were not required to take the usual oaths of allegiance and supremacy, according to Delamere, because without their removal the Convention could not be regarded as a free assembly. This, as with the elections to the court of aldermen in London, freed up dissenters to take up places in the Commons. Realising that the lower house was dominated by Whigs and supporters of William's claim to the throne, on 22 January the Tory Seymour attempted to shift discussion of the succession to the Lords, where the loyalists were stronger, on the grounds that not all MPs had yet assembled in Westminster. The motion was successful but the objective of allowing the loyalist Lords to seize control of the debate was thwarted by Halifax, who managed to convince the upper house that they should discuss the succession at the same time as the Commons.

On 28 January the debate began in earnest. The declaration issued by the Commons aimed at terminating James's kingship with a blunderbuss shot. There was a nod to Lockeian contract theory in the statement that James had broken 'the Original Contract between the King and People'; acknowledgement of the idea of a Popish Plot in the phrase 'the advice of Jesuits'; and reference to notions of an ancient constitution in the claim that he had 'violated the fundamental Laws'. At this early stage there was already a clear preference among MPs that William rather than Mary should occupy the executive office. The Whig Boscawen stated that, as France was likely to declare war, 'we have reasons to make use of our best weapon, to chuse a king to go before us and fight our battells (which was the first occasion of kingly government) and that a woman cannot so well do'.[14] Boscawen's remarks underline the importance of the sexual politics of the revolution: despite the deification of Elizabeth I, feminine rule was still seen as an unnatural anomaly. Particularly in times of war, it was vital that states should have virile, martial, masculine rulers. The declaration announcing that the throne was vacant was followed the next day by a further resolution that asserted that it was 'inconsistent with the Safety and Welfare of this Protestant Kingdom, to be governed by a Popish Prince'.[15]

The Lords gave their agreement to this last resolution, effectively ending, at least for the time being, the dynastic aspirations of the Catholic wing of the Stuart royal family. In any case the claims of James's son, the legitimate heir, were barely discussed by either Whigs or Tories. Clarendon had urged in the Lords' debate on 29 January that the 'matter' of the Prince of Wales should be investigated further, but this was not followed up.[16] Some Whigs did raise the issue of the Prince of Wales in order to ridicule the Tory attachment to the hereditary succession. Treby made the point in the committee meeting to discuss the Commons' resolution: 'You are persons that usually are, or ought to be, present at the delivery of our Queens, and the proper witnesses to the birth of our Princes. If then your Lordships had known who was on the Throne, we should certainly have heard his name from you, and that had been the best reasons against the vacancy as could have been given.'[17] In spite of the promise in William's Declaration that a parliamentary committee would investigate the circumstances of the Prince of Wales's birth, most members of the Convention preferred conveniently to forget that a legitimate male heir to the throne, James Francis Edward Stuart, already existed.

However, hopes of a rapid agreement on conferring the crown on William were quickly thwarted by the Lords response to the Commons' judgement that James's actions constituted an 'abdication' and that the crown was now 'vacant'. These debates could be seen as an exercise in pedantry, and there was certainly a fair degree of filibustering involved, but in seeking precise definitions of these terms, peers were coming to the nub of some thorny political issues. 'Abdicate' could be taken, in the common, modern understanding of the term, to mean a voluntary renunciation of office (as in the case of Edward VIII's abdication in order to marry

Wallace Simpson). This was also common usage in the seventeenth century and, as applied to the case of James II's flight, many Tories viewed it as an acceptable description. For the Earl of Pembroke, James's quitting the kingdom was no 'more than a man's running out of his house when on fire, or a seaman's throwing his goods overboard in a storm, to save his life, which could never be understood as a renunciation of his house or goods'.[18] However, there were other, relatively common, usages of the word in seventeenth-century England. It had a long-standing significance in civil law to cover the actions of fathers in disinheriting their children. It could also be used as a transitive verb, meaning to put off or to cast away, and it also had a more obscure meaning, which equated it with deposing from office. It was in its use as a transitive verb that the term was applied by some Whigs. The Whig lawyer John Somers explained in committee with the Lords that

> the word abdicate doth naturally and properly signify, entirely to renounce, to throw off, disown, relinquish any thing or person, so as to have no further to do with it; and that whether it be done by express words or in writing (which is the sense your Lordships put upon it, and which is properly called resignation or cession), or by doing such acts as are inconsistent with the holding and retaining of the thing, which the Commons take to be the present case.[19]

So in Somers's interpretation, echoed by the veteran Sir John Maynard, it was the illegal actions of James II, taken collectively, which amounted to a casting off of kingly office. This was not mere semantics, but made better sense of the Commons' resolution of 1688, where 'abdication' followed the King's breach of contract, collusion with Jesuits and violation of the fundamental laws.[20]

To declare the crown 'vacant' appeared to be a violation of the established laws of succession which did not recognise an interregnum (so the reign of Charles II was taken as beginning after the execution of his father in January 1649, rather than in 1660). A further implication of this was that if the throne was vacant, then in debating who should succeed to it, the Convention was turning England from a hereditary to an elective kingdom. There was strong support in the Lords, led by the Earl of Nottingham, for the idea of a regency, with Mary as the preferred regent. The advantages of the regency scheme were that it could put aside deciding whether James had 'abdicated' or whether the throne was 'vacant'. It also offered a possible back door to Mary ruling (as Queen Elizabeth II does) with William as only her consort. If, as was anticipated, James rejected the plan of a regency, the Princess of Orange could be installed as monarch in his place.

There were also anticipated political and religious advantages to supporting Mary's candidacy, namely her staunch Anglicanism (in contrast to her husband's Calvinism) and her connections with some leading Tories, such as Danby. However, the prospect of rule by Queen Mary II again jarred with the patriarchal culture of early modern England. Henry Pollexfen complained that it was 'not possible, nor ought to be in nature', that a man, let alone a prince, should be governed by his wife.[21] The rule of women over men, and wives over husbands, belonged rather to the nightmare of the world turned upside down, where fish swam through the air, and birds flew through the sea.[22] A vote on establishing a regency was lost by a mere three votes, but another motion, to declare William and Mary joint monarchs, was also defeated. However, successful amendments in the upper house replaced the word 'abdicated' with 'deserted' and removed the clause referring to the throne being vacant.

At the same time as the peers were rejecting offering the crown to William and Mary, at a private meeting at the Earl of Devonshire's house on 31 January clear indications were given that the Prince was unwilling to accept the role of consort. A Dutch spokesman for William informed the gathering of English peers, which included Halifax and Danby, that the Prince was not content to be 'his wife's gentleman usher'. Danby, the leading spokesman for a regency at the meeting, took umbrage at these comments and departed immediately afterwards. The Princess of Orange herself remained in Holland, delayed from coming over first by the frozen state of the rivers and then by strong winds, so there was as yet no clear indication of Mary's own feelings.[23]

While pressure was being indirectly exerted from above to resolve the issue of succession in William's favour, the practice of mass petitioning was revived to lend pressure from below. Crowds surrounded the House of Lords in great numbers to demonstrate their disgust at the obstructionism of the Tory peers. Lord Lovelace and Anthony Rowe, a former Monmouth rebel, presented a petition for William and Mary to accept the crown to the Lords and Commons. In both cases the petition was not read, as it had yet to be signed. (Lovelace claimed this was because of the disorder gathering subscriptions might provoke.) The rejection of the petition by the Convention led Lovelace to seek signatures from the populace. It was reported that fifteen thousand names had been collected, with the petition circulating in many of London's coffee-houses, and that ten thousand men would deliver the signed petition on Monday 4 February. However, by this date, following belated pressure from William, the Lord Mayor had ordered that the petition be suppressed as a threat to public order.[24] Some Williamites in the Lords were nonetheless explicit in stating that their duty of loyalty to James was well and truly at an end. The hot-tempered Delamere stated that 'if King James came again, he was resolved to fight against him, and would die single, with his sword in his hand, rather than pay him any obedience'.[25]

While loyalist peers picked apart the Commons resolution of 28 January, the lower house began discussing on what grounds the monarchy would be settled, whoever the crown should fall to. The debate was initiated by the Tory Lord Falkland, spurred into action by the motion of Thomas Wharton that William and Mary should immediately be offered the crown. Falkland said that the House should 'take such care, that, as the Prince of Orange has secured us from Popery, we may secure ourselves from Arbitrary Government. The Prince's Declaration is for a lasting foundation of the Government. I would know what our foundation is. Before the question be put, who shall be set upon the Throne, I would consider what powers we ought to give the Crown, to satisfy them that sent us hither.' The fact that the discussion of a declaration of rights was instigated by a Tory has led some historians to suggest that it was simply a delaying tactic, designed to prevent attempts by Wharton and others to have the crown speedily offered to the Prince and Princess of Orange. However, Falkland's intervention was quickly followed up by the Williamite Whig William Garroway, who agreed that as there had been 'such a violation of Liberties in the last reigns' the Prince of Orange could not object 'if we make conditions, to secure ourselves for the future'.[26] William himself had suggested the idea of a declaration of the subject's rights in his second declaration, issued on 14 October 1688. It is also worth remembering that Tories had supported placing limitations on the royal prerogative as means to secure the Church and State against the actions of a popish successor during the Exclusion Crisis.

Arguably it was Anglican-Tory interests that were hardest hit by James's perceived invasions of the law: displacing the Fellows of Magdalen College; suspending clergy via the Commission for Ecclesiastical Causes and purging Tory corporations and county benches through the issuing of *quo warranto* writs. There were certainly some supporters of William's claim, such as Wharton and Colonel John Birch, who wanted the issue of a declaration of rights put aside until after the succession had been settled. Despite their opposition, a Commons committee was set up on 30 January to deal with the matter. This committee may have had a predominately Whig membership, and certainly in its original form, as the heads of grievances, the draft document contained some radical proposals, including some for preventing the Crown from curtailing or perpetuating sessions of Parliament, for religious toleration and for appointing judges on good behaviour rather than at the King's pleasure. This draft document was presented to the Commons on 2 February.[27]

The following day, however, William decided that he could endure no further delay from loyalists and Maryites in the Lords. France had since declared war on the United Provinces, and William and Bentinck had already put in place plans to deploy the English army and navy to help protect the Dutch Republic from the anticipated French invasion.[28] The Prince summoned six or seven peers, including Halifax, Shrewsbury, Mordaunt, Winchester and Danby, and informed them that he would not act as regent or as consort to Mary. He did not, he said, wish to hold 'any thing by apron strings'. Finally, he said, he did not think 'it reasonable to have any share' in government, 'unless it was put in person, and that for a term of life'.[29] If they would not do this he would return to Holland, taking his army with him. Aside from this blunt ultimatum, William offered Parliament two (minor) concessions: Mary would be admitted to share the title (but not the exercise) of sovereignty with him, and Anne's children would be next in line to succeed, irrespective of whether he had children by another marriage in the event of Mary's death. (The concessions regarding Anne involved little sacrifice, given William's relative lack of interest in women – compared with his Stuart predecessors – and Anne's own medical history.)

The meeting revealed the fundamental weakness of the position that English politicians, both Whig and Tory, were in. As Halifax remarked, 'as nobody knew what to do with him [the Prince of Orange], so nobody knew what to do without him'.[30] If William and his Dutch troops departed, they had no protection from the revenge of their former king, should James return with French military help. A traitor's fate might befall even some of those now branded loyalists. Even if James did not return immediately, they would be left again in the situation the country found itself in on the night of 11 December, descending into anarchy, yet this time there would be far less prospect of bringing the mob under control. The absence of William might also encourage the hopes of those who favoured far more radical political solutions, in the shape of a republic. It was also soon made clear that neither William's wife nor his sister-in-law Anne would consider breaking ranks with the Prince of Orange. In a letter to Danby, Mary had severely reprimanded him for presuming to advance her as her husband's competitor for the throne. She was, she said, the Prince's wife, and she had no other wish than to be subject to him. After initial intransigence Anne, sweetened by the overtures of John Tillotson, Dean of Canterbury, and Lady Rachel Russell, widow of the executed Rye House plotter, contented herself with the belief that a child of hers might succeed to the throne, given the unlikelihood now of William and Mary ever having offspring of their own. The offer of a generous state pension by William further softened any blow Anne's own ambitions had taken. On 6 February she sent a message to the Lords via Churchill in which she urged the peers to concur with the Commons in settling the crown on William and Mary.

Far more than any of the half-baked arguments advanced in the Convention, the unified front presented by the Protestant wing of the Stuart family served to break the loyalist party in the Lords. On 4 February they managed to sustain opposition to the Commons vote of 'abdication' instead of 'desertion' but by only two votes. The majority for rejecting the vacancy of the throne fell even further, from fourteen votes to one. After Anne's letter had been received, the Lords voted to accept the abdication and the vacancy of the throne. Winchester then moved that William and Mary should be offered the throne, to which there was no opposition, despite an attempt by Clarendon to stage a walkout of loyalist peers. The Earl of Thanet condemned this suggestion as highly dangerous in the current climate, warning, 'we must not leave ourselves to the rabble'.[31]

The question of how to square the circle of giving obedience to William and Mary with oaths of allegiance already taken to James was resolved by the formulation of new oaths of loyalty to the joint monarchs. The new oath of allegiance to William and Mary passed in 1689, unlike those to previous monarchs, made no reference to their being 'rightful and lawful' sovereigns. Instead, subscribers were asked to swear that they would 'be faithful and bear true allegiance to their Majesties, King William and Queen Mary'. The oath was drawn up by Bishop White of Peterborough at the behest of the Earl of Nottingham. Ironically, White would be one of the first to refuse the new pledge of loyalty and was apparently so displeased with his handiwork that he had thrown the draft of it out of his window.[32] Framed in this way, the oath was supposed to provide a salve to the consciences of Tories who continued to view James as the king *de jure* (by right) but who acknowledged that William and Mary were the monarchs de facto (in fact). As we will see, it was only partially successful in this regard.

It was now clear that the crown would pass to William and Mary jointly, but with William as effective head of state. There remained one obstacle in the path of his assuming power: the list of grievances and constitutional reforms that the Commons were preparing. It was now time for William's anger to be turned from loyalist Tories to revolutionary Whigs, who, it was alleged, wished to clip the wings of their new monarch. It has been argued that the Declaration of Rights was connected to the offer of the crown, effectively making William's accession to the throne conditional on his acceptance of limitations to his power. Sir Richard Temple had stated that the Commons were not to 'go up with your vote to the Lords, to declare the Prince and Princess King and Queen, and nothing with it. If you will give the committee leave, they will connect it all at once.'[33] Certainly some of the Tories attempted to brief against the Whigs, by suggesting to William at a meeting held on 7 February that they were planning to place 'fetters' upon the crown. However, it had already been decided three days earlier, in the committee drafting the Declaration of Rights, that those elements of it which were deemed to involve making new law should be separated from the main document. Instead the Declaration of Rights should be only a statement of the law as it was deemed it already stood, a reaffirmation of existing rights, not an attempt to acquire new ones. The model here that many MPs had in mind was the Petition of Right tendered to Charles I in 1629, which, as John Wildman stated, did not claim 'new Laws, but claimed what they demanded *ab origine*'.[34] It should be added that Temple also stated that the 'Throne must be actually filled before you deliver that Petition'.[35]

The framers of the declaration averted a collision course with the Prince by assuring him that the document was only declarative of old laws and did not constitute conditions placed upon the throne. They made a further concession to William by amending the text so that the Prince was described as having the 'sole and full exercise of the regal power' rather than merely the 'administration of the Government', making a clear distinction between his status as King and his previous role as *custos regni*. Any final doubt as to whether the Declaration of Rights amounted to a condition of accepting the throne was dispelled by William's speech at his coronation on 13 February. Here he made clear that he and Mary accepted the crown first and then promised to preserve the people's religion, laws and liberties.

Much of the Declaration of Rights was, in any case, retrospective, denouncing the perceived excess of James II's rule. In its final form it affirmed the illegality of the independent exercise of the royal suspending and dispensing power, the Court of High Commission, the levying of money without parliamentary consent and the keeping of a standing army without parliamentary consent. It asserted the right of petitioning, the need for the free election of MPs, the privileges of freedom of speech and debate in Parliament and the need for frequent Parliaments. There were specific criticisms of the judiciary under James, against the imposition of excessive bail, the infliction of cruel and unusual punishments (with the aftermath of the Monmouth rebellion and the punishments handed out to Johnson and Oates in mind), against jurors who were not freeholders serving in trials for high treason (a specific criticism of the conduct of the trial of the Rye House plotters) and against all 'grants and promises of fines and forfeitures of particular persons before conviction' (here again referring to the Bloody Assizes and the sale of rebels as indentured servants before trial and sentencing).[36]

Edmund Burke described the Declaration of Rights as the cornerstone of the English constitution. For Burke, writing at the end of the eighteenth century, the fact that the Revolution settlement purported to do no more than reaffirm existing law was one of its greatest strengths, particularly when compared with the bloody social and political upheaval of the French Revolution. However, it is precisely these qualities which make the Declaration appear such an irrelevancy now. It is not a part of the historical record, like the Putney Debates or the American Declaration of Independence, which appears to speak to posterity. To be sure, making these demands explicit in 1689 had some importance. However much the members of the Convention might stress that they were only making old laws explicit, they were in fact making clear pronouncements on matters which were either legal grey areas (such as the suspending or dispensing powers) or which were not really illegal at all (James's attempt to 'pack' Parliament). Overall, they expressed a bipartisan agreement that English monarchs were obliged to act within the rule of law and reign in cooperation with Parliament. Yet there were no safeguards, even after the Declaration had been enshrined in law as the Bill of Rights, to ensure that its demands would be observed. For example, there were no mechanisms in place to ensure regular Parliaments until the passage of the Triennial Act in 1694.

This is not to say that the Declaration did not have a lasting influence. Strong echoes of its assertions can be found in the Constitution of the United States, particularly in the second and eighth amendments, affirming the right to bear arms, and freedom from cruel and unusual punishment.[37] However, we can draw a comparison between the Declaration and the new coronation oath taken by William and Mary. Whereas previous monarchs had sworn only to observe 'such laws as the commonalty have', indicating an endorsement of laws already passed, William and Mary were required to promise to govern 'according to the statutes in parliament agreed on, and the laws and customs of the same'. The notion that the coronation oath formed an original contract between monarch and people had been a staple of parliamentarian thought in the Civil War and was revived by Whigs during the debates in the Convention. John Somers argued that James had broken the original contract by failing to be 'such a king as he swore to be at his coronation, such a king to whom the allegiance of an English subject is due'.[38] But the changes in the coronation ceremony did not change it from an acclamation of the monarch to an election, nor were there procedures of impeachment established whereby monarchs could be brought to account for infracting their oaths. Both the Declaration and the new coronation oaths were symbolically important statements that lacked any legal machinery to back them up.

By 1689, then, the only thing that had been established with any sort of permanency was the Protestant succession. The changes that had been enacted could not even reliably be described as a parliamentary revolution, given the uncertain legal status of the Convention itself (for instance, it was objected that it had not been summoned by royal writ). It was only after considerable debate and, again, pressure from William, that the members resolved to agree that the Convention did constitute a Parliament and could continue to sit after the settlement of the crown.[39] All along, the key driver of events was William, backed by Mary and

Anne. However, to concede that the Revolution was effected by only a very small number of political actors (plus, of course, the very important supporting cast of the Dutch army), and focus only on their activities, is to leave a great deal out of the picture. As William had recognised even before his armada had landed in England, it was of vital importance, both domestically and internationally, that the Revolution be seen as being at the invitation of the English people and consented to by them. More than this, the crowd, particularly in London, played a very significant role in encouraging both James to leave his kingdom and the Convention to seek a speedy political solution to his departure. By requiring oaths of allegiance of office holders and clergy, and appointing loyal prayers and days of thanksgiving, the new monarchs required frequent and widespread public testimonies of loyalty. The responses William and Mary received to these demands are revealing of the extent to which the English people supported the Revolution settlement.

As we have already seen, the Convention attempted to frame oaths of allegiance to William and Mary which would ease their taking by those who continued to feel bound by their previous oath of loyalty to James. The tendering of the new oaths nonetheless sparked a considerable controversy which was largely dominated by arguments about giving allegiance to the king in possession of the throne.[40] Apologists for the government tended to use a hotchpotch of arguments based on the various claims of divine providence, possession, conquest and a historically located 'original contract' to justify giving allegiance to the new regime. John Locke's *Two Treatises of Government* (1689) is the most famous work of political thought to emerge during the debate over giving allegiance to the new monarchs. Yet the book, with its natural-rights-based contract theory, and its justification of popular rights of resistance against tyranny, was an anomaly in this pamphlet discussion. Indeed it has been suggested that the publication of the tract, originally written during the Exclusion Crisis, may have been a vain attempt to turn the tide of arguments based on expediency, necessity and divine intervention.

Over four hundred clergy, the so-called 'non-jurors', and an indeterminate number of lay office holders refused to take the oaths. Originally it had been intended that the oath would be imposed only on new incumbents among the lower clergy and members of Parliament, but the matter of the oaths became a bargaining counter in the debate over the religious settlement. The unwillingness of Tory lords to agree to removing the sacramental test, designed to bar dissenters from taking public office, led the Commons to withdraw the proposal that the oath would only be tendered to new clergy. Under the final provisions of the oath bill, all clergy, academics and schoolmasters were to take the oaths before 1 August 1689 on pain of suspension from office. If they did not take the oaths by 1 February 1690 they would be deprived of their posts. Many others, however, chose to swear allegiance to William and Mary in a 'reserved' sense, amounting only to a promise of obedience under de facto rulers, rather than lose their offices. Leading ministers, including the Earl of Nottingham, were known to have made only a limited promise of allegiance.[41] Petitions were sent to Parliament requesting confirmation of whether such subscriptions were permissible.[42] No reply was forthcoming but this did not prevent many who took the oaths from using declared reservations. The author of the pamphlet *Melius inquirendum* (1689) offered: 'that which . . . I am to Swear in taking this Oath'. He took it that he was not being required to deny or assert William and Mary's or James's legal right to the crown, nor was he required to declare that he would never bear allegiance to James II though he might legally recover his crown. The author would instead promise only that he would obey the new monarchs in 'all things lawful and honest'.[43] Others who subscribed in a limited sense 'informed by discourses with severall of the members of both Houses of Parliament' swore only to offer 'such a peaceable acquiesance and submission to the p[re]sent Governm[en]t as the law requires.'[44]

Despite the use of such equivocations, and the blandishments of government spokesmen who encouraged subscription in a limited sense, the issue of giving allegiance to William continued to trouble individuals long after 1689 and even split families. Although the oaths might have been framed to ease tender consciences, the obligation upon clergy to say loyal prayers for the King and Queen made a further test of allegiance. In 1702 Susanna Wesley, mother of John Wesley, the founder of Methodism, wrote to Lady Yarborough to ask for her help in a terrible situation. One night at family prayers her husband Samuel noticed that Susanna 'did not say "Amen" to his prayer for k[ing] W[illiam] as I usually do to all others'. In response to this expression of political defiance, Samuel 'kneeled down and imprecated the divine vengeance upon himself and all his posterity if he ever touched me more or came into a bed with me before I had begged God's pardon and his for not saying "Amen" to his prayer for the k[in]g'. Susanna tried to persuade him otherwise: 'I've unsuccessfully represented to him the unlawfulness and unreasonableness of his oath: that the man in that case has no more power over his own body than the woman over hers: that since I'm willing to let him quietly enjoy his opinions he ought not to deprive me of my little liberty of conscience.'

Samuel made arrangements to separate from his wife and six children by enlisting as ship's chaplain on a man-of-war. In the meantime Lady Yarborough referred Susanna to George Hickes, a non-juring divine. He assured her that her husband's oath was a rash one and 'wholly contrary to the prior obligation of his marriage promise and the relative duties of a husband resulting from thence. It was perjury of him to make it, and it will be perjury for him to persist in the performance of it.' But this was not the view of Samuel, who apparently said that 'if we have two kings we must have two beds'.[45]

Of course, although the oaths were tendered to more individuals than originally intended, this was largely a debate which concerned the clergy. Indeed, there was evidence that public opinion was losing patience with clerical prevarication over giving allegiance to William and Mary.[46] It has been argued that, in general, below the level of the gentry, the English public were essentially uninterested in the outcome of the Revolution and that certainly the political elite made little attempt to court them.[47] Unquestionably it is possible to find examples of the staggering disregard, and often overt distaste, that those in power had for the middling and poorer sort. Famous Whigs such as Daniel Defoe and John Locke were keen advocates of child labour to curb the increase in the 'idle poor'. Defoe was delighted to find that around Halifax 'hardly anything above four years old' was unemployed. Locke, the founder of English liberalism, urged the establishment of work schools for poor children above the age of three so that youths should no longer by 'maintained in idleness' in their infancy and their labour 'lost to the public till they are twelve or fourteen years old'.[48] The post-Revolutionary penal code grew ever more draconian in its treatment of crimes against property to secure the land and possessions of the haves from the grasping hands of the have-nots. In 1688 around fifty crimes were punishable by death but by 1800 about two hundred were deemed capital offences.[49]

Many factors of life in the late seventeenth century militated against the lower classes developing a political consciousness of their own. Especially in rural areas, many were illiterate, with even those who occupied minor public offices, such as churchwardens, overseers of the poor and so on, often unable even to write their own names. The rural communities in which most of the population still lived were also isolated and when those within spoke of 'the country' they usually meant their own parish and its immediate environs rather than the nation. Church, State and school worked together to instil into the masses values of obedience to social and political superiors. Beyond this intellectual conditioning there were plenty of 'safety valves' in English society after 1689 which ensured that social tensions did not spill over into overt opposition to authority or rebellion. Alcohol was one, with fairs such as Bartholomew Fair in London becoming so notorious in the 1690s for the consumption of drink that the authorities made several attempts to curb its activities. Theatre, too, according to John Dennis in 1698, diverted 'mens minds from thoughts of rebellion or disobedience'.[50] Moreover, the regular Parliaments and elections of William's reign gave many opportunities for the increasing number who met the forty-shilling threshold for the vote to air their political voices, if only for the Whig and Tory parties, which essentially served the wealthy, landed classes.

However, this picture of ordinary men and women in the post-Revolutionary period as being essentially apolitical needs serious revision. Research has shown that even as early as the reign of James I, England had a thriving 'news culture' which fed the public appetite for information on current affairs. In the 1620s members of the provincial gentry, such as John Rous, paid individuals known as 'intelligencers' to send them information from the capital on political events. For poorer social groups the same function was often performed by word of mouth as travelling tinkers or peddlers would hawk not only their goods but also the latest titbits of information from London to their customers. In a less formal way private correspondence that reflected upon the news was often copied and circulated in manuscript. Printed news-sheets mirrored these manuscript productions but by the 1640s had far exceeded them in terms of the volume of material generated. The illiterate were not excluded from this burgeoning news culture. Literate members of the community would often read aloud pamphlets and news-sheets for the benefit of those who could not. Moreover, much information was originally conveyed in oral form, as ballads or verse libels, or simply through conversation in sites popular for the exchange of news, such as St Paul's Walk in London. This oral discussion often formed the basis for printed or manuscript material.[51]

This news culture, which both James II and his brother Charles II had attempted to censor and control, was rapidly resuscitated during the Glorious Revolution, as political chaos and the propaganda needs of the differing factions loosened state restrictions on the press. Aside from the revival of mass petitioning and the illicit reporting of votes and debates in the Convention, there was a huge expansion in the number of cheap weekly newspapers. Titles such as the *Orange Gazette*, the *Harllum Currant*, the *London Courant*, the *London Intelligence*, the *London Mercury*, the *English Currant*, the *Universal Intelligence*, jostled for space alongside the official *London Gazette*, which continued to supply an official spin on events but this time told from the perspective of the Williamite court. Prints of William were also produced before the meeting of the Convention Parliament which glossed over the Prince's rather unappealing physical make-up – his short stature, spindly legs, little feet, crooked back, huge, beak-like nose and black teeth – and emphasised instead his personal virtues and military prowess.

By the end of the seventeenth century as much as 70 per cent of the adult male population may have been able to read. Even for the illiterate, however, there was an increasing number of avenues through which the news could be distributed by word of mouth. The public spaces for discussing and disseminating news of current events were expanding during the seventeenth century and becoming more socially inclusive. Two key places where the public gathered to hear the latest goings-on at court or in Parliament were the pub and the coffee-house.[52] Consumption of beer remained high after the Restoration, despite competition, as we will see, from newer stimulants. According to the statistician Gregory King, in 1695 about 28 per cent of annual per capita expenditure in England was devoted to ale and beer. The clientele of the alehouse remained distinctly lower-class. Writing in the 1690s, Anthony Burnaby argued that the victuallers' trade was supported by the 'more inferrior part . . . as tailors, weavers, smiths, bricklayers . . . labourers . . . drovers of cattle, carters, coachmen,

Titus Oates, engraving by R. White (1679). Oates was the chief fabricator of stories of a 'Popish Plot' to assassinate Charles II. This print displays Oates' unusual appearance: 'his nose was snub, his mouth in the very centre of his face, for his chin was almost equal in size to the rest of his face.' *(Mary Evans)*

England's Grand Memorial (1679). The 'murder' of Sir Edmund Godfrey, the magistrate who had heard Oates and Tonge's account of Catholic subterfuge, sparked panic in London. In fact, Godfrey may well have taken his own life.
(Private Collection/Bridgeman Art Library)

King Charles II, attributed to Thomas Hawker (*c.* 1680). Charles seriously doubted the existence of a Popish Plot, aware of factual inconsistencies in Oates' story. *(National Portrait Gallery)*

James Scott, Duke of Monmouth, by Sir Godfrey Kneller (1678). Charles's eldest illegitimate son, Monmouth led a serious revolt against his uncle James II in 1685. Captured and sentenced to death, it took five blows from the executioner's axe to behead the Duke. *(National Portrait Gallery)*

James II, by Sir Godfrey Kneller (1684–5). James, a devout Catholic, had a strong, authoritarian personality shaped by his early military career. *(National Portrait Gallery)*

Catherine Sedley, studio of Peter Lely (*c.* 1675). Despite his religious beliefs, James, like his brother, had a string of mistresses. James's relationship with Catherine Sedley was the most long-lasting of his adulterous liasions (despite Charles's barbed comments about her plainness). *(National Portrait Gallery)*

Queen Mary Beatrice, Prince James Francis Edward in the cradle, and Father Petre. Claims that James's son, the Prince of Wales, was not his own, or had been smuggled in in a warming-pan, were given credence by the Prince of Orange's Declaration, in which he promised a Parliamentary investigation into the child's paternity and birth.
(British Museum)

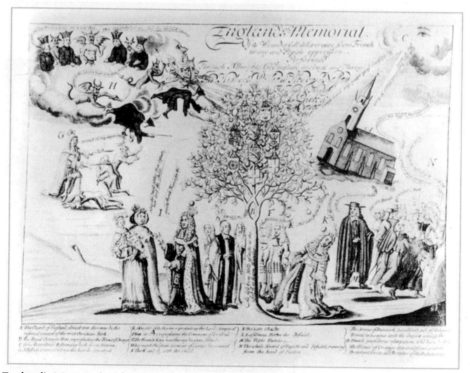

England's Memorial. Of its wounderfull deliverance from French tirany and popish oppression (1688). Prints of this kind gave visual representation to the claim that William had saved England from popery and its political equivalent, arbitrary government.

(Private collection/Bridgeman Art Library)

Mary II, by Sir Godfrey Kneller (1690). Mary, a statuesque 5′ 11″, was as famed for her beauty as she was for her piety and devotion to her husband. *(Sotheby's/AKG Images)*

William III, by Gottfried Schalken (1692). This portrait of William not only conveys his sombre and reserved character but also displays his greatest facial characteristic, his enormous hooked nose.
(Crown Estate/Bridgeman Art Library)

The Battle of the Boyne, by Jan Wyck (1690). Although the war in Ireland continued for another two years, William's victory at the Boyne effectively ended James's personal involvement in the Jacobite cause. *(National Army Museum/Bridgeman Art Library)*

The Battle of La Hogue, by George Chambers Senior (1692). The crushing naval victory for the British and Dutch over the French at La Hogue led Louis XIV to turn his nation's seaborne efforts to privateering to damage British trade. *(National Maritime Museum)*

Queen Anne, studio of John Closterman (*c.* 1702). A doughty, irascible character, Anne's decision to side with her sister rather than her father during the Revolution was swayed by the desire to preserve her own and her children's dynastic inheritance.
(National Portrait Gallery)

John Churchill, First Duke of Marlborough, by Sir Godfrey Kneller (1700). Churchill rose through the army ranks under James II, but was a key member of the 'Orangist' conspiracy against the King and would be ennobled by William for his role in the revolution in 1689.
(National Portrait Gallery)

Prince Charles Edward Stuart, by Hugh Douglas Hamilton (1785). 'Bonnie Prince Charlie', the most charismatic of the Stuart pretenders and the one, in the 1745 rebellion, to pose the most serious threat to the Hanoverian dynasty.
(National Portrait Gallery)

Prince James Francis Edward Stuart, by Louis Gabriel Blanchet (1741). A portrait of the elderly 'Old Pretender': 'a tall lean blak man, loukes half dead alredy, very thine, long faced, and very ill cullored and melancholy'.
(National Portrait Gallery)

porters and journeymen of all sorts'. Women were customers of the alehouses, too, though they were usually expected to come only with their husbands. However, drinking dens were not solely the preserve of the plebeian orders. In Oxford in the 1670s it was reported that members of Balliol College were habitués of a nearby tippling establishment 'fit for none but draymen and tinker' and here 'continually lie and by perpetual bubbing add art to their natural stupidity to make themselves perfect sots'. Samuel Pepys was an inveterate frequenter of pubs, in November 1664 recording that he put on a 'poor black suit' and went with Bagwell's wife 'to a blind alehouse and there I did caress her and eat and drank'.

Yet, far from being places where the lower orders could anaesthetise themselves against the cruelties of everyday life and let off steam in harmless, drunken revelry, alehouses were often the settings for seditious talk among the labouring poor. Heated by alcohol, men and women discussed the claims to the throne of William or James over their cups and hurled accusations of treason or sedition at one another. The term 'seditious words' refers only to verbal expressions, not to writing, which was seditious libel.[53] The evidence that we can gather from cases brought for speaking seditious words is not without its problems and it is likely that some prosecutions were politically motivated. In post-Revolutionary Norwich the mayor, Thomas Cooke, rigorously prosecuted a number of such cases in an effort to ingratiate himself with the Williamite regime. Joseph Smith, a labourer of the city, alleged before Cooke that having gone 'to drinke a pott of Beer at his Master Cromes seller in St Gregory p[ar]ish', his drinking companions fell to 'discourse of King William', one 'William Symonds saying, "God Bliss King William King of England. God of the first place saved us, And King William in the next place saved all our Lives."' However, another drinker, Robert Poynter 'replyed and said that King William was none of the King of England but a Deputy and fitt for no better And that he did nott Question but once in a moneths time to see a hundred such Rogues as the s[ai]d

Informant was should be hanged for speaking ag[a]inst King James'. Barnard Barratt, another customer in Crome's cellar that day, reported that Poynter had said that 'King William was but an Elective King and that the Late King James would be here againe within halfe a yeare'. Symonds's information was even more damning, reporting that Poynter had claimed 'that he had rather be und[e]r the power of the Devill then und[e]r the presbeterian [meaning Williamite] Goverment'. Poynter admitted that he had described William as an elective king but denied that he had said that Smith and Symonds would be hanged when James returned. It may be that a mere expression of political judgement on the part of Poynter, albeit an injudicious one, that William was an 'elective', not a hereditary monarch, had been transformed by the zeal of the mayor into something that could be prosecuted as an act of sedition.[54]

Alehouse keepers, as well as their customers, could find themselves in trouble. At Epiphany Quarter Sessions in Buckinghamshire Ralph Lacey was fined £5 for 'speaking scandalous words against the King and Queen', his alehouse at Princes Risborough was suppressed and he was fined a further 3s and 4d for keeping a 'disorderley alehouse'.[55] The growing social respectability of alehouse keepers often led them to become informers against their fractious customers in order to preserve good relations with local authorities, this in turn resulting in their becoming targets for mob violence themselves, as in London (1720), Norwich (1731) Shoreditch (1736), Sundridge (1734) and Tiverton (1738).[56]

In private homes, too, alcohol acted to loosen tongues and embolden its imbibers to make seditious statements. On 18 August 1691 William West of Atworth in Wiltshire, a baker, alleged that 'upon a certain Sunday about a moneth past, being Box revells he was in the house of John Cottle of Box where was present one Thomas Hibbert of Bath'. West asserted that 'the said Hibbert taking a glass of beer severall times in his hands began and drank severall healths to ye late King James saying withall our present

King William was brought in to England with a East wind and was driven out again by a West wind [probably a reference to the King's going to Ireland] as ye locusts were from off the earth. And this informant further saieth that Hibbert spoke severall approbrious words against the present King and Queen and their government.' Cottle admitted the presence of the two men in his house but denied hearing of this conversation and stated that he always urged his guests 'not to talke of ye government'.[57]

Some of the remarks ascribed to those convicted of speaking seditious words display a surprisingly sophisticated understanding of politics and political ideas. Peter Webb, a nailer from Wolverhampton, demonstrated considerable knowledge of hereditary right when in December 1689, while carol singing in Albrighton in Shropshire, he told a weaver friend that 'wee ought to live in a rule and obedience under Kinge James as well as where hee is as if hee were amongst us & that hee that is yor King Meaninge Kinge William is a Usurper to the Crowne, & has noe more to Doe with [it] then I have'. In this brief statement Webb had distilled almost the entirety of the non-jurors' arguments for refusing to give allegiance to William III. Some of the convicted had got into trouble by exploring the full implications of the de facto theory often used to support William's title. Margaret Steene, a Roman Catholic of Burslem in Staffordshire and wife of a yeoman, or gentleman farmer, was asked by her neighbour in 1689 to return a shearing hook that had been loaned to her. Steene replied that if she had the hook 'she would keepe it by the same Right as King William kept his Crowne, ffor itt was none of his owne for he was an outcomling [a stranger or foreigner] a Rouge [sic] & A Bastard, And that they would have his head as soone as the [sic] Could'. Others demonstrated knowledge of the lack of constitutional propriety in the way that the Convention Parliament had been summoned. In Wiltshire an unnamed individual was committed to prison for saying that 'the present majesties [William and Mary] are not lawfully King and Queen and that the present Parliament is not a Parliament but a parcel of fools met together who make themselves a Parliament'.[58]

Just as important as these political arguments to the content of seditious speech were the personal politics of the Revolution. William was often described in recorded seditious speech as a 'rogue', meaning that he was a thief who had stolen the crown. Simon Lynch, a gentleman of St Andrew's, Holborn, and probably Irish, was fined and imprisoned in 1690 for saying King William was 'a Rogue & a Sonne of a Whore & that he took his father's Right from him'. Others spoke of William's criminality in more literal terms. Rumours circulated that William had stolen treasures from royal palaces and sent them to the Netherlands. Robert Jefferson of Hexham in Northumberland was accused in 1689 of saying that the Prince of Orange had purloined King James's 'rich Hangings' and that he had 'Rob'd Whitehall of King James Plait & had Smelted itt and some of itt had Coyned into money and the rest he made into Piggs Like Lead and sent into Holland'.[59] The fact that William had taken his father-in-law's title was often alluded to in Jacobite propaganda and seditious words accusations, his act making the Prince of Orange guilty of the crime of petty treason. Henry Ellyott of St Paul's, Covent Garden, whose words begin this chapter, was pilloried five times, fined and imprisoned for calling William 'a Sone of a Whore' who ate the 'bread out of his fathers mouth'. Casting doubt on William's paternity threw back in their faces the Whigs' accusations concerning the Prince of Wales's birth.[60]

It was not the demon drink alone that loosened tongues and enflamed political passions. A voguish new beverage, coffee, also appeared to stimulate and enliven talk of the news. According to the Oxford antiquarian Anthony Wood, the first English coffee-house was established in that city in 1650 by one of the Jews readmitted into England by Oliver Cromwell. A few years later the owner relocated to London and opened a coffee-house in

Holborn. By the late seventeenth century there were nearly eight thousand coffee-houses in London. John Macky, a Scottish visitor to the capital, noted that they were nearly always full in the evening. By the period of the Exclusion Crisis it was estimated that a hundred tunnes of coffee were consumed in England each year and most cities and boroughs in England had coffee-houses of their own. These catered for a variety of political opinions, with Tories meeting at the Cocoa Tree and Osinda's and Whigs in the Coffee House of Saint James.[61] Historians have seen coffee-houses as part of a burgeoning 'public sphere', providing a 'forum where even the socially humble could have access to the latest pamphlets and newspapers'. But coffee-houses also had their secretive, closed side as well. The Grecian coffee-house in Devereux Court doubled as both a meeting place for members of the Royal Society, including Newton, Sir Hans Sloane and Edmund Halley, and for secret meetings of radical Whigs and commonwealthsmen like Walter Moyle and John Trenchard, who gathered to produce anti-standing-army tracts. Even so, coffee-houses were remarkably socially inclusive establishments. One seventeenth-century commentator stated that a 'coffee-house is free to all comers, so [long as] they have human shape'. In a time of rising prices for beer and wine, which pushed out poorer customers, coffee-houses offered cheap refreshment as well as newspapers and gazettes to read.

Coffee-houses, even more than alehouses, were identified as hotbeds of political discourse. As early as 1661 Anthony Wood was complaining about the effect that coffee-houses had had upon the intellectual life of Oxford. Scholarly topics had given place to 'nothing but news, and the affairs of Christendome is discoursed off and that also generally at coffee houses'. In the late 1690s the minister of Epworth in Lincolnshire told his neighbour, Abraham de la Pryme, that when he had been in London he knew a parrot who was sent to a coffee-house and within six months 'could say nothing but "Bring a dish of coffy", "Where's the news?", and such like'. The English state quickly turned its attentions upon the political debates taking place in English coffee-houses. The Cromwellian protectorate appears to have employed spies to monitor coffee-houses, despite the infancy of the trade. The Earl of Clarendon reported discussions with Charles II concerning coffee-houses as early as 1666 in which the King complained of the freedom of speech allowed there.

In 1675 it was said that *A Letter from a Person of Quality to his Friend in the Country* (probably written by John Locke under the instruction of the Earl of Shaftesbury and a severe censure of Charles II's government and the policies of his chief minister, the Earl of Danby) was the talk of all the coffee-houses. The circulation of this pamphlet seems to have prompted a royal proclamation in December of that year 'For the Suppression of Coffee Houses'. Among the problems caused by coffee-houses, it mentioned 'that in such Houses . . . divers, False, Malicious and Scandalous Reports are devised and spread abroad, to the Defamation of his Majesties Government and to the Disturbance of the Peace and Quiet of the Realm'. The crown's attempt to suppress London's café society failed.[62] However, the role of coffee-house owners as intelligencers and spreaders of news meant that they continued to attract the attention of the authorities. In 1678 Chillingworth, master of a coffee-house in Leadenhall Street, together with Kid, keeper of the Amsterdam in Bartholomew Lane, the principal gathering place for Whig sympathisers, and Rebecca Weeden, by the Exchange, were all censured for dispensing letters of false news. Coffee-houses were also suppressed outside of London. In January 1681 orders were issued to shut down the coffee-house of William Pearce at Warminster in Wiltshire as he 'hath of late made it his dayly practice to expose to the view of the inhabitants divers seditious pamphlets and libells against the government now established in both Church and State'.[63]

Suppression during the 'Tory reaction' did not prevent coffee-houses from returning as key forums for political discussion during the Glorious Revolution. Already aware that they were becoming venues for distributing Orangist propaganda, James attempted to have them suppressed in October 1688. The greatest public celebration of the coronation of William and Mary took place outside of Watt's coffee-house on 13 February. During a debate in the Convention on 9 March it was argued that the votes of the Commons may as well be printed as they were common discourse in coffee-houses.[64]

It was not only seditious speech or illicit printed libels and pamphlets that these establishments generated. Some periodical publications sprang directly from the coffee-house milieu. John Dunton's *Athenian Gazette, or Casuistical Mercury* made use of the theological works of Robert Sanderson, Henry Hammond and William Perkins in the novel setting of the problem page. But Dunton's gazette was more in the vein of 'Notes and Queries' than a religious treatise. The publication stemmed directly from the emerging coffee-house culture, as the editor and his collaborators met in Smith's coffee-house in Stocks Market to compose answers to questions they had received in the post from readers. It was published twice weekly, on Tuesdays and Saturdays, on both sides of a folio sheet, priced at a penny a copy. The questions raised by readers ranged from the sublime to the ridiculous: 'Why fish that live in salt water as Whitings etc. taste fresh?', 'What's the reason that some Men have no beards?' and 'Why a Horse with a round Fundament emits a square Excrement?' Aside from dealing with more familiar moral problems, such as whether it was 'lawful for a man to marry his cousin German [*sic*]' or 'whether a person that is divorced may lawfully marry another, while those they were first marryed to are yet living?', the *Athenian Gazette* also touched upon questions of political obedience, such as 'whether what Dr Sherlock cites out of Bishop Overall's Convocation-Book, and his other Assertions, be sufficient to Ground an oath of allegiance upon?' and 'what is the meaning of the new word "Abdication"?'[65] The moral dilemmas of those faced with the choice of giving their allegiance either to James or to William and Mary were being resolved in the pages of a forerunner to the advice column.

It is clear that by the end of the seventeenth century England had experienced a 'news revolution'. The range and volume of printed media had expanded dramatically since the 1660s. With coffee-houses springing up in virtually every major town in the country, the spaces for public discussion of the news had also proliferated exponentially. It is important, however, to recognize that this increase in the availability of news, and the obvious exploitation of the press and public opinion by the crown and political parties, does not represent the acceptance by the political elite of the people's freedom to discuss affairs of state. Secrecy norms continued to officially govern parliamentary proceedings and those, like Henry Sacheverell, whose views challenged political or religious orthodoxy could face severe punishment by the courts. Despite this, all sides, Williamites and Jacobites, saw the absolute necessity of winning over the hearts and minds of the public in the struggle for the British crown.

The dynastic revolution in England took place with remarkable rapidity and with little blood being spilt. From December 1688 it was being driven by William's clear wish to accept nothing less than the effective exercise of sole monarchical authority. With both Mary and, later, Anne supporting William's candidacy, and with the legitimate monarch, James II, having fled the country, there was little alternative for English politicians other than to acquiesce to the Prince's claim to the throne. Attempts at limiting monarchical authority were undercut by the desire of William and his supporters for a speedy settlement, and by the lack of mechanisms of enforcement being incorporated into the Bill of Rights. However, the need for William to present the image of an English settlement to the nation and Europe as a whole meant that compromises had to be made with both Tory and Whig opinion to an extent that left the exact nature of the Revolution settlement highly contested. On what grounds could William be said to have a right to the English throne? How limited were the powers of the monarchy after 1689? These were questions that were debated not only at Westminster or among the social and political elite, but in pubs and coffee-houses and at home.

Moreover, this ambiguous Revolution settlement extended only to England and Wales. In Scotland and Ireland the dynastic contest between William and James would be both more emphatic in its constitutional and religious outcomes and far more bloody in its resolution.

7

THE REVOLUTION IN SCOTLAND AND IRELAND

Bar a few minor skirmishes, the Revolution in England had been a largely bloodless affair. The absence of armed conflict would later form an important part of the mythology of the 'sensible revolution' (a mythology which glossed over the overtly martial nature of William's 'expedition'). However, in James II's other kingdoms of Ireland and Scotland, the Revolution unleashed waves of warfare, sectarian violence and bloody clan rivalry, and was characterised by far more explicit (and thereby far more divisive) political and religious settlements. The revolutionary wars in Ireland and Scotland featured examples of great bravery: the obstinate defence made by the besieged Protestants of Londonderry; and of great perfidy: the brutal slaughter of the men, women and children of clan MacDonald at Glencoe. The scars left by these wars and the exclusive nature of the settlements in Scotland and Ireland helped to create and sustain Jacobitism as a force that would seriously threaten the Protestant succession in Britain up to its military defeat at Culloden in 1746. In Ireland the post-Revolution establishment of Protestant hegemony, in flagrant breach of the peace terms negotiated between Williamites and

Jacobites, had an even further-reaching impact, dividing Irish society sharply along sectarian lines and consigning the majority of its population to the status of second-class citizens.

As king of Scotland and Ireland, James II pursued policies that shared clear objectives with those that he initiated in England. Again, in his other kingdoms, James's overriding aim was to secure the religious and political emancipation of his Catholic subjects. The methods that he used to do this were also basically the same as those deployed in England: the exploitation of his prerogative powers to dispense with laws barring Catholics from holding civil, ecclesiastic and military office, the 'packing' of the Irish and Scottish Parliaments in order to ensure the statutory repeal of penal legislation against Catholics, and the issuing of edicts of toleration for both Catholic and Protestant dissenters. These measures were accompanied, as in James's southern kingdoms, with words and actions that often raised fears of arbitrary government (even if, as in England, this was expressly not the monarch's stated aim). Yet though some aspects of his other kingdoms might have raised James's hopes of success (in Scotland the less independent nature of Parliament and the loyalty of the Highland clans; in Ireland the fact that the majority of the population were Catholics), these different contexts also meant that advocating the same policies in all three kingdoms did not mean getting the same outcome in England, Scotland and Ireland. In particular, the stark contrast in religious make-up between Scotland and Ireland meant that James's aim of emancipating his Catholic subjects was seen as too extreme and too limited, respectively.

James was proclaimed James VII, King of Scotland, on 10 February 1685, breaking with tradition by failing to take the part of the coronation oath which obliged him to defend the Protestant religion. As in England, there was evidence of popular joy at his accession: 'Never King succeeded to a throne more with the love and esteem of his subjects than your Majesty,' observed the earl of Balcarres.[1]

The new King himself felt that exercising his rule in Scotland would be easier than in England. Having spent a long time in exile in his northern kingdom during the Exclusion Crisis, James II was probably, after his grandfather James I and VI, the Stuart monarch with the greatest contacts in Scotland. This greater knowledge of Scottish affairs led James to believe that he would be more able to rule alone here than in England, given the comparative weakness of the Scottish Parliament. This was reflected in his decision to call a Scottish Parliament before the English one of 23 April 1685. James's faith in the loyalty of this institution appeared to be rewarded when it voted the king a very generous financial settlement, granting the crown excise revenues in perpetuity, along with voting other sources of income to the royal purse calculated to total £60,000. This financial settlement was followed by the passage of a series of acts which one historian described as the 'Nuremberg decrees of seventeenth-century Scotland'.[2] James's first Parliament declared war on those who attended 'field conventicles', unofficial outdoor Presbyterian meetings, making it a capital offence not only to go to such meetings but also to harbour those who did. Further statutes made it a treasonable offence to refuse to give evidence in treason trials, indemnified royal officers against suits and complaints made against actions carried out under the royal seal and placed the lives and property of James's male subjects aged from sixteen to sixty at the ultimate disposal of the crown. The draconian nature of these laws was intensified by the strong insinuation that they were not the product of parliamentary deliberation but rather created by the King's absolute prerogative. The preamble to the Excise Act affirmed that these laws were made by the King's 'sacred, supreme and absolute power' and promised 'the hearty and sincere offer' of his subjects' 'lives and fortunes to assist, support, defend and maintain King James the seventh . . . against all mortals'. James congratulated the Duke of Queensberry, commissioner for the estates, on the success of the Parliament, which he said would 'be a very good precedent to the English one'.[3]

This harsh policy against conventiclers has been justified on the grounds that the Cameronians, the extreme wing of the Scottish Presbyterians, were effectively terrorists bent on the overthrow of the Stuart monarchy, and as a consequence could scarcely be tolerated. Certainly the threat of armed covenanter rebellion was real, and in the Sanquhar Declaration published in June 1680 (a year after the defeat of Presbyterian rebels at Bothwell Bridge), the Cameronians had declared war on Charles II as a tyrant and covenant breaker, and disowned their new overlord in Scotland, his brother James, then Duke of York.[4] However, it was also the case that James's government used the reality of Cameronian extremism as a means to persecute all Presbyterians, including moderates who usually attended church, had little to do with house conventicles and disassociated themselves from field conventiclers. Presbyterians of this ilk were subject nonetheless to rigorous fines and periodic quartering of troops.[5] To be sure, emotive histories of the so-called 'killing time', like some treatments of the Bloody Assizes, may lose a sense of the generally brutal responses of Tudor and Stuart governments to sedition or the mere threat of it. However, there can be little doubt that some of the crown's agents, in particular the notorious John Graham of Claverhouse, took a sadistic pleasure in enforcing the new hard line against conventiclers.

Claverhouse was a professional soldier who had taken part in the battle of Bothwell Bridge and played an active part in Monmouth's removal from Scottish command on the grounds of his leniency to the defeated rebels. He was made a Privy Councillor by James in 1685, a major general in 1686, Provost of Dundee in 1688 and, after the Dutch invasions, Viscount Claverhouse. Graham was placed in charge of raiding parties against conventiclers, showing no mercy against ringleaders 'lest', he said, 'rebellion be thought cheap here'. In May 1685 he summarily executed John Brown, shot dead after being discovered with arms in his house. Claverhouse reported: 'I caused to shoot him dead, which he suffered very inconcernedly.'[6] In the same month Dunottar Castle was commandeered as a new fortress to keep the growing numbers of captured conventiclers – it was reported that in one dungeon 110 men and women were kept in near darkness. Argyll's ill-fated rebellion was as fiercely repressed as that undertaken by Monmouth south of the border. Government troops were ordered to 'either kill or apprehend all those who joined with the late Argile against the king'. Argyll himself, like Monmouth, was executed without trial, following an act of attainder. One English rebel who joined Argyll's rising was returned to his home town in boiled and tarred quarters.[7]

As in England, the rebellion was used as a pretext to bring Catholics into the civil and military administration in Scotland. The Earl of Dumbarton was made commander in chief of the Scottish army and a further twenty-six Catholics, including the Duke of Gordon and the Earl of Seaforth, were appointed as commissioners of the excise. To Scottish Presbyterians these appointments represented a clear breach of James's promise before Parliament to defend the 'Religion as established by law'. Government was placed further in the hands of Catholics by the politic conversions of the Drummond brothers, the Earls of Perth and Melfort, who initiated a steady campaign against Queensberry. Perth had flagrantly flouted Scottish law (attendance at mass was a criminal offence carrying the death penalty for the third offence) by opening a Catholic chapel in Edinburgh. The Drummonds attempted to implicate Queensberry in anti-Catholic demonstrations, having an Edinburgh fencing master put to death when he refused to give false evidence that Queensberry had been involved in these disturbances. The King was behind the policy to suppress anti-Catholic preaching in Scotland, as he had been in England. The apparent romanising policies of James brought stern reactions from Protestant ministers, one preacher being silenced after declaring that he 'would as soon believe that the moon was made of green cheese as in transubstantiation'. When James Glen, a bookseller, received an order not to sell any anti-Catholic books, 'he answered the Masters of the Privy Counsell, that he had one book in his shop which condemned Popery very directly, and he desired to know if he might sell it, meaning the Bible'.[8] These attempts at censoring anti-popish sermons and books provoked further Protestant reaction, including anti-Catholic rioting in Edinburgh on 24 January 1686 as apprentices insulted Catholics leaving the house of a priest, calling them papist dogs. On 31 January the same house was stoned during a communion service, and Perth's wife, who was in attendance, was pelted with mud. The ringleader of the mob was arrested and ordered to be flogged through the streets of Edinburgh on 1 February but was rescued by the crowd as the punishment was being carried out. The government's reaction to these anti-Catholic riots and demonstrations had reached outright paranoia. Hugh Maxwell was imprisoned for, as it turned out, completely uncontroversial marginal annotations he had made on theological works in a shorthand that was indecipherable and (so the Privy Council reasoned) must be seditious. He was kept in prison for seventeen months before it was confirmed that the notes were harmless.[9]

It seems hard to reconcile the legislation passed in the first session of James's Scottish Parliament, and the harsh enforcement of it, with his apparent life-long commitment to the idea of religious toleration. Here it is important to consider another element of the King's personal belief system, his almost pathological hatred of disloyalty. The Protestant dissenters to whom James appeared to be most ready to grant toleration, both in England and in his other kingdoms, were those, like the Quakers and Baptists, who adopted a quietist approach and retreated from involvement in public life.[10] These groups represented a small yet significant minority in early modern England. In Scotland, however, such sects were represented by tiny numbers of followers, whereas the majority of those outside the worship of the Church of Scotland were Presbyterians who had been implicated in fomenting rebellion against the crown from the reign of James II's great-grandmother, Mary Queen of Scots, onwards. These differences in the religious make-up of the two kingdoms had serious repercussions for the success of James's project to repeal the tests and penal laws.

Though Perth and Melfort failed to implicate Queensberry in the rioting, the disturbances nonetheless persuaded James that he had lost control of the government and encouraged him to put his faith in the Drummond brothers instead. Queensberry was removed as commissioner for the estates and Melfort put in his place. It led the King to place urban government further under the control of Catholics. The Catholic Duke of Gordon was made governor of Edinburgh because according to James, 'I thought that necessary at this tyme to make that towne have more regard for my commands and civiler to the Catholicks, by seeing it in the hands of one of that persuasion.'[11] As a result of the Drummonds' influence James was convinced that the new session of his Scottish Parliament would see him win agreement to the repeal of the tests and penal laws. More reliable advice came from members of the secret committee of the Privy Council, led by the Duke of Hamilton, a leading Presbyterian peer. He warned that repeal was unlikely unless it was accompanied by some form of toleration for Protestants. Toleration, however, was looked at askance by the Episcopalian clergy of Scotland, who feared both the threat of a resurgent Presbyterianism, should the arguments of men like Hamilton win the day, and the actions of a popish King who had suspended the Bishop of Dunkeld for expressing anti-Catholic views. As a result of the fears of Presbyterians and the jealousies of the Episcopalians, the second session of Parliament, begun on 29 April 1686, proved far less tractable than the first. MPs were prepared to consider only giving liberty of private worship to Catholics, a mere extension of liberty of conscience, not the full emancipation that James demanded. Their answer to the king's letter requesting them to consider a toleration, in which they promised to do only as much as their consciences would allow, was suppressed, given its pointed statement that they did not doubt that the King would 'be careful to secure the Protestant Religion established by law'. Disheartened, James prorogued Parliament on 15 June.

The methods adopted by James to overcome the obstacles placed in his path by the legislature were essentially the same as those he deployed in his southern kingdom. As in England, James began engineering town councils so as to elect a more pliant Parliament. He also replaced five of his Privy Councillors, installing Dundonald, a Presbyterian, and the Earls of Seaforth and Traquair, both Catholics, made it clear that he would institute a Catholic chapel at Holyrood and ordered judges not to molest his Catholic subjects. A public display of the King's intentions was made on 23 November 1686 when his yacht arrived from London at Leith 'with the Popish altar, vestments, images, Priests, and other dependents, for the Popish Chapell in the Abbcy'. Again, as in England, in the short term James circumvented the failure to achieve a toleration through parliamentary means by effecting religious liberty through the use of his prerogative.

On 12 February 1687 he issued his Edict of Toleration, which, aside from suspending all penal laws against Roman Catholics, extended freedom of private worship to 'moderate Presbyterians' and allowed Quakers to worship in public. James asserted that the Proclamation was effective as law on the grounds of the recognition of the King's absolute power in the excise act. On 10 March he clarified even this very limited offer of toleration to his Protestant subjects by insisting that in order to benefit from the provisions as relating to Presbyterians, they were to take an oath of non-resistance which also confirmed the King in the exercise of absolute power. However, few were prepared to swear to this, and the need to build bridges with the Presbyterians was evident in James's rapid extension of the concessions offered. In April the King permitted Presbyterian ministers to preach without taking the oath and in July he granted an unconditional toleration. As Sir John Lauder observed, 'This was great instability of counsell.'[12]

The problem for James was that in Scotland he never succeeded in converting Presbyterians into part of an alliance with Catholics, as he had been able to do to a degree with English dissenters. This led to the impression that the edict was really only a grant of toleration to Scottish Catholics, an impression fostered by the revival of the Order of the Thistle in June 1687, the Scottish equivalent of the Order of the Garter. James gave preference to Catholic peers like the newly converted Drummonds in the granting of this honour.

Despite the poor reception of his plans for toleration in Parliament, James nonetheless attempted to poll public opinion, as he had done in England concerning the repeal of the tests and penal laws, only to receive equally depressing returns. Balcarres informed him that 'most of them, though they consented and signed it, yet had such cruel apprehensions of other things further to be pressed upon them, that it kept them in constant concern and uneasiness.'[13] Gilbert Burnet alleged that the edict was part of a plan to establish absolute power in Scotland, an accusation which James later refuted. It was taken to mean that he meant 'either the usurping of my subjects' property or constraining any body in matters of religion. For the first, nobody can accuse me of ever having done it and for the second everyone can see . . . that it is not my intention.'[14] However, as in England, the process of public canvassing was meant less to test the water for support for repeal than to identify its opponents and prepare the way for political purges that would produce a compliant Parliament. Rumours intensified that the King would be calling for fresh elections.

Discontent among most of James's Protestant Scottish subjects remained subdued until the news of the birth of a Catholic heir reached his northern kingdom. There was very little public celebration of the Prince of Wales's arrival and suspicions concerning his paternity were raised almost immediately. One of William's spies reported that the 'business of the new Prince is so much suspected in Scotland that when the news of it were, with great solemnity, made known to the people by the Chancellor, as he was attended with very few of the nobility . . . so in his acclamations of joy and waving of his hat he was scarce seconded by one of a great multitude of spectators'.[15] Despite this very public affront to the King, resistance in Scotland remained muted until James was forced to draw his northern army south in order to counter William's invasion force. In December of 1688 rioting broke out anew in Glasgow and Edinburgh, with mass pope-burning processions, and crowd attacks on Roman Catholic chapels and mass-houses. Presbyterian mobs also drove around two hundred Espicopalian clergy from their livings in the south-west of Scotland.

If it was true that James's Scottish subjects had generally waited until the Revolution was underway in England before demonstrating their overt opposition to the King's rule, it was also the case that the Scottish were prominent in William's invasion party. In addition to his chief propagandist, Burnet, William was accompanied by the 'plotter' (and future Jacobite) Robert Ferguson, Archibald, 10th Earl of Argyll, William Carstares, the Prince's chaplain, Sir James Dalrymple, later Viscount Stair, and James Johnston. It was these exiled Scots who suggested to William at a meeting at Whitehall in early 1689 that he should summon a Scottish Convention to decide the political settlement north of the border. As in England, the Convention was so ordered that only a minimum number of those who had sat in James's Parliament would be included. The Convention met in Edinburgh on 14 March 1689 under Hamilton's presidency. Claverhouse, now Viscount Dundee, attended for a while before making his Jacobite credentials plain by withdrawing from the Convention and setting up a rival body at Stirling.

Following a month of fierce debate, the Convention agreed on 11 April 1689 to offer the crown to William and Mary and drafted a Claim of Right, which justified their actions. In contrast to the fudge that was the English Declaration of Rights, the Scottish claim explicitly stated that James had 'forfaulted' his Scottish throne through having 'invaded the fundamental constitution of the Kingdom and altered it from a legal limited monarchy to an arbitrary despotic power'. Unlike the English Declaration, the Scottish claim was also distinctly Presbyterian in character, involving a condemnation of 'prelacy'. In July 1689 the Convention passed an act abolishing prelacy and in 1690 the Presbyterian ministers who had lost their livings in 1662 as a result of the Act of Uniformity were restored to their parishes. The Convention's abolition of episcopacy had the concomitant effect of immediately creating a natural constituency of support for James in Scotland. Support for Jacobitism became strongest in the lowland coastal strip between Fife and Aberdeen, where Episcopalianism was most heavily entrenched. At the same time, the Convention asserted Scottish legislative independence from England by abolishing the Lords of the Articles, through whom English monarchs since James I had managed to control much of the business of the Scottish Parliament. Consequently, although both England and Scotland were now governed by the same Protestant king (and politically the Act of Union was only seventeen years away), the initial effect of the Revolution was to loosen the bonds between the various parts of the British Isles.

Meanwhile in Ireland events were producing a Jacobite revolution as religiously and politically exclusive as that occurring across the Irish Sea in Williamite Scotland and, as with the revolution in Scotland, it was pushing the Irish nation further towards independence from the British state. The central figure in effecting this Jacobite revolution was Richard Talbot, created Earl of Tyrconnel in May 1685. A former comrade in arms of the King, Talbot had a reputation for duplicity, heavy drinking, lying, swearing and verbal, if not physical, violence (though he was fond of issuing challenges and once had the audacity to challenge the then Lord Lieutenant of Ireland, the Earl of Ormonde, to a duel). Tyrconnel's secretary, Thomas Sheridan, described his master as

a tall proper handsome man, but publicly known to be most insolent in prosperity and most abject in adversity, a cunning
dissembling courtier of mean judgement and small understanding,
uncertain and unsteady in his resolutions, turning with every wind
to bring about his ambitious ends and purposes, on which he was
intent that to compass them he would stick at nothing and so false
that a most impudent notorious lie was called at Whitehall and St
James's one of Dick Talbot's ordinary truths.

The Earl of Clarendon was equally damning in his assessment:

I do assure you truth, even in bare matter of fact, will never be
known from my Lord Tyrconnel ... It is impossible you can
believe, unless you found it as we do here, how wonderfully false
he is in almost everything he does. What he desires to be done one
day, or avers he has done, he will positively deny another, though
witnesses can prove him in the wrong: nay, though sometimes his
own hand is shown against him; really his passion and rage (we
know not for what) makes him forget what he says and does; and
when he is convinced that he is in the wrong he is then in such a
fury that the like is not usual.[16]

During the Monmouth and Argyll rebellions, Tyrconnel used
the excuse of the alleged disloyalty of the Ulster Presbyterians to
disarm them and purge some from the army. While attempting to
hobble the Protestants in the north, Tyrconnel also worked against
the newly appointed Lord Lieutenant of Ireland, the Earl of
Clarendon, telling the King that his appointment 'dos soe terreffye
your Catholick subjects hear ... by lodging your authority in a
person from whom they have so little to expect any favour'.[17]

When Clarendon arrived in Ireland, Tyrconnel immediately set
off for England so that he could brief against the new Lieutenant
at court, exhibited articles of impeachment against the Vice-
Treasurer of Ireland and even raised charges of a criminal nature

about Rochester's conduct. In this, Tyrconnel was supported by court Catholics such as Sunderland, seeing it as a good way of further weakening the influence of the Protestant Hydes. For his part, Clarendon was exasperated by the appointment of Tyrconnel to oversee military affairs. He wrote to his brother, 'It is a new method of doing business that all that the King thinks fit to have done should be performed by those in subordinate authority, and he, who is vested in all the power the King can give him, must sit like an ass and know nothing.'[18]

Tyrconnel proceeded to replace 'English' soldiers with 'Irish natives', while Clarendon was instructed to alter the judiciary so as to favour the Catholic 'Old English'. In private he complained that 'it was never yet known, that the sword and the administration of justice were put into the hands of a conquered people'.[19] Clarendon attempted to soothe English fears by issuing proclamations assuring them that their property was safe and that the terms of the Act of Settlement would not be abrogated. However, Tyrconnel was already urging the King in August 1686 that he had been mistaken in confirming the Act of Settlement. It was clear that Clarendon was out of favour with the King when in October of that year he received a list of 'five heads', complaints about his conduct as Lord Lieutenant which Tyrconnel had laid before James. On 8 January 1687 Clarendon learnt that his brother had resigned, that he had been recalled to England and that Tyrconnel was to be appointed Lord Deputy for the government of Ireland.

The task that James had set for Tyrconnel was similar to that assigned to the Drummonds in Scotland. The end goal was an Irish Parliament that would be dominated by Catholics, a goal the King 'was persuaded no English peer could effect'. To this end Tyrconnel called the old charters in and remodelled the corporations as had been done in James's other two kingdoms. Catholics were commissioned as officers in the army and appointed to the government and judiciary. The Catholic Sir Richard Nagel was made Attorney General and in January 1687 Sir Alexander Fitton was made Lord Chancellor (though he had to be released from prison to take up his post as he had been put in gaol for forgery). The Catholic Archbishop of Cashel wrote to the Vatican that Tyrconnel had made 'the army nearly all Catholics, as well commanders and officers as ordinary soldiers. The royal council in Dublin is for the greater part Catholic. The civil officials, both judges and magistrates, are for a greater part Catholic.'[20] The Catholic Church itself in Ireland was given increasing support. Livings in the Church of Ireland were left vacant and the money redistributed to Catholic priests, mass-houses were opened in Dublin castle and the Royal Hospital, while Kilmainham was reconsecrated for Catholic use.

The policies undertaken in Ireland mirrored those pursued in England and Scotland as, again, for James the objective was the emancipation of Catholics and the creation of a pliant representative body, not the immediate conversion of the whole state to Romanism. To an extent the activities of Tyrconnel were little more than a continuation of the policies undertaken in the 1670s, when restrictions on Catholic trade were lifted in some areas and rumours spread among Protestants that papists were being allowed back into county government as sheriffs and JPs.[21] However, Tyrconnel's objectives diverged from those of either Charles II or James II in two important ways: first, he wished to see the Act of Settlement reversed and English overlordship of Ireland overthrown; and secondly, as a consequence of the first aim, he was not interested in the outcome of the Jacobite struggle in James's other two kingdoms. As early as 1686 Tyrconnel appears to have been considering what the Catholics in Ireland should do if James should die without leaving an heir. He told Sheridan that the Irish would be 'fools or madmen if, after his death, they should submit to be governed by the Prince of Orange or Hyde's daughter or be longer slaves to England'. They should 'rather set up a King of their own, and put themselves under the protection of France'.[22]

Here Tyrconnel probably had in mind James's eldest illegitimate son, the Duke of Berwick.

This vision of an independent Ireland, ruled by a Catholic Stuart king, clashed with the vision of both James and his Catholic advisers in England. Sunderland, though happy to use Tyrconnel as a means to undermine the Hydes at court, had no wish to unsettle Protestant settlers in Ireland, and urged the King to issue a proclamation confirming the titles to land of those then in possession (a request which Tyrconnel managed to have rejected). For James's English Catholic advisers, a policy of reversing the Act of Settlement was correctly seen as being absolutely disastrous for their project of gaining Protestant assent to the repeal of the test acts and penal laws in England. Similarly, James, fundamentally an Anglocentric monarch who happened also to be King of Ireland and Scotland, did not see the Protestant Irish as interlopers, colonisers, thieves and oppressors but as his wealthiest subjects within Ireland, who could not be dispossessed without greatly damaging royal revenue. As James advised his son James Francis in 1692, 'for the good of trade and improvement of that kingdom, the English interest must be supported', although he warned him that 'there must be great care taken not to trust them too far, they being generally ill-principled and republicans'.[23]

The birth of a legitimate son to James in 1688 removed the need for Tyrconnel to look for an alternative candidate to take the Irish throne should the King die, but in most other respects the Earl's plans of 1686 were put into effect at the Revolution. In February 1689 Tyrconnel sent an embassy to France led by William Stewart, Lord Mountjoy, a Protestant supporter of James, and chief baron Rice, a Roman Catholic. Mountjoy told James that Ireland was untenable, but Rice denounced his fellow envoy as a traitor and instead conveyed Tyrconnel's warm imprecations to James to come to Ireland, begging him to consider 'whether you can with honour continue where you are, when you possess a kingdom of your own plentifull of all things for human life'.[24] (There was irony in this appeal to personal honour, with its echoes of similar pressure exerted upon an earlier royal exile to the continent, the Duke of Monmouth.) Mountjoy was imprisoned in the Bastille. The pleading of the Lord Deputy alone might not have been enough to convince James to leave his exiled court at St Germain en Laye, absorbed as he now was in the practice of private Catholic devotion. The King was convinced that the Revolution represented a temporal punishment from God for his own failings and sinfulness, and that his own sincere penance was necessary to assuage the wrath of the Lord.

James may well have preferred to remain at St Germain in quiet contemplation but Louis XIV saw an opportunity to use a Jacobite revolution in Ireland to open up a second front in the Continental war that he was fighting against William. However, the French king had little interest in James's using Ireland as a launching pad to reconquer England and Scotland. Firstly, he did not have resources to support such an operation, and secondly, his primary aim to was to divert William from his Continental theatre of operations to deal with problems nearer to home, rather than to recover James's possessions for him. This was reflected in the limited initial help that James was given by the French. No troops were sent though James was accompanied by French officers, but these clearly remained under French command and were instructed to return to France if they judged that Ireland favoured William of Orange, and that the expedition was untenable. Otherwise, they could give assurance to Tyrconnel and James that French troops would follow the next winter. This emphasis on the preservation of French resources, which was present right through the revolutionary wars in Ireland, severely limited the strategic value of French assistance to James during the conflict.

James left St Germain on 15 February and sailed from Brest the following day. He landed at Kinsale on 12 March 1689 and Tyrconnel joined him at Cork on the 14th. The King greeted Tyrconnel warmly, breaking with usual protocol by embracing him with open arms, appointing him to a dukedom and allowing him to sit to his right at table with the Duke of Berwick sitting to the monarch's left. There was widespread jubilation in Ireland at James's arrival, the first English king to set foot in Ireland since Richard II, though this was to prove short-lived. It was reported that the Irish celebrated the King's arrival at Kinsale in 'rude and barbarous manner, by bagpipes, dancing, throwing their mantles under his horse's feet, making a garland of a cabbage stump'.[25] However, the success of the Jacobite mission in Ireland was compromised from the beginning by the divided objectives of its leaders. Tyrconnel's aim was to secure Ireland under Catholic government with James as king. This was a more realistic policy but one which would seriously hamper the task of regaining England and Scotland because of the likely effect this would have in hardening Protestant resistance in the other kingdoms and weakening any support for a policy of toleration. James, however, anticipated that his Irish sojourn would be a mere staging post on a triumphal military progress that would take him next to Scotland, where, he was encouraged to believe by Melfort, an army of twenty-five thousand was ready to join him, and from there to England and a final confrontation with his treacherous son-in-law William. James even entertained pie-in-the-sky notions that the war might become part of an international Catholic crusade, hopes that were doused by the failure of either the Pope or the Holy Roman Emperor (both allies of William) to endorse his plan.

The French ambassador, D'Avaux, took a dim view of James's leadership in Ireland. He reported that James often changed his mind and rarely settled on what the ambassador considered the best course of action. There were also concerns about the strength and effectiveness of the military force that James had in Ireland. Tyrconnel had managed to raise an army of forty-five thousand but these men were untrained and very poorly equipped, with the majority armed only with spikes on sticks. The English Jacobite John Stevens recorded that 'most of them had never fired a musket

in their lives'. As they were 'people used only to follow and con-
verse with cows', it was, he said, hard to make them 'sensible of the
duty of a soldier or be brought to handle their arms aright' and 'to
make many of them understand the common words of command,
much less to obey them'. They would 'follow none but their own
leaders, many of them men as rude, as ignorant, and as far from
understanding any of the rules of discipline as themselves'.[26] James
issued new coinage to provide funds to equip his forces, the so-
called 'gun money', made from melted-down old brass cannons
and to become practically worthless after the battle of the Boyne.

A new Irish Parliament was called on 7 May and, thanks to the
management of Tyrconnel, most of its members were Catholics
and only five or six Protestants. About two-thirds of members were
Old English and the remainder Gaelic Irish. James, however, had
chosen to attempt to break the resistance of the Protestants of
Londonderry, rather than prepare for Parliament's opening. The
Jacobites' victory over Protestant forces at Dromore gave them
control of most of east Ulster, and in the wake of their advance
northwards many Protestants fled towards Derry as a last resort.
The Jacobites were jubilant at their successes so far but, aware that
William was preparing a force to relieve the city to embark from
Liverpool, James himself considered turning back at this news but
was brought back after pleading from the Duke of Berwick, who
reported that the English fleet had not yet appeared. Surely the
sight of the King outside the walls of Derry would be enough to
make the besieged inhabitants surrender? Certainly the signs were
good for the Jacobite forces. Their cavalry had routed a force of
Protestant foot soldiers led out by Robert Lundy, the military governor of the city and a veteran of siege warfare in Tangier, who had
attempted a pre-emptive strike against their besiegers. Lundy was
deeply pessimistic about the chances of defending the city, with its
thin defensive walls, against a properly equipped siege train, and
had advised the commanders of the reinforcements from England
that it was not worth disembarking their regiments. Indeed, when

James approached the city walls with the French commander, Conrad de Rosen, on 18 April, peace terms had already been concluded between the Jacobite force led by Richard Hamilton and the city's inhabitants. Consequently James's appearance outside Derry seemed to be a breach of these negotiations. Troops stationed in the church bastion let out a volley of musket and cannon fire 'proclaiming defence and hostilities, with the triumphant shout of "No Surrender"'. One of James's aides-de-camp, a Captain Troy, was cut down by the hail of shot and killed at the King's side. Not only was Derry no longer ready to capitulate but its inhabitants would resist the Jacobite besiegers for a further 105 days until relieved by Williamite forces.

James retreated to Dublin in the rain. His speech at the opening of the Irish Parliament promised relief for those who had suffered as a result of the Act of Settlement but stopped short of promising outright repeal. The Parliament passed acts which acknowledged James as rightful sovereign and condemned the Revolution in England as an usurpation. However, further acts struck out for the Irish Parliament's independence. One declared that the English Parliament could not legislate for Ireland. James registered his disapproval of an attempt to have Poyning's Law (by which all laws considered by the Irish Parliament had first to be approved by the English Privy Council) repealed. The Parliament was prepared to offer the King a generous financial settlement of £20,000 a month for thirteen months, on condition that the Act of Settlement should be repealed. On 22 June the Parliament voted to repeal the Act, going far beyond what James had been prepared to promise Tyrconnel in 1687, and provoking another fit of nosebleeds from the King. James's obvious displeasure did not slow down the Parliament in voting an act of attainder against twenty thousand Protestants: those who had declared for William of Orange, those who had left Ireland since the arrival of William in England and those who had crossed the Irish sea before the Dutch invasion. This summary death sentence placed on the heads of so many Protestants undercut the King's offer liberty of conscience in the Irish Toleration Act passed at the same time.

Far from getting the pliant Parliament that he had wished, James had summoned a body that was determined to put Irish Catholic interests first and those of their British monarch second. The resolutions of the 'Patriot Parliament', as it came to be known, and the plight of Ulster Protestants, heightened the already intense fear of popery in Scotland and England. After the defiance of the inhabitants of Derry and the recklessness of his Irish Parliament, further bad news was to come which effectively crushed James's hopes of a Jacobite counter-revolution in Scotland. Claverhouse had raised the standard for James in his northern kingdom and, together with Scottish loyalists and an Irish Gaelic contingent from the Isle of Rathlin, had laid siege to the fortress at Blair Atholl. On 27 July Claverhouse defeated the Williamite force sent to raise the siege, under the command of Hugh Mackay, at the battle of Killiecrankie. However, Killiecrankie was a Pyrrhic victory. Claverhouse used traditional Highland fighting techniques, such as the Highland charge, and the steep terrain, to decimate his Williamite opponents, inflicting over two thousand casualties on them. Mackay gave a good description of what the Highland charge entailed: 'They come on slowly till they be within distance of firing, which because they keep no rank or file, doth ordinarily little harm. When their fire is over, they throw away their firelocks, and everyone drawing a long broadsword, with his terge [target, a light shield] (such as have them) on his left hand, they fall a running toward the enemy.'[27] Mackay recorded in his journal that the Highlanders were of 'such quick motion' that they were upon and in among the Williamite musketeers before they had a chance to use their second line of defence, the cumbersome plug bayonets that could be fixed only after firing. Lochiel reported that as the Highlanders engaged in hand to hand combat with the Williamite soldiers, a deathly hush seemed to come across the battlefield: 'nothing was heard . . . but the sullen and hollow clashes of broadswords, with the dismal groans and cries of dying and wounded men'. Killiecrankie was the last battle in which the famous two-handed Scottish broadsword, the claymore, was used. It left its heavy marks upon the Williamite dead, with many 'officers and soldiers . . . cut down through the skull and neck, to the very breasts; others had skulls cut off above the ears. Some had both their bodies and cross belts cut through at one blow; pikes and small swords were cut like willows.'[28]

Yet this bloody victory had cost the Jacobites over a third of their forces, including their leader, Claverhouse, in the battle. The Highland charge had won them the fight but was highly costly in human terms. Most of the Highland troops were shot at a range of just fifty to one hundred yards, though, as Lochiel reported, the Highlanders, 'with a wonderful resolution, kept up their own, as they were commanded'. Moreover, its usefulness as a tactic diminished with every passing year, as the rifles of the government forces got lighter, more accurate and more reliable, and the plug bayonet was replaced by the socket bayonet, which could be attached before firing.[29]

Worse was to come the following month, when the Scottish Jacobites were routed at the battle of Dunkeld on 21 August 1689. The town of Dunkeld protected the Perthshire lowlands from Jacobite depredations and was defended by Cameronian Presbyterians. Cannon, taking over command of the Jacobite forces from Claverhouse, commanded from the rear, arousing clan fury at his lack of courage (though this was the position most professional military commanders adopted in order to better coordinate their forces). However, Cannon did little to effectively marshal the Jacobite artillery and, forced into house-to-house fighting, the Jacobite troops, accustomed to shock frontal assaults, fared badly. As the Glencoe poet recorded: 'They were not accustomed to stand against a wall for protection, as was done at Dunkeld. The stalwart young men fell . . . felled by bullets fired by cowherds.'[30] The Presbyterian defenders trapped Jacobite snipers in houses and set them aflame. By eleven in the morning the Jacobites were running out of ammunition and the soldiers retreated complaining that they could not fight against 'mad and desperate men' or 'devils'.

The prospects for James in Scotland looked dire, though for a time he was still being fed misinformation concerning his followers' successes and failures. In Ireland, too, the tide appeared to be turning against him. The actions of the Catholic Parliament had strengthened resolve in the Protestant strongholds of Londonderry and Enniskillen. For his part, James was not prepared to see this as an all-out war between Protestants and Catholics, continuing to regard Ulster Protestants as his subjects, and he was horrified when the French commander Rosen issued a draconian edict to the men of Londonderry to capitulate or no quarter would be given when starvation forced them to submit.[31] This attitude did not soften the outlook of the citizens who wrote to James that they questioned not 'but your lands will be forfeited rather than ours, and confiscated into our possession, as recompense for this signal service to the crown of England and for the inexpressible toil and labour, expence of blood and treasure, pursuant to their sacred Majesties declaration to that purpose; a true copy whereof we herewith send you to convince you how little we fear your menaces'.[32] By June, however, the defenders were in a dire state. The inhabitants were reduced to living on a diet of dogs, cats, mice, tallow, salted hides, horse blood and seaweed. (The one benefit of the beef-tallow diet was that it appeared to lead to constipation, a welcome relief from dysentery.) Even cannibalism was considered: 'A certain fat Gentleman conceived himself in the greatest danger, and fancying several of the Garrison lookt on him with a greedy Eye, thought fit to hide himself for three days.'[33] However, after much delay, on 28 July Colonel Percy Kirke's relief force from England broke through the boom placed by the Jacobites across the River Foyle. The Jacobite forces, themselves ravaged by hunger and disease, left over the next few days.

Worse news came soon after of the landing of a large Williamite army at Bangor in Ulster on 13 August, led by the veteran French commander the Duke of Schomberg. However, Schomberg's forces were heavily depleted during their first six months in Ireland by disease: by February 1690 5674 out of 18,728 troops had died. News-sheets of the time reported that some of the soldiers were delirious with fever, a Colonel Hewett was reported to have shot himself in the head, a Captain Garet stabbed himself in the throat and a French Huguenot officer in Lisnegarvy (Lisburn) threw himself out of a third-storey window. The Reverend George Story, a chaplain to the army, recorded that the lack of adequate shoes had caused the toes or feet of some of the men to drop off from gangrene on the march towards Belfast. Schomberg himself was afflicted with the 'flux', or dysentery. The army also appeared to have been inadequately provisioned, and once they moved away from the fertile land around Bangor towards Dundalk, where they made camp, they found a land that had been deliberately laid waste by the enemy.

James, then, still had a chance of defending Ireland. His army of thirty-five thousand had been reinforced in the spring of 1689 by five to six thousand French troops, plus supplies of arms for the Irish troops. (Tyrconnel complained, however, that the weapons that the French had given them were too old and too few. He estimated that his army was short of twenty thousand firearms and that two-thirds of his soldiers never fired a shot because of lack of powder.) Given these conditions, John Stevens was forced to revise his opinions of the Irish troops. It was, he said, 'really wonderful, and will perhaps to after ages seem incredible, that an army should be kept together above a year without any pay . . . And what is yet more to be admired, the men never mutinied nor were they guilty of any disorders more than what do often happen in those armies that are best paid.' What was more remarkable was that these men had had

neither beds nor so much as straw to lie on, or any thing to cover them during the whole winter, and even their clothes were worn to rags, insomuch that many could scarce hide their nakedness in the daytime, and abundance of them were barefoot or at least so near it that their wretched shoes and stockings could scarce be made to hang on their feet and legs, I have been astonished to think how they lived and much more that they should voluntarily choose to live so, when if they would have forsaken the service they might have been received by the enemy into good pay and want for nothing, But to add to their suffering the allowance of meat and corn was so small that men rather starved than lived upon it.[34]

William recognised that Schomberg's position and his advanced age (he was in his eighties) were threatening the success of the Williamite war effort and arrived to take control in person at Carrickfergus in June. The pressure was increased by the fact that William knew that a speedy conclusion to the civil wars in his kingdoms was necessary to convince his European allies to support him wholeheartedly in his offensive campaigns against Louis XIV on the Continent. Determined not to repeat the logistical errors of Schomberg's expedition, William came with both a field bakery and a field hospital, artillery and fifteen tons of small coin. His force amounted to over sixteen thousand foot soldiers and nearly ten thousand cavalry, which, combined with Schomberg's remaining troops and reinforcements from the Protestant Irish, gave him a field army of around thirty-five thousand. James's French advisers were counselling him not to attempt to tackle this force head on but to retreat to the Jacobite strongholds in the west of Ireland, around the River Shannon, but James, as he had at Derry, ignored this advice and advanced to meet William at the River Boyne.

The battle of the Boyne was fought on 1 July 1690. Historians remain divided over whether the site James chose to engage William was defensible. What does appear clear is that James mistook a move to cross the Boyne from the west by the Williamite cavalry, led by Schomberg's son Meinhard, as the main assault, and directed the majority of his forces to the left of the battlefield to meet them, leaving a depleted remnant open to a frontal attack on Oldbridge village by the main Williamite force. The Irish, in particular the cavalry, fought bravely for some three hours before the greater strength in numbers of the enemy, plus the morale boost of William's personal presence at the forefront of the attack, began to tell. One French observer, Intendant D'Esgrigny, stated, 'This is the sixth battle that I have seen, but I have never seen such a rout.'[35] For their part, the French, under the command of the courtier Lauzun, followed to the letter their orders not to engage the enemy forces unless there was a reasonable chance of success. The French were in no doubt either that William's troops were far better equipped and disciplined than the Irish they faced. Major General Boisseleau stated that in 'all the movements which I saw the enemy make, they conducted themselves in a soldierly fashion, and their troops went bravely into the firing line. These savages here, who are unaccustomed to war, were taken completely by surprise, and terror soon took hold of them. The officers did no good and showed bad example. Such terror and such a rout were never heard of.'[36] Indeed, without the presence of the disciplined French troops, protecting the Jacobite rear as they retreated, the carnage may have been even worse. As it was, the Jacobites who did not escape were shot, according to one observer, 'like hares amongst the corn',[37] while William's forces suffered only five hundred casualties (though these included Schomberg himself; William was grazed by a Jacobite cannon ball and had to ride among his troops to assure them that he was alive and well).

The Boyne is often seen as the decisive battle in the revolutionary wars in Ireland. Certainly it signalled the end of James's personal involvement in the Jacobite cause, as he fled back to France, never again to set foot in his former kingdoms. James, in contrast to William, took a conspicuously rearguard approach to command at the Boyne. There is a story that on his return to Dublin he met Lady Tyrconnel, and complained to her that his

Irish troops had run away, to which the lady was said to have replied, 'I see you have preceded them yourself, your majesty.'[38] In fairness, the relative caution William had shown in not throwing more of his forces into an encircling movement (as Schomberg had recommended) prevented the Boyne from leading to the complete destruction of the Jacobite army. Consequently the war in Ireland continued for over a year. The Williamites' first attempt to storm the stronghold of Limerick had to be abandoned at the end of August when a frontal assault led to the death and injury of over two thousand troops. Only with Marlborough's campaign to capture Cork and Kinsale in the autumn of 1690, as part of a plan to open up a second front in Ireland, did William's forces enjoy further successes. (Cork was taken on 29 September and Kinsale on 12 October.) The Jacobite resistance was effectively brought to an end in 1691 with defeat at the battle of Aughrim on 12 July, the surrender of Galway in the same month and the final capitulation of Limerick after a second siege on 3 October. As described by one Danish observer, the aftermath of Aughrim was even bloodier than the Boyne:

> The Irish fled all over the fields . . . not knowing what to do or where to turn, since from all sides the inescapable violence meets them . . . throwing away their arms and finding no place to make a stand within a distance of seven miles. The women, children, waggoners, like madmen, filled every road with lamentation and weeping. Worse was the sight after the battle when many men and horses pierced by wounds could have neither flight nor rest. Sometimes trying to rise they fell suddenly, weighed down by the mass of their bodies, others with mutilated limbs and weighed down by pain asked for the sword as a remedy, but the conqueror would not even fulfil with sword or musket the desire of him who implored him; others spewed forth their breath mixed with blood and threats, grasping their bloodstained arms in an icy embrace, as if in readiness for some future battle and that I may say it in brief,

from the bodies of all, blood . . . flowed over the ground, and so inundated the fields that you could hardly take a step without slipping . . . O horrible sight![39]

In Scotland, too, the Jacobite cause was faltering. By September 1690 the lack of further French help had caused James to urge his Scottish supporters to look out for themselves:

> that if they cannot any longer . . . stand out but are forced by the pursute . . . of the rebels to some kind of Outward submission or Complyance, we shall not think the worse of ym for keeping quiet, but shall [be] compassionate and not condemne yr suffering condition, being perfectly assured of their hearts at all tymes, and of their hands too, whenever the Condition of Our affairs shall require ym to appear for us. And as to those of our officers who cannot bend . . . to any kind of compliance & perhaps would not be received . . . tho they should, we desire all such to make use of . . . the ship . . . to retire to . . . Ireland.[40]

In October 1690 the Earl of Seaforth, who had taken over command of the Jacobite forces from Claverhouse, surrendered to William's forces. By this point the ability of the Jacobites to fight a major pitched battle against the Williamite forces had diminished, but skirmishes continued in the Highlands, and in a bid to improve security Mackay established a new fort at Inverlochy, which henceforth would be known as Fort William. Finally generous peace terms were concluded with the clans at the Treaty of Achallader in June 1691. In return for a sum of £12,000 as recompense for their war expenses, along with a full indemnity from actions undertaken in war and the continued right to wear arms, the clans would agree to take the oath of allegiance to William and end their war against him. Again external pressures had led William to sue for peace. He was now preparing for campaigns in Flanders and in Savoy and needed the full cooperation of his allies for these to be effective. The opposition in Parliament was placing serious obstacles in William's way as regards supply for the war and there was real danger in any case of financial collapse if England alone were made to bear the burden of the costs of the Continental campaign.

However, William's Secretary of State in Scotland, Sir John Dalrymple, saw in the peace terms an opportunity to eliminate some of the Highland clans. Writing to Breadalbane, he stated that the King should 'rather to have made the Hylanders examples of his justice by extirpating them (. . . as much as some men's designe, as it's now practicable, tho' perhaps it was not so likely when you entered in this negotiation) . . . he can gratify many by destroying them with as little charge. And certainly, if there do remain any obstinancy, . . . by their ruin, he will be rid himself of a suspicious crew.'[41] Dalrymple was aided in his plan by the continued refusal of some clans to accept the generous peace terms on offer, choosing instead to wait and see if events, such as further help from France, would turn in their favour. In a further letter to Breadalbane, he noted that all

> the papist chieftains stand forfaulted by act of Parliament, and it ought to be made effectuall. My Lord, you have done very generously, being a Campbell to have procured so much for McDonalds, who are the inveterate enemies of your clan; and both Glengary and Keppoch are papists, and that's the only papist clan in the Hylands. Who knows but by God's providence they are permitted to fall into this delusion, that they only may be extirpate, which will vindicate their Majesties justice, and reduce the Hylands without further severities to the rest?[42]

The opportunity Dalrymple had hoped for in exterminating the Catholic Highland clans was presented by that late subscription to the oath of allegiance by MacIain of Glencoe. MacIain entered Fort William on 31 December to take the oath, and signed a certificate confirming his submission which was sent on to Colin Campbell at Edinburgh. Meanwhile Argyll's regiment marched to Glencoe, where 'they were ceivilie and kyndlie intertain'd'. The clerks of the Scottish Privy Council refused to accept MacIain's certificate as it was taken after the deadline had passed and Campbell was informed that he should not present the list in its present state before the council, so he erased the record of MacIain's oath. On 7 January Dalrymple ordered the destruction of Lochaber, Appin and Glencoe, adding, 'I hope the souldiers will not trouble the Government with prisoners.' Three days later he drew up further orders for the commander Livingston to attack the rebel areas 'by fire and sword', burning their houses, destroying their goods and killing all the men. Final instructions sent by Dalrymple on 16 January, stated, 'If M'Kean of Glencoe, and that tribe, can be well separated from the rest, it will be a proper vindication of the publick justice to extirpate that sept [tribe] of thieves.'[43] The document was laid before William, who superscribed and subscribed it. However, the King was at this time preoccupied by his split with Marlborough, who was leading a strike of English officers and intriguing with Jacobites, and was unlikely to have given much thought to what he had signed.

The high mountain walls that surrounded the glen made escape difficult once the passes were guarded, so that it was, in the words of one historian, an 'excellent scene for slaughter'.[44] One government detachment, under the command of Glenlyon, pretended that they had come to be quartered in Glencoe, a pretext which Iain MacIain accepted and welcomed them. He nonetheless took the precaution of hiding the clans' weapons in case the soldiers had orders to disarm them, a decision which would have disastrous consequences. Hamilton ordered Duncanson to attack Glencoe at 5 a.m. repeating that neither 'the old fox [MacIain], nor none of his cubs' must be allowed to escape, and added that he should take no prisoners and spare nobody under seventy.[45]

MacIain was shot at point-blank range in his back by soldiers and two of his servants were also murdered. At Inverrigan Glenlyon had nine men who had been bound brought out and shot one by one, then personally finished them off with his bayonet. However, he later attempted to stop his soldiers committing further atrocities, but to no avail. Drummond had a boy shot joking that a nit if allowed to grow would turn into a louse. Some women who managed to escape the slaughter, including MacIain's widow, died later from exposure: a storm was raging while the massacre was taking place. Of the forty-five people killed in the massacre, it was reported that all but thirteen were women. Neither the sick nor the very young were spared. Campbell of Aird's company discovered at Achnacone a man dying of fever and his five-year-old son, and killed them both. To cover their activities they hurled the boy's body into the river, but his corpse was so badly mutilated that his arm came off.

Glencoe has with good reason lived on in infamy. However, most historians are agreed that William played little or no active part in the decisions which led up to the massacre. Rather, that the massacre was allowed to happen reflected the English administration's lack of interest in, and control over, Scottish affairs at this time. Nonetheless, it is true that the King obstructed investigations into Glencoe and, when a public inquiry was finally launched into the atrocity in 1695, William chose to indemnify and reward its main architect, Dalrymple, rather than expose him to prosecution. The King displayed a similar indifference to the feelings of his non-English subjects by his failure to see that the terms of the Treaty of Limerick were upheld. According to the treaty, Catholics were to enjoy the same freedoms of worship they had received in the reign of Charles II (an admittedly vague definition of religious liberty) and were also given guarantees concerning their property rights. However, the Williamite Irish Parliament, as Protestant in its character as James's Parliament had been Catholic, never fully ratified the treaty. Instead, it set about establishing a Protestant (and mainly Anglican) monopoly over land ownership and political power. Harsh penal laws were passed which prevented Catholics from owning arms, or even horses over a certain value, and which banished the Catholic clergy from Ireland.

The outcomes of the revolutions in Scotland and Ireland revealed the extent to which these kingdoms were only a minor concern to William. They mainly impinged on his consciousness as areas of civil unrest that could distract him militarily and financially from his grander project of defeating Louis XIV. Because of this European focus, William's main concern was with the management of his English kingdom, the richest and most populous part of his new British territories. Similarly, James was guilty of essentially seeing Ireland and Scotland as staging posts on the road to the recovery of what he saw as the main prize, the English crown. However, it may be said in his defence that at least James had attempted to pursue policies of toleration in both Scotland and Ireland. The conflicts in Ireland and Scotland, though not as serious in terms of loss of life as those that both kingdoms had endured during the 1640s, were bloody enough, and each contained incidents of brutality and cruelty that lingered long in the public memory. In the case of Ireland, the battle of the Boyne and the siege of Londonderry remain an integral part of Ulster Protestant identity. The immediate outcome of the revolutions in the two countries was a greater degree of political independence, but within each of these kingdoms this greater freedom from English interference was exploited as a means to marginalise and persecute certain ethnic and religious groups. In neither Ireland nor Scotland could the outcome of the Revolution be said to be 'glorious'.

8

WILLIAM AND MARY

King William thinks all, Queen Mary talks all, Prince George
drinks all, and Princess Ann eats all.

ABRAHAM DE LA PRYNE ON THE COURT OF WILLIAM III[1]

Most, if not all the nations in Europe in a flame; wars, rumours of
wars, great preparations everywhere for blood and slaughter, many
countries dreadfully involved already in war, the Lord of Hosts
mustering up His armies this day, shaking of kingdoms and monarchs.[2]

In 1689 the English were presented with a unique phenomenon
in their history, that of dual monarchy. Though executive power
was officially lodged with the King, the fact that William and
Mary ruled as joint monarchs was vitally important to legitimating the Revolution. Mary's hereditary claim to the throne helped
ease the consciences of Tories in giving their allegiance to the new
monarchs. As we will see, the Queen's warmth, beauty and piety

also helped to counter her husband's colder, more distant character. Moreover, though Mary practically always deferred to William's authority, his continued personal involvement in military campaigning in Ireland and Flanders meant that she had nonetheless, under the terms of the Regency Act, to take up the reins of government for long periods of time. However, the broad political coalition that had brought William and Mary to the throne had fragmented in the wake of the Revolution and the dual monarchs now governed a country that was both politically and religiously divided. These divisions were in part created, and certainly exacerbated, by William's continued pursuit of his central objective, the military defeat of Louis XIV's France. In the early years of his reign, though the threat of invasion was effectively ended by the naval victory over the French at La Hogue, William's land campaigns in Flanders did not go well. The massive cost of these wars raised taxation to levels that it had not reached since the civil wars, yet taxes alone could not pay for the King's wars and public borrowing also escalated to new heights. To manage growing government debt, a new national bank was founded in 1694 to underwrite long-term loans to the crown. Yet, though Britain was now managing to fund land wars of an unprecedented scale, the political and social consequences of these was leading some to fear for the moral well-being of the nation. For these reformers the Revolution's gift of religious toleration was in danger of being squandered. In their eyes, instead of fostering Protestant unity it was leading to the growth of irreligion, immorality and atheism. The weakening of the authority of church courts, had, it was felt, permitted the growth of vice, lewd behaviour and idleness. While the Bank of England had saved the crown from bankruptcy, it had also encouraged avarice, greed and self-interest. Without actions to suppress this behaviour, such as the creation of Societies for the Reformation of Manners, the nation stood in grave danger of divine punishments, punishments that could already be detected in the military losses that William suffered.

At the beginning of his reign, however, William's situation appeared more favourable. England's new king had a number of qualities which ought to have made him an appealing character and fostered public loyalty towards him. William more than fulfilled the martial capabilities expected of a king, for he was a warrior prince of European standing whose grit and determination had played a large part in resisting French aggression in the Dutch Republic's crisis year of 1672. Nor was he an armchair general, for he displayed considerable personal courage, at times leading his men from the front, as at the battle of the Boyne. Aside from these military talents, the new King was politically astute, and although he was keen to defend his monarchical authority, using the royal veto to override Parliament on a number of occasions, overall his reign was characterised by cooperation with the two Houses. At least in the early years of his reign, William also attempted to include within his administration a broad spectrum of political opinion in England (a policy, however, which, as we will see, eventually proved divisive). Perhaps most important of all, William was a committed Protestant, albeit of the Dutch Calvinist variety. Although he shared with James II a principled belief in the efficacy of religious toleration, and employed both Jews and Catholics in his service, William was a practising member of the Dutch reformed church who attended daily prayers and followed rigorous regimes of moral self-examination. There could be little doubt that the Protestant faith in England was more secure with William upon the throne, though his lack of personal commitment to the Anglican form of it would cause problems.

Nevertheless, the positive military, political and religious aspects of William's character were undercut by a number of other factors which diminished his appeal to the English public. First, despite his bravery and military prowess, William did not cut a very regal figure. In 1695 George Dent, a Southwark glover, was accused of saying that 'King William is not Lawfull King, and that he is a Nasty Little Fellow'.[3] William was indeed short, almost four inches shorter than his wife Mary, who stood a statuesque five foot eleven tall. His best feature, his long auburn hair, which in his youth had allowed him to dispense with fashionable periwigs, could not compensate for William's other less appealing characteristics. He had a large, hooked nose, the sole benefit of which was that it at least made him easy to recognise in profile on coins and medallions. His teeth were blackened, his back hunched and his legs spindly. These features provided ample scope for those with axes to grind to deride the King. William's sister-in-law, Princess Anne (following his public snubbing of her favourites, the Churchills, as a result of Marlborough's suspected Jacobitism), nicknamed the King 'Caliban' and, worse, 'the Dutch abortion'.[4] William was also in poor health. A bout of smallpox in 1675 and his continual campaigning took its toll upon his lungs and he suffered from asthmatic attacks which made it impossible for him to reside at Whitehall, so that he chose instead to live in apartments at Hampton Court.

William's physical weakness, and the retreat from public life it sometimes necessitated, compounded a reserved and taciturn personality that distanced him from his subjects. Even those relatively close to him complained about William's frosty demeanour. Gilbert Burnet remarked that the King had 'a coldness in his way, that damps a modest man extreamly for he hears things with a dry silence that shows too much of distrust of those to whom he speaks'.[5] He chided his master for his lack of effort in winning the affections of the nation and these personality traits were hardly helped by the fact that the King was frequently out of the kingdom on his military campaigns, as he pursued the defeat of Louis XIV. Equally, reform of the royal court instigated by both William and Mary, which created a more sober, less magnificent regal style, while, as we will see, being welcomed by some moral campaigners as a necessary change from the debauched institution presided over by Charles and James, also created a less public, less accessible monarchy.

The King's preference for a more private existence fed into other concerns. His possession of an English wife never completely obscured the fact that he was a foreigner with only a weak hereditary claim to the throne. English mistrust of William as an outsider was increased by the King's reliance on a small band of mainly Dutch advisers, in particular William Bentinck, whom he created Earl of Portland, and Arnald van Keppel, who became Earl of Albemarle. Not only did these Dutchmen monopolise the King's attention, they also took the lion's share of royal patronage, something that English courtiers viewed with great jealousy. There was evidence of hatred of the Dutch at a popular level too. William Pennington, a London labourer, was accused in 1689 of calling William a 'Dutch Dogg' and Mary his 'Dutch Bitch'.[6] Jacobite writers alleged that the favour that William held Bentinck and Keppel in was more than platonic, and the former Williamite turned Jacobite plotter Robert Ferguson claimed that Englishmen were filled with 'contempt and hatred of themselves, for enduring a Catamite to rule over them'.[7] There is no conclusive evidence to support such claims. It was true that both Bentinck's and Keppel's rooms interconnected with the King's apartments and that William was known to stay up late into the night with them, although this was not an unusual arrangement for royal servants. Bentinck did warn William, in a letter, about the rumours his closeness to Keppel was generating, but this can be seen as a product of jealousy at the younger courtier's increasing influence upon his royal master. Perhaps the greatest argument against these allegations, however, was the very clear affection that William held for Mary.[8]

The strong attachment that developed between the royal couple had not been evident at the beginning of their marriage in 1677. Then, their union had clearly been, as most royal matches were, a piece of statecraft. William hoped that by marrying Mary, then aged only fifteen, his junior by twelve years, he would gain greater influence over English politics and thereby bring Britain into an alliance against France. Conversely, his English uncle, Charles II, hoped that the match would give him greater leverage over the Dutch Stadtholder. The political nature of the marriage was rein-forced by the fact that it was the King, not her father, the Duke of York, who gave Mary away. For the time being the political aspi-rations of both parties were frustrated. During the Exclusion Crisis William developed links with the Whig opponents of James and Charles, while, in response, both Charles and James took to remodelling their Parliaments into a more loyal mode. Initially the marriage seemed no more successful on a personal level. Mary wept 'all that afternoon and the following day' when she was informed that her uncle and father had agreed that she should marry the Prince on 21 October 1677. For his part, William appeared to take little interest in his wife: at a ball given in honour of her birthday on 15 November it was noted that William danced only once with the princess and appeared sullen. When the royal party left Margate on 19 November, Mary was again in tears, com-plaining to the Queen, who attempted to sympathise with her plight, 'but madam you came into England; but I am going out of England'.[9] Marital relations were not helped by Mary's miscar-riages, first in the spring of 1678 and then again a year later (she would not conceive again) and by William's adultery with one of her ladies-in-waiting, Elizabeth Villiers.

Gradually, though, the royal couple developed affection for each another. The change was most evident in Mary and may in part have been a result of her fairly lonely and isolated life in the Netherlands, where she had spent most of her time in religious devotions and playing cards and doing needlework with her female companions. The Prince, too, at least began to show greater respect for his wife's feelings, becoming more discreet about his infidelities after Mary had confronted him concerning his rela-tionship with Villiers in 1685. Especially for William, however, the couple were really brought together by Mary's response to the crisis of 1688. The Princess's decision to choose loyalty to her husband above her duty of obedience to her father convinced William of her absolute devotion to him, a conviction only made stronger by Mary's almost complete deference to him on becoming Queen.

Mary's Anglican faith was integral to making this crucial decision to honour William rather than her father. As her father's policies for the repeal of the Test and Corporation Acts became clear, Mary, despite her personal inclination to retire from public life, became more politically involved. She had already asked James to intercede with Louis XIV on behalf of the French Huguenots, a request which she later claimed her father refused. Mary then complained to the King about the arraignment before the Ecclesiastical Commission of Henry Compton, the bishop who had confirmed her in the Anglican faith and married her to William, but James responded only by chastising her for interfering in matters of state. She rebuffed her father's attempts to convert her, telling him that the more she heard of his religion 'the more pleased I am with my own'.[10] God had chosen her, she believed, to be the instrument for preserving the Church but yet she had not been gifted an heir. For Mary, heavily influenced by the testimony of her sister Anne, the only logical explanation was that the Prince of Wales must be supposititious, for a Protestant God could not have gifted a popish King a legitimate son.

This same intense piety also informed Mary's understanding of her duties as wife, beliefs that had serious political implications. Burnet claimed that he raised with Mary the point that in English law, she as regnant Queen, and not William, would hold the reins of government. He asserted that after he had pointed this out, Mary had reassured William that, according to God's law, 'she did not think that the husband was ever to be obedient to the wife: she promised him he should always bear rule; and she asked only, that he would obey the command of "husbands love your wives", as she should do that, "wives be obedient to your husbands in all things"'.[11] The growing bond between the royal couple led to emotional scenes as William left for England alone in the winter of

1688. The Prince told Mary on departing that if he died in battle she should marry again (though not to a papist) – to which Mary replied tearfully that she loved him only and could never love another.

Allied to a natural grace and beauty, these qualities of wifely obedience and deep, but orthodox, piety contributed to the markedly deeper affection that the public held for their English queen than for their Dutch king. Although they ruled in name as joint monarchs, it was clear from the outset of William and Mary's reign that it was the King who wielded the real power. It was William who spoke at the coronation – Mary's sole contribution was 'her looks and a little curtsy' – and the symbols of sovereignty were reserved for William. He was first to be anointed, the first to receive the crown and ring and only he took the sword and spurs.[12] Though, early in their marriage, William was worried about his wife's political ambitions, Mary never seems to have wished for a greater share in government. Hostile observers recorded her apparently indiscreet excitement on entering Whitehall for the first time as queen, hinting that personal ambition, rather than religious principle, drove her to betray her father: 'She ran about it [the palace], looking into every closet and conveniency, and turning up the quilts of beds, just as people do at an inn.'[13] However, the new Queen's private feelings about her coronation were far more mixed. She explained her behaviour at Whitehall as necessary to convince doubters that she was happy with the government of the kingdom being entirely in her husband's hand:

> so that I was fain to force my self to more mirth than became me
> at that time, and was by many interpreted as ill nature, pride, and
> the great delight I had to be queen. But, alas, they did little know
> me, who thought me guilty of that; I had been only for a regency,
> and wisht for nothing else; I had ever dreaded being queen, liking
> my condition much better (and indeed I was not deceived); but

the good of the public was to be preferd and I protest, God knows
my heart, that what I say is true, that I have had more trouble to
bring myself to bear this so envied estate than I should have had to
have been reduced to the lowest condition in the world. My heart
is not made for a kingdom and my inclination leads me to a retired
quiet life, so that I have need of all the resignation and self denial
in the world, to bear with such a condition as I am now in. Indeed
the princes being made king lessened the pain, but not the trouble
of what I am like to endure.[14]

Elsewhere in her memoirs Mary declared her opinion 'that
women should not meddle in government'. However, her husband's consuming obsession with defeating Louis XIV meant that
she was forced to act against her own inclinations. The Regency
Act placed regal power and administration of government into the
Queen's hands when the King was absent from the realm. As a
result of William's absences on campaign in Ireland and Flanders,
Mary ruled as regnant Queen for a total of thirty-two months.[15]
In December 1689 the low ebb that his public popularity had
reached even led William to consider whether he should not
return to Holland and leave government in the hands of his wife.
Although there were some disagreements between the royal couple
as a result of Mary's actions as regent – namely over the appointment of William's candidate, Thomas Tenison, as Archbishop of
Canterbury in 1694, instead of the Queen's favourite, Edward
Stillingfleet, and over Mary's overall preference for Tory ministers
above Whigs – the King's confidence in his wife's ability to act as
regent reflected both her considerable political nous and her willingness to defer to his authority. Although initially hesitant about
speaking in Privy Council discussions, Mary was savvy enough to
spurn the attempts of the council president, Thomas Osborne, the
Earl of Carmarthen, to monopolise her attention by telling the
Whig Edward Russell that she needed to see him to explain business to him. In her letters to her husband Mary reiterated her

unquestioning readiness to do William's will: 'That which makes me in pain is for fear what is done may not please you. I am sure it is my chief desire . . . as much as may be to act according to your mind.'[16]

Her actions as regnant Queen, with their winning combination of submission to male authority (in conformity with patriarchal orthodoxy) and her practical competence (sustaining public faith in the effectiveness of the regime) won widespread approval. Mary's resolution in response to the crisis brought about by military defeat at Beachy Head in 1690 led some news-sheets to argue that she was 'deserving the character of another Elizabeth'. (Such comparisons were not new: Mary had been touted as another Elizabeth in the 1670s when she was being promoted as a potential regent in place of her father, James.) In many ways Mary was an even more appealing character than Elizabeth, to male opinion at least, as her marital status and submissiveness allayed traditional worries about the dangers of feminine rule. Some of her public statements seemed to consciously echo Elizabeth. There were resonances with the Virgin Queen's words at Tilbury, in Mary's morale-boosting message to naval officers before the battle of La Hogue, 'that she reposes an entire confidence in them all, and will never think that any brave English seaman will betray her or his country to the insolent tyranny of the French, and as it is their duty and their glory to defend the government, it shall be her part to reward their service'.[17] After the battle the Queen made good her word by rewarding the seamen with a substantial sum of money, and pledged herself to establish a hospital at Greenwich for those who were disabled. She received the thanks of both houses of Parliament for her government of the kingdom in the King's absence.

Another benefit to William was his wife's Anglicanism, which strengthened her appeal to Tories who might have distrusted their Calvinist king. Mary's attachment to the Church of England and her determination to defend and strengthen it were deep and genuine. Her royal chaplain, William Payne, stated that she was devoted to 'Building up and Repairing the whole Church of England and making it like Mount Sion, the joy of the whole Earth'. However, though she was a committed Anglican, Mary was generous in her relations with dissenters and helped foster cooperation between Protestant denominations. The Presbyterian William Bates stated that she 'was not fetter'd with Superstitious Scruples, but her clear and free Spirit was for the Union of Christians in Things essential to Christianity'.[18] This was reflected in her ecclesiastical appointments, in which William allowed her an almost completely free hand. The episcopate under William and Mary was dominated by latitudinarian bishops who favoured the toleration of nonconformity and were prepared to enter into constructive dialogue with dissenters.

Mary, like her husband, displayed a strong belief in divine providence and feared that the betrayal of her father, though necessary, would occasion God's wrath. When splits developed between William and Anne in 1691–2, Mary viewed these events as the Lord's chastisement. Her commitment to moral reform was highly motivated by a powerful belief in the reality of divine vengeance. She pursued part of this programme through her efforts to reform the court. Burnet recorded:

> She took the Ladys off from that Idleness, which not only wast their time but exposes them to many temptations [hinting at the excesses of Charles II's reign], and engaged them to work; She wrought many hours a day her self, and had her Maids of honour and Ladys working about her: And whereas the female part of the Court had been in the former reignes subject to much just scandal, She has freed her Court so entirely from all suspitions, that there is not so much as colour for discourse.[19]

As will be shown later, Mary was also committed to the moral reform of the nation as whole, viewing this as essential to avoid further divine opprobrium falling upon the country.[20]

This campaign for national reformation was all the more necessary in some eyes because of the disorder and division in both
Church and State. The broad coalition of Whigs and Tories that
had brought William to the throne quickly disintegrated as the
objective shifted from restraining or removing James II to delin-
eating the full form of the Revolution settlement and the national
government that would administer it. At least in the early years of
his government, the King attempted to avoid favouring one party
over another in a bid to defuse partisan tensions. However, the
bitter political struggles of the past decade, extending to armed
rebellion and assassination attempts on the Whig side, and the
brutal suppression of such efforts on the Tory side, through executions, corporal punishment, imprisonment and transportation,
had scarcely left a well of goodwill between the parties and, in fact,
the policy proved ultimately divisive. William's appointment of
ministers who had been loyal to James – such as Sidney, Lord
Godolphin, moderates such as Halifax, and Daniel Finch, Earl of
Nottingham, and Thomas Osborne, Earl of Danby and recently
Marquis of Carmarthen, who, though a staunch Orangist, was
also associated with the policies of Charles II's 'tory reaction' –
raised Whig heckles. Thomas Wharton, Whig Comptroller of the
Household, complained of this in a letter to the King:

> it is visible to all men & the meanest People reason upon it, That
> we must expect the same Councills and the same Government
> from the same Men. If you did not come over to support our
> Religion & repair the breaches that were made in our Laws and
> Constitution, what can you urge but Force to justify what you
> have done, which would destroy the Glory of your Enterprise? We
> have made you King, as the greatest return we could make for so
> great a blessing, taking this to be your Design; and if you intend to
> govern like an Honest Man, what occasion can you have for knaves
> to serve you? Can the same Men who have contrived and wrought
> our Ruin be fitt Instruments for our Salvation?[21]

William's efforts to pour oil on troubled waters were further undermined by demands for vengeance from Whigs for the deaths of Whig 'martyrs' such as Algernon Sidney, the Earl of Essex, and the Monmouth rebels, fired, as we have already seen, by the propaganda of men such as John Tutchin which revived memories of the barbarism of the Bloody Assizes. The veteran Presbyterian MP and former parliamentarian colonel John Birch, stated: 'That which lies heaviest upon the Nation is Blood, I would have some Blood, though little, rather than be stained with what they have shed.'[22] The King attempted to block Whig schemes for revenge through a very generous indemnity bill but this was voted down in Parliament. However, Parliament's committee of grievances, established to look into the misdemeanours of the Tory reaction, did little other than to convince William of the divisiveness of some Whigs and push him further into an alliance with Nottingham. The final straw came for the King as Whig peers opposed the campaign in Ireland, convinced that by removing troops from England it would place the country at risk. In response, William prorogued Parliament on 27 January 1690 and called for a fresh Parliament to meet on 20 March, making it known that he looked for the return of 'moderate men of the Church party' to the new House of Commons.

The election was dominated by strong party feeling, with Whigs using the press to publicise the names of 151 Tories who refused to declare the crown 'vacant', while the Tories had printed the names of 146 commonwealthsmen who had voted in favour of disabling from sitting in the House all those who had supported Charles II's *quo warranto* campaign (an attempt to effect a mass purge of Tories from the House). The final result saw a general swing towards the Tories, particularly in London, where the four Whig incumbents for the capital were replaced wholesale by Tory candidates, giving Nottingham a working majority in the Commons. The increasing Tory influence in government and in the House led the Whig Secretary of State Shrewsbury to resign his offices.

The growing power of Nottingham and the Tories led to concerns about the independence of the Commons, fears which MPs attempted to counter through 'place' bills, to bar crown officers from sitting in the House, and 'triennial' legislation, to force the King to hold fresh elections every three years. However, William resisted this legislation as an infringement of his monarchical authority and used the royal veto to torpedo first a Triennial Bill in 1693 and then a place bill the following year. Disenchantment at the King's actions was particularly evident among radical Whigs such as John Hampden and John Wildman, the former Leveller leader who lost his office as Postmaster in March 1691. It seemed to show that Algernon Sidney had been right to warn of the danger posed by the dynastic ambitions of the House of Orange in his unpublished *Court Maxims*. The climax of Whig fury with William followed his use of the royal veto to kill the Triennial Bill in February 1693. It seemed to one writer that the Revolution had merely effected a 'Change, without an Alteration'. The outspoken Whig peer Henry Booth, formerly Lord Delamere, now Earl of Warrington, an individual who had been one of the first English lords to raise arms for William when Prince of Orange, told the Chester Grand Jury in April 1693 that it appeared that 'his [William's] Design in assisting them was only to get into the Throne, and not ease the Nation's Oppressions. So that in such Cases a Revolution does the People no Good; for he that hath got the Crown, thinks that whatsoever is done for the Good and Security of the People, is so much Loss to him of what he hop'd to get by coming over.'[23] The following year, as William again used his veto to kill a place bill, the Commons sent an address to the King which argued that, after the Revolution, the monarch had no power of veto, and which accused him of listening to 'evil counsellors'. (This was a reference to Sunderland, 'the oily Earl', who had managed to ingratiate himself back into royal favour despite having been excluded from William's Act of Grace in 1690 and exiled in the Netherlands for his role as the main architect of James II's scheme to 'pack' Parliament and repeal the Test and Corporation Acts.)

Disappointment at the King's choice of ministers and distrust of his attitude to Parliament led some Whigs to consider more radical courses. There had, ironically, been a resurgence of domestic Jacobitism in the wake of James's failures in Ireland and after the French naval defeat at La Hogue in 1692. After this point James's proclamations took on a more moderate air as he began to accept that if he were to return to the throne at all it might be upon conditions.[24] James's subsequent appeals were tailored to suit 'compounders' like the Earl of Sunderland, the Earl of Shrewsbury and Admiral Russell, who were prepared to consider James's return provided that their former monarch would be ready to countenance greater limitations on his prerogative than William was at present. Key defectors to William in 1688 were now tempted to play the turncoat again. John Churchill, Duke of Marlborough, was overlooked for commands in the military campaigns of 1691, probably because William, rightly, did not trust him. In January 1692 further humiliation came as Marlborough was stripped of all his court posts and in April of that year sent to the Tower. Churchill was released in September but still ostracised, and the treatment meted out to him drove a wedge between William and Princess Anne, whose close confidante was Churchill's wife, Sarah. In May 1694 Churchill took the momentous step of disclosing to the French the planned English raid on Brest. Here he may have been animated by personal jealousy: Thomas Talmarsh – the only Englishman given a senior command by William – was in charge of the raid, and he was one of the fatal casualties of Marlborough's betrayal. Thwarted ambition played a part in the defection of other former Orangists to the Jacobite cause, such as Sir James Montgomery and Robert Ferguson. On the other hand, the intriguing of Shrewsbury, Russell, the Earl of Monmouth (formerly Lord Mordaunt) and John Wildman was largely born of political disgust at William's apparent betrayal of the Revolution.

With opposition turning to treason in some quarters, William was not helped by the fact that the court was itself divided. The King's continued pursuit of a bipartisan ministry meant that Whig members of the administration, such as Wharton, John Somers and Richard Hampden, were keen to get the Earl of Nottingham ousted from the King's councils. Narrow legislative defeats of place bills and the royal veto of the Triennial Act combined with military defeats in the summer of 1693 (in July William was defeated at Landen in Flanders and the same month a richly laden merchant fleet fell into French hands while en route to the Turkish port of Smyrna) and allegations of maladministration to increase the pressure on Nottingham to resign. On 6 November William asked for the Earl's resignation, though he assured him that he was convinced of the Earl's 'fidelity and zeal to his service', believing that Nottingham's continued presence in the administration was beginning to weaken support for war. William told the Queen he thought 'his case so bad that he was forced to part with the Lord Nottingham, to please a party who he cannot trust'. The Whigs nonetheless returned to office, with Shrewsbury returning to government in March 1694, having won the King's assurance that he would assent to a Triennial Act.[25]

Religious disagreements accompanied these political divisions. The summer of 1688 had seen an atmosphere of détente between the Church of England and dissent as members of James's episcopate began to recognise the danger they faced from a union of nonconformists and Catholics. Yet the events of 1688 and the demand to swear allegiance to William and Mary in 1689 caused an immediate fissure in this Protestant alliance. Some four hundred Anglican clergy refused to take the new oaths, viewing those who did so as perjured by breaking their oaths of loyalty to James II. As a proportion of the Church of England, with around ten thousand clergy, the non-jurors represented only a small fraction of the religious establishment. In their number, though, they included some of the most high-ranking and intellectually respected churchmen of the age: William Sancroft, the Archbishop of Canterbury, Robert Frampton of Gloucester, Thomas Ken of Bath and Wells, John Lake of Chichester, William Lloyd of Norwich, William Thomas of Worcester, Francis Turner of Ely and Thomas White of Peterborough. The principled stand that these men had taken, to lose their offices rather than overlook their continuing duty of allegiance to their monarch *de jure*, was reflected in the fact that five of the non-juring bishops had been among the seven sent to the Tower for refusing to read James II's second Declaration of Indulgence.

In contrast, it was noted that the majority of the clergy, who often took the oaths to the new monarchs with the casuistic reservation that they were only recognising William as king in fact, not by law, were increasingly being viewed by the public as 'partial, cowardly and perjured'.[26] The majority of non-jurors were deprived of their posts on 1 February 1690 and some of their number refused subsequent opportunities to conform, by taking further oaths of allegiance, well into the eighteenth century.

Even greater divisions emerged over the question of what the national church's relationship should be with nonconformity. After the Revolution most agreed on the need for some form of religious toleration. However, the fact that the pre-revolutionary rapprochement between dissent and the Church was based largely on expediency glossed over major points of disagreement between the parties on religious policy. Whigs argued that toleration should be generous and permanent; Tories felt that it should perhaps be temporary, and certainly that it should be limited to a bare freedom to worship and closely supervised to ensure religious liberty did not encourage sedition, immorality or blasphemy. Secondly, Whigs and Tories disagreed about the need for comprehension, meaning not only the toleration of non-Anglican Protestant worship but also the acceptance of dissenters back into the Church. While many Whigs felt that the Church of England should offer compromises to nonconformists to attract them back, such as modifying the liturgy and softening its line on the need for bishops to ordain ministers, Tories were generally opposed to the readmission of dissenters, viewing the doctrine and discipline of Anglicanism as already a moderate middle way that needed no further revision. Finally, there was disagreement over the Anglican monopoly upon public office. Tories were adamantly against nonconformists taking up public office and insisted on retaining the test acts of the 1670s, which had ruled that people could be sworn into offices only once they had taken Anglican communion. Whigs, conversely, pressed for the abandonment of the sacramental test.

There was widespread Tory unease at what William's plans for the Church might be, and this was not simply as a result of his attachment to a faith, Dutch Calvinism, that appeared to have more in common with English Puritanism than the national church. During the 1680s William had publicly supported the stance of the Whigs in their demands for greater toleration and given Whig exiles sanctuary in the Netherlands. In his declaration he had been careful to avoid any religious controversy, to placate both his English and Continental audiences. The issue of the relationship between Anglicans and dissenters was to be left to a 'free Parliament', though he urged it to consider 'such Laws as may establish a good Agreement between the Church of England and all Protestant Dissenters'.[27] To appease his Catholic allies on the Continent, William's declaration also promised his good intentions to all peaceable English Romanists. The Prince also made sure that he was clearly seen to be a friend of the Church of England, appointing the Anglican Burnet as his chaplain, making sure he was visible at Anglican services such as the act of thanksgiving in Exeter cathedral soon after his landing, attending Anglican prayers and communion regularly once he was in London and making early contact with the clergy of the capital to thank them for their opposition to James over the preceding years.

This policy was successful in stifling religious debate in the early days of the Convention, but this led William to be overconfident, and in the spring of 1689 the King made his own religious preferences clearer. A group of latitudinarian ministers, including John Tillotson, Simon Patrick and Edward Stillingfleet, with the support of their patron the Earl of Nottingham, produced two parliamentary bills in January and February 1689, one for comprehension that would offer concessions on Anglican liturgy and on episcopal ordination and another that would offer toleration to those Protestants who could not be included in the broader church settlement. Their vision of a national church both more tolerant and more inclusive was pushed forward by William in a speech of 16 March in which he 'urged the admission to public office of all Protestants that are willing and able to serve'.[28] These words, with their explicit hope of bringing to an end the Anglican ecclesiastical and political hegemony, provoked an angry response from Tory MPs, 150 of whom met that evening in the Devil's Tavern. Over their cups they vowed to fight any further erosion of the Church's position.

The Tory backlash scored some immediate successes in reversing William's declared policy. In the Commons debate over the coronation oath the Tories successfully insisted not only that the King should promise to defend the Church of England but also that he must defend the church 'as by law established'. This was intended to bind William to uphold the present form of the liturgy and episcopal government. The strength of resistance to a dual policy of comprehension and toleration led William to pull back from his attempt to break the Anglican monopoly on public office. He dropped the idea of repealing the test acts and sacrificed the idea of comprehension by arguing that such changes should be considered by Convocation, not by Parliament. Convocation met in November 1689 but no proposals even reached a vote. William himself made a number of sycophantic public statements about the Anglican Church, describing it as the 'best constituted in the world' and an 'eminent part of the Reformation'. He promised he would 'venture his life' in its defence and had resolved to die in its communion. As a further sop to the 'Church party', after 1689 William surrendered control of the Church of England to solid Anglicans. During Mary's lifetime she, not he, essentially handled ecclesiastical patronage and policy. However, William refused to back down on the point of toleration and it was largely royal pressure that ensured that Nottingham's Toleration Act got on to the statute book in April 1689. The act granted Protestant dissenters the freedom to worship outside of the Church of England, so long as they registered their meetings with local magistrates, kept their doors unlocked during services and swore to uphold the doctrinal (but not the liturgical and episcopal) ideals of the establishment.

The toleration enshrined in the act was not as extensive as that which James had sought in 1687–8, as it officially excluded Catholics, Quakers and Unitarians from its terms. Yet it was nonetheless welcomed as something little short of miraculous by some dissenters, such as the members of the Axminster Congregational church: 'O what a mercy is it when kings are nursing fathers, and queens nursing mothers to the churches of Christ; when rulers are ministers of God for good, to encourage piety, that the people of the Lord may lead quiet and peaceable lives in all godliness and honesty under their rule and government.'[29] And the actual degree of religious toleration under William's government was broader than the letter of the law allowed. Both Catholics and nonconformists who fell outside the terms of the act also enjoyed in practice a relatively high level of religious freedom. Again, with his eye on his main goal of overcoming Louis XIV, the King wished to quell religious controversy at home as far as possible, both to avoid it becoming a distraction and to appease his Catholic European allies.

During the 1690s both religious and political controversy were stirred and prolonged by the cost and conduct of William's Continental wars. Government propaganda through sermons and monthly public fasts stressed that these were wars to defend

Protestantism. Huge amounts of religious literature were published after the Revolution, more than at any time since the
1640s.[30] Pro-war divines such as Dean Comber of Durham liked
to emphasise the religious elements to this struggle: the sword that
the French king brandished against Britain was 'yet reeking with
the Gore of a Sister Reformed Church', said Comber, meaning the
Huguenots. Some even infused this vision of a religious war with
apocalyptic elements. Judge Thomas Rokeby said in May 1689 that
the 'cause wherein King William and Q. Mary and the Parliament
of England are now ingaged' was 'the cause of God and Christ
against Satan and Antichrist'.[31] Toleration fitted in with William's
war aims and Whigs, albeit unsuccessfully, used national security
as an argument for doing away with the Anglican sacramental
test, contending that Protestant union was necessary to defend
England. Comprehension measures were also argued for in a
European context, in that they would show that the Church of
England saw itself as part of a broader community of Protestants.

However, presenting the war as a religious crusade was not
without its problems, given that William was in an international
alliance with Catholic Austria and Spain. Even those amenable to
viewing the war as part of a divine struggle noted the King's odd
military bedfellows: 'The Lord seemed to be doing great things,
great work upon the wheel, the nations in a reeling, staggering
posture, Europe seemed to be in a flame, great armies appearing
in divers parts, the Lord of Hosts still mustering up the hosts
to battle. Contrary interests seemed to be united, papists and
protestants combining, and yet agreeing interests were divided,
papists against papists, the Lord setting Egyptian against Egyptian,
kingdom against kingdom.'[32]

Jacobite writers complained that it was nonsense to argue that
French popery was 'so much worse than the Spanish; and the
House of Bourbon more an Enemy to Protestants, than the
Bloody House of Austria'.[33] Rather, they argued, with some justi-
fication, England had been dragged into the war simply for the

benefit of the Dutch. Indeed, William had largely steered clear of portraying the war as having a confessional purpose in propaganda developed for European consumption. Consequently the argument that this was a war against popery was coupled with warnings about the threat from Louis XIV's ambitions to become 'universal monarch' with pretensions to suzerainty over Europe as a whole. The French king was rechristened as the 'most Christian turk', playing on the contemporary image of the Turkish empire as the quintessence of anti-Christian barbarism, a view strengthened by Louis's actual diplomacy with the Ottoman Empire, making common cause with Sultan Suleiman II against Emperor Leopold.

An added difficulty was that, until 1694 at least, William's land war against Louis was not going well and, with the exception of the cannonball that grazed the King's shoulder at the Boyne, there was little sign of providential favour to the Orange cause. At sea, it was true, the English navy fared better. Anxiety about a French invasion attempt had been high since the defeat of English and Dutch ships at the hands of Louis's navy off Beachy Head on 30 June 1690. That victory had given the French effective control of the Channel and fears were raised further by French ships' bombardment of the Devon village of Teignmouth on 26 July. Aside from this sabre-rattling, the French admiral, Tourville, made little effort to press home his military advantage, to the annoyance of his royal master (who if not contemplating an invasion attempt at this time, still wished his commander to take a more serious toll of English shipping). Meanwhile the defeat gave impetus to a programme of shipbuilding and naval reorganisation: the Commons voted money for twenty-seven new men-of-war, and new shipyards and dry docks were built at Plymouth and Portsmouth. New instructions were issued to commanders which were designed to maximise the strengths of British ships (greater firepower over greater manoeuvrability) by encouraging attack only when there was opportunity for a close-range confrontation in which British ships were at a numerical advantage.

By the summer of 1691 preparations were being made on both sides of the Channel for invasion attempts. The Jacobite intrigues of leading political, military and naval figures had encouraged Louis to believe that there would be domestic support for restoring James by force, with a planned landing of twenty thousand troops at Torbay – the Stuart king would begin the recovery of his crown where William had begun his design to steal it. News of these efforts leaked out to England in April 1692. Easterly winds which kept the invasion force at bay in La Hogue gave time for the English fleet to assemble under Russell with ninety ships and around forty thousand men. Joined shortly afterwards by the Dutch, William's force now had a distinct numerical advantage, with a combined force of ninety-nine ships, thirty-eight fireships and 6736 guns against forty-four ships, thirty-eight fireships and 3240 guns on the French side. Russell's guns inflicted such damage on the French flagship the *Soleil Royal* that she had to be towed off. As the French fleet dispersed in retreat, the British set fire to the enemy fireships and transports in the bay. The threat of invasion of England had been averted but, as with the French after Beachy Head, there was no firm decision as to how this victory should be pressed home. A plan to turn defensive success into offensive advantage, via a 'descent' on France, was abandoned as Russell dithered, reluctant to land his ships on the treacherous French Atlantic coastline. La Hogue also brought about a change of strategy by the French. Realising that, outnumbered and outgunned, they could not compete with the English and Dutch in a full-scale naval war, they turned their ships to attacking English trade, with great success. French privateering led to an overall collapse in English overseas trade: by 1693–4 English exports to the Iberian Peninsula, the Canary Islands and the Mediterranean region had fallen by 25 per cent of their pre-1686 levels and colonial merchants also experienced heavy losses of cargoes.[34]

William, in any case, believed the crucible of his war against Louis would not be the Channel but on land in Flanders. With the end of the Irish campaign, the King was able to bring another forty thousand English troops into the Low Countries. The King was now engaged in the kind of Continental land war that he and most European generals were familiar with, one dominated by the besieging and bombarding of massively fortified towns, a slow, costly, attritional form of warfare of which the English had far less experience, even after the civil wars. William's lack of success in the early part of the Nine Years War did not endear the Flanders campaign to the English public either. Heavy rains and flooding which swept away pontoons prevented the King from relieving the French encirclement of Namur and after a month-long siege the fortress surrendered in June 1692. Further defeat was experienced at Steenkirk in July as William attempted to engage the French army in a pitched battle, but in the close fighting the King lost around three thousand men, with around half of the troops in the Scottish regiments of Mackay and Lanier killed. The opinions of the Newcastle nonconformist Ambrose Barnes on the Flanders campaign were not uncharacteristic: 'Our Revolution has cost us more millions than all our warrs, I had almost said since William the Norman's time put them together. We have had forces enow to have subdued the world, yet all has ended in marches and counter-marches, loyal camps, and the taking and retaking a town or two.'[35]

English ministers, particularly Nottingham, felt that war in Flanders would not bring a decisive victory and instead went back to the idea of a 'descent'. MPs continued to vote William money, agreeing to give him a further £4 million in supply, but largely on the rather negative argument, used by Sir William Temple, that it was at least better that the war was fought in Flanders rather than in England. But William's war continued to go badly. In July 1693 he suffered another heavy defeat at Landen, which was followed by the French capture of Charleroi. Worse news still came with the French capture of the wealthy Smyrna fleet off the coast of Portugal. As will be shown in the next chapter, this humiliation played a large part in killing off William's hopes of governing through a joint ministry of both parties and led him to turn reluctantly towards the Whigs.[36]

War not only transformed politics and shaped the religious settlement but also altered the constitution, arguably in ways more profound than the Revolution settlement of 1688. William's wars necessitated a massive increase in government expenditure; while under King James government spending had been about £2 million a year, under King William it was £5.5 million per annum. In part this expenditure was funded by raising taxation to unprecedented levels. In the 1680s taxation had amounted to about 3–4 per cent of national income, but by the first decade of the eighteenth century this was around 9 per cent. The most important of these taxes was the land tax, which accounted for no less than 52 per cent of the government's tax revenue in 1696. Other major sources of revenue were customs duties, providing around 22 per cent of government tax income in the 1690s, and the excise (a form of sales tax), giving around 25 per cent. In contrast with the early seventeenth century, the vast majority of the Crown's taxes now required parliamentary approval (the King had conceded further parts of the Revolution financial settlement in 1690) and, in order to smooth the financing of his war machine, William allowed greater and greater public scrutiny of government spending. Commissions of public accounts were established which looked into the State's budget, routing out corruption and waste. The King's aim here was to convince the Parliament that the vast costs of the war were not masking peculation by crown officers and that the money was, in fact, going into arms, ships and men.

Taxation alone was not enough, though, to support the huge costs of major European land war. Tax revenue was consequently heavily supplemented by government borrowing, but short-term loans were not sufficient to make up the difference, particularly given the wariness of creditors about lending money to a regime that had only recently been established and remained under the threat of a Jacobite invasion. Lenders were not encouraged any further by the inability of William and Mary to pay their IOUs. The government was left to resort to new methods to raise credit, including state lotteries such as the Million Lottery of 1694, the prizes for which were to be paid for out of future duties on salt and alcohol.

By far the most important of these new institutions was the Bank of England, established in the summer of 1694, initially as a private company. A scheme for a joint-stock company, lending money to the crown on an indefinite basis in return for a fixed-interest rent, had first emerged in 1692 from the London-based Scottish merchant William Paterson. Legislation for founding the Bank was presented to Parliament in April 1694 by the Treasury commissioner, Charles Montague, working with Michael Godfrey, its future deputy governor (killed in 1695 at the battle of Namur while discussing Bank business with the King). The Bank would raise a stock subscription of £1.2 million, a sum which would, in turn, be lent by the Bank to the crown for an indefinite period in return for an annual 'rent' amounting to 8 per cent interest (6 per cent lower than the rate charged on the 'Million Loan' of 1693). The subscription was taken up eagerly by English merchants whose other investments were suffering as a result of war.

Thomas Addison, the editor of the *Spectator*, retrospectively portrayed the Bank as one of the founding stones of the Revolution settlement, envisaging 'public credit' as as much a part of the English constitution as Magna Carta. Indeed, it has recently been argued that some of those merchants who were the earliest advocates of the Bank were also key players in effecting the Revolution of 1688. Perhaps precisely because its creation was politically charged, set against the downfall of Nottingham's ministry, not everyone, and Tories less than most, was happy with the creation of the Bank of England. There were complaints that it represented, along with the heavy burden of the land tax, another assault by mercantile capital against the landed interest. Indeed, the

Tories attempted to set up a rival institution, the Land Bank, in 1696 in order to create a new source of public credit based on landed wealth. Beyond these arguments motivated by politics and economic self-interest, there were broader, less partisan complaints about the social and moral implications of the financial revolution. The new world of stock speculation and public lotteries seemed to some to be diverting the energies of merchants and traders away from 'real' business into what was little more than state-sponsored gambling. (In fact, conflict in Flanders caused its own betting craze, as vast sums of money were wagered with so-called 'insurers' on the outcomes of sieges.[37])

The war itself, which had been the catalyst for these financial innovations, was linked by some individuals to national sinfulness. George Berkeley stated that 'it is very remarkable that luxury was never at so great a height, nor spread so generally through the nation, as during the expense of the late wars'.[38] William's lack of success in the Flanders campaign was attributed by some to divine disfavour provoked by the nation's sinfulness. Natural disasters were also interpreted as the product of God's wrath. The earthquake at Port Royal in Jamaica on 7 June 1692, in which around fifteen hundred people died, and another tremor felt in London in September the same year, were seen as signs of the Lord's anger with England. 'O that now Gods judgments are in the earth,' wrote Abigail Harley from London on the day of the quake, 'the inhabitants may learn righteousness & not go on presumptuously in sin.' A pamphlet of the time stated that though the tremor had done little damage 'who can tell, this is not the last Warning; and that the next time he shall visit us, he will not in his Fiery Indignation utterly consume us, and swallow us up quick?'[39] Jacobites alleged that these misfortunes were divine punishment for the unlawful deposition of James II. Williamites urged rather that the Revolution was a divine blessing, but one which might be transformed into a curse if the nation did not mend its ways: 'God can create destruction upon a People, which he hath created Salvation and Deliverance for, that will not accept of it, nor be saved nor delivered by him.'[40]

Concerns about the impact of war on society were combined with fears about the ramifications of the Revolution's religious settlement upon the public's faithfulness. Though toleration was limited, at least on paper, some consequences of the Toleration Act raised anxieties that the 1690s were witnessing the rise of irreligion, immorality and atheism. Churchwardens were still theoretically obliged to present parishioners to the church courts who had failed to attend communion but they increasingly failed to do so on the basis that non-communicants might instead be attending services in nonconformist meeting houses. There is certainly some evidence of a decline in communicants after the passage of the Act. In Clayworth in Nottinghamshire perhaps 85–90 per cent of parishioners of an age to communicate did so before the Glorious Revolution but by 1701 figures were perhaps only 55 per cent.[41]

The role of church courts in regulating moral behaviour and monitoring religious observance was also undermined by the Act. Though individuals were still being presented for irreligious activity as flagrant (but not fragrant) as pissing in the parish church, punishments such as excommunication were obviously of little worth in the case of individuals who were no longer Anglican worshippers. It seemed to some more logical for these nonconformist churches to apply their own sanctions on recalcitrant followers. However, many churchmen suspected that a large proportion of the public simply used the terms of the Toleration Act as a cover to avoid attending religious services of any kind, instead, it was alleged, spending their time drinking, gaming and whoring. Perceived public religious indifference was all the more worrying as it appeared to form part of a larger movement of intellectual scepticism about religion, headed by freethinkers like John Toland, a close associate of Locke, who argued for the discarding of all parts of Christian faith that could not be supported by reason. Feelings of concern were not limited to Church of England men.

There was evidence of disenchantment among Protestant dissenters, in particular Presbyterians, who felt that the Williamite reformation had not gone far enough; popery was tolerated too much, and old members of James's regime were allowed to slink back into office. The King had failed to foster the Protestant union which was essential to the successful reformation of the nation.

The apparent threat posed by religious pluralism, moral indifference and atheism was made more palpable by the fact that Protestantism appeared at this point to be under threat internationally. The revocation of the Edict of Nantes by Louis XIV in 1685, and the harsh persecution that followed, led to the emigration of fifty thousand Huguenots to England. The following year the Duke of Savoy attacked fifteen thousand Protestant Vaudois (Waldenses), killing many, forcing the conversion of others, and leaving the remainder to flee to the safety of Switzerland. In response to these assaults on European co-religionists, the English public gave generously to charitable funds to aid distressed Protestants. Towards the end of the seventeenth century and around the start of the eighteenth century £64,713 was raised for Huguenots, £59,146 for Irish Protestants, £27,606 for the Vaudois, £22,038 for the Palatines and £19,548 for Orange Protestants. These charitable endeavours were encouraged by William and Mary, who gave £39,000 to Huguenots between 1689 and 1693 and prompted a Royal Bounty of £15,000 supplied by Parliament from 1696 onwards.[42]

Consequently the 1690s saw a cross-denominational movement to counter public vice and religious ignorance and indifference. As the Toleration Act had tied the hands of the State to act in this regard, these energies were now directed into voluntary societies. Some, such as the Religious Societies, begun by Anthony Horneck, the pastor of the Savoy chapel in London, before the Revolution, the Society for the Propagation of the Gospel in Foreign Parts and the Society for the Propagation of Christian Knowledge (SPCK), founded in 1700, were exclusively Anglican.

Yet others, such as the Societies for Reformation of Manners, which will be discussed in greater detail below, benefited from the involvement of the Crown, the Church and Protestant dissent.

William's more latitudinarian bishops were committed to promoting national moral reformation. In December 1691 they petitioned the King to issue a proclamation for the implementation of the laws against vice, which was published at the end of January 1692. Fifty-three Anglican ministers, among them several bishops, preached to the Society for Reformation of Manners between 1696 and 1739. The societies were particularly linked with low-church figures such as Gilbert Burnet, Simon Patrick, White Kennett, William Wake and Edmund Gibson. Bishops also sponsored moral legislation, Tenison successfully backing a blasphemy act that became law in 1698.[43] There was also clear political value for the crown in promoting reformation. The historian Tony Claydon has pointed to the role of the reformation of manners campaign in legitimating William and Mary's rule. The unprecedented series of monthly fasts which the monarchs established to promote national reformation also reminded the people that God's cause and King William's were one and the same. Here they fitted in with the overall Williamite effort to present the new King as a providentially appointed deliverer to rescue the nation from popery. Yet it was also the case that Queen Mary in particular sincerely believed that the campaign for reformation of manners was necessary to avert divine punishment. Mary had been shocked by what she had seen when she arrived in England in 1689: 'The first thing that surprised me at my coming over, was to see so little devotion in a people so lately in such eminent danger.'[44] Burnet claimed that Mary was heavily weighed down by the prospect that divine judgement upon the land might be imminent.

The first Society for Reformation of Manners was formed in 1690 in Tower Hamlets in London's East End to deal with the problem of the growing number of bawdy houses (brothels) in the area.[45] Prostitutes and prostitution at this time (and perhaps still)

were closely linked in the public's perception with crime and crim-
inality. Josiah Woodward, the first historian of the Societies for
Reformation of Manners, stated that the impetus to the Tower
Hamlets householders forming a society was that they were

> much perplexed by pilfering People, Pick-locks, House-breakers,
> and such ill Persons: some of them began to inquire into the Places
> which were suspected to harbour that sort of People. And by trac-
> ing out their places of Rest, they soon div'd in to the true Source
> of their Grievances, namely That these vicious Persons living in
> shameful Lewdness and Idleness, and having no Income by trade
> or Estate to maintain them in it, they betook themselves to
> Robbery, Shop-lifting, Burglery and picking of Locks and Pockets
> to maintain their expensive Lusts and Lewd Companions.[46]

However, the impetus to form these Societies really gathered
pace with the intervention of Edward Stillingfleet, who petitioned
the Queen on behalf of five prominent gentlemen who had
formed a society based in the Strand. Some of these gentlemen had
strong links with dissent. Maynard Colchester was influenced by
his Presbyterian lawyer grandfather, Sir John Maynard, while the
Irish gentleman Sir Richard Bulkeley was influenced by the mil-
lenarian group the French prophets. The eccentric barrister turned
priest Edward Stephens was a nonconformist critic of the regime,
who believed that, in neglecting to punish sin, William had failed
to honour the trust placed in him by God. Yet, at the prompting
of Stillingfleet, the Crown was pressed into action. In July 1691
Queen Mary issued a letter to the Middlesex bench demanding
they implement the laws against vice. The following year William
wrote an open letter to Bishop Compton of London saying that 'as
our duty requires, we most earnestly desire, and shall endeavour a
general reformation of lives and manners of all our subjects, as
being that which must establish our throne, and secure to our
people their religion, happiness, and peace, all which seem to be in

great danger at this time, by reason of that overflowing of vice, which is too notorious in this as well as other neighbouring nations'. The new monarchs also strengthened the laws against immoral behaviour, passing four statutes against profanation of the Sabbath, swearing and blasphemy.[47]

Some of these directions provoked ridicule. Lord Dartmouth noted against the passage relating to the Queen's pious activities in Burnet's *History of My Own Time*

> There came forth at this time several puritanical regulations for observing the Sabbath in London, savouring so much of John Knox's doctrine and discipline, that Burnet was thought to have been the chief contriver. One was that hackney coaches should not drive upon that day; by another, constables were ordered to take away pies and puddings from anybody they met carrying of them in the streets; with a multitude of other impertinences so ridiculous in themselves, and troublesome to all sorts of people, that they were soon dropt, after they had been sufficiently laughed at.[48]

Others objected to the Societies' apparent supplanting of the Church's role in regulating moral behaviour and were suspicious of the religious aspirations of some members. As has already been stated, some founding members of the movement were dissenters or had close links with nonconformist groups. Some certainly hoped that the Societies would have a role in fostering religious union. Edmund Calamy wrote that it was 'an hopeful Prognostick in the Present Case, that those who differ in Rituals but with too much Vehemence, should unanimously join together in forming those Societies for Reformation, who aim at the Checking those Vices which threaten to over-run us, which are heartily detested by Good Men of all Perswasions'.[49]

The possibility of the Societies being a route to comprehension by the back door was picked upon, and objected to, by some Anglicans. William Nicolson, Archdeacon of Carlisle, stated that they smacked too much of the 'associations of the Presbyterians and Independent Ministers in the days of the Rebellion'.[50] Then, there might have been some role for these voluntary associations, as the national church had been demolished by the Long Parliament, but this was not now the case. The Anglican controversialist Henry Sacheverell described the Societies as places wherein 'every Tradesman and Mechanick is to take upon him the Gift of the Spirit, and to expound the difficult Passages of Scripture, and every Justice of Peace is allow'd to settle its Canon, and Infallibly Decide what is Orthodox or Heretical'.[51] However, Josiah Woodward argued that in fact the Societies had helped bring people back within the communion of the Church of England: 'For they have been instrumental to bring several Quakers and Enthusiastick people to Baptism, and to a sober Mind; and the Conversion of many profane Persons.'[52]

It was also the case that some advocates of the Societies attempted to make partisan capital out of their work. Thomas Papillon stated: 'Under the name of Whigs is comprehended most of the sober and religious persons of the Church of England that . . . are willing that there might be a Reformation to take away offence, and that desire that all Swearing, Drunkeness, and Ungodliness should be discountenanced and punished . . . As also all dissenters of the several persuasions are included under this title.' On the other hand, the Tory party was made up of those who 'press the forms and ceremonies more than the Doctrines of the Church, which are sound and Scriptural; and that either in their own practice are Swearers, Drunkards, or loose in their Conversation, or do allow of and are unwilling such should be punished, but give them all countenance, provided they stickle for the forms and ceremonies and rail against and endeavour to discountenance all those that are otherwise minded'.[53] The Whig writer and publisher John Dunton, in his *The Night-walker, or Evening Rambles in Search after Lewd Women*, an early piece of tabloid journalism in which sexual titillation masqueraded as moral exposé, addressed his pamphlet to the aged Duchess of Cleveland, Barbara Villiers, Charles II's former mistress, 'as being the first after the Re[storation], who in an avowed and daring manner polluted this Nation by your bad Example. It had been a greater Instance of your Loyalty, to have rejected the unchast Embraces of [Charles II] than to have complied with him, in turning the Grace of God towards him into Wantoness; and infecting other Ladies by your Example.'[54] His clear intent was to link the Societies to a campaign to overturn the excesses both political and moral of Charles II's reign. Dunton denied that his work was 'a Satyr against one Party more than another . . . but if the Tories will need have it that a Satyr against Whoreing is a Satyr against them, we cannot hinder them to apply it as they please'.[55] It was notable, however, that many of the prostitutes and brothel-keepers that Dunton accosted seemed to have Tory or Jacobite political sympathies. Dunton alleged that one madam told him she would 'rather have half a dozen of King James' Officers, they Drink and Carouse, and make all the house merry; and not only pay my Girls well for their Company, but gratifie me for my procurement'. To which Dunton replied that he had 'often heard that all the Whores in Town are Jacobites, and now I perceive something of the reason of it'.[56] A remarkable number of the 'lewd-women' Dunton interviewed were also Catholics, one whore telling him that she did not fear heavenly punishment for her activities:

such Bug-bears might well frighten us who were Protestants, but for her part she was a Roman Catholick, and could be absolved when she pleased; and having the Eucharist brought her on her death bed, which was a never failing Viaticum: I answered her that I found the Church of Rome might properly enough be called the Mother of Harlots in a literal sense, seeing by her Doctrines and Pardons people were incouraged to lead loose lives, adding that those Pardons and Absolutions of their Priests were meer Cheats, which would stand in no stead at the bar of God, and therefore advised her to have recourse to the Word of God where she would find that he would judge Whoremongers and Adulterers.[57]

Nonetheless, despite attempts to hijack the campaign for reformation of manners for particular political and religious groups and causes, many people responded positively to this initiative. By 1701 there were more than a dozen Societies in London and the rest of England. In 1738 they claimed they had prosecuted 101,638 people for disorderly and lewd behaviour. Campaigns to regulate the nation's moral behaviour were nothing new, for movements of this kind went back to at least the fourteenth century, one of the most recent and famous (or infamous) being the puritanical rule of the major generals under the Cromwellian Protectorate. Three factors distinguished the Societies from previous attempts to suppress vice. First, there was the long duration of the movement, with formal reports of the Societies' activities continuing until 1738. Secondly, the supporters of moral reformation were for the first time organised into independent Societies which not only lobbied for better enforcement of the laws but also assumed (to a certain extent) the duties of parish officers. Members of the Societies were encouraged to observe their surroundings carefully and inform JPs of any profanity, drunkenness, Sabbath-breaking, lewdness or other immorality. To facilitate this process, the Societies printed up blank warrants and paid agents to hear informers' complaints and fill out the warrant forms correctly. The informer then took the warrant to a JP, who would sign it and seal it after examining him or her under oath to ensure that their story was true. Constables received the warrants and would arrest offenders, who would be brought before the Justices and either prosecuted by indictment, committed to a house of correction or asked to enter into a recognisance, depending on their circumstances. Some of the punishments meted out were fairly severe; keepers of bawdy houses could be fined 10 shillings or more and sentenced to be whipped along the Strand from Charing Cross to Somerset House and ordered to stand in the pillory. The names of 'Delinquents' were published in 'Black Lists' to shame in particular those offenders who could not be punished by the courts (that is, mainly the better-off). The Eleventh Black List, published in 1706, listed 830 'Lewd and Scandalous Persons' who had been legally prosecuted.

Finally, this moral reformation, while tackling familiar vices such as drunkenness, loose swearing and blasphemy, also addressed new problems. Although, as we will see, the Societies spent considerable energy in prosecuting 'lewd' heterosexuals, indicting female prostitutes and their male clients, they also attempted to suppress the emerging homosexual 'molly culture' of this time. Some satirists alleged that 'he-whores' were now so common that they were putting their female counterparts out of business. *The Women's Complaint to Venus* (1698) alleged

> Poor Whores may be Nuns
> Since Men turn their Guns
> And vent on each other their passion.
> In the Raign of Good *Charles* the Second
> Full many a Jade
> A Lady was made
> And the Issue Right Noble was reckon'd:
> But now we find to our Sorrow
> We are overrun
> By Sparks of the Bum
> And peers of the Land of Gommorah.

To curb homosexual activity, the Societies even employed agents provocateurs to expose and convict gay men. Captain Edward Rigby was accused of soliciting one Minton by taking him by the hand in St James's Park on Bonfire Night and putting his 'Privy Member Erected into *Minton*'s Hand; kist him, and put his Tongue into *Minton*'s Mouth'. Minton attempted to run away but was pursued by Rigby, who 'after much Discourse prevailed with

Minton to tell him where he lodged, and to meet him the *Monday* following about Five a Clock, at the *George-Tavern* in the *Pall mall,* and to Enquire for *Number 4*'. Minton then went to a Middlesex JP, Thomas Rialto, 'who being informed of what past between *Rigby* and *Minton,* appointed his Clark with a Constable, and two other Persons, to go with *Minton* to the *George-Tavern,* who were to stay in some Room adjoyning to the Room whereinto *Minton* should go: and if any Violence should be offered to him, upon crying out " *Westminster*" the Constable and his Assistance should immediately enter the Room'. Minton went to Rigby's rooms at the George Tavern as arranged but with the constables lodged in the adjoining room.

> *Rigby* seemed much pleased upon *Mintons* coming, and drank to him in a glass of Wine and kist him, took him by the Hand, put his Tongue into *Mintons* Mouth, and thrust *Mintons* hand into his (*Rigby*) Breeches, saying, 'He had raised his Lust to the highest degree,' *Minton* thereupon askt, 'How can it be, a Woman was only fit for that,' *Rigby* answered, 'Dam'em, they are all Port, I'll have nothing to do with them.' Then *Rigby* sitting on *Mintons* Lap, kist him several times, putting his Tongue into his mouth, askt him, 'if he should F[uck] him'.

When Minton objected, Rigby attempted to convince him by stating that it was 'no more than was done in our Fore-fathers time' and that, moreover, the French king did it, and so did Peter the Great, who Rigby himself said he had seen through the port-hole of his ship 'lye with Prince Alexander'. Minton allowed Rigby to continue to fondle him until it was clear that the Captain intended to bugger him (providing the evidence for a conviction for assault with sodomitical intent). Giving the appointed sign, the constables and their assistants rushed into the room and appre-hended Rigby. The Captain was sentenced to stand in the pillory for three days, fined £1000 and imprisoned for a year.[58]

It was not coincidental that the first Societies for the Reformation of Manners emerged in the capital. In addition to dealing with moral or sexual offences, they attempted to deal with some of the social problems that came with increasing urbanisation and commercialisation. Many of those convicted of breaking the Sabbath were not alehouse tipplers but traders and shopkeepers who now opened their businesses on a Sunday. Woodward reported that the Societies had had success in closing down several Sunday markets. The Societies' attack on vice was also linked to the problems of the confusion of status and identity produced by a consumer culture in which, as Defoe complained, a whore could afford to dress like a gentlewoman. Dunton often described the prostitutes that he met as wearing 'genteel attire' and complained about 'Tradesmens wives dressing as Ladies', which, he said, proved a great temptation to men.[59] There is also good evidence that the Societies endeavoured to tackle the perceived threat to law and order posed by the urban poor. Under the offence of 'lewd and disorderly conduct', informers often included a variety of activities, not only prostitution and soliciting but also 'idleness', vagrancy and theft. Of course, as we have already seen, there was a link in the public imagination between prostitution and crime and equally poverty was seen to increase the temptation to sin (many charitable endeavours were motivated mainly by the desire to check immorality rather than out of a commitment to social justice or to provide a safety net). However, parish officers of St Martin in the Fields who called for the suppression of brothels also did so because they contributed to the 'daily increase of poor in the said parish' and had caused 'several great disorders and misde-meanors . . . against the peace'. Some individuals were convicted of 'lewd and disorderly conduct' on the basis of little evidence of actual misbehaviour besides the fact that they were poor, lacked a proper job and were found in suspicious circumstances (which could mean as little as walking the street at night). The minister John Shower admitted that the Societies tended to prosecute poorer people but hoped that the punishment of meaner persons would 'so far influence the greater sort, as to bring them to be more private, and less scandalous in their crimes'.[60]

Historians have been divided as to the level of public support for the work of the Societies. The Societies' informers not only lay in wait for men soliciting prostitutes on the street, or lone 'lewd women' night-walking, but also went into the brothels to catch individuals engaging in sexual acts. Seventy-five per cent of all arrests of prostitutes' clients in Middlesex and Westminster in the 1720s were 'inside a well-known bawdy house' rather than on the street. One John Walker was bound 'for being . . . in a Notorious house with a woman of known ill fame and Reputation she standing between his Leggs and him . . . having his briches [sic] down and his Privy parts Bare'. Richard Lary was taken with '2 lewd women in an obscene posture', while Samuel Hornby was found 'in Bedd with a whore bigg with child'. Justice of the Peace John Sully arrested a whore, 'Having my Selfe taken my sunn in Bed with her'. Unsurprisingly, a number of the accused attacked the constables who interrupted their activities. Thomas Cowper, listed as a gentleman, was accused of 'picking up a woman in the streete, and goeing along with her'. He resisted arrest and was also bound for 'assaulting, striking, kicking and very much abusing' the constable and his assistants.[61]

However, if some prostitutes' clients naturally objected to the activities of the Societies, there was a strong level of condemnation in the press of men who went whoring. Some authors even began to see women as the victims, and Joseph Addison condemned that 'loose tribe of men . . . that rambles into all the Corners of this great City, in order to seduce such unfortunate Females as fall into their Walks'. John Dunton also pointed out a moral double standard, that whores' clients 'would be ill pleas'd to have [their] Wives follow [their] own Examples . . . which is a plain Demonstration that [they] hate[d] that vice in others, which [they] indulge[d] in [them]selves'. Sexual vice was now seen as damaging to gentle

reputation and *The Gentleman's Library* instructed men to avoid
sexual 'Adventures' or they would render themselves 'more vile and
despicable than any innocent man can be, whatever [his] low sta-
tion'. Dunton stated that only a 'Porter, Common-Soldier, trooper
or Common Carmen [*sic*]' would hold himself so low as to resort
to 'bawds'. In investigating sexual crimes, JPs were also urged not
to exhibit an overly puerile interest in the details of the case lest
they be seen to taking 'too much pleasure in the inquiry'. The JP's job
in such situations was to encourage the woman's 'Natural Modesty'
otherwise he would 'effectually teach instead of Correcting the
Crime'.

As to the general public, there are hints here too that there was
some popular support for the campaign against sexual vice.
Dunton reported that young 'sparks' were jeered at for bringing
prostitutes into taverns. An angry group of spectators killed
Mother Needham, an infamous procuress, when she was put in
the pillory in 1730 and the same year Colonel Charteris, a notorious whoremonger who was known as the 'Rape Master General of
Great Britain', was beaten by a mob when spotted in Chelsea with
two young women. There may, though, have been less enthusiasm
for the Societies' prosecution of other offences.[62] Two reforming
constables were killed while attempting to apprehend offenders. At
the funeral of one of the officers, John Dent, it was claimed that he
had 'often been much abused, beaten, mobbed and wounded; and
in a very great danger of his life in detecting and bringing to justice, the lewd and disorderly persons'. John Disney noted that the
stocks, a form of punishment which attempted to embarrass a
criminal in front of his friends and neighbours, was 'of little or no
effect' in punishing persons who were 'guilty of vice'.[63]

Members of the Societies also complained that the judiciary
were often more a hindrance than a help in prosecuting offenders.
Woodward complained that 'where either the Informer or the
Magistrate fails in his respective Duty, Justice is obstructed, the
Efficacy of the Law null'd, Iniquity cherish'd, and the Wrath of

God provoked'.[64] Yet, he said, some informers had complained that they 'had spent above half [a day] going from the House of one Justice of Peace to another, before they could get a Warrant signed'.[65] Many members of the magistracy complained, however, that the use of unpaid informers was producing all sorts of legal sharp practice. The Middlesex JP Ralph Hartley, an enthusiastic supporter of the Societies' activities – he had even convicted and fined one of his fellow justices for profane swearing at a JP's dinner – was ejected from the commissions of the peace for irregular conduct. The main objection against him was that he had convicted and sentenced offenders without summoning them to appear before him. Magistrates also questioned the powers of constables to arrest persons for 'disorderly conduct' without good grounds. The killers of John Dent in 1709 were convicted of the lesser charge of manslaughter only because, Chief Justice Holt argued, the constable had had no good grounds for arresting them, the three soldiers only being in the company of Anne Dickens, who was labelled a 'nightwalker', disorderly woman and the like. Holt invoked Magna Carta, stating: 'If a man is oppressed by an officer of justice, under a mere pretence of an authority, that is provocation to all the people in England.' He went on: 'I like a religious zeal for reformation very well, but let this zeal be according to knowledge and consistent with the laws of our country, not furious and mistaken. No man ought to think himself so far more righteous than his neighbours as to enter into such voluntary societies for reformation of manners, as contradict our laws and endanger our rights and liberties.'[66]

It is almost impossible to evaluate the success or failure of the Societies in their campaign to reform the nation's morals, given the nature and breadth of the crimes prosecuted. It is also, obviously, rather difficult to ascertain whether society under William and Mary was more or less virtuous than it had been under James II. For contemporaries, however, there was no clearer evidence that God's wrath at the nation's sinfulness had not been assuaged than his taking away of England's blameless Queen. Mary died of small-pox on 28 December 1694. She was thirty-two. The Duke of Newcastle's chaplain had no doubt that her death was a divine judgement upon the kingdom: 'God in his goodness sent us such a princess as was both a patroness and an example of goodness: a glass by which this crooked age might have rectified itself; and seeing he has waited divers years, and found no amendment, what was it but just to take the mirror from us? What should they do with a light who will not walk by it?'[67]

Mary's funeral procession was the largest and most expensive (at a cost of £50,000) held yet for an English monarch. Henry Purcell, who had enjoyed the Queen's patronage, composed a special funeral anthem. William had grown much closer to Mary by the end of her life, risking infection to minister to her on her deathbed. Her passing devastated him. For almost a month the King was inconsolable, Burnet recording that his spirits had 'sunk so entirely that there was great reason to apprehend that he was following her. For some weeks he was so little Master of himself that he was not capable of minding his affaires, nor of seeing any Company. He gave himself much to the meditations of Religion and Prayer.' Burnet himself was crushed by the Queen's passing: 'I never felt my self sink so much under any thing that had happened to me as bey her death . . . for I am afraid that in loosing her, we have lost both our strength and our glory.'[68]

There is little doubt that the King's grief was sincere but he had other, less personal, reasons to mourn Mary's passing. Through her, William had had a link with both Anglicanism and moderate Tory opinion. The Queen had also been generally popular with the public in a way that he had never been. Significantly, Mary's death destroyed the argument that the King enjoyed a 'hereditary right by proxy' to the English throne and, as we will see in the next chapter, made him more vulnerable to Jacobite plotting. Fighting a war in Europe that was going badly and proving increasingly unpopular at home, with Parliament and Church both often hostile to him, William appeared to be at a crisis point as monarch. His solution was to abandon the attempt to govern by a bipartisan administration and rule in cooperation with a 'Junto' of Whig MPs and peers. However, rather than avert catastrophe, the King's decision brought England close to dynastic, military and economic disaster.

9

William Alone

If the overwhelming reaction to Mary's death was widespread public expression of grief, in Bristol there was much revelry on the occasion of the Queen's death as crowds of people celebrated to the refrain of 'The King [James] shall enjoy his own again'.[1] The threat to security potentially posed by a reinvigorated Jacobitism led to a doubling of the guards on the palace of Whitehall in the wake of the Queen's passing.

Sixteen ninety-four represented not only a personal watershed but also a political and military turning point for William. For the remainder of the Nine Years War the King would govern in cooperation with Junto Whigs, abandoning the attempt at a bipartisan administration. In Flanders the fighting turned in the favour of the Grand Alliance of England, the United Provinces of the Netherlands and the Austrian Habsburgs, though both England and France were struggling to continue to pay and supply their armies and navies. In political and religious terms England was more divided than ever and the burden of war almost brought down the government, as a Jacobite assassination attempt was followed by a coinage crisis that practically brought military operations to a halt in the summer of 1696 and threatened serious civil disorder at home. William emerged from this crisis year with his personal reputation not only intact but enhanced. Public subscription to an 'association' to defend his person from Jacobite threats revealed a deep well of popular support for the regime, if little personal affection for William himself. With war on the Continent reaching an effective stalemate, peace was secured in 1697, but the end of war, if anything, exacerbated political divisions, as 'country' politicians argued for a return to 'normality': a much-reduced military establishment, smaller government and lower taxes.

The King again trimmed his sails, at points favouring the Tories, at others the Whigs, depending on which party was most likely to allow him to keep the largest army and, as the truce between England and France broke down over the Spanish succession, which would support war. However, in the face of renewed French aggression and the sudden death of the heir to the throne, the Duke of Gloucester, it was clear that the political nation was committed to maintaining the Protestant succession, though the experience of the 1690s also left Parliament determined to place greater shackles on the monarchy.

The turning point in the Nine Years War came less as a result of victory on the battlefield than as a product of harvest failure in France. By 1694 one French soldier claimed France was suffering 'the severest famine known for many centuries'. The food shortages were so severe that the French army was unable to mount offensive manoeuvres for the whole of the 1694 campaign. The following year brought even better news for the Grand Alliance. In 1695 William's old adversary the Duke of Luxembourg died, depriving Louis of one of his best generals, and William retook the fortified town of Namur after a two month-siege, despite Vauban's reinforcing the garrison to sixteen thousand men. Britain was also enjoying success against the French at sea. In July of that year Russell's navy compelled the French fleet to lift its blockade of Barcelona and sent it scuttling back to its base at Toulon, leaving the western Mediterranean, with Russell's ships overwintering at Cadiz, effectively under English control.

Military success made Parliament more ready to lend money. Equally, the closer alliance that William was forming with the Whig party was mainly intended to help him prosecute his war against Louis more effectively. The Whigs' ideological opposition to French 'popery' and 'absolutism', and their greater connections with mercantile and trading interests, made them stauncher supporters of the conflict in Europe than the Tories. However, this alliance came at the price of William's assent to the Triennial Act of 1694, which ensured regular Parliaments and ushered in a period of feverish electioneering and deeply partisan politics. Between 1689 and 1715 there were twelve general elections: in 1689, 1690, 1695, 1698, 1701 (two), 1702, 1705, 1708, 1710, 1713 and 1715. Each of these saw on average 100 out of 269 seats contested. To modern eyes this may seem a small proportion. However, over that period only nineteen constituencies managed to avoid having contests at all, meaning that in almost every constituency in England the local electorate was at some point asked to decide between rival candidates. Both within and outside Parliament politics was increasingly being governed by loyalty to one or other party. There is strong evidence that after 1695 voting in the Commons was conducted largely along party lines, with only 14 per cent of MPs regularly engaging in cross-party voting, and a similar, if slightly less rigid, pattern was evident in the Lords.

William's decision to align himself with the Whigs for the time being did not make Parliament any more manageable. The strength of the division between Whigs and Tories made it difficult for the court to establish itself as an alternative power base within Parliament, even though the war, through massively increasing the size of the government, had greatly expanded the opportunities for dispensing royal patronage. There were certainly a large number of 'placemen' (men who held government office or enjoyed a royal pension) in the Commons at this time, probably amounting to between 97 and 136 MPs between 1692 and 1698. Yet, though regularly tendered 'place' bills reflected Parliament's concern about the impact of these MPs on legislative independence, very few placemen were prepared to vote consistently with the court across party lines. Indeed, appointment to government office was now more often used as a way for the majority party to reward its followers after an election victory, and was accompanied by purging of political rivals from their positions.

Parliament continued to display its independence of the executive, even if the strength of an identifiable 'country party' had been weakened by the ministerial changes of 1693–4. Between 1691 and 1695 a group of 'country' Whigs, led by Robert Harley and Paul Foley, in cooperation with dissident Tories such as Sir Thomas Clarges and Sir Christopher Musgrave, had formed a significant third force in Parliament, the cross-party ties so formed being helped by collaboration on the Commission of Public Accounts. However, after Mary's death the 'country' position was increasingly identified with Tory interests as the Whigs were brought into government and the Bank of England, essentially a Whig enterprise, was founded, while war in Europe drew its main support from Whigs, for reasons of trade and confessional shared interest. Nonetheless, though this led to a weakening of 'country' opinion, bills against placemen were again tendered in the 1694–5 session and Parliament undertook a series of investigations into government corruption. The Speaker of the House of Commons, Sir John Trevor, was found to have received 1000 guineas from the City of London to help smooth the passage of a Bill for the Relief of London Orphans. On 12 March he was stripped of his office and expelled from the House, and Foley was put in his place. Thomas Osborne, now Duke of Leeds, was implicated in corrupt dealings over the renewal of the East India Company charter and impeached. Though he was not successfully prosecuted, the impeachment effectively brought to an end his political career.

William's alliance with the Junto Whigs also raised religious tensions. For supporters of the Church of England it awakened fears of a return to the policies of James II's reign. The Earl of Sunderland was again involved at the heart of government, though he preferred to have the safety of the role of unofficial adviser rather than accept a titled post that might leave him open to impeachment proceedings. 'The Church Party' worried that the 'oily Earl' was again counselling the crown to further the goal of securing religious toleration by favouring 'fanaticks'. They looked askance at the King's apparent reliance on Scottish Presbyterians like James Johnston, his Scottish Secretary of State, and William Carstares, his chaplain. High Anglican rhetoric adopted a noticeably shriller tone in the mid-1690s, with the slogan 'Church in Danger' a popular rallying cry. William Stephens observed that in the 'sermons Preached at Visitations, and the constant ordinary Discourse of the Clergy . . . the Church of England is always represented'.[2] Debate was further stirred by Francis Atterbury's famous *Letter to a Convocation Man* of 1696, in which he argued that the only way to stem the growth of heresy and blasphemy was through Convocation, the Church's own deliberative and legislative body. Convocation had traditionally sat whenever Parliament had been assembled, but had not met since 1689. The debate revolved around whether Convocation could be summoned only by the King or had to be convened as of right when Parliament sat. The controversy therefore raised questions concerning the autonomy of the Church and the extent of the Crown's ecclesiastical prerogatives. When the Junto ministry finally collapsed in 1700 William was forced to admit into office the Tory Earl of Rochester and his High Church followers, who successfully demanded that Convocation should sit.

The markedly different character of the Williamite episcopate from its Jacobite predecessors also shifted the targets of High Church rhetoric. Before the Revolution the Whigs and the supporters of dissent frequently directed their invective against persecuting 'prelates'. Now, with the dominance in the Church of England of latitudinarian figures such as Tenison and Stillingfleet, it was the 'Convocation men' who attacked the ecclesiastical hierarchy. In 1694 the High Tory journalist Charles Leslie complained that 'we see among the newmade Bishops those who were formerly Fanatical Preachers; and those who, of all our Number, are least Zealous for the Church, and most Latitudinarian, for Comprehension of Dissenters, and a Dispensation with our Liturgy and Discipline'.[3]

Nonetheless, despite the King's governing over a society that was divided both religiously and politically, the internal threats to his regime were limited given the weakness of domestic Jacobitism as a force – a fact reflected in William's readiness to leave the country repeatedly, either to go on campaign or to return to the Netherlands. Jacobite insurrections or assassination attempts had little chance of success without French military assistance. However, the stalemate reached in Flanders encouraged Louis to look again at supporting James in recovering his crown. An invasion force of some sixteen thousand troops would be ready by the spring of 1696 but would be deployed only in coordination with English risings. Even so, the leading English conspirator Sir George Barclay correctly decided that there was not enough popular support to foment a serious rebellion and that consequently an assassination plot was the only realistic way to destabilise the regime. Together with his colleagues in the 'Select Number', the secret Jacobite organisation modelled on the royalist 'Sealed Knot' of the 1650s, Barclay planned to murder William while he was riding in his carriage through Richmond Park.

However, Barclay was betrayed by some of his companions and the plot was discovered. On 24 February 1696 William informed both Houses of Parliament of the attempt upon his life. Three hundred Jacobites were arrested after the plot was revealed, although retribution for the plot was limited, with seven of the plotters executed immediately, a further five sentenced to life imprisonment by Parliament and in January 1697 the execution of Sir John Fenwick (appointed by James to lead the originally planned rebellion) after a failed attempt to implicate Marlborough, Godolphin and Shrewsbury and Russell in Jacobite activity. The involvement of the Duke of Berwick, who had visited London to help organise the plot, implicated James in the scheme. The result was a disaster for James, whose public standing sank to a new low. The diarist John Evelyn recorded that this was a defining moment in William's kingship: 'tho many did formerly pitty K. James's Condition, this designe of Assasination, & bringing over a French Army, did much alienate many of his Friends, & was like to produce a more perfect establishment of K. William'.[4] News of the assassination attempt caused a wave of public sympathy for William and a rapid upswing in his popularity. A correspondent of Lord Hatton wrote that it had 'renewed the affections of the generallite of the people to this King'. Others saw the foiled plot as providing further evidence of God's providential blessing on William. Sir Richard Cocks, a Gloucestershire JP and MP, stated that there had 'been almost as visibly the hand of god in our revolution as was in bringing the Children of Israell out of the Aegyptian thraldom'.[5]

The thwarting of the plot allowed the Whigs to push through a sworn 'association' in defence of the King. According to this, the subscribers were to 'heartily, sincerely, solemnly profess, testify and declare, That his present Majesty, King William, is rightful and lawful King of these Realms'. They promised to assist one another in revenging the King's death should any assassination plot prove successful.[6] Unlike the oaths of allegiance passed in 1689, which were imposed only on the clergy and those in public office, the association was tendered to the public at large.[7] In wording and form the oath harked back to the 1584 Bond of Association, and contemporaries noted the parallel.[8] In the later instance, however, the anxiety caused by the assassination plot was relatively minimal, owing to its early discovery, and it was even rumoured that the whole conspiracy had been fabricated to serve the government's purposes.[9]

The 1696 Association, in the words of one historian, was a 'bitter faction instrument'. It offered a means for court Whigs to cut off a ministerial challenge from Tories, like the Earl of Nottingham, who felt able only to swear to William as de facto monarch and, by imposing the oath nationally, cripple the opposition in England as a whole. (William himself gave no support to the Association as, despite having abandoned the device of a joint ministry, he still refused to tie himself permanently to one party.) Certainly a large number of Tory MPs and peers had considerable problems in swearing to William as a 'rightful and lawful' monarch, rather than simply king 'for the time being'. A total of 113 MPs and more than twenty peers refused to take the oath, though initially there were no penalties for failing to subscribe.[10] By April, though, legislation had made the Association mandatory for office holders. Three Privy Councillors were dismissed for refusing, Nottingham, John Sheffield, Duke of Normanby, and Edward Seymour, Lord Treasurer, in 1692. By the end of July one Lord Lieutenant, eighty-six JPs and 104 Deputy Lieutenants had also been dismissed for failing to subscribe.

In the localities the Association was used to oust the 'disaffected' from public office.[11] Occasionally whole towns deemed politically suspect were left off the Association's returns. In Radnor, Wales, Sir Rowland Gwyn would only allow 'friends' to sign the Association, as a means to help him form a new county committee in opposition to the clients of Sir Robert Harley.[12] In a number of returns the inhabitants promised in future to elect only MPs who had subscribed to the Association and/or were deemed loyal to the present government. In Nottinghamshire subscribers vowed only 'to elect such members, and not other, but those who have before signed the Association made and contrived so loyally and reasonably by the Hon[our]able House of Com[m]ons'.[13] Indeed, in the 1698 election, the electorate generally tended to turn their backs on members who had not signed the 1696 Association.

Aside from being used as an instrument to exclude the 'country' opposition from both central and local government, the Association was also intended to bolster William's title. As has been discussed previously, the death of Queen Mary in 1694 had deprived the King of the argument, which had been popular with Williamite Tories, that he had a hereditary right by proxy to the throne. The notion that the failure of Fenwick's plot demonstrated 'God's signal providence' towards William strengthened the claims of earlier court propaganda that the King, like Elizabeth I, was the divinely appointed deliverer of the nation from popery. A royal proclamation appointed 16 April as a day of national thanksgiving for William's salvation from the Jacobite plot. Published sermons given in response to the proclamation, numbering dozens of titles, hammered home the theme that God's hand could again be seen at work. Nicholas Brady, in a sermon given at St Catherine Cree church in London, stated that God's favour to the nation could be seen not only in the revolution,

> by which our Religion and our Liberties were secured; but also by watching over it in a peculiar manner, and defeating all designs which were devised for its destruction. For, not to look backwards to former deliverances, which are much too numerous to be insisted upon at present, how wonderful a mercy have we lately experienced! If an attempt be made to surprise us unprovided (as in the invasion at this time designed) the Winds and the Weather conspire to keep back our enemies til their intentions are discovered, and their contrivances are laid open. If *Secret Practices are levelled against the Government and Plots* are carried on for imbroiling us again (as in the *Horrid Treason* so freshly discovered) *the Providence of God* interposes for us visibly.[14]

In protecting William, these sermons insisted, God had saved not only England but Europe as a whole: 'Providence therefore appeared signally, in preventing so common a ruine; wherein not a single Nation, though powerful and numerous, but the whole interest of Divers States were concerned; and from which, had it taken effect, many Nations might have dated their misery.'[15] Edward Fowler, the Bishop of Gloucester, called the discovery of the assassination plot a greater divine blessing than the averting of the Gunpowder Plot, as in 1605 only Catholics had been involved but in 1696 Protestants were among the conspirators. A number of ministers stressed that the plot proved the worthlessness of promising allegiance to William only as de facto monarch. William Stephens hoped that 'the Knavish Distinction of De Facto, which was the foundation-stone of the late designed Assassination, Insurrection and Invasion, will be left out of his title'. According to Stephens, the scruples of de factoist Tories about swearing to William as 'rightful and lawful' monarch were no more than a cover for Jacobite political sympathies.[16]

Aside from the sermons' promotion of the Association, the oath returns themselves formed part of the regime's propaganda. Hundreds of printed copies of the text of the Association were made on vellum or parchment, ready to be signed. The returns for some counties were vast: the historian David Cressy estimates that those for Suffolk contained over seventy thousand signatures.[17] Loyal addresses provided the public with an opportunity to demonstrate their fidelity to the King. The officers of the Shropshire militia hoped that 'the gratious providence that hath sav'd you, from so many imminent dangers ever watch over you and preserve you long the impregnable bulwark of our Religion, Lives, Liberties and Properties'.[18] Many of these addresses referred to William as the saviour of the Protestant religion, not only in Britain but also throughout Europe. The signatories to the Lichfield Association described William as 'the defender of our fayth, the deliverer of our Church and Nation, the Preserver of the Reformed Religion and Libertyes of Europe'.[19] Others commented on the threat of invasion from France. The subscribers for Malmesbury in Wiltshire wrote that, by their 'Villanous and detestable conspiracy', Louis XIV and James II had hoped they might 'with more ease and felicity Invade this Kingdom, subvert its Government, plunder its Cities, alter its laws and religion and make it the miserable seat of Warr and Desolution'.[20] The inhabitants of Brackley in Northamptonshire added a humble address to their Association so that the King might know 'that not onely our Persons but alsoe our principles (without which mistaken men tender but a doubtfull Allegiance) are for the support of your government'.[21] An Oxfordshire watchmaker, John Harris, felt that merely signing the Association was an inadequate expression of loyalty and added to his subscription that he did 'ack[n]o[w]ledg[e] and o[w]ne my sovran Lord King William to be Rightfull and Lawfull King of England'.[22] In some areas subscription to the Association was accompanied by great pomp and ceremony. Edward Canby wrote to John Roades in April 1696 with news of subscription at Doncaster, where for 'the honour of my Lord and the credit of our lordship, we marched in with 200 horse . . . It made a great noise in the town so that the streets were filled and windows decked with fair ladies.'[23]

The 1696 Association represented a considerable coup for William and the court Whigs, both in terms of its value as propaganda for the regime and its effectiveness as a political purgative. However, the sheer volume of returns alone cannot be taken to indicate that the whole nation was united in its loyalty to William III. Many subscribed out of fear or self-interest. The Whig leaders of Norfolk told weavers in Norwich that the more zeal they showed for the King, the more support there would be from the court for a bill prohibiting the import of Indian silks.[24] Loyal declarations, while presenting the public with an opportunity to declare its support for the government, also allowed it to make professions of allegiance on terms different from those offered in the Association itself.

The oath was taken in Britain's colonies and by British merchants in Europe, and their declarations reflected the different political relationship with the monarchy. The address from the mainly Catholic-Irish population of Montserrat made no mention of William being rightful and lawful king but hoped only that his survival would allow the colonists to continue to go about their business freely and 'eate our Breade with more safety'.[25]

In Malmesbury the declaration referred to William as 'lawfull and rightfull' king. This may have been simply an accidental inversion of the phrase in the Association itself, but it could also be taken as meaning that William only had a 'right by law' to the throne.[26] The address produced by the officers and sailors of Trinity House, Newcastle upon Tyne, made no reference to the King's legal, providential or hereditary right to the throne and described William only as the 'deliverer of these nations' whom they promised to assist 'against the force and power of France'. There were far more signatures to this loyal declaration than to the text of the Association itself, though the subscribers to the oath claimed they were signing for the rest of Trinity House.[27]

Aside from the ambiguous wording of some of the humble addresses to the King, the Association was also refused by a large number of people and many others would subscribe to it only on equivocal terms. English Catholics very rarely appear as refusers of the Association. Yet, despite the apparent loyalty of English Catholics, the Buckinghamshire militia harried their recusant population with such zeal that Robert Throckmorton, a prominent local Catholic, who had asked to stay at home with his sick wife, she 'havving binn lately lyke to Dye', and had offered profuse expressions of loyalty to the King, was nonetheless placed in custody in London.[28] Quakers, on the other hand, regularly appear as refusers of or equivocators with the Association. Friends are recorded as declining to take it in Brainford in Norfolk, Hoston in Middlesex, Mundon Magna in Herefordshire, Whitechurch near Southampton, Hilsham and Holipstow in Suffolk and

Hawkeshead then in Lancashire.[29] Suffolk Quakers followed the declaration adopted by the London members of the sect on 28 March 1696 which stated that the setting up of 'Kings and Governments' belonged to 'God's peculiar Prerogative' and that they had no part in it but to 'pray for the King and for the safety of the Nation'. Treacherous designs, they said, were the works of 'the Devil and Darkness'. They blessed God and were 'heartily Thankful to the King and Government, for the Liberty and Priviledges we Enjoy under them by law'.[30] The historian Mary Geiter has argued that the Quaker declarations were part of a political bargain, in return for which the government would promote the passing of the Affirmation Bill, allowing Friends (Quakers) to avoid having to swear oaths.[31] If so, William ought to have felt somewhat short-changed. Stripped of its hyperbole, this declaration represents little more than a promise of passive obedience. Given some Friends' previous cooperation with James II's religious policies, and the fact that the Quaker leader William Penn was probably a Jacobite conspirator and had been implicated in the 1696 plot, this was less than reassuring.[32]

By far the most equivocal response to the demand for a show of allegiance to the King came from the Anglican clergy. Parochial ministers figure regularly in county returns as either refusing or placing limitations on the Association. In Bedfordshire several ministers refused to take the oath. Edward Gibson, Vicar of Hawnes in the county, would subscribe only 'as far as by ye laws of God and those of this Realm doe oblige or allow'.[33] Hugh Owen, the vicar of Sevenoaks in Kent, took the Association 'according to my own sense and judgement'.[34] These individual returns, thick with Anglican bromide, might be deemed relatively insignificant were it not for the fact that, with the exception of Beacon in the diocese of St Davids,[35] none of the deans and chapters actually put their names to the text of the Commons' Association. What they signed instead were two variant forms of a loyal address to the King, which significantly diluted the meaning of the original oath.

The first 'Canterbury version' of this address left out the promise to revenge or even punish would-be assassins and was taken by not only the clergy in the diocese of Canterbury, but also those in Shropshire, Rochester, Worcester, Bath and Wells and Lincoln.[36] The 'York version' was identical to that taken at Canterbury except that it described the King as having only a 'Right by Law to the Crowne'[37] and was followed by all the remaining deaneries and archdeaconries that delivered returns with the exception of Exeter cathedral. Here the bishops, dean and chapters acknowledged that William was invested 'with a legall Right and Title'. In Exeter it was even alleged that clergymen were encouraging locals to refuse the oath by putting 'scruples into people's heads' about the words 'rightful and lawful' and 'revenge'.[38]

It is perhaps understandable that the clergy would have had problems with swearing to personally take revenge for the death of the King, but the omission of the word 'revenge' was a consequence of more than just clerical scruples, as returns from some laymen demonstrate. In Norwich, the original association of the corporation used the term 'punish' instead of 'revenge'.[39] Humphrey Prideaux's letters suggested an alternative reason for this unease at the idea of 'revenging' William's death. He was concerned that those carrying out any post-assassination vengeance 'would draw their swords and cut the throats of all the Jacobites' and that 'Jacobite' might be interpreted by these vigilantes to mean all 'whom the rabble shall think fit to plunder and abuse'.[40] Tory clerics (and perhaps Tory politicians) who scrupled at acknowledging that William had anything other than a legal claim to the throne would, Prideaux suspected, be among the first to suffer reprisals.[41]

In terms of the sheer volume of signatures, the Association of 1696 seemed to represent a massive public vote of support for William. Yet, when examined more closely, the loyalty being offered to the King seems in some instances highly equivocal. Even those who did offer their allegiance without any qualification did so in many cases on the basis of what William was deemed to represent or defend, rather than out of any sense of personal loyalty to the King. William of Orange was to be supported because he protected parliamentary government and Protestantism, not because of any legal or hereditary claim to the throne or a deep sense of public affection. For his part, though, William felt secure enough to leave the country in May 1696 to go on campaign. The summer saw a number of military advances for the French. Peace with Savoy allowed Louis to concentrate military efforts on Spain, the Spanish Netherlands and the Rhineland, with the result that he seized Ath and Alost in the Spanish Netherlands and captured Barcelona in August. Despite these gains, there had been no military action of great consequence since William's retaking of Namur and both sides were now looking to sue for peace.

Although the end result of the Jacobite plot of 1696 had been a resurgence of support for William, as the Axminster Congregational church recorded,

> the Lord was distressing this nation by other means. The coin of the nation being spoiled, there was a great want of current money; besides there was a considerable price on corn and other provisions for the outward man. Likewise the Lord was breaking men in their earthly trades and interest, bringing the nation low, giving it up into the hands of spoilers. The Lord was emptying the nation, making it waste . . . As with the servant so with the master, as with the buyer so with the seller – men earn[t] wages and put it into a bag with holes, look[ed] for much and it came to little.[42]

Coin-clipping had been around as an organised criminal activity since the 1670s. Criminals took rimless pre-Restoration silver coins and sheared off their edges, selling on the clipped metal to unscrupulous goldsmiths. This activity was given a massive boost by the need for silver bullion to pay for the English army's supplies in Flanders. Indeed, without this illicit activity it is likely that there would not have been enough bullion to meet the army's needs, given the decline in trade. So, in the words of one historian, 'England's war effort had come to depend in large measure upon organised crime'.[43] Yet this activity also debased the coinage, with some coins losing 40–50 per cent of their original metal content. With public confidence in the clipped money waning, a recoinage was deemed necessary and in January 1696 Parliament passed legislation providing for the progressive demonetisation of the clipped coin and its melting down and recoining by the Mint. On 4 May 1696 the clipped coin was accepted in payment of tax for the last time, triggering a financial crisis as the circulation of money virtually ceased; some hoarded old clipped coins in anticipation of sterling devaluation, others refused to accept either clipped or unclipped coins.

In south-east Wales the JP Charles Price complained that many people were in 'A great Consternation About the Money, not being able to Have any Commoditys for it, tho much of it to my apprehension being good money.'[44] The Tory former licenser of the press, Edmund Bohun, now a Suffolk JP, reported from Ipswich in July 1696 that the picture looked bleak, 'no trade is Managed but by trust . . . Our tenants pay no rent, our Corne factors can pay nothing for what they had and will trade no more so that all is at a stand; and the People are discontented to the utmost. Many self Murders [suicides] happen in sevrall families for want and all things look very black and should the least accident put the Mobb in motion no man can tell where it would end.'[45] In the north of England the problems caused by the recoinage did lead to unrest. There were disturbances in Kendal in Lancashire, where magistrates struggled to restrain a crowd of rowdy and drunken alehouse keepers, finally resorting to placating them with more drink. However, in the aftermath of the assassination plot it was noted that most anger was directed at the King's ministers rather than the King himself. Hugh Todd noted that in Newcastle the 'Rabble spoke dutifully of his Majesty, but were very seditious in their

Expressions toward the Ministers of State & their Representatives'.[46] In Lincolnshire Abraham de la Pryne recorded that in
June

> the country people has been up at Stamford, and marched in a
> great company, very lively, to the house of S[i]r John Brownley.
> They brought their officers, constables, and churchwardens
> amongst thm, and as they went along they cryd 'God bless King
> William, God bless K[ing] W[illiam]' etc. When they were come
> to S[i]r John's he sent his man down to see what their will was,
> who all answered – 'God bless K[ing] W[illiam], God bless the
> Church of England, God bless the Parliament, and the Lords
> Justices and S[i]r John Brownley! We are King William's true ser-
> vants, God forbid that we should rebel against him, or that
> anything that we now do should be construed ill We come only to
> his worship to besieech him to be mercifull to the poor, we and our
> familys being all fit to starve, not having one penny ith' the world
> that will go' etc. S[i]r Jo[hn] hearing all this (as soon as his man) at
> a window where he was viewing them, sent them a bagg with fif-
> teen pound in it of old mill'd [unclipped] money, which they
> received exceedingly thankfully, but sayd the sum was so little, and
> number and necessitys so great, that they feared it would not last
> long, therefore must be forced out of meer necessity to come to see
> him again, to keep themselves and their families from starving.
> Then they desired a drink, and S[i]r Jo[hn] caused his doors to be
> set open and let them go to the cellar, where they drunk God bless
> King William, the Church of England, and all the loyal healths
> they could think on, and so went their ways.[47]

Although these problems did not lead to social revolution or
even rebellion, they had a serious impact on the government's war
machine. The coinage crisis brought English military operations
almost to a standstill in the summer of 1696. In July the country's
fiscal problems forced the Bank of England to renege upon its

commitment to its Continental creditors, leaving the army pay-master in Flanders penniless. With its credit in tatters, William's government had to rely on loans from the Dutch to keep it afloat.

The Nine Years War had been a conflict of attrition from the beginning and by 1697 a financially and materially depleted France and England were both ready to agree peace terms. In September 1697, after four months of negotiations, hostilities were officially brought to an end by the Treaty of Ryswick. The major political gain for William was that Louis acknowledged him as king of Great Britain *par la grace de Dieu* and promised not to assist anyone either directly or indirectly who might trouble him in the possession of his kingdoms. Jacobitism in England, heavily dependent on Louis's military support, was thereby dealt a serious blow. In territorial terms, France kept Strasbourg but restored William's princely lands in Orange to the boundaries of 1678. Though militarily the war had been a bloody and expensive stale-mate, the peace appeared distinctly to William's credit. French territorial ambitions had been checked and his title to the British throne had been publicly recognised. The end of war was cele-brated in England by a great firework display held in St James's Square on December 1697 but the pyrotechnics got out of control and several spectators were killed.

The noisy, bloody chaos of the peace celebrations proved omi-nous. In England peace raised rather than eased political tensions. Between the winter of 1696 and the summer of 1697 the Whig character of the ministry had become more pronounced with the resignation of the Tory Godolphin in October 1696 and the advancement of Somers to Lord Chancellor, Montague to first Lord of the Treasury and James Vernon to Secretary of State in 1697. The Junto Lords, Somers, Russell, Wharton, Montagu and Sunderland, held regular meetings to agree policy. Overall, the impact of the assassination plot had been to see a closing of Whig ranks in Parliament against the Tories, who had now been suc-cessfully tainted by Jacobitism.

Nonetheless, peace presented William with the problem that he wished to retain a large standing army, correctly seeing the treaty secured at Ryswick as little more than a temporary truce, particularly given the unresolved issue of the Spanish succession. In his opening speech to Parliament on 3 December 1697 he said that England could not be 'safe' without a significant permanent military presence (in William's estimation a force of about thirty-five thousand). Many in Parliament, however, associated large standing armies with the threat of royal absolutism and the reign of James II. Aside from their association with tyranny, large permanent military establishments were costly and MPs were eager to see a reduction in the heavy burden of taxation on their constituencies. However, this was problematic as the crown's indebtedness meant that heavy taxation was necessary just to pay off the national debt, let alone to meet the costs of a standing army. William had to accept large reductions in the size of his peacetime force, as Robert Harley succeeded in getting through a vote in the Commons to cut it down to ten thousand troops (though in the end a lack of funds prevented full disbanding and the army was actually kept at sixteen thousand men).

The defeat over the army was one sign of a growing loss of control over Parliament, in part caused by the slow disintegration of the Whig ministry. Sunderland resigned his office in December 1697 (he had finally been appointed to a named post, as Lord Chamberlain, in April of that year), to avoid anticipated impeachment proceedings being instigated in the Commons (MPs had attacked Sunderland, viewing him as a key advocate of keeping a large standing army, one describing him as 'a man who was the standard bearer of despotism in the last two reigns').[48] Another of the King's ministers, the Earl of Shrewsbury, was incapacitated by illness. William was also frustrated at his ministers' failure to fully support his aim of retaining a large standing army, rejecting compromise proposals which would have left him with a force of fifteen thousand soldiers. Meanwhile the King complained to

Anthonie Heinsius in Holland that Parliament was 'now engaged in private animosities and party quarrels, and thinks very little of public affairs. God knows when this session will terminate.'[49] The King left the country for Holland on 7 July, not returning until five months later, and thereby taking no part on behalf of the Whigs in the general election of that year.

When he returned the new Parliament again turned its attention to the problem of standing armies. The Commons, incensed that the King had attempted to dupe the House by losing higher than agreed numbers of English troops in the figures for the Irish establishment and officer corps, would support a force of no more than seven thousand, none of them foreigners, meaning that the King's prized Dutch guards would have to be disbanded. William was infuriated by the Commons' actions and by his ministers' continued attempts to get him to compromise by suggesting that he argue for retaining a force of ten thousand. He even spoke of abdication, telling Somers on 29 December that he intended to leave England given that the nation he had saved from popery still viewed him with jealousy and distrust. Somers managed to talk the King out of this course of action and on 1 February 1699 William gave his grudging assent to the Disbanding Bill, but only after having told the Commons that in doing so he left the nation 'too much exposed'.

The breach with his Junto ministers which had developed as a result of the debate over standing armies was not repaired. William had sided with the Whigs, viewing them as the most committed party to furthering his struggle with Louis XIV. Constant talk of compromise with the House, however practical, led the King to see his ministers as lacking resolve in this matter. He accepted without demur the resignation of a number of ministers now fearful of Commons' impeachment proceedings. There were further signs of assaults on William's government: the Admiralty commission was censured, another 'place' bill was framed, Parliament expelled a number of office holders from the Commons and considered again the King's actions in disposing of confiscated Irish estates to his supporters. The failure of Somers to stop these Commons investigations led William to dismiss him on 27 April 1700. (Somers had already been smeared with promoting piracy as a result of the commission that he, Shrewsbury and Orford had been involved in granting to the notorious Captain Kidd, ostensibly for protecting East India Company shipping from Indian Ocean pirates.)[50] William was still feeling isolated, increasingly an outsider in his own kingdom. He felt keenly the loss of his Dutch guards, and the retirement of the Earl of Portland, upset at Keppel's growing influence, was a further blow. The loss of his principal Dutch adviser was compounded by a Commons bill passed on 10 April 1699 which stated that no foreigners should serve on the King's councils.

With Whigs discredited in his eyes, William reluctantly turned to the Tories, though he held 'country' figures like Robert Harley largely responsible for the disbanding of his forces. Nonetheless, Harley had impressed the King with his handling of supply through the Commons and William appears to have been brought round to the idea that, pragmatically, a Tory administration, if less committed to his European objectives, might be more effective in managing Parliament. Three Tory peers, the Earl of Jersey, the Earl of Pembroke and Viscount Lonsdale, had already been brought into the ministry. Tory confidence was further boosted by the fact that at this point the political future appeared to belong to them. William was an heirless widower and would be succeeded by the Duke of Gloucester, the Tory Princess Anne's son. The prospects looked favourable for a long period in the political ascendancy under a succession of Tory monarchs.

This situation was dramatically changed by the death of the Duke of Gloucester in July 1700 while William was out of the kingdom on another visit to the Netherlands. Robert Harley recounted the sudden death of the heir to the throne: 'The Duke of Gloucester danc'd on his [eleventh] birth day, was ill the next, fryday Dr Harnes orderd him to be let blood, & blister'd, he had some spots, had eat fruit, small pox was suspected, he had looseness al the time, dyed this morning at one a clock.'[51] The issue of the succession was at once again thrown wide open, a situation made more uncertain by the apparent revival of Louis XIV's dynastic and territorial ambitions. The death of Carlos II of Spain in October 1700 left Louis's second grandson, Philip of Anjou, the sole inheritor of his lands. The will was accepted by the French king, though this was a breach of the second partition treaty that Louis had signed with William, by which he had agreed to give Spain's empire (with the exception of its Italian possessions) to the Austrian emperor's second son. William attempted to broker a compromise in which Philip would take Spain and her American possessions, while the Austrian Habsburgs would gain the Spanish territories in Italy: effectively a reversal of the second partition treaty. However, Louis proved intransigent and the prospect of Britain becoming involved in another European war seemed likely.

On his return to England William continued to move towards the Tories and appointed Godolphin and Rochester to the government in December 1700 and promised Harley his support in the MP's campaign for speakership of the Commons. To secure a greater number of supporters for the ministry, fresh elections were held in January and February 1701 which witnessed, according to John Evelyn, 'extraordinary strivings among the Candidats' but resulted in no clear majority for either party.[52] However, the new ministry did succeed in May 1701 in steering through Parliament the Act of Settlement, which secured the Protestant succession by declaring that the crown would pass to the Lutheran heirs of electress Sophia of Hanover. The Act passed without a single division on a vote, reflecting near unanimity in Parliament over not only the dangers from readmitting the Catholic Stuarts to the succession but also the threat posed by the crown's being in the hands of another Protestant foreigner. The terms of the Act of Settlement put heavy limitations on the powers of the Hanoverian monarchs:

non-native-born kings would not be able to wage war without the consent of Parliament and would not be allowed to leave the British Isles without parliamentary consent (reflecting unhappiness at William's frequent absences); and foreigners were prohibited from sitting on the Privy Council or in Parliament, holding crown office or receiving crown lands, irrespective of whether or not they were naturalised. All monarchs were obliged to 'join in communion with the church of England as by law established'.

However, this success did not ensure the longevity of William's new alliance with the Tories. In February French troops had occupied the Dutch barrier fortresses in the Spanish Netherlands and Continental conflict appeared inevitable. Yet, rather than make preparations for war, the Commons concentrated on attempting to impeach members of the Whig Junto. Kentish freeholders, who had submitted a petition to the lower house calling for them to supply the King with funds so that he could provide for the security of the nation, were committed to prison. The parliamentary session ended on 24 June 1701 and William spent the summer and early autumn in the United Provinces. In September of that year James II died and Louis explicitly broke the terms of the Treaty of Ryswick by recognising his son James Francis Edward as James III. French aggression allowed William to overcome initial European reluctance and form on 6 September the second Grand Alliance between Britain, the United Provinces of the Netherlands and Austria against Louis XIV. The behaviour of the Commons in the last session, the imminence of war and the advice of Sunderland, still pulling strings behind the scenes, convinced William to turn once more to the Whigs. Elections were called the week after his return. They did not secure the Whigs an overall majority, but the House did vote money for the war and passed a bill requiring office holders to abjure the title of the Stuart Pretender.

The political fluctuations of William's last years appear bewildering, but they reflected the King's overriding concern with defeating Louis XIV in Europe. William chose whichever combination of English politicians appeared best able at a particular time to secure funds from Parliament for his army and navy. Although he had abandoned early in his reign the attempt to govern via a joint ministry, he remained fundamentally unwedded to one particular party. For him the Tories were too tainted with Jacobitism and too strident in their defence of Anglicanism to be fully trusted. Equally, the radical wing of the Whigs led William to view the party as a whole as suspiciously attached to republican principles. His lack of trust in either party was mirrored in a similarly detached attitude towards William among both the general public and Parliament. At key moments of crisis, such as the 1696 assassination plot, in the wake of the Duke of Gloucester's death and finally, in 1702, with the renewed threat of French invasion, the nation united around its King. However, while these moments of national unity reflected a public belief in William's ability to defend the country from the threat of popery and French absolutism, they did not reflect the same level of public affection that the King's wife, Mary, had enjoyed. William remained, in the eyes of the people, a foreigner, and in 1701, at the same time as the nation rallied to the defence of the Protestant succession, they placed further shackles on the freedom of action of future, non-native-born British heads of state.

THE END OF THE LINE

King William's friends say he did all that he could for us, and they are not his enemies who say, he did not all that the necessities of our nation required to be done for us. That Prince left us in a morning strangely overcast with clouds. Our deliverance was not more amazing, than the unaccountable stop put to the success of it.

AMBROSE BARNES[1]

William and Mary (1689–1702)
Par-li-a-ment made Will-i-am and Ma-ry joint King and Queen.
For a time all went well
Ma-ry won all hearts by her bright ways, but Will-i-am was stern
   and rough.

THE HISTORY OF ENGLAND MOSTLY
IN WORDS OF ONE SYLLABLE (LONDON, 1869)
[A VICTORIAN CHILDREN'S
HISTORY PRIMER]

While William was riding in Hyde Park on 21 February 1702, his horse tripped over a molehill, throwing the King to the ground and breaking his collarbone. Afterwards it became popular with Jacobites to toast 'the little gentleman in black velvet' who had succeeded where invasion attempts and assassination plots had failed. However, the King's riding accident did not immediately look life-threatening and for the next fortnight he appeared to be making a good recovery, but on 5 March 1702 he collapsed while walking in the gallery of Kensington House. His condition deteriorated rapidly and by the 7th the King was convinced that he was dying. Attended by Archbishop Tenison, Gilbert Burnet and his closest friends, Keppel and Bentinck, William died on the morning of 8 March 1702. The true cause of death was pulmonary fever, possibly brought on by the accident and aggravated by William's long-term respiratory problems. The King was buried in a private ceremony at Westminster Abbey on 12 April. Significantly, plans laid by the Privy Council for monuments to him in the Abbey and in other public places were never brought into effect.

In Britain the succession passed smoothly to Queen Anne, while in the Netherlands William was thwarted in his hope that his cousin, John William Frisco, would inherit the position of Stadtholder, as republicans blocked his accession and kept the office vacant. In contrast to the public reaction to Mary's death, deep mourning for the King's passing was rare. At Worcester there were 'few mourners', at Bath 'so short a sorrow' and in Buckinghamshire 'severall expressions of Joy publickely spock'.[2] Despite William's many military, political and constitutional successes, in Britain he has not been much better or more fondly remembered by subsequent generations. In nineteenth- and twentieth-century schoolbooks he was portrayed as miserable, ugly, stand-offish and above all, foreign. A School History of England (1901) stated that William was 'never popular in England. His cold and formal manner, his affection for his old Dutch friends, and above all, his love for Holland, his own country, together', it claimed incorrectly, 'with his slight knowledge of English, made men look on him as a foreigner.'[3] Warner and Marten's *Groundwork of British History* described William as 'diminutive in stature, thin and fragile-looking, his appearance was only redeemed by the brightness and keenness of his eyes. His manner was cold and repellent, and his habits unsociable; and the few friends he possessed were all Dutchmen. Moreover, his health was wretched, and inclined to make him irascible and peevish.'[4] To employ the idiom of Sellar and Yeatman's classic *1066 and All That*, William III was a 'good thing' but a 'bad king'.

Whig historians such as Edmund Burke, Lord Macaulay and G. M. Trevelyan wished to present the Revolution of 1688 as an essentially English affair, fundamentally effected by native politicians. The fact that the nation had to be rescued from popery and arbitrary government by the military intervention of another European head of state did not sit easily with a teleological story of national political self-determination. As Trevelyan remarked, there was 'indeed a certain ignominy in the fact that that a foreign fleet and army, however friendly and however welcome, had been required to enable Englishmen to recover the liberties they had muddled away in their frantic faction feuds'.[5] Recent historiography, though correcting this picture in stressing the importance of the Dutch role in events, has done little to resurrect a positive image of the Revolution in, conversely, viewing the events of 1688 and after as little more than a dynastic power grab.[6]

The problems encountered in commemorating William's death reflected wider difficulties in celebrating the Revolution itself. In the early Hanoverian period a number of equestrian statues of William were commissioned (possibly because the first two Georges were even less charismatic than the Dutch king). One still stands in Queen's Square in Bristol and another can be seen outside Kensington Palace. Equestrian statues were also raised by public subscription in Petersfield in Hampshire and in Glasgow. A life-size statue of William was commissioned by the Bank of England in 1732 to mark the opening of its first purpose-built offices, in Threadneedle Street. However, these statues themselves became points of contention, particularly as a result of the lionisation of William by Ulster Protestants. A statue of the King erected on College Green in Dublin and unveiled on 1 July 1701, in celebration of his victory at the Boyne, was routinely bedecked with Orange ribbons, with Protestants often accompanying this with a rifle salute across the memorial. The city's Catholic population exacted its revenge on the statue, stealing William's sword and baton, and in 1805 covering the whole edifice with thick black grease. After repeated attempts by nationalists to blow it up, the statue was eventually removed. Even in England the linkage between William and Ulster Protestantism made the celebration of this King's life more difficult than in the case of other monarchs. In commemoration of William's landing there, a foundation stone for a statue of the King was laid in Brixham in Devon on 5 November 1888. The Dutch royal family contributed £100 to the cost, and the Dutch ambassador, Count de Bylandt, performed the ceremony of laying the stone. At the celebratory dinner after the event Bylandt stated that the current Dutch king hoped that the statue 'would tend more to cement and strengthen the historical and traditional feelings of friendship and sympathy between the two nations'. The ambassador went on to discuss the importance, from a Dutch perspective, of English assistance in the struggle against Louis XIV. Among William's 'many great deeds' during his 'too short reign' might also be included 'the Battle of the Boyne; but he feared that that would be treading just now on delicate ground, and he believed that foreign representatives had to abstain in the countries where they resided from touching upon questions of home politics which they must only watch with respectful interest'.[7]

If, owing to his essential 'foreignness' and the linkage of the Orange cause with the Irish Troubles, William has been denied a cherished place in the national memory, his Catholic Stuart rivals have fared rather better in the popular consciousness. After the naval defeat at La Hogue, James had largely abandoned the notion of personally regaining his kingdoms, instead choosing an existence of quasi-monastic retreat at St Germain (though there, as throughout his life, he could never quite shake off the temptations of the flesh and continued to keep several mistresses). The former King viewed the setbacks of 1691, 1692 and 1696 as divine judgements for his 'almost perpetuall course of sin'.[8] Towards the end of the 1690s his health visibly declined, one commentator in 1698 describing his appearance as 'lean and shrivelled'. He endured a stroke in 1701 which paralysed his right side and he became subject to frequent fainting fits. He suffered a final fit on 22 August of that year. After his death on 5 September James's body, as befitted a man now, ironically, whispered of as a suitable candidate for sainthood, was dismembered and his parts sent to various Catholic churches (his brain went to Paris, his heart to a nunnery at nearby Chaillot).

However, though, by the end of his life, James may have given up on recovering the British crown himself, his son, James Francis Edward Stuart (the 'Old Pretender', recognised on his father's death as James III by Louis XIV) and grandson, Charles Edward Stuart, 'Bonnie Prince Charlie', headed serious Jacobite rebellions in 1715 and 1745 respectively. These uprisings, and the strength of Jacobite feeling throughout the eighteenth century revealed the shaky foundations upon which the Hanoverian monarchy in England rested. Some groups were never able to reconcile themselves fully to the Revolution for conscientious and/or ideological reasons. Although, as the Williamite regime became more established, a number of non-jurors conformed and took the oaths to the new monarch(s), others, such as Charles Leslie and Luke Milbourne, continued to produce masses of pamphlet literature attacking the legitimacy of the Revolutionary regime. Some non-jurors conformed only after decades of soul-searching. William

Higden, rector of Shadwell and prebend of St Paul's, took the oath to Queen Anne in 1708 after years of debating with himself and others his original decision to refuse giving allegiance to William and Mary.[9]

On the opposing side of the political and religious spectrum, for radical dissenters and republicans and commonwealthsmen, the Revolution had clearly failed to fulfil its promise either to instigate national reformation or to effectively safeguard the liberties of the subject and limit the powers of the crown. Most threatening of all to the post-Revolutionary regime were those who continued to regard the exiled Stuarts as the legitimate ruling dynasty. A significant number of Tory MPs were active Jacobites, while many others continued to have divided loyalties.

By the time Queen Anne ascended to the throne she was already a very sick woman. Her seventeen pregnancies had seen only five children born alive, with the remainder either miscarried or stillborn. The death of her only surviving child, the Duke of Gloucester, in 1700, left the Queen seriously weakened both physically and mentally. By the 1690s she was seriously affected by rheumatism, obesity and gout and by the new century could barely walk unaided. Not without reason did Sellar and Yeatman commemorate her as 'the memorable dead queen, Anne'. Her physical status as an invalid, unable to produce healthy Protestant Stuart heirs, encouraged the pursuit of the restoration of her half-brother to his rightful throne, by either peaceful or violent means. A Jacobite invasion attempt was launched in 1707 which was intended to exploit dissatisfaction with the union with England. The expedition, however, turned into a fiasco as James Francis's departure for Scotland was delayed for a week by a bout of measles, giving English and Dutch spies time to alert the authorities in Britain. The French fleet itself, commanded by a man with no faith in the success of the mission, missed the entrance to the Forth by some distance and sailed home without landing troops.

In the early years of her reign and later, during the negotiations between 1711 and 1713 to end the War of Spanish Succession, English politicians made overtures to the exiled court at St Germain, offering the tempting prospect of inheriting the British crown in return for James Francis's conversion to Protestantism. The sincerity of these promises is debatable, and Robert Harley, Earl of Oxford, may well have made them simply to play along Tory-Jacobites while preventing military preparations being made by the exiled court in anticipation of Anne's death. Moreover, the 'Old Pretender', like his father, never thought England 'worth a mass', and refused this expedient. Queen Anne herself, driven by the same ambition and self-belief which had permitted her to betray her father, was less malleable than her poor health indicated. She resisted the efforts of her former favourite, Sarah, Duchess of Marlborough, to exclude the Tories from office. The dispute between the two formerly close friends became increasingly bitter. Sarah promoted rumours circulating at court that the Queen was engaged in a lesbian relationship with one of her servants, Abigail Hill, who was also Sarah's first cousin. The breach between the two widened as the decade progressed, and only the importance of the Duke of Marlborough as a commander kept the Queen and the Duchess on speaking terms. Anne and Sarah's last meeting came on 6 April 1710. When the Queen refused to respond to any of the Duchess's questions, Sarah left, telling Anne that 'God would punish her, either in this world or in the next, for what she had done to her this day'.[10] Her 'liberation' from Sarah's 'tyranny', according to some contemporaries, made the Queen even more intractable. Jonathan Swift remarked that 'after the usuall Mistake of those who think that they have often been imposed on', the Queen 'became so very suspicious that She overshot the mark and ered in the other Extream'.[11]

Towards the end of Anne's reign the threat of Jacobite insurrection appeared to have dissipated. English Jacobites under the last Stuart Queen, many of whom were Protestants, had faced a difficult political choice between acquiescing in the rule of the

Anglican Anne, an Englishwoman born and bred, or chancing everything on supporting the cause of a Catholic Prince who had spent virtually all of his life in the France of the absolutist monarch *par excellence*, Louis XIV. The Treaty of Utrecht, which ended the War of Spanish Succession, forced the Catholic Stuarts to leave France. However, there remained a strong well of support for the 'Old Pretender', with around eighty Tory MPs elected to Anne's last Parliament being convinced Jacobites. Pressure over the issue of the succession was further exerted by the House of Hanover itself, which in April 1714 formally requested that Prince George be admitted to Parliament under his English title of Duke of Cambridge.

Anne fell seriously ill on 30 July. Most saw that she would not recover, and the Privy Council quickly put security measures in place, seizing Catholic arms, closing ports, moving troops to London and bringing the representatives of the House of Hanover into the government's discussions. The Queen died on 1 August, aged forty-nine. The Privy Council breathed a sigh of relief as there was no active attempt to resist the implementation of the Act of Settlement or dispute the proclamation of George as the new monarch. As a contemporary remarked, 'All the nobility attended the proclamation, and there was not the least disturbance, The Parliament met, and the Lords and commons took the oaths. Thank God everything is quiet.'[12]

The initial peace surrounding the accession of George I was shattered first by the vindictiveness of the Whig party, newly restored to government by the elections to the new King's first Parliament. Former ministers such as Oxford, Bolingbroke and Ormonde, who were suspected of Jacobite intrigues during the peace negotiations, were lined up for impeachment. Oxford stayed to face down his accusers and was released from the Tower because not enough evidence could be gathered against him. Bolingbroke and Ormonde, however, fled to the continent and with the Pretender and his half-brother, James Fitzjames, Duke of Berwick, began to plot a Jacobite insurrection in England and Scotland. The exiled court was encouraged by news of rioting in thirty towns in southern and western England, which, it was said by some, had been raised to 'try the affections of the people and discover the pretenders fire'.[13] Their plans were cut down by the death of Louis XIV and the establishment of a regency under the government of Philippe, Duc d'Orléans. The regent refused to countenance giving any aid to the conspirators, aware that the fortunes of the French Bourbon dynasty hung by a thread (three of Louis XIV's heirs had died in quick succession, leaving only the sickly two-year-old child king Louis XV as a barrier against the Spanish monarch, Charles V, inheriting the throne). Without foreign aid or a popular uprising, a Jacobite rebellion was unlikely to succeed. The English conspirators were thrown into further confusion by the independent decision of the Earl of Mar to declare for the Pretender at Braemar on 6 September 1715. Though this caught the Hanoverian government unawares, stringent security measures had already been put in place as a result of anxieties over George's succession, leaving English Jacobites effectively powerless. The Pretender admitted in September that his dynastic ambitions had 'a very melancholy prospect'.[14] Ormonde's attempt to land in the West Country, that favoured site for rebellious amphibious expeditions, was thwarted by customs officers. A small rising in Northumberland did manage to link with Scottish forces under the Earl of Mar, but this tiny army surrendered unconditionally to government troops at Preston on 13 November, signalling the end of the ''15' in England. The rebellion sputtered on in Scotland, with an inconclusive battle being fought at Sherrifmuir on the same day as the engagement at Preston. False reporting of this skirmish as a crushing Jacobite victory encouraged James Francis to leave France, and he landed at Peterhead on 22 December 1715. A Jacobite Privy Council was formed incorporating Mar and some of his followers, and the Pretender moved south with his entourage as far as Perth, where one observer recorded a very negative description of the would-be James III and VIII, reporting him to be 'a tall lean blak man, loukes half dead alredy, very thine, long faced, and very ill cullored and melancholy'.[15] Establishing the semblance of a royal court there, James Francis was already convinced of the hopelessness of the military situation and this gloomy outlook did not help to inspire support from those around him. The news of the surprise advance of a government force towards Perth at the end of January 1716 convinced the Pretender that it was now time to flee. On 3 February, giving no warning to his Jacobite commanders, James Francis boarded a waiting French vessel and left Scotland.

James Francis's humiliating flight to France not only permanently discredited him in the eyes of English and Scottish Jacobites but also seriously weakened the Tory party politically. The complicity of some Tory politicians in the rebellion allowed Walpole and his allies to tar the whole party with the same brush. Combined with the preference of the new king for the Whig party, the linkage between the Tories and the Jacobites allowed Walpole to get through the Septennial Act of 1716. This act extended the life of Parliaments from three to seven years, providing greater opportunities for the Whigs to increase their control of the executive through government patronage. By 1717 pressure exerted on France had forced James Francis first to seek refuge in the papal enclave of Avignon and finally to relocate the Jacobite court to Rome. Further Jacobite plots hatched in 1719 and 1722 proved stillborn.

By the 1730s the 'Old Pretender' had abandoned any hope of personally leading a Jacobite rebellion to recover Britain for the Stuart dynasty. Instead, he passed the baton of military leadership to the 'Young Pretender', his son, Charles Edward Stuart, the charismatic 'Bonnie Prince Charlie'. In the early 1740s Charles Edward began to cultivate his image as a serious pretender, adopting Highland dress to appeal to the main remaining base of Jacobite support, the Highlands and islands of Scotland. In the winter of 1743 a French invasion attempt of England was being planned which, if it were to prove successful, would see the subsequent installation of Charles as regent. The Young Pretender made his way to Paris, narrowly evading capture by the Royal Navy en route, in anticipation of this scheme being put into effect. He arrived there on 8 February 1744, only for Louis XV to pour cold water on the plan once it became clear that British intelligence had been tipped off (possibly as a result of Charles's departure from Italy). The invasion attempt was formally called off on 11 March, much to the anger of Charles Edward, who decided to attempt to force the French to come to his assistance by making an independent landing in Scotland. Raising loans with the help of his father, the Young Pretender was able to amass a considerable cache of weapons, and on 22 June 1745 he set sail from Nantes aboard the frigate *Du Teillay* to rendezvous with the man-of-war *Elizabeth*. However, the *Elizabeth* was badly damaged in an encounter with the Royal Navy and was forced to return to France with most of the Jacobites' weapons and supplies on board. In spite of the loss of this ship, Charles decided to press on towards Scotland and landed at Ericksay on 23 July.

It was not until late August that Charles was able to amass an army of any considerable size, but rather than wait to gather more troops, it was decided that this force would march south as soon as possible to prevent giving the Hanoverian government time to mount an effective military response. By 15 September the Jacobites had reached Edinburgh and by the 17th, after the city's negotiators with the army had left the gates open (perhaps deliberately), the Scottish capital was theirs. Although Charles's propaganda adopted a pro-Scots, anti-union tone and his public image stressed the Stuart dynasty's Scottish roots, the Young Pretender was aware that the military strength of the Hanoverian state made any plan of simply remaining in Scotland unfeasible, particularly as the government was already recalling troops from Europe to combat the Jacobite invasion. Charles managed to secure an agreement to continue the march south towards London, though by only one vote.

With the English militia in disarray and hastily raised volunteer defence forces proving a wholly inadequate substitute, the Jacobites made rapid progress. Carlisle was taken on 15 November, Manchester on the 23rd and Preston on the 26th. By 4 December they had reached Derby. At this point, however, anxiety set in among the Young Pretender's mainly Scottish supporters. The Jacobites did not know that London was poorly defended by an army of only two thousand regular troops, or that the French had begun, as the Prince had hoped, to form an invasion fleet to come to his assistance, nominally headed by Charles Edward's brother, Henry Benedict. Charles could provide his supporters with no firm evidence that either French support or an English Jacobite uprising was in the offing. Against the Prince's wishes, it was decided that the army would retreat to Scotland, and on 6 December they turned north again. His hopes thwarted, Charles sank into depression and drink, leaving the task of marshalling his army's retreat to his general, Lord George Murray. Murray's advice, exaggerating the scale of desertion from the army, led the Jacobite forces to fall back to their Highland strongholds on reaching Scotland.

To defend the last major city, Aberdeen, that the rebels held, the Jacobites fought a pitched battle against the troops commanded by George II's son, the Duke of Cumberland (later known as 'the Butcher' for his brutal suppression of the rebels) on 16 April 1746. The Duke's troops outnumbered the Jacobites almost two to one and were more heavily armed. The Jacobites sustained a massive artillery assault for ten to fifteen minutes before making a suicidal charge at the Hanoverian infantry lines. Those not mown down by grapeshot or impaled on bayonets (which proved far more effective than the Jacobites' broadswords) were caught by the Duke's cavalry on their retreat. In all 3600 Jacobite casualties were recorded, the vast majority being fatalities. In the following days, after Cumberland's orders to give no quarter to remaining rebels, many survivors were tracked down and summarily executed. Prince

Charles himself narrowly avoided capture, but only by taking extreme measures, including disguising himself as the Irish servant girl, Betty Burke, of a Jacobite sympathiser, Flora MacDonald, in order to escape to the Isle of Skye. After virtually six months of playing hide and seek with government hunting parties, Charles finally managed to leave Scotland aboard a ship for France on 20 September.[16]

Despite the crushing defeat at Culloden, Charles continued to actively pursue invasion plans in the 1750s, travelling Europe incognito (often dressed as a priest) in his attempts to drum up support. However, when these schemes came to nothing Charles gradually succumbed to despondency and became increasingly reliant on alcohol. His drinking in turn crippled his health and led him to make violent attacks on his wife, Louisa. Charles suffered a stroke in January 1788 and died on the 30th of that month. With his passing, his brother, Henry Benedict became the next Stuart claimant to the British crown. Yet Henry, made Cardinal of York by Pope Benedict XIV in 1747 (much to the anger of Charles, who wished to distance the Jacobite cause from Catholicism), had carved out for himself in the Catholic Church a successful alternative career to that of royal pretender, becoming papal treasurer in the 1750s and a leading figure in Roman literary and artistic circles. On his brother's death Henry nonetheless adopted the title of Henry IX and touched for the King's evil to stress the thaumaturgical powers attributed to the Stuart royal dynasty.[17] By this point he was a man of considerable wealth and status, but all of this was lost in the French Revolutionary Wars. He invested virtually all of his personal wealth in attempting to aid the Pope in resisting Napoleon's invasion of the papal states. Unable to hold back Bonaparte's forces, Henry fled to Venice, seeking sanctuary in a monastery. Left a homeless and penniless old man, he became the object of a rather unexpected source of charity. Through the British envoy in Rome, Sir John Coxe Hippisley, the Prime Minister, Sir William Pitt, was alerted to Henry's plight.

On 7 February 1800 the last Stuart claimant to the British throne was informed by letter that George III had decided to grant him an annual pension of £4000. As a gesture of gratitude Henry left the remaining royal jewels to the King on his death on 13 July 1807.

So ended any even nominal Catholic Stuart claim to the British crown (though impostors posing as descendants of Bonnie Prince Charlie appeared in the Victorian era).[18] Though Charles Edward came closest to challenging the Hanoverian succession, it is debatable how long he could have maintained control of England even if he had seized London. The exiled Stuarts nonetheless succeeded in capturing the popular imagination, particularly the Young Chevalier, whose exploits in the '45 and after would feed the imagination of nineteenth-century romantic novelists, notably Sir Walter Scott in his *Waverley; or 'Tis Sixty Years Since*, published in 1814. By contrast the first two Georges would inspire little public devotion. Yet by 1745 George II could draw upon a far more reliable wellspring of loyalty than his (very limited) personal magnetism. As the Jacobite army headed towards Derby, pulpits across England rang out with loyal sermons. Yet the preachers rarely spent much time discussing the virtues of George II himself. Instead, they stressed the need to preserve England's post-Revolutionary constitution, which ensured stability, the rule of law and, above all, economic prosperity.[19] The financial catastrophe that would follow a Jacobite victory was repeatedly emphasised, the Bishop of Chester even managing to link the Catholic doctrine of transubstantiation to high taxation. The greatest number of loyal addresses came from large trading ports such as Liverpool and Bristol. In the words of the Archbishop of Canterbury, the public were urged, not to defend their monarch, George II, but instead 'our happy constitution in Church and State'.[20] The Hanoverian monarchy may not have wormed its way into the hearts of the English people, but it had, more importantly, fattened many people's wallets. The stability and prosperity secured by the Revolution settlement proved far stronger than any emotional attachment to an exiled dynasty.

From its immediate aftermath to the present day, public debate about the Revolution has, through all its permutations and controversies, cohered around at least one fact: 1688 was a struggle over the English constitution. In academic circles, however, the interpretation of 1688 as an English constitutional revolution has been under threat for a long time. In 1984, in response to a suggestion from the cross-bench peer Baron Henderson of Brompton that there should be some public celebration of the tercentenary of the revolution in order to promote 'patriotic' history, a correspondent to the *Times*'s letters page wrote that it was not only 'questionable whether 1688 bequeathed us the modern parliamentary system' but also commemoration might have the unfortunate effect of 'awakening emotions that have laid dormant within the national psyche'. The Revolution, it was pointed out, hardly improved 'Anglo-Scottish relations', nor, given the fact that William of Orange was welcomed 'by many because he would not pursue the Stuart policy of religious toleration', was it the 'advent of parliamentary democracy'. Given that the Revolution was, in any case, bound to be celebrated in one part of the United Kingdom, the correspondent wondered whether it would be wise for the government to sponsor 'what would appear to be an undiluted Orange-flavoured brand of history'.[21]

While they might use slightly less strident terms, many historians would agree with this interpretation of the Glorious Revolution. The constitutional changes effected, at least in 1688–9, as a result of the Revolution settlement were minimal. The religious liberty granted under the Toleration Act was far more limited than that which James II had attempted to get Parliament to approve in the final year of his reign (a policy which had played a large part in leading to his 'abdication'). To adopt a less Anglocentric view, it was less than glorious, too, with serious conflict, loss of life and even incidents of military atrocities in Ireland and Scotland. Taking a broader perspective has also encouraged historians to view this as an event with essentially European causes. The English political revolution could not have happened without the intervention of Dutch arms. The reasons for William's involvement in English affairs had far less to do with the invitation sent to him by the 'immortal seven' (necessary though it was for the Prince's propaganda purposes) and far more to do with the need for English financial and military assistance in the Dutch struggle with Louis XIV. Once installed as British monarch, William used his new kingdom, in the words of one historian, as a 'milch cow' to fund war against the French.[22] By 1697 Britain was contributing 45 per cent of the costs of William's army in Flanders and making up a quarter of that army's manpower.

There is much to support the view that 1688 represented a Dutch invasion and occupation of England, albeit one with considerable support from a fifth column of English politicians, soldiers and clergymen. Such an interpretation has the advantage of reminding us how close England itself came to serious armed conflict, with only James's loss of nerve preventing the country from experiencing another, perhaps more bloody civil war. However, if we see the Glorious Revolution simply from the perspective of William III and his Dutch advisers we will miss much that is significant about the events of 1688 and after. Contemporaries called this a revolution and there remains significant evidence to support this view. First, this was not merely a palace coup or piece of European *realpolitik*. The English people were deeply involved in the changes brought about during the Revolution. It was ordinary people, not the gentry, who first flocked to William's cause in the west of the country. It was the London crowd, so virulent in its anti-popery, which played a large part in James's decision to flee his kingdom rather than attempt to stay and fight. The massive amount of ink spilt in attempting to legitimate or to contest William's right to the throne revealed the importance placed by both sides upon winning over public opinion.

Secondly, if the Revolution did not represent the advent of parliamentary 'democracy' it certainly enshrined parliamentary government. Through its increasing control over government expenditure, its power to scrutinise public accounts and later through the statutory device of the Triennial Act, Parliament became an integral, permanent institution at the heart of government. This revolution in Parliament was accompanied by a financial revolution which laid the foundations for Britain's emergence as a great power in the eighteenth century, through the creation of new institutions such as the Bank of England (which owed a good deal to existing Dutch joint-stock companies). The Revolution not only established the Westminster Parliament as the pre-eminent political body in the British Isles, but also heralded its emergence as an imperial authority. The years following 1689 saw a significant tightening of Parliament's control of colonial administration. A revised Navigation Act (1696) authorised colonial vice-admiralty courts, legislation was issued to help suppress piracy (1700) and regulate privateers (1708) and, in 1710, a general post office with branches in England, Ireland, Scotland and the American colonies was created. The consequence of this legislation was a growing sense of interconnectedness, politically as well as economically, between the constituent parts of the British Empire and the metropolitan centre. The increasing involvement of Westminster in the colonies' internal affairs also brought about the extension of rights and privileges enjoyed in Britain to the Americas. Parliament compelled colonial assemblies to grant religious toleration in terms modelled on the English Toleration Act and the Naturalisation Act of 1740 offered the same rights as enjoyed by natural-born British subjects to foreign Protestant and Jewish settlers.

The end result of these changes was a growing feeling among many white, English-speaking colonists that they held the same rights as Crown subjects in Britain (a view, however, not shared by many in Westminster). As tensions over trade and taxation between Britain and its American colonies increased over the course of the eighteenth century, many colonists looked to the constitutional inheritance they shared with the British, the Revolution of 1688–9, to offer them the means to defend themselves from the perceived predations of an over-mighty and unrepresentative empire. In particular, they looked to that clause of the Bill of Rights of 1690 which affirmed that 'Subjects which are Protestants may have Arms for their Defence suitable to their conditions, and as allowed by Law.' This novel *right* to bear arms, shorn of the element of religious discrimination, would later form the basis for the second amendment to the Constitution of the United States: 'A well-regulated militia, being necessary to the security of a free state, the right of the people to keep and bear arms shall not be infringed.'[23] However, while the impact of the Glorious Revolution upon the white inhabitants of the British Atlantic was, in the long term, to furnish them with the ideological ammunition necessary to throw off imperial rule, for the non-white inhabitants 1688 heralded a massive increase in unfreedom in the first British Empire. The Revolution effectively ended the Royal African Company's monopoly on the transatlantic slave trade. In 1698 the African trade was opened up to other companies on the payment of a 10 per cent duty on exports and by 1712 all restrictions had been done away with, leading to a doubling in human traffic. If the Glorious Revolution marked a watershed for Britain as a colonial and trading power, the nation's rise to greatness was, in part, built upon the labour of enslaved Africans.[24]

Thirdly, the change of monarchs ushered in cultural, as well as political, change. Many contemporaries spoke as much of a Williamite 'reformation' as 'revolution': 1688 was seen as an opportunity to return divine blessings upon the nation in terms of its salvation from popery, through a thorough reformation of public morals and manners. The popularity of this campaign remains a matter of historical debate, but it is a reminder that the Glorious Revolution did not represent the abrupt dawn of a secular age. Christian religion remained at the core of public and private life and religious controversy could be as raw and vindictive as it had been in the 1640s. However, these conflicts were increasingly tempered by a growing conviction that what was important was sincerity rather than correctness of belief.

Advice sheets like the *Athenian Mercury* dished out the kind of moral guidance on sensitive topics that had previously only been offered in private and it was now left up to the anonymous individual reader whether or not to heed such counsel. The decade after the Revolution did see an upsurge in national and local efforts to regulate moral behaviour. Yet it was arguably the case that communities cracked down on prostitution, drunkenness and 'idleness' as much out of a desire to curb criminality and social disorder, as out of a fear of divine judgements for leaving sin unchecked. However limited in scope, the Toleration Act represented a significant retreat by the Church-State. A plurality of religious beliefs was accepted which went far beyond earlier pragmatic recognitions of religious diversity (such as the French Edict of Nantes). The British state was moving closer to the ideas of radical thinkers like John Locke, who argued that the civil authorities should not seek to regulate religious worship or belief: 1688 may have represented a 'Godly revolution', in that it inspired a religious and moral revival, but its architects did not attempt to create a 'Godly commonwealth' of 'saints' as some Englishmen had sought to do in the 1650s.

Finally, the Revolution imposed real limitations on the power of the monarch. Ironically, fetters were placed upon the crown less as a means of protecting Parliament and the public from the threat of Catholic Stuart absolutism than as a defence against the likely succession to the throne of more foreign Protestant princelings. The 1701 Act of Settlement, with its limitations upon royal powers of appointment and royal power to wage war independently, effectively ended the threat of royal tyranny. What the Revolution did not prevent, as one historian has recently pointed out, was the possibility of legislative tyranny.[25] The threat of an over-mighty Parliament became a reality as the Septennial Act effectively destroyed the Revolution's commitment to regular elections, ushering in the rule of a Whig oligarchy. While our constitution remains such a nebulous (or as Edmund Burke would have had it, immemorial) entity, we may continue to suffer under the government of what Lord Hailsham memorably described as an 'elective dictatorship'.

NOTES

PREFACE: THE QUIET REVOLUTION

1 *Hansard,* 7 July 1988, col. 1233.
2 Quoted in A. L. Morton, *A People's History of England* (London, 1938), pp. 277–88.
3 On the role of the *Stadtholder* or *Stadholder* see J. Israel, *The Dutch Republic: Its Rise, Greatness and Fall* 1477–1806 (Oxford, 1995), pp. 300–07.
4 *Hansard,* 7 July 1988, col. 1262.
5 Ibid., col. 1237.
6 Ibid., col. 1234–5.
7 Ibid., col. 1239–40.
8 Ibid., col. 1245–6.
9 Ibid., col. 1253–4.
10 Ibid., col. 1258.
11 H. T. Dickinson, 'The Eighteenth-Century Debate on the "Glorious Revolution"', *History,* 61 (1975), pp. 28–45, at p. 34.
12 Ibid., p. 35.
13 Dickinson, p. 36.
14 Ibid., p. 7.
15 D. Szechi, 'Mythistory versus History: The Fading of the Revolution of 1688', *The Historical Journal,* 33 (1990), p. 143.
16 Dickinson, p. 40.

17 Ibid., p. 45

18 *The Times*, 21 November 1788, p. 4.

19 Pp. 117–18. (Baldwin was a pseudonym for the radical political philosopher William Godwin, husband of Mary Wolstonecraft and father of Mary Shelley.)

20 P. 164.

21 B. M. Gardiner, *The Struggle against Absolute Monarchy* (London, 1908), p. 78.

22 Pp. 163–4.

23 P. 44.

24 Gardiner, p. 79.

25 P. 446.

26 G. M. Trevelyan, *The History of England* (3rd edn., 1945), p. 472.

27 Ibid., p. 475.

28 Morton, p. 277.

29 C. Hill, *The Century of Revolution, 1603–1714* (London, 2nd edn., 1972), p. 210.

30 Ibid., pp. 237–8.

31 C. Hill, 'A Bourgeois Revolution?' in J. G. A. Pocock (ed.), *Three British Revolutions: 1641, 1688, 1776* (Princeton, 1980): 'If the Revolution of 1640 was unwilled, the *coup d'état* of 1688–9 and the peaceful Hanoverian succession were very much willed. The self-confident landed class had now consciously taken its destiny into its own hands.'

32 Hill in a letter to the *Independent*, February 1988.

33 Quoted in J. Morrill, 'The Sensible Revolution', in his *The Nature of the English Revolution* (Harlow, 1993), ch. 20., p. 421.

34 J. P. Kenyon (ed.), *Dictionary of British History* (Ware, 1994).

35 R. A. Beddard, 'The Unexpected Whig Revolution of 1688', in his *The Revolutions of 1688* (Oxford, 1991), p. 97.

36 See J. Israel, *The Anglo-Dutch Moment* (Cambridge, 1991), esp. chs. 3 and 10.

37 Ibid., p. 100.

38 P. 312.

1 A POPISH PLOT?

1 J. P. Kenyon, *The Popish Plot* (London, 1972), p. 56.
2 Ibid., p. 59.
3 Ibid., p. 86.
4 Ibid., p. 88.
5 Ibid., p. 106.
6 J. Spurr, *England in the 1670s: 'This Masquerading Age'* (Oxford, 2000), p. 266.
7 A. Marshall, *The Strange Death of Sir Edmund Bury Godfrey* (Stroud, 1999); Alan Marshall, 'To Make a Martyr, The Popish Plot and Protestant Propaganda', *History Today* (1997), pp. 39–45; P. Hammond, 'Titus Oates and Sodomy', in J. Black (ed.), *Culture and Society in Britain 1660–1800* (Manchester, 1997).
8 Kenyon, *The Popish Plot*, p. 101.
9 Op. cit.
10 Ibid., p. 149.
11 Spurr, *England in the 1670s*, p. 271.
12 Kenyon, *The Popish Plot*, p. 175.
13 Spurr, *England in the 1670s*, p. 279.
14 Ibid., p. 280.
15 Ibid., p. 282.
16 Ibid., p. 283.
17 Ibid., p. 286.
18 Ibid., p. 289.
19 Ibid., p. 291.
20 Kenyon, *The Popish Plot*, p. 111.

2 THE PROTESTANT DUKE AND THE POPISH PRINCE

1 *The Axminster Ecclesiastica 1660–1698*, ed. K. W. H. Howard (Sheffield, 1976), pp. 93–4.
2 J. G. Muddiman (ed.), *The Bloody Assizes* (1934), p. 54. Muddiman's text is from the fifth edition (1705).
3 *The Autobiography of Sir John Bramston* (Camden Society, o.s. 32, 1845), p. 192.

4 J. W. Ebsworth, 'Thomas Dangerfield', *Dictionary of National Biography* (1888), vol. 14, pp. 16–18. See also *Duke Dangerfield declaring how he represented the D. of Mon— in the Country* (1685); *Dangerfields Dance. Giving an Account of several Notorious Crimes by him Committed; viz. He pretended to be a Duke and feigned himself to be Monmouth* (1685).

5 B. Sharp, 'Popular Political Opinion in England 1660–1685', *History of European Ideas*, vol. 10, no. 1 (1989), pp. 13–29, at p. 23.

6 The best account of Monmouth's rebellion is R. Clifton, *The Last Popular Rebellion: The Western Rising of 1685* (Hounslow, 1984). See also W. MacDonald Wigfield, *The Monmouth Rebellion: A Social History* (Bradford-on-Avon, 1980); P. Earle, *Monmouth's Rebels* (London, 1977).

7 *C.S.P.D.*, 1685, p. 180.

8 Ibid., pp. 30–1. Hollwell was said to have surveyed the moor on which it was anticipated that the battle would take place and to have seen 'the stone which lies on that moor which they say the crown shall sit on and drink man's blood'. Monmouth's own commonplace book reveals that he maintained a keen interest in astrology, casting his own nativity.

9 T. Harris, 'London Crowds and the Revolution of 1688' in E. Cruickshanks (ed.), *By Force or By Default? The Revolution of 1688–89* (Edinburgh, 1989), ch. 4.

10 See Clifton, chs. 1 and 2; Wigfield, chs. 2 and 3.

11 *The Declaration of James, Duke of Monmouth, & the noblemen, gentlemen, & others now in arms* (1685), p. 5. P. 1 asserts that the British constitution is one of limited monarchy. However, the proclamation issued from Taunton on 20 June recognises Monmouth as 'lawful and rightful sovereign'; see J. N. P. Watson, *Captain-General and Rebel Chief, the Life of James, Duke of Monmouth* (London, 1979), p. 278.

12 *C.S.P.D.*, 1685, pp. 61, 137, 140.

13 Sharp, pp. 21–4.

14 *County of Buckingham Calendar of the Sessions Records, Vol. 1. 1678 to 1694*, ed. W. H. Hardy (Aylesbury, 1933), p. 176.

15 Clifton, p. 129.

16 *An Account of what Passed at the Execution of the Late Duke of Monmouth* (1685).

17 The best discussion of Monmouth's character is in Clifton, chs. 3–4.

18 See below.

19 My narrative here is indebted to Clifton's account, chs. 5–7.

20 *C.S.P.D.*, 1685, p. 239. See also *Axminster Ecclesiastica*, p. 96.

21 Clifton, p. 224.

22 S. A. Timmons, 'Executions following Monmouth's Rebellion: A Missing Link', *Historical Research*, 76 (2003), pp. 286–91.

23 He has even been the subject of a horror movie, Franco Nero's *The Bloody Judge*, in which he was played by Christopher Lee.

24 *Axminster Ecclesiastica*, p. 99.

25 *C.S.P.D.*, 1685, pp. 327, 335.

26 H. Pitman, *A Relation of the Great Sufferings and Strange Adventures of. . .* (London, 1689), in C. H. Firth (ed.), *Stuart Tracts*, pp. 434–5.

27 Muddiman, p. 28.

28 Wigfield, p. 44.

29 *The Glory of the West, or the Virgins of Taunton-Dean* (1685).

30 J. H. Bettey, 'Andrew Loder: A Seventeenth-Century Dorset Attorney', *Southern History*, 17 (1995), pp. 40–7.

31 Muddiman, p. 40.

32 *Axminster Ecclesiastica*, p. 103.

33 *Quarter Sessions from Queen Elizabeth to Queen Anne . . . drawn from Original Records (Chiefly of the County of Devon)*, ed. A. H. A. Hamilton (London, 1878), p. 238.

34 *C.S.P.D.*, 1685, pp. 353–4. Confirmed by *Quarter Sessions . . . Devon*, p. 239.

35 Clifton, p. 240.

36 Muddiman, p. 41.

37 *C.S.P.D.*, 1685, pp. 332–3.

38 Pitman, pp. 436–44.

39 Ibid., pp. 445–53.

40 Ibid., pp. 455–60.

41 Ibid., pp. 461–8.

42 Ibid., pp. 468–76.

43 M. S. Quintilla, 'Late Seventeenth-Century Indentured Servants in Barbados', *The Journal of Carribean History*, 27 (1993), pp. 114–29.

44 A. Fletcher, *Tudor Rebellions* (2nd edn., 1977), pp. 68–9, 100–2.

45 J. Miller, *James II: a Study in Kingship* (Hove, 1977), p. 120.

46 T. Harris, 'London Crowds and the Revolution of 1688', p. 47.

47 *Quarter Sessions . . . Devon*, p. 242.

48 Clifton, pp. 228–9.

49 Muddiman, p. 22.

3 THE ANGLICAN REVOLT

1 *The Axminster Ecclesiastica 1660–1698*, ed. K. W. H. Howard (Sheffield, 1976), pp. 125–7.

2 *The Autobiography of Sir John Bramston* (Camden Society, o.s. 32, 1845), pp. 234, 248–9.

3 *C.S.P.D.*, 1686–7, p. 313.

4 *Halifax: Complete Works*, ed. J. P. Kenyon (Harmondsworth, 1969), p. 107.

5 Ibid., p. 106.

6 *C.S.P.V.*, 1673–5, pp. 316–17, 324, 327, 330–1, 334, 357–9, 390–1, 401. See also Andrew Barclay, review of Louis G. Schwoerer, *The Ingenious Mr Henry Care, Restoration Publicist*, H-Albion, H-Net Reviews, April 2004.

7 Quoted in W. A. Speck, 'James II', *Oxford Dictionary of National Biography* (2004).

8 *C.S.P.D.*, 1686–7, p. 13.

9 G. V. Bennett, 'Loyalist Oxford and the Revolution', in L. S. Sutherland and L. G. Mitchell (eds.), *The History of the University of Oxford: Vol. V. The Eighteenth Century* (Oxford, 1986), ch. 1, pp. 16–17.

10 T. B. Macaulay, *The History of England from the Accession of James II*, ed. C. H. Firth (London, 1913–15), vol. II, p. 752.

11 *C.S.P.D.*, 1686–7, pp. 56–7.

12 J. P. Kenyon, 'The Commission for Ecclesiastical Causes 1686–1688: A Reconsideration', *The Historical Journal*, 34 (1991), pp. 727–36.

13 *C.S.P.D.*, 1686–7, pp. 233, 254.

14 T. Harris, *Politics under the Later Stuarts: Party Conflict in a Divided Society 1660–1715* (London, 1993), pp. 125–6.

15 *C.S.P.D.*, 1686–7, pp. 62, 71.

16 Ibid., p. 145.

17 Bennett, p. 17.

18 J. Twigg, *The University of Cambridge and the English Revolution,* (Woodbridge, 1990), p. 278.

19 Ibid., p. 277.

20 This is the conclusion of Andrew Barclay, 'The impact of James II on the departments of the royal household' (Cambridge University PhD, 1994)

21 Bramston, pp. 268–70.

22 J. P. Kenyon, *The Stuart Constitution, 1603–1688* (2nd edn., Cambridge, 1986) p. 389.

23 Harris, *Politics under the Later Stuarts*, p. 126.

24 *Axminster Ecclesiastica*, p. 133.

25 No. 2243.

26 No. 2250.

27 No. 2258.

28 No. 2284, Somerset clothworkers, no. 2276, Stroud water clothiers, no. 2273, Master builders of London, offer some examples.

29 Bramston, p. 272.

30 Ibid., p. 275.

31 No. 2266.

32 No. 2246.

33 No. 2264.

34 No. 2268.

35 *Penal Laws and Test Act. Questions Touching Their Repeal Propounded in 1687–8 by James II*, ed. Sir George Duckett (2 vols. London, 1882–3), vol. II, p. 22.

36 M. J. Short, 'The Corporation of Hull and the Government of James II, 1687–8', *Historical Research,* 71 (1998), pp. 172–92, at p. 177.

37 Kenyon, *The Stuart Constitution*, p. 390.

38 See, for examples, no. 2243, address of Bishop, Dean and Chapters of Durham, no. 2246, address from the Bishop of Chester, no. 2256, Bishop, Dean and Chapters of Lincoln, Ripon, no. 2258, Coventry and Lichfield diocese.

39 Bennett, p. 17.

40 No. 2273.

41 No. 2250.

42 No. 2271.

43 W. A. Speck, *James II* (Basingstoke, 2002), p. 56.

44 Bramston, p. 284.

45 Ibid., pp. 284–96; *C.S.P.D.*, 1687–8, p. 70; Bennett, p. 18.

46 Twigg, pp. 283–4.

47 W. A. Speck, 'The Orangist Conspiracy Against James II', *The Historical Journal*, 30 (1987), pp. 453–62.

48 *A letter writ by Mijn Heer Fagel, pensioner of Holland, to James Stewart, advocate, giving an account of the Prince and Princess of Orange's thoughts concerning the repeal of the Test* (1688 [i.e., 1687]).

49 *Penal Laws and Test Act*, vol. I, pp. 222–3, vol. II, pp. 219–20.

50 Harris, *Politics under the Later Stuarts*, pp. 126–7; V. Alsop, *Mr Alsop's Speech to King James II* (1687); R. A. Beddard, 'Vincent Alsop and the Emancipation of Restoration Dissent', *Journal of Ecclesiastical History*, 24 (1973), pp. 161–84.

51 M. Goldie, 'John Locke's Circle and James II', *The Historical Journal*, 35 (1992), pp. 557–86.

52 *C.S.P.D.*, 1687–9, p. 66.

53 H. Newcome, *The Autobiography of Henry Newcome*, ed. R. Parkinson (2 vols., Manchester, Chetham Soc., 1852), p. 265.

54 D. Ogg, *England in the Reigns of James II and William III* (Oxford, 1969), p. 184.

55 *Penal Laws and Test Act*, vol. I, p. 74 (Duckett's editorial insertions here, as elsewhere, are misleading).

56 Ibid., vol. I, p. 218.

57 Ibid., vol. I, p. 182.

58 John Carswell, *The Descent on England: A Study of the English Revolution of 1688 and its European Background* (London, 1969), pp. 238–43.

59 W. A. Speck, 'The Revolution of 1688 in the North', *Northern History* 25 (1989), pp. 188–204, 200.

60 Speck, 'The Orangist Conspiracy Against James II', p. 254.

61 Bramston, p. 306: 'Unto the two first I said I could not preingage; to the third I sayd I would always pay all duty and obedience to the King, and endeauour what in my lieth to lieu peaceably with all

men. Mr Petre of the Park who acted the part of Secretary to my Lord in all the procedure of this matter, set down my answer, "I would live peaceably with my neighbours of all perswasions", which I sayd were not my words, tho' much to my sence.'

62 *Penal Laws and Test Act,* vol. I, p. 196.

63 Ibid., vol. I, p. 156.

64 Ibid., vol. I, p. 285.

65 Bramston, p. 302.

66 *Penal Laws and Test Act,* vol. II, pp. 19–26.

67 Speck, 'The Revolution of 1688 in the North', p. 197.

68 M. Short, 'The Corporation of Hull and the Government of James II, 1687–8', *Historical Research,* 71 (1998), pp. 174–5.

69 Ibid., p. 187.

70 This point is well made by Mark Goldie, 'John Locke's Circle and James II', p. 573.

71 *C.S.P.D.,* 1687–9, p. 127.

72 Ibid., p. 66. Clarendon, on the other hand, thought that even those who had been intruded were no more likely to do James's wishes than the original officers and judges they had displaced, p. 118.

73 *Penal Laws and Test Act,* vol. II, p. 219.

74 Harris, *Politics under the Later Stuarts,* p. 128.

75 Bramston, p. 310.

76 *C.S.P.D.,* 1687–9, pp. 224–5.

77 *An Account of the Reasons of the Nobility and Gentry's Invitation of His Highnesse the Prince of Orange into England* (1688). The pamphlet went into intimate detail about the Queen's pregnancy, noting that it was alleged that she had continued menstruating and that her breasts had not been seen to swell, nor leak milk. See ibid., pp. 18–19.

78 I am basing my discussion of the warming-pan myth on Rachel Weil's excellent *Political Passions, Gender, the Family and Political Argument: 1680–1714* (Manchester, 1999), ch. 3.

79 Speck, 'Revolution in the North', p. 196; Speck, *James II,* p. 148.

80 J. L. Malcolm, 'The Creation of a "True Antient and Indubitable" Right: the English Bill of Rights and the Right to be Armed', *Journal of British Studies,* 32 (1993), pp. 226–49, at pp. 242–3. An

earlier test case brought against a magistrate, Sir John Knight, who had been over-zealous in enforcing the recusancy laws, for riding armed, failed to secure a conviction.

81 Which did not make it illegal, as declarations of the House do not carry the force of law. But it did make it *unwise*.

82 The history of James's government in New England requires further research. A starting point is ch. 7 of Speck's *James II*. See also the references for the North American reaction to the Glorious Revolution given below.

83 *C.S.P.D.*, 1686–7, pp. 147, 149; on James's relationship with the Huguenots see Robin D. Gwynn, 'James II in the light of his treatment of Huguenot refugees in England 1685–1686', *English Historical Review*, 92 (1977), pp. 820–33.

4 THE DUTCH INVASION

1 *The Axminster Ecclesiastica 1660–1698*, ed. K. W. H. Howard (Sheffield, 1976), p. 135–6.

2 *C.S.P.D.*, 1687–9, p. 191.

3 W. A. Speck, *James II* (Basingstoke, 2002), p. 70.

4 Henri and Barbara Van der Zee, *1688 Revolution in the Family* (Harmondsworth, 1988), p. 104.

5 Ibid., p. 96.

6 Ibid., p. 111.

7 J. Israel, 'The Dutch Role in the Glorious Revolution', in J. Israel (ed.), *The Anglo-Dutch Moment* (Cambridge, 1991), ch. 3, p. 121.

8 Van der Zee, p. 90.

9 Ibid., p. 104.

10 J. P. Kenyon, *Robert Spencer, Earl of Sunderland* (London, 1958). p. 219.

11 A. Browning, *Thomas Osborne Earl of Danby and Duke of Leeds, 1632–1712, Vol. II Letters* (Glasgow, 1944), p. 135.

12 Ibid., p. 136.

13 On the northern risings see Speck, 'Revolution of 1688 in the North'; D. H. Hosford, *Nottingham, Nobles and the North* (Hamden, Conn, 1976); A. Browning, *Thomas Osborne Earl of*

Danby and Duke of Leeds 1632–1712, vol. 1 *Life* (Glasgow, 1951), pp. 389–410.

14 *Memoirs of Sir John Reresby*, ed. Andrew Browning (Glasgow, 1936), pp. 514–5, 524.

15 Van der Zee, p. 122.

16 On the Williamite and Jacobite propaganda efforts see L. G. Schwoerer, 'Propaganda in the Revolution of 1688–9', *American Historical Review*, 82 (1977), pp. 843–74; idem, 'The Glorious Revolution as Spectacle: A New Perspective', in S. B. Baxter (ed.), *England's Rise to Greatness, 1660–1763* (Los Angeles, 1984), ch. 4; T. Claydon, 'William III's Declaration of Reasons and the Glorious Revolution', *The Historical Journal*, 39, 1 (1996), pp. 87–108.

17 Speck, *James II*, p. 74; Van der Zee, *Revolution in the Family*, p. 123.

18 *Memoirs of Sir John Reresby*, p. 502.

19 Van der Zee, p. 125.

20 Ibid., p. 126.

21 Historical Manuscripts Commission, *Kenyon MSS* (London, 1894), p. 204. See also p. 197, Earl of Dunmore to the Earl of Derby: 'our forces are in so good order, and so much encreased, that I believe they will find it very difficult, if not impossible, to compasce their designe, especially since there is a fleet out, which my Lord Dartmouth goes tomorrow to command'.

22 Van der Zee, p. 126.

23 Speck, *James II*, p. 76.

24 Historical Manuscripts Commission, *Kenyon MSS* (Lomdon, 1894), p. 207.

25 Speck, *James II*, p. 75.

26 G. Burnet, 'The Expedition of His Highness the Prince of Orange for England' in *A collection of papers relating to the present juncture of affairs in England* (1688), p. 3.

27 The story is unlikely given that, thanks in part to his wife, William's English was excellent.

28 Van der Zee, p. 146.

29 Burnet's account, from which the quotation is taken, describes these men as 'Blacks brought from the Plantations of the Netherlands in America', i.e., Surinam, Burnet, 'Expedition', p. 6.

30 Van der Zee, p. 151.

31 Historical Manuscripts Commission, *Kenyon MSS* (London, 1894), p. 207.

32 *C.S.P.D.*, 1687–9, p. 316.

33 *The Lord Delamere's letter to his tenants in Warrington, Lancashire, answered* (1688), p. 2.

34 G. Burnet, *A collection of papers relating to the present juncture of affairs in England* (1688), p. 19.

35 Text in *Penal Laws and Test Act*, vol. II, pp. 113–15.

36 *Memoirs of Sir John Reresby*, p. 526.

37 Speck, 'Revolution in the North', pp. 188–91.

38 Van der Zee, p. 157.

39 Ibid., p. 172. Ironically, Seymour would refuse the 1696 Association which recognised William as rightful and lawful king.

40 J. P. Kenyon, *Revolution Principles* (Cambridge, 1977), p. 6; W. A. Speck, *Reluctant Revolutionaries: Englishmen and the Revolution of 1688* (Oxford, 1988), pp. 230–2.

41 *C.J.*, vol. x, p. 6.

42 R. A. Beddard, 'The Unexpected Whig Revolution of 1688', in R. A. Beddard (ed.), *The Revolutions of 1688* (Oxford, 1991), pp. 11–102, at pp. 40, 45, 52. See BL Add MS 28252, f. 53, 'List of members that refused the association to the Prince of Orange'.

43 Speck, *James II*, p. 76. Indeed, from contemporary accounts, it appears that James was suffering from posterior, as opposed to anterior, nosebleeds, which can indicate the presence of a tumour. Another, and in the King's case more likely, cause of such regular bleeding from nose and throat can be high blood pressure.

44 Van der Zee, p. 177.

5 PANIC AND FLIGHT

1 *The Letters and Diplomatic Instructions of Queen Anne*, ed. B. C. Brown (London, 1935), pp. 33, 44–5.

2 M. Waller, *Ungrateful Daughters: The Stuart Princesses Who Stole Their Father's Crown* (London, 2002), p. 81. Waller discusses Anne's conversion to the Williamite cause in ch. 2.

3   F. Harris, *A Passion for Government, The Life of Sarah, Duchess of Marlborough* (Oxford, 1991), p. 47. Sarah described the Queen as having 'no fault but being govern'd by Priests'.

4   On Anne's flight see D. H. Hosford, *Nottingham, Nobles and the North* (Hamden, Conn., 1976), pp. 101–8.

5   T. B. Macaulay, *The History of England from the Accession of James II*, ed. C. H. Firth (London, 1913–15), vol. III, p. 1185.

6   Henri and Barbara Van der Zee, *1688 Revolution in the Family* (Harmondsworth, 1988), p. 184.

7   Quoted in W. A. Speck, *James II* (Basingstoke, 2002), p. 78.

8   Van der Zee, p. 195.

9   On the Catholic rioting of December 1688, see J. Miller, 'The Militia and the Army in the Reign of James II', *The Historical Journal*, 16 (1973), pp. 659–79, at p. 675.

10   *Memoirs of Sir John Reresby*, p. 536.

11   Sir James Dalrymple remarked that 'Heaven seemed by this accident to declare that the laws, the constitution, and the sovereignty of Great Britain were not to depend on the frailty of man'. Physical evidence supports the idea that the Great Seal was at some point recovered. The new seal made for William and Mary was in fact little more than a crude alteration of the reverse side of James II's original seal with 'part of a female figure and some indications of a horse clumsily inserted in inadequate space, and with a new legend', H. Jenkinson, 'What happened to the Great Seal of James II?', *Antiquaries Journal*, 12 (1943), pp. 1–13.

12   Van der Zee, p. 197.

13   According to Reresby, *Memoirs*, p. 539.

14   Van der Zee, p. 198.

15   Ibid., p. 199.

16   Macaulay, *History*, vol. III, p. 1178. However, Macaulay gets the dating of this incident wrong; see R. Howell, *Puritans and Radicals in North England: Essays on the English Revolution* (Lanham, Md., 1984). On the desacralisation of monarchy in the seventeenth century see R. Zaller, 'Breaking the Vessels: the Desacralization of Monarchy in Early Modern England', *Sixteenth Century Journal*, 29 (1998), pp. 757–78.

17 Van der Zee, p. 201.

18 Ibid., p. 202.

19 G. H. Hilton, 'The Irish Fright of 1688: Real Violence and Imagined Massacre', *Bulletin of the Institute of Historical Research*, 55 (1982), pp. 148–53, at p. 149.

20 Op. cit.

21 Van der Zee, p. 203.

22 Hilton, p. 149.

23 Van der Zee, p. 209.

24 Op. cit.

25 Hilton p. 152.

26 T. Harris, 'London Crowds and the Revolution of 1688', in E. Cruickshanks (ed.), *By Force or By Default? The Revolution of 1688–9* (Edinburgh, 1989), ch. 4; W. K. Sachse, 'The Mob and the Revolution of 1688', *Journal of British Studies*, 4 (1964), pp. 23–41.

27 T. Harris, 'The People, the Law, and the Constitution in Scotland and England: A Comparative Approach to the Glorious Revolution', *Journal of British Studies*, 38 (1999), pp. 28–58, 32–3.

28 A. Fox, *Oral and Literate Culture* (Oxford, 2001), pp. 381–2.

29 S. Pincus, '"To Protect English Liberties": The English Nationalist Revolution of 1688–9', in *Protestantism and National Identity*, eds. T. Claydon and J. McBride (Cambridge, 1999), pp. 81–2.

30 *A Relation of the bloody massacre in Ireland* (1689), p. 4.

31 *A Full and True Account of the Inhumane and Bloudy Cruelties of the Papists to the Poor Protestants in Ireland in the Year 1641* (1689), p. 20.

32 Ibid., p. 24.

33 Ibid., p. 28.

34 Ibid., p. 1.

35 *An Abstract of the Unnatural Rebellion and Barbarous Massacre of the Protestants in the Kingdom of Ireland in the Year 1641* (1689), p. 5.

36 Ibid., p. 3.

37 W. Lamont, 'Richard Baxter, "Popery" and the origins of the English Civil War', *History*, 87 (2002), pp. 336–52, p. 348.

38 M. Zook, '"The Bloody Assizes" Whig Martyrdom and Memory after the Glorious Revolution', *Albion*, 27 (1995), pp. 373–96, at pp. 385–6.

39 Van der Zee, p. 204.

40 *Memoirs of Sir John Reresby*, pp. 540–1.

41 Van der Zee, p. 214.

42 Speck, *James II*, p. 80.

43 *The Diary of John Evelyn*, ed, E. S. de Beer (6 vols., Oxford, 1955), iv, 612.

44 Speck, *James II*, p. 81.

6 SELLING THE REVOLUTION

1 W. A. Speck, *Reluctant Revolutionaries; Englishmen and the Revolution of 1688* (Oxford, 1988), p. 96.

2 P. Monod, *Jacobitism and the English People, 1688–1788* (Cambridge, 1989), p. 258.

3 A. Fox, *Oral and Literate Culture* (Oxford, 2001), p. 358.

4 I. K. Steele, 'Communicating an English Revolution to the Colonies, 1688–1689', *Journal of British Studies*, 24 (1985), pp. 333–57.

5 R. A. Beddard, 'The Unexpected Whig Revolution of 1688' in R. A. Beddard (ed.), *The Revolutions of 1688* (Oxford, 1991), pp. 27–39.

6 Interestingly, the appointment of a *custos regni* in the absence of the ruling monarch had previously been mooted in 1641 when Charles I left for Scotland, *C.J.*, iii, 4 August 1641.

7 G. R. Elton, *The Tudor Constitution* (Cambridge, 1972, reprint), p. 2, describes this act as being 'over-ingeniously explained'. In fact, its limited intention was to indemnify, retrospectively, acts of obedience to 'kings for the time being' (meaning Richard III) from later charges of treason. It did not effectively distinguish between de facto and *de jure* powers and, thanks to a sub-clause, did not free subjects of Henry VII from subsequently giving their loyalty to a Perkin Warbeck or Lambert Simnel. For the text of the act see pp. 4–5.

8 G. Burnet, *A Pastoral Letter* (1689), p. 21. These arguments were later suppressed by the Williamite government. In 1693 Edmund Bohun was condemned for licensing Charles Blount's *King William and Queen Mary Conquerors* for publication.

9 Speck, *Reluctant Revolutionaries*, pp. 92–4.

10 Lords Journals, vol. 14, 22 Jan 1689, pp. 101–3.

11 *A Parliamentary History of the Glorious Revolution*, ed. D. L. Jones (HMSO, 1988), p. 79. The Bishop of Oxford did read the prayers to the King, which caused consternation, particularly with the speaker of the House, the Earl of Halifax.

12 Ibid., p. 27. Despite objections the House did offer a vote of thanks to Sharp for his sermon.

13 Beddard, 'The Unexpected Whig Revolution of 1688', p. 91.

14 Danby's notes in *A Parliamentary History of the Glorious Revolution*, ed. D. L. Jones (HMSO, 1988), p. 94.

15 Ibid., p. 239.

16 Beddard, 'Unexpected Whig Revolution', p. 78.

17 Ibid., p. 34.

18 Quoted in Speck, *Reluctant Revolutionaries*, pp. 101–2.

19 T. P. Slaughter, '"Abdicate," and "Contract" in the Glorious Revolution', *The Historical Journal* 24 (1981), pp. 323–37.

20 For the various meanings, see *OED*. Disputes over the meaning of the term have led to a rather unnecessary controversy among historians, see T. P. Slaughter, pp. 323–37; John Miller, 'The Glorious Revolution: 'Contract' and 'Abdication' Reconsidered', *The Historical Journal*, 25 (1982), pp. 541–55; Slaughter's reply, '"Abdicate" and "Contract" restored', *The Historical Journal*, 28 (1985), pp. 399–403. It should be noted that Miller and Slaughter actually agree that abdicate was a term of some ambiguity.

21 Miller, '"Contract" and "Abdication" Reconsidered', p. 552.

22 On this idea of the inversion of gender stereotyping as a metaphor for disorder see, N. Z. Davis, 'Women on Top', in her *Society and Culture in Early Modern France* (London, 1975), Chap. 5.

23 T. B. Macaulay, *The History of England from the Accession of James II*, ed. C. H. Firth (London, 1913–15), vol. III, p. 1287. The spokesman was wrongly identified by Dartmouth as Fagel but he had died in Holland over a month earlier.

24 L. G. Schwoerer, 'Press and Parliament in the Revolution of 1689', *The Historical Journal*, 20 no. 3 (1977), pp. 545–67, 551–2.

25 *A Parliamentary History*, p. 82.

26 Ibid., pp. 125–6.

27 Speck, *Reluctant Revolutionaries*, pp. 105–7.

28 J. Israel (ed.), *The Anglo-Dutch Moment* (Cambridge, 1991). p. 134; Beddard, 'The Unexpected Whig Revolution of 1688', p. 85.

29 Beddard, 'The Unexpected Whig Revolution of 1688', p. 85.

30 Speck, *Reluctant Revolutionaries*, p. 108.

31 Beddard, 'The Unexpected Whig Revolution of 1688', p. 92.

32 J. C. Findon, 'The Non-Jurors and the Church of England 1689–1716' (Oxford University D.Phil thesis 1978), pp. 6–14; E. N. Williams, *The Eighteenth Century Constitution 1688–1815* (Cambridge, 1960), pp. 29–30; H. Horwitz, *Revolution Politicks: The Career of Daniel Finch, 2nd Earl of Nottingham, 1647–1730* (Cambridge, 1968), p. 82; idem, *Parliament, Policy and Politics in the Reign of William III* (Manchester, 1977), pp. 21–2, 24–5, 26.

33 Speck, *Reluctant Revolutionaries*, p. 111.

34 *A Parliamentary History*, p. 147.

35 Ibid., p. 148.

36 The text of the Declaration can be found at http://www.nationalarchives.gov.uk/pathways/citizenship/rise_parliament/making_history_rise.htm

37 Although it could equally be said that neither of these amendments has been very well observed.

38 Miller, '"Contract" and "Abdication" Reconsidered', p. 546.

39 See *A Parliamentary History*, pp. 188–202.

40 M. Goldie, 'The Revolution of 1689 and the Structure of Political Argument', *Bulletin of Research in the Humanities*, lxxxiii (1980), pp. 473–564.

41 J. P. Kenyon, *Revolution Principles* (Cambridge, 1977), p. 21.

42 Findon, p. 44.

43 *Melius Inquirendum, or a further modest and impartial enquiry into the lawfulness of taking the new oath of allegiance* (1689), 'That which (I suppose) I am to swear in taking this Oath.'

44 Bodleian Library, Oxford, MS Rawl. D 1232 fo. 1.

45 R. Weil, *Political Passions, Gender, the Family and Political Argument: 1680–1714* (Manchester, 1999), pp. 1–2.

46 'London in 1689–90 by the Rev. R. Kirk', trans. D. Maclean, *Transactions of the London and Middlesex Archaeological Society*, n.s. VII (1937), p. 313.

47 A. McInnes, 'The Revolution and the People', in G. Holmes (ed.), *Britain after the Glorious Revolution* (Macmillan, 1969), ch. 3.

48 Quoted in ibid., p. 86.

49 On this see E. P. Thompson's classic *Whigs and Hunters* (Pantheon, 1976).

50 McInnes, p. 91.

51 On this 'news culture' see A. Fox, *Oral and Literate Culture in England, 1500–1800* (Oxford, 2001).

52 It was during the seventeenth century that the term 'public house' first became popular, reflecting a growing convergence between the style of premises of the inn, tavern and alehouse (formerly an ordinary dwelling house that also served home-brewed beer). Overall, drinking was becoming a more civilised affair. There was a trend towards more rooms and the addition of stables to aid travellers, with the development of 'drinking booths' to give customers more privacy. This process of gentrification was not in evidence everywhere. Fairs continued to be a peak time for old-fashioned shabby, uncivilised boozing. Ned Ward, author of *The London Spy*, on a visit to St James's Fair soon after 1700, spoke of a 'parcel of scandelous boozing kens where soldiers and their trulls were skipping and dancing to the most lamentable music performed upon a cracked fiddle by a blind fiddler'. Victuallers after the Restoration nonetheless tended to be older and wealthier than their Civil War predecessors. The proportion of alehouse keepers who were women had risen slightly since the Civil War, and many now appeared to be widows of alehouse keepers who had inherited the business rather than newcomers. Women accounted for 17 per cent of licensed victuallers in Oxford in 1708–9. This figure alone does not represent the true importance of women in the drink trade and their involvement was in fact a good deal greater. Often the licensee was only formally in charge. When Leonard Wheatcroft took over the licence of a house at Ashover in Derbyshire he wrote in his journal: 'there did my wife begin to sell ale and so did continue for many years after'.

53 Occasionally spoken words were called 'treasonable' and the famous treason statute of 25 Edward III (1362) had drawn no distinction

between speaking and writing. This statute was strengthened by Richard II and Henry VIII but their statutes were soon repealed. It was not until 1628 in Pine's case that the common law definitely and finally decided that seditious words were not to be tried as high treason. They constituted thereafter a crime of misdemeanour, with penalties ranging from flogging and pillorying to imprisonment and fines. Cases were tried at Quarter Sessions, Assizes and King's Bench, with transferral to a higher court, depending on how serious examining judges considered the crime to be and whether or not local juries were seen as politically trustworthy. On seditious words see B. Sharp, 'Popular Political Opinions in England 1660–1685', *History of European Ideas*, 10 (1989), pp. 13–29; Monod, *Jacobitism*, ch. 8. Unless otherwise indicated instances of seditious speech are taken from Monod's work.

54 Norfolk Record Office, NCR 12 B (1), 1684–9.

55 *County of Buckingham Calendar of the Sessions Records, Vol. 1 1678 to 1694*, ed. W. H. Hardy (Aylesbury, 1933), pp. 364, 365, 368.

56 My discussion of the seventeenth-century alehouse is indebted to P. Clark, *The English Alehouse: A Social History* (London, 1983), ch. 9.

57 *Records of the County of Wilts being extracts from the Quarter Sessions Great Rolls of the Seventeenth Century*, ed. B. H. Cunnington (Devises, 1932), p. 276.

58 Ibid., p. 275.

59 Monod, p. 259.

60 Hannah Bromfield of Upton Warren in Worcestershire was indicted for calling King William 'a sonne of a whore and if ever King James comes in Ile be one that shall help put down Justice Cheke's house or sett fire on it, but Ile have it downe'. Worcestershire Record Office, Worcestershire Quarter Session 1/1/176 1695–8.

61 Some Tories, however, saw the temperate culture of the coffee-house as antithetical to their masculine, health-drinking lifestyle. One defender of alehouse culture proudly retold a recent visit to an alehouse 'in Petty France, where after a bottle or two, I grew so strong, that I call'd for a convenient room, went upstairs had a fresh bottle, flung [the barmaid] on the bed, and gave her as good a meal's meat as ever she ate since the prime of her understanding'. Such

triumphs, the author said, could never be had in a coffee-house, 'for that curs'd liquor disable the most valiant hector in the universe'. *The Women's Petition Against Coffee, Representing to Public Consideration the Grand Inconveniences Accruing to their Sex from the Excessive Use of the Drying and Enfeebling Liquor* also complained that through drinking the black brew their husbands had become 'as unfruitful as the deserts, from where that unhappy berry is said to be brought'.

62 The initial proclamation was followed ten days later by an amendment which stated that in return for a humble confession of their abuses and misdeeds, and provided the coffee-men took the oaths of allegiance and supremacy, and entered into recognisances to the amount of £500, the Crown would allow coffee retailers to remain open until 24 June 1676. An additional proclamation 'for the better discovery of Seditious Libellers' dropped the cash demand of £500, with the government declaring that it would be waived if coffee-men would cooperate with them in barring entry to unsavoury individuals.

63 On coffee-houses in this period see S. Pincus, '"Coffee Politicians Does Create": Coffeehouses and Restoration Political Culture', *Journal of Modern History*, 67 (1995), 807–35; J. Harris, 'The Grecian Coffee House and Political Debate in London 1688–1714', *London Journal*, 25 (2000), pp. 1–13; H. Berry, 'An Early Coffee-House Periodical and its Readers: the Athenian Mercury, 1691–7', *London Journal*, 25 (2000), pp. 14–33; A. Ellis, *The Penny Universities: A History of the Coffee Houses* (London, 1956); B. Lillywhite, *London Coffee Houses* (London, 1963).

64 See Schwoerer, 'Press and Parliament in the Revolution of 1689', pp. 549–50.

65 [J. Dunton], *The Athenian Gazette or Casuistical Mercury resolving all the most nice and curious questions proposed by the ingenious*, i (1691), no. 4, no. 10, no 21, no. 22.

7 THE REVOLUTION IN SCOTLAND AND IRELAND

1 W. A. Speck, *James II* (Basingstoke, 2002), p. 85.

2 D. Ogg, *England in the Reigns of James II and William III* (Oxford, 1969), p. 172.

3 Speck, *James II*, p. 86.

4 Charles II had been forced to take the Solemn League and Covenant at his coronation at Scone in 1650, as well as make a humiliating confession of his father's sins, in order to win Scottish covenanter military support against the English republican regime.

5 A. I. MacInnes, 'Repression and Conciliation: The Highland Dimension 1660–1688', *The Scottish Historical Review*, LXV (1986), pp. 167–95, 167; I. B. Cowan, *The Scottish Covenanters 1660–1688* (London, 1976).

6 Speck, *James II*, p. 78.

7 *C.S.P.D.*, 1685, p. 337.

8 Speck, *James II*, p. 90.

9 Ogg, pp. 173–4.

10 Some Quakers, such as William Penn, were both involved in public life and, at times, in breach of the 'peace principle' established by George Fox for the movement in 1661.

11 Speck, *James II*, p. 90.

12 Ibid., p. 94.

13 Ibid., p. 95.

14 Ibid., p. 94.

15 Ibid., p. 96.

16 Sheridan and Clarendon did both have an axe to grind: Sheridan was dismissed from Tyrconnel's service on trumped-up charges of corruption and Clarendon lost office directly as a result of Talbot's machinations. However, positive portraits of the Earl are hard to come by. J. Miller, 'The Earl of Tyrconnel and James II's Irish Policy, 1685–1688', *The Historical Journal*, 20 4 (1977), pp. 803–23, 805–6.

17 Speck, *James II*, p. 103.

18 Ibid., p. 104.

19 Ibid., p. 104.

20 Ibid., p. 106.

21 T. C. Barnard, *The Kingdom of Ireland, 1641–1760* (Basingstoke, 2004), p. 37.

22 Speck, *James II*, p. 107.

23 J. Miller, 'The Earl of Tyrconnel and James II's Irish Policy, 1685–1688', *The Historical Journal*, 20 (1977), p. 810.

24 Speck, *James II*, p. 108.

25 P. Le Fevre, 'The Battle of Bantry Bay, 1 May 1689', in special edition of *Irish Sword*, 18 (1990), 'The War of the Kings, 1689–91', p. 2.

26 *The Journal of John Stevens Containing a Brief Account of the War in Ireland 1689–1691*, ed. R. H. Murray (Oxford, 1912), p. 63.

27 J. Michael Hill, 'Killiecrankie and the Evolution of Highland Warfare', *War in History*, 1 (1994), pp. 125–39, at p. 127.

28 Ibid., pp. 137–8.

29 Ibid., p. 136.

30 P. Hopkins, *Glencoe and the End of the Highland War* (Edinburgh, 1986), p. 188.

31 Rosen was, in fact, doing no more than following accepted European rules of war in the conduct of a siege. Defenders who refused offers to surrender peacefully were at the mercy of the besieging force once a town had been subdued.

32 R. Doherty, *The Williamite War in Ireland 1688–91* (Dublin, 1998), p. 58.

33 Ibid., p. 69.

34 Quoted in D. and H. Murtagh, 'Irish Jacobite Army, 1689–91' in *Irish Sword*, 18 (1990), p. 38.

35 S. Mulloy, 'French eye-witnesses of the Boyne', *Irish Sword*, 15 no. 59 (1982), pp. 105–13, at p. 107.

36 Ibid., p. 108.

37 Doherty, p. 124.

38 Op. cit.

39 J. MacGuire, *Kings in Conflict: The Revolutionary War in Ireland and its Aftermath, 1689–1750* (Belfast, 1990), p. 88.

40 Hopkins, p. 253.

41 Ibid., p. 310.

42 Ibid., p. 311.

43 Ibid., p. 328.

44 Ibid., p. 332.

45 Ibid., p. 335.

8 WILLIAM AND MARY

1 J. Hoppitt, *A Land of Liberty: England, 1689–1727* (Oxford, 2000), p. 132.
2 *The Axminster Ecclesiastica 1660–1698*, ed. K. W. H. Howard (Sheffield, 1976), p. 143.
3 T. Harris, *Politics under the Later Stuarts: Party Conflict in a Divided Society 1660–1715* (London, 1993), p. 216.
4 Quoted in W. A. Speck, 'Mary II', *Oxford Dictionary of National Biography* (Oxford, 2004).
5 C. Rose, *England in the 1690s* (Oxford, 1999), p. 38.
6 Harris, *Politics under the Later Stuarts*, p. 217.
7 Rose, *England in the 1690s*, p. 2. It is interesting to note that Jacobites sought to portray William as the passive partner in these alleged relationships.
8 My discussion of William's attributes is based on T. Claydon, *William III: Profiles in Power* (Basingstoke, 2002); idem, 'William III', *Oxford Dictionary of National Biography*; Rose, *England in the 1690s*, ch. 1; S. B. Baxter, *William III* (London, 1966).
9 Quoted in Speck, 'Mary II', *Oxford Dictionary of National Biography*.
10 M. Waller, *Ungrateful Daughters: The Stuart Princesses Who Stole Their Father's Crown* (London, 2002), p. 114.
11 Ibid., p. 116.
12 L. G. Schwoerer, 'Images of Queen Mary II, 1689–95', *Renaissance Quarterly*, 42 (1989), pp. 717–48, 730.
13 W. A. Speck, 'Mary II'.
14 Rose, *England in the 1690s*, p. 44.
15 Schwoerer, 'Images of Queen Mary II, 1689–95', p. 717.
16 Speck, 'Mary II'.
17 Ibid.
18 Rose, *England in the 1690s*, p. 41.
19 Ibid., p. 42.
20 This assessment of Mary is indebted to W. A. Speck's article in the *Oxford Dictionary of National Biography*; Schwoerer, 'Images of Queen Mary II, 1689–95'; Rose, *England in the 1690s*, ch. 1.

21 Rose, *England in the 1690s*, pp. 73–4.

22 Ibid., p. 73.

23 Ibid., p. 81.

24 D. Szechi, 'The Jacobite Revolution Settlement, 1689–1696', *English Historical Review*, 108 (1993), pp. 610–28.

25 On the party politics of the 1690s see Rose, *England in the* 1690s, ch. 3; Claydon, *William III*, ch. 4; D. Rubini, *Court and Country 1688–1702* (London, 1967); H. Horwitz, *Revolution Politicks: The Career of Daniel Finch, Second Earl of Nottingham* (Cambridge, 1968); idem, *Parliament, Policy and Politics in the Reign of William III* (Manchester, 1977); R. D. McJimsey, 'A Country Divided? English Politics and the Nine Years War', *Albion*, 23 (1991), pp. 61–74.

26 'London in 1689–90 by the Rev. R. Kirk', trans. D. Maclean, *Transactions of the London and Middlesex Archaeological Society*, n.s., VII (1937), p. 313.

27 Claydon, *William III*, p. 100.

28 Ibid., p. 102.

29 *Axminster Ecclesiastica*, pp. 141–2.

30 V. Barrie, 'The Church of England in London in the Eighteenth-Century', *Proceedings of the British Academy*, 107 (2001), pp. 211–21, at p. 218.

31 Rose, *England in the 1690s*, p. 107.

32 *Axminster Ecclesiastica*, p. 146.

33 Rose, *England in the 1690s*, p. 110.

34 For the engagements at Beachy Head, Barfleur, La Hogue (or La Hougue) see J. Guttman, 'Battlers Becalmed', *Military History*, 7 (1991), pp. 38–44; N. Thornton, 'Guarding the Glorious Revolution', *Quarterly Journal of Military History*, 13 (2001), pp. 78–86; P. Villiers, 'Victoire de Barfleur ou Defaite de la Hougue: 29 Mai–2 Juin 1692', *Revue du Nord*, 74 (1992), pp. 53–72; E. Taillemaite, 'Un Conflict Vauban-Louvois', *Histoire, Economie et Société*, 15 (1996), pp. 113–15.

35 Ambrose Barnes, *Memoirs of the Life of Mr Ambrose Barnes*, ed. W. H. D. Longstaffe (Surtees Society, 50, 1867), p. 225.

36 On the Nine Years War see J. Childs, *The Nine Years War and the*

British Army, 1688– 1697: The Operations in the Low Countries (Manchester, 1991).

37 J. Childs, 'Fortune and War', *History Today*, 53 (2003), pp. 51–5.

38 Rose, *England in the 1690s*, p. 220.

39 Ibid., p. 197.

40 Ibid., p. 198. On providential discourse in this period, see Rose, *England in the 1690s*, ch. 6; idem, 'Providence, Protestant Union and the Godly Reformation in the 1690s', *Transactions of the Royal Historical Society*, 3 (1993), pp. 151–69; T. Claydon, *William III and the Godly Revolution* (Cambridge, 1996).

41 Hoppitt, p. 225.

42 Ibid., pp. 214–15.

43 T. Isaacs, 'The Anglican Hierarchy and the Reformation of Manners 1688–1738', *Journal of Ecclesiastical History*, 33 (1982) pp. 391–411.

44 Rose, *England in the 1690s*, p. 204.

45 On the Societies see ibid., ch. 6; Isaacs, 'Anglican Hierarchy'; Jennine Hurl-Eamon, 'Policing Male Heterosexuality: The Reformation of Manners Societies' Campaign Against the Brothels in Westminster, 1690–1720', *Journal of Social History*, vol. 37, no. 4 (2004), pp. 1017–35; R. B. Shoemaker, *Prosecution and Punishment: Petty Crime and the Law in London and Rural Middlesex, c. 1660–1725* (Cambridge, 1991); D. W. R. Bahlman, *The Moral Revolution of 1688* (New Haven, 1957); E. G. Rupp, *Religion in England 1688–1971* (Oxford, 1986); J. Spurr, 'The Church, the societies and moral revolution in England, 1688', in J. Walsh, C. Haydon and S. Taylor (eds.), *The Church of England c. 1688–c.1833: from Toleration to Tractarianism* (Cambridge, 1992); T. C. Curtis and W. A. Speck, 'The Societies for the Reformation of Manners: A Case Study in the Theory and Practice of Moral Reform', *Literature and History*, 3 (1976), pp. 45–64; S. H. Gregg '"A Truly Christian Hero": Religion, Effeminacy and Nation in the Writings of the Societies for Reformation of Manners', *Eighteenth-Century Life*, 25 (2001), pp. 17–28.

46 J. Woodward, *Religious Societies (Dr Woodward's 'Account')*, ed. D. E. Jenkins (Liverpool, 1935), p. 53.

47 Isaacs, p. 403.

48 Quoted in Speck, 'Mary II', *ODNB*.

49 Rose, *England in the 1690s*, p. 207.

50 Ibid., p. 209.

51 Isaacs, p. 401.

52 Woodward, p. 69.

53 Rose, *England in the 1690s*, p. 202.

54 [J. Dunton], *The Night-walker*, ed. G. Stevens Cox (Guernsey, 1970), p. 1.

55 Ibid., p. 3.

56 Ibid., pp. 17–18.

57 Ibid., p. 16.

58 *An Account of the Proceedings against Captain Edward Rigby* (London, 1698). This single-sheet account of the case can be found on Rictor Norton's excellent on-line sourcebook on homosexuality in eighteenth-century England, http://www.infopt.demon.co.uk/eighteen.htm.

59 Dunton, *The Night-walker*, pp. 13, 15.

60 Shoemaker, *Prosecution and Punishment*, pp. 250–1.

61 Hurl-Eamon, 'Policing Male Heterosexuality', pp. 1021–3.

62 Ibid., pp. 1025–6.

63 Shoemaker, *Prosecution and Punishment*, p. 241.

64 Woodward, *Religious Societies*, p. 52.

65 Ibid., p. 56.

66 Shoemaker, *Prosecution and Punishment*, pp. 261–2.

67 Quoted in Speck, 'Mary II', *ODNB*.

68 Rose, *England in the 1690s*, p. 43.

9 WILLIAM ALONE

1 T. Harris, *Politics under the Later Stuarts: Party Conflict in a Divided Society 1660–1715* (London, 1993), p. 218.

2 Ibid., p. 153.

3 Harris, *Politics under the Later Stuarts*, p. 156.

4 Hoppitt, p. 153.

5 C. Rose, *England in the 1690s* (Oxford, 1999), p. 52.

6 *C.J.*, vol. xi, p. 470.

7 D. Cressy, 'Literacy in 17th Century England, More Evidence',

Journal of Interdisciplinary History, viii (1977), pp. 141–50, at p. 144; J. S. W. Gibson, *The Hearth Tax, Other Later Stuart Tax Lists and the Association Oath Rolls* (Federation of Family History Society Publications, 1985).

8 *The Parliamentary Diary of Sir Richard Cocks*, ed. D. Hayton (Oxford, 1996), p. 36.

9 'Association Oath Rolls for Wiltshire', ed. L. J. Acton Pile, *Wiltshire Notes and Queries*, vi (1908–10), pp. 197–201, at 198. On the plot see J. Garrett, *The Triumphs of Providence, the Assassination Plot, 1696* (Cambridge, 1980).

10 D. Cressy, 'Binding the Nation: the Bonds of Association, 1584–1696', in *Tudor Rule and Revolution, Essays for G. R. Elton from his American Friends*, ed. D. J. Guth and J. W. McKenna (Cambridge, 1982), pp. 211–37, at p.228.

11 Ibid., p. 230, states that eighty-six JPs and 104 Deputy Lieutenants lost their posts for failing to subscribe or failing to do so quickly enough.

12 Ibid., p. 66.

13 PRO C213/204.

14 N. Brady, *A Sermon Preached at St Catherine Cree Church* (1696), pp. 22–3.

15 A., S., *God glorified, and the wicked snared* (1696), p. 21.

16 William Stephens, *A thanksgiving sermon preach'd before the Right Honourable the Lord Mayor, Court of Aldermen, sheriffs, and companies of the city of London at St Mary-le-bow, April 16, 1696, upon occasion of His Majesty's deliverence from a villanous assassination in order to a French invasion* (1696), the Dedication. See also T. Dorrington, *The Honour due to the Civil Magistrate* (1696); Peter Newcome, *A sermon preached in the parish church of Aldenham* (1696).

17 Cressy, 'Binding the Nation', p. 231.

18 PRO C213/213.

19 PRO C213/263B.

20 PRO C213/201.

21 PRO C213/191.

22 PRO C213/208.

23 Historical Manuscripts Commission, *Various MSS*, viii (London, 1913), p. 81.

24 D. Rubini, *Court and Country 1688–1702* (London, 1967), p. 66.

25 *The Association Oath Rolls of the British Plantations*, ed. W. Gandy (London, 1922), pp. 60, 67.

26 PRO C213/301.

27 PRO C213/196.

28 Ibid., pp. 328, 330. Steve Pincus, in his forthcoming book on the Revolution of 1688–89, has found MS sources indicating great interest among Catholics to associate, including lobbying foreign diplomats to beg Secretary Somers to allow them to present separate Catholic lists.

29 C213/181 pt. 5; /121 f. 90, 105; /251; /264 pt 8; /152; *Lancashire Association*, ed. Gandy, p. 85.

30 PRO C213/170b; for similar returns see C213/264 pt 1.

31 M. Geiter, 'Affirmation, Assassination and Association'; idem, 'William Penn and Jacobitism: A Smoking Gun?', *Historical Research*, LXXIII, 181 (2000), pp. 213–19.

32 Geiter, 'Affirmation, Assassination and Association', p. 277, 281. See also M. Goldie, 'James II and the Dissenters Revenge: The Commission of Enquiry 1688', *Historical Research*, LXVI (1993), pp. 53–88.

33 C213/2, ff. 3v, 4v, 7v, 9.

34 C213/129. Edward Browne, another Kent minister, would only take the oath in 'the sense of my Diocesan, Lord Archbishop of Canterbury.' See also C213/152 pt 4 for the subscription of Robert Ivory, vicar of Hoston parish, Middlesex: 'In ye sense I understand this association, and as farr as it concerns me, I subscribe it.'

35 C213/420.

36 C213/402; /417[same roll as Stafford clergy]/419/430/431/448/452.

37 C213/404.

38 Historical Manuscripts Commission, *Fitzherbert MSS* (London, 1893), pp. 38–9.

39 NRO, NCR 16 d/8, fos. 200v-1. In the end two association oath rolls were produced for the city, with another headed by the Mayor, Nicholas Bickerdike, following the Association's original wording,

NRO, NCR 13d/1. I thank Mark Knights for pointing me to these references.

40 Rubini, p. 66.

41 H. Prideaux, *Letter to J. Ellis, Under-Secretary of State, 1674–1722*, ed., E. M. Thompsom (Camden Soc, new series, 15, 1875), p. 174.

42 *The Axminster Ecclesiastica 1660–1698*, ed. K. W. H. Howard (Sheffield, 1976), p. 156.

43 Rose, *England in the 1690s*, p. 136.

44 Ibid., p. 137.

45 Ibid., p. 138.

46 Ibid., p. 139.

47 Ibid., p. 140. The evidence from the *Axminster Ecclesiastica* somewhat contradicts this picture, noting that many looked to blame the King for their misfortunes, though it concluded that in this 'few that spake aright, few that lamentingly say "What have I done?"', p. 157.

48 Kenyon, *Sunderland*, p. 297.

49 Hoppitt, p. 157.

50 The initial plan was that Kidd would defeat the pirates and seize their treasure, which would then be sold and the profits divided among the investors, including the 'hidden partners', Shrewsbury, Orford and Somers. Kidd, however, attacked shipping, including an East India Company vessel, that was clearly outside of his commission and also murdered a shipmate after mutinous rumblings among his crew. Kidd was eventually arrested in New York and transported back to England. He was hanged (after two attempts – the first rope broke) at Execution Wharf in Wapping on 23 May 1701. A very nice pub, the Captain Kidd, now marks this spot.

51 Rose, *England in the 1690s*, p. 59.

52 Hoppitt, p. 162.

CONCLUSION: THE END OF THE LINE

1 Ambrose Barnes, *Memoirs of the Life of Mr Ambrose Barnes*, ed. W. H. D. Longstaffe (Surtees Society, 50, 1867), p. 224.

2 J. Hoppitt, *A Land of Liberty: England, 1689–1727* (Oxford, 2000), p.

164.

3 P. 239.

4 Pp. 449–50. Of course, James II fared little better. Edward Baldwin's *The History of England for the Use of Schools* described the King as 'a gloomy bigot; he was very fit for a monk, but had no notion how to govern a kingdom'.

5 G. M. Trevelyan, *The History of England* (3rd edn., 1945), p. 472.

6 Similarly, immediately after the Revolution, the argument that William had acquired his title by conquest was officially suppressed by the government, as both the Crown and its ministers, for a variety of reasons, sought to emphasise the autonomy of the English political actors in events. Despite the fact that in 1689 Gilbert Burnet had asserted William's right to the throne via lawful conquest, in 1693 the Tory Edmund Bohun was publicly censured and stripped of his office as licenser of the press by Parliament for permitting the publication of Charles Blount's pamphlet *King William and Queen Mary Conquerors*; G. Burnet, *A Pastoral Letter* (1689), p. 21; J. P. Kenyon, *Revolution Principles* (Cambridge, 1977), p. 31.

7 *The Times*, 6 November 1888, p. 9. The statue was unveiled a year later and still stands on Victoria Embankment, Brixham. My thanks to Dr Philip Armitage of the Brixham Heritage Museum for this information and the postcard of the statue.

8 W. A. Speck, *James II* (Basingstoke, 2002), p. 145.

9 On Higden see my *Oxford Dictionary of National Biography* article and my 'The Decline of Conscience as a Political Guide: William Higden's *View of the English Constitution* (1709)', in H. E. Braun and E. Vallance (eds.), *Contexts of Conscience in Early Modern Europe, 1500–1700* (2004), ch. 6.

10 E. Gregg, *Queen Anne* (London, 1980), p. 308.

11 Ibid., p. 322.

12 Hoppitt, p. 311.

13 Ibid., p. 393. Hoppitt suggests that the actual reason for this rioting may have been disatisfaction with the Whig party's attempts to reverse the democratic advances after the Revolution and create one party rule in its place.

14 Ibid., p. 395.

15 E. Gregg, 'James Francis Stuart', *Oxford Dictionary of National Biography* (2004).

16 On 'Bonnie Prince Charlie', the '45 and Culloden see F. J. McLynn, *Charles Edward Stuart: A Tragedy in Many Acts* (London, 1988); idem, *The Jacobite Army in England* (Edinburgh, 1983); W. A. Speck, *The Butcher: The Duke of Cumberland and the Suppression of the '45* (Oxford, 1981); E. Cruickshanks, *Political Untouchables: The Tories and the '45* (London, 1979).

17 On the exiled Stuarts' continued practice of dispensing the royal touch, see M. Bloch, *The Royal Touch: Sacred Monarchy and Scrofula in England and France*, trans. J. E. Anderson (London, 1973), pp. 221–2.

18 The brothers Charles Manning Allen and John Carter Allen claimed to be the legitimate sons of Prince Charles, who had been fostered by their father, Thomas Gatehouse Allen, a lieutenant in the navy. The Allens were also leading figures in the Victorian revival and reinvention of Highland culture.

19 On the preaching effort see F. Deconinck-Brossard, 'The Churches and the "'45"', in *The Church and War*, Studies in Church History, 20 (1983)

20 *The Gentleman's Magazine For September* (1745), p. 483.

21 *The Times*, 5 September 1984.

22 D. Szechi, 'Mythistory versus History: The Fading of the Revolution of 1688', *The Historical Journal*, 33 (1990), p. 150.

23 On this see J. L. Malcolm, *To Keep and Bear Arms: The Origins of an Anglo-American Right* (Cambridge, Mass., 1994). On the impact of the Glorious Revolution in the Americas see R. S. Dunn, 'The Glorious Revolution and America', in *The Oxford History of the British Empire, Vol 1. The Origins of Empire*, ed. N. Canny (Oxford, 1998), pp. 445–67; D. S. Lovejoy, *The Glorious Revolution in America* (New York, 1972); J. M. Sosin, *English America and the Revolution of 1688* (Lincoln, Nebr., 1982); S. S. Webb, *Lord Churchill's Coup: The Anglo-American Empire and the Glorious Revolution Reconsidered* (New York, 1995).

24 The exact relationship between British industrialisation and the slave trade remains historically contested, but it is hard to argue that

slave labour and the profits of human traffic did not play a significant part in Britain's economic growth in the eighteenth century. See
E. Williams, *Capitalism and Slavery* (Chapel Hill, 1944) for the classic Marxist thesis, recently reaffirmed by J. E. Inikori, *Africans and
the Industrial Revolution in England* (Cambridge, 2002).

25 This point was made by Professor John Morrill in his recent Aylmer
Memorial Lecture, 'Rethinking Revolution in Seventeenth-Century
Britain'.

ACKNOWLEDGEMENTS

I would like to thank a number of people who offered me help and advice while I was writing this book. First, I must thank Tim Whiting at Little, Brown for taking on the project and offering such good editorial advice as the writing progressed. Bill Hamilton of A. M. Heath and Company made some valuable suggestions when I was struggling to think how to begin and end my story. Mark Knights, Steven Pincus, Justin Champion, Philip Armitage and Matthew McCormack were all very generous in providing me with information and references at various points. Martin O'Neill checked my Marx. The staff of the British Library, the National Archives, Kew, and the Special Collections department of the Sydney Jones Library, University of Liverpool, gave a great deal of help. As a work of synthesis, this book could not have been written without the efforts of previous scholars of the Glorious Revolution. Further acknowledgements are given in the footnotes but I am particularly indebted to the work of Robert Beddard, Tony Claydon, Tim Harris, Alan Marshall, Craig Rose, Lois Schwoerer, Julian Hoppitt, Barbara and Henri Van der Zee, John Spurr, Jonathan Israel, W. A. Speck, J. P. Kenyon, John Miller, David Ogg, T. B. Macaulay and Robin Clifton. Any errors in the text, are, of course, solely the result of authorial incompetence.

I would also like to thank the personnel of Staff House,

Abercromby Square, for seeing to my coffee and muffin needs. My wife Linnie bore the lost weekends spent writing with great stoicism and offered love and encouragement throughout. I hope the end result will be a book that is genuinely a pleasure to read.

BIBLIOGRAPHY

PRIMARY SOURCES

Bodleian Library, Oxford, MS Rawl. D 1232

British Library Add MS 28252, f. 53, 'List of members that refused the association to the Prince of Orange'

Calendar of State Papers Domestic Series (*C.S.P.D.*)

Calendar of State Papers Venetian Series (*C.S.P.V.*)

Commons Journals (*C.J.*)

Lords Journals

National Archives, Kew, PRO C213/ 1–476

Norfolk Record Office, NCR 12 B (1), 1684–9

    NCR 13d/1

    NCR 16 d/8, fos. 200v–1

Worcestershire Record Office, Worcestershire Quarter Session 1/1/176 1695–8

BOOKS AND PERIODICALS

(Unless otherwise stated the place of publication for works printed before 1700 is London.)

An Account of the Reasons of the Nobility and Gentry's Invitation of His Highnesse the Prince of Orange into England (1688)

An Account of what Passed at the Execution of the Late Duke of Monmouth (1685)

An Account of the Proceedings against Captain Edward Rigby (1698)

Alsop, V., *Mr Alsop's Speech to King James II* (1687)

Anne, Queen of Great Britain and Ireland, *The Letters and Diplomatic Instructions of Queen Anne*, ed. B. C. Brown (London, 1935)

The Association Oath Rolls of the British Plantations, ed. W. Gandy (London, 1922)

'Association Oath Rolls for Wiltshire', ed. L. J. Acton Pile, *Wiltshire Notes and Queries*, vi (1908–10)

The Axminster Ecclesiastica 1660–1698, ed. K. W. H. Howard (Sheffield, 1976)

Barnes, Ambrose, *Memoirs of the Life of Mr Ambrose Barnes*, ed. W. H. D. Longstaffe (Surtees Society, 50, 1867)

The Bloody Assizes, ed. J. G. Muddiman (1934)

Brady, N., *A Sermon Preached at St Catherine Cree Church* (1696)

Bramston, Sir J., *The Autobiography of Sir John Bramston* (London, Camden Society, o.s. 32, 1845)

Burnet, G., *A collection of papers relating to the present juncture of affairs in England* (1688)

Burnet, G., *A Pastoral Letter* (1689)

Cocks, Sir R., *The Parliamentary Diary of Sir Richard Cocks*, ed. D. Hayton (Oxford, 1996)

County of Buckingham Calendar of the Sessions Records, Vol. 1 1678 to 1694, ed. W. H. Hardy (Aylesbury, 1933)

Dangerfields Dance. Giving an Account of several Notorious Crimes by him Committed; viz. He pretended to be a Duke and feigned himself to be Monmouth (1685)

The Declaration of James, Duke of Monmouth, & the noblemen, gentlemen, & others now in arms (1685)

Dorrington, T., *The Honour due to the Civil Magistrate* (1696)

Duke Dangerfield declaring how he represented the D. of Mon— in the Country (1685)

[Dunton, J.], *The Athenian Gazette or Casuistical Mercury resolving all the most nice and curious questions proposed by the ingenious*, i (1691)

[Dunton, J.], *The Night-walker*, ed. G. Stevens Cox (Guernsey, 1970)

Elton, G. R., *The Tudor Constitution* (Cambridge, 1972, reprint)

Evelyn, John, *The Diary*, ed. E. S. de Beer (6 vols, Oxford, 1955).

Fagel, Caspar, *A letter writ by Mijn Heer Fagel, pensioner of Holland, to James Stewart, advocate, giving an account of the Prince and Princess of Orange's thoughts concerning the repeal of the Test* (1688 [i.e., 1687])

The Gentleman's Magazine For September (1745)

Gibson, J. S. W., *The Hearth Tax, Other Later Stuart Tax Lists and the Association Oath Rolls* (Federation of Family History Society Publications, 1985)

The Glory of the West, or the Virgins of Taunton-Dean (1685)

Halifax: Complete Works, ed. J. P. Kenyon (Harmondsworth, 1969)

Historical Manuscripts Commission, *Fitzherbert MSS* (London, 1893)

Historical Manuscripts Commission, *Kenyon MSS* (London, 1894)

Historical Manuscripts Commission, *Various MSS*, viii (London, 1913)

Kirk, Rev. R., 'London in 1689–90 by the Rev. R. Kirk', trans. D. Maclean, *Transactions of the London and Middlesex Archaeological Society*, n.s. VII (1937)

The Lord Delamere's letter to his tenants in Warrington, Lancashire, answered (1688)

The London Gazette (1687–8, nos. 2218–23)

Melius Inquirendum, or a further modest and impartial enquiry into the lawfulness of taking the new oath of allegiance (1689)

Newcome, H., *The Autobiography of Henry Newcome*, ed. R. Parkinson (2 vols., Manchester, Chetham Soc., 1852)

Newcome, P., *A sermon preached in the parish church of Aldenham* (1696)

A Parliamentary History of the Glorious Revolution, ed. D. L. Jones (HMSO, 1988)

Penal Laws and Test Act. Questions Touching Their Repeal Propounded in 1687–8 by James II, ed. Sir George Duckett (2 vols., London, 1882–3)

Pitman, H., *A Relation of the Great Sufferings and Strange Adventures of . . .* (1689), in *Stuart Tracts 1603–1693*, ed. C. H. Firth (London, 1903)

Prideaux, H., *Letter to J. Ellis, Under Secretary of State, 1674–1722*, ed. E. M. Thompson (Camden Soc., n.s., 15, 1875)

Quarter Sessions from Queen Elizabeth to Queen Anne . . . drawn from Original Records (Chiefly of the County of Devon), ed. A. H. A. Hamilton (London, 1878)

Records of the County of Wilts being extracts from the Quarter Sessions Great

Rolls of the Seventeenth Century, ed. B. H. Cunnington (Devizes, 1932)

Reresby, Sir J., *Memoirs of Sir John Reresby*, ed. Andrew Browning (Glasgow, 1936)

S., A., *God glorified, and the wicked snared* (1696)

Stephens, William, *A thanksgiving sermon preach'd before the Right Honourable the Lord Mayor, Court of Aldermen, sheriffs, and companies of the city of London at St Mary-le-bow, April 16, 1696, upon occasion of His Majesty's deliverence from a villanous assassination in order to a French invasion* (1696)

Stevens, John, *The Journal of John Stevens Containing a Brief Account of the War in Ireland 1689–1691*, ed. R. H. Murray (Oxford, 1912)

Williams, E. N. (ed.), *The Eighteenth Century Constitution 1688–1815* (Cambridge, 1960)

Woodward, J., *Religious Societies (Dr Woodward's 'Account')*, ed. D. E. Jenkins (Liverpool, 1935)

SECONDARY WORKS

Bahlman, D. W. R., *The Moral Revolution of 1688* (New Haven, 1957)

Baldwin, E., [William Godwin], *The History of England for the Use of Schools* (London, 1840)

Barnard, T. C., *The Kingdom of Ireland, 1641–1760* (2004)

Barrie, V., 'The Church of England in London in the Eighteenth-Century', *Proceedings of the British Academy*, 107 (2001)

Baxter, S. B., *William III* (London, 1966)

Beddard, R. A., 'Vincent Alsop and the Emancipation of Restoration Dissent', *Journal of Ecclesiastical History*, 24 (1973)

Beddard, R. A. (ed.), *The Revolutions of 1688* (Oxford, 1991)

Bennett, G. V., 'Loyalist Oxford and the Revolution' in *The History of the University of Oxford: vol. V. The Eighteenth Century*, eds. L. S. Sutherland and L. G. Mitchell (Oxford, 1986)

Berry, H., 'An Early Coffee-House Periodical and its Readers: the Athenian Mercury, 1691–7', *London Journal*, 25 (2000)

Bettey, J. H., 'Andrew Loder: A Seventeenth-Century Dorset Attorney', *Southern History*, 17 (1995)

Bloch, M., *The Royal Touch: Sacred Monarchy and Scrofula in England and France*, trans. J. E. Anderson (London, 1973)

Browning, A., *Thomas Osborne Earl of Danby and Duke of Leeds, 1632–1712* (2 vols., Glasgow, 1944, 1951)

Carswell, J., *The Descent on England: A Study of the English Revolution of 1688 and its European Background* (London, 1969)

Childs, J., *The Nine Years War and the British Army, 1688–1697: The Operations in the Low Countries* (Manchester, 1991)

Childs, I., 'Fortune of War', *History Today*, 53 (2003)

Clark, P., *The English Alehouse: A Social History* (London, 1983)

Claydon, T., 'William III's Declaration of Reasons and the Glorious Revolution', *The Historical Journal*, 39, 1 (1996)

Claydon, T., *William III and the Godly Revolution* (Cambridge, 1996)

Claydon, T., *William III: Profiles in Power* (Basingstoke, 2002)

Clifton, R., *The Last Popular Rebellion: The Western Rising of 1685* (Hounslow, 1984)

Cowan, I. B., *The Scottish Covenanters 1660–1688* (London, 1976)

Cressy, D., 'Literacy in 17th Century England, More Evidence', *Journal of Interdisciplinary History*, viii (1977)

Cressy, D., 'Binding the Nation the Bonds of Association, 1584–1696', in *Tudor Fall and Revolution, Essays for G. P. Elton from his American friends*, eds. D. J. Guth and J. W. McKenna (Cambridge, 1982)

Cruickshanks, E., *Political Untouchables: The Tories and the '45* (London, 1979)

Curtis, T. C. and Speck, W. A., 'The Societies for the Reformation of Manners: A Case Study in the Theory and Practice of Moral Reform', *Literature and History*, 3 (1976)

Davis, Natalie Zemon, *Society and Culture in Early Modern France* (London, 1975)

Deconinck-Brossard, F., 'The Churches and the "'45"', in *The Church and War* (Studies in Church History, 20, 1983)

Dickinson, H. T., 'The Eighteenth-Century Debate on the "Glorious Revolution"', *History*, 61 (1975)

Doherty, R., *The Williamite War in Ireland 1699–91* (Dublin, 1998)

Dunn, R. S., 'The Glorious Revolution and America', in *The Oxford*

History of the British Empire, Vol. 1. The Origins of Empire, ed. N. Canny (Oxford, 1998)

Earle, P., *Monmouth's Rebels* (London, 1977)

Ellis, A., *The Penny Universities: A History of the Coffee Houses* (London, 1956)

Fletcher, A., *Tudor Rebellions* (2nd edn., 1977)

Fox, A., *Oral and Literate Culture in England, 1500–1800* (Oxford, 2001)

Gardiner, B. M., *The Struggle against Absolute Monarchy* (London, 1908)

Garrett, J., *The Triumphs of Providence, the Assassination Plot, 1696* (Cambridge, 1980)

Geiter, M., 'Affirmation, Assassination and Association: the Quakers, Parliament and the Court in 1696', *Parliamentary History*, 16 (1997)

Geiter, M., 'William Penn and Jacobitism: A Smoking Gun?', *Historical Research*, 73 (2000)

Goldie, M., 'The Revolution of 1689 and the Structure of Political Argument', *Bulletin of Research in the Humanities*, lxxxiii (1980)

Goldie, M., 'John Locke's Circle and James II', *The Historical Journal*, 35 (1992)

Goldie, M., 'James II and the Dissenters Revenge: The Commission of Enquiry 1688', *Historical Research*, 66 (1993)

Gregg, E., *Queen Anne* (London, 1980)

Gregg, S. H., '"A Truly Christian Hero": Religion, Effeminacy and Nation in the Writings of the Societies for Reformation of Manners', *Eighteenth-Century Life*, 25 (2001)

Guttman, J., 'Battlers Becalmed', *Military History*, 7 (1991)

Gwynn, Robin D., 'James II in the light of his treatment of Huguenot refugees in England 1685–1686', *English Historical Review*, 92 (1977)

Hammond, P., 'Titus Oates and Sodomy', *Culture and Society in Britain 1660–1800*, ed. J. Black (Manchester, 1997)

Harris, F., *A Passion for Government, The Life of Sarah, Duchess of Marlborough* (Oxford, 1991)

Harris, J., 'The Grecian Coffee House and Political Debate in London 1688–1714', *London Journal*, 25 (2000)

Harris, T., 'London Crowds and the Revolution of 1688', in *By Force or By Default? The Revolution of 1688–89*, ed. E. Cruickshanks (Edinburgh, 1989)

Harris, T., *Politics under the Later Stuarts: Party Conflict in a Divided Society 1660–1715* (London, 1993)

Harris, T., 'The People, the Law, and the Constitution in Scotland and England: A Comparative Approach to the Glorious Revolution', *Journal of British Studies*, 38 (1999)

Hill, C., *The Century of Revolution, 1603–1714* (London, 2nd edn., 1972)

Hill, C., 'A Bourgeois Revolution?', in J. G. A. Pocock (ed.), *Three British Revolutions: 1641, 1688, 1776* (Princeton, 1980)

Hill, J. Michael, 'Killiecrankie and the Evolution of Highland Warfare', *War in History*, 1 (1994)

Hilton, G. H., 'The Irish Fright of 1688: Real Violence and Imagined Massacre', *Bulletin of the Institute of Historical Research*, 55 (1982)

Hopkins, P., *Glencoe and the End of the Highland War* (Edinburgh, 1986)

Hoppitt, J., *A Land of Liberty: England, 1689–1727* (Oxford, 2000)

Horwitz, H., *Revolution Politicks: The Career of Daniel Finch, 2nd Earl of Nottingham, 1647–1730* (Cambridge, 1968)

Horwitz, H., *Parliament, Policy and Politics in the Reign of William III* (Manchester, 1977)

Hosford, D., *Nottingham, Nobles and the North* (Hamden, Conn., 1976)

Houghton, T., *A Summary of the Principal Events in English History* (London, 1875)

Howell, R., *Puritans and Radicals in North England: Essays on the English Revolution* (Lanham, Md., 1984)

Hurl-Eamon, Jennine, 'Policing Male Heterosexuality: The Reformation of Manners Societies' Campaign Against the Brothels in Westminster, 1690–1720', *Journal of Social History*, 37, no. 4 (2004)

Inikori, J. E., *Africans and the Industrial Revolution in England* (Cambridge, 2002)

Isaacs, T., 'The Anglican Hierarchy and the Reformation of Manners 1688–1738', *Journal of Ecclesiastical History*, 33 (1982)

Israel, J. (ed.), *The Anglo-Dutch Moment* (Cambridge, 1991)

Israel, J. (ed.), *The Rise and Greatness of the Dutch Republic* (Oxford, 1995)

Jenkinson, H., 'What happened to the Great Seal of James II?', *Antiquaries Journal*, 23 (1943)

Kenyon, J. P., *Robert Spencer, Earl of Sunderland* (London, 1958)

Kenyon, J. P., *The Popish Plot* (London, 1972)

Kenyon, J. P., *Revolution Principles* (Cambridge, 1977)

Kenyon, J. P., *The Stuart Constitution, 1603–1688* (2nd edn., Cambridge, 1986)

Kenyon, J. P., 'The Commission for Ecclesiastical Causes 1686–1688: A Reconsideration', *The Historical Journal*, 34 (1991)

Kenyon, J. P. (ed.), *Dictionary of British History* (Ware, 1994)

Lamont, W., 'Richard Baxter, "Popery" and the origins of the English Civil War', *History*, 87 (2002)

Le Fevre, P., 'The Battle of Bantry Bay, 1 May 1689', *Irish Sword*, 18 (1990)

Lillywhite, B., *London Coffee Houses* (London, 1963)

Lovejoy, D. S., *The Glorious Revolution in America* (New York, 1972)

Macaulay, T. B., *The History of England from the Accession of James II*, ed. C. H. Firth (London, 1913–15)

MacGuire, J, *Kings in Conflict: The Revolutionary War in Ireland and its Aftermath, 1689–1750* (Belfast, 1990)

McInnes, A., 'The Revolution and the People', in *Britain after the Glorious Revolution*, ed. G. Holmes (Macmillan, 1969)

MacInnes, A. I., 'Repression and Conciliation: The Highland Dimension 1660–1688', *Scottish Historical Review*, LXV (1986)

McJimsey, R. D., 'A Country Divided? English Politics and the Nine Years War', *Albion*, 23 (1991)

McLynn, F. J., *The Jacobite Army in England* (Edinburgh, 1983)

McLynn, F. J., *Charles Edward Stuart: A Tragedy in Many Acts* (London, 1988)

Malcolm, J. L., 'The Creation of a "True Antient and Indubitable" Right: the English Bill of Rights and the Right to be Armed', *Journal of British Studies*, 32 (1993)

Malcolm, J. L., *To Keep and Bear Arms: The Origins of an Anglo-American Right* (Cambridge, Mass., 1994)

Marshall, A., *The Strange Death of Sir Edmund Bury Godfrey* (Stroud, 1999)

Marshall, A., 'To Make a Martyr, The Popish Plot and Protestant Propaganda', *History Today*, 47 (1997)

Miller, J., 'The Militia and the Army in the Reign of James II', *Historical Journal*, 16 (1973)

Miller, J., 'The Earl of Tyrconnel and James II's Irish Policy, 1685–1688', *Historical Journal*, 20 (1977)

Miller, J., *James II: a study in kingship* (Hove, 1977)

Miller, J., 'The Glorious Revolution: 'Contract' and 'Abdication' Reconsidered', *The Historical Journal*, 25 (1982)

Monod, P., *Jacobitism and the English People, 1688–1788* (Cambridge, 1989)

Morrill, J. S., 'The Sensible Revolution', in his *The Nature of the English Revolution* (Harlow, 1993)

Morton, A. L., *A People's History of England* (London, 1938)

Mulloy, S., 'French eye-witnesses of the Boyne', *Irish Sword*, 15 (1982)

Murtagh, D. and H., 'Irish Jacobite Army, 1689–91' in *Irish Sword*, 18 (1990)

Ogg, D., *England in the Reigns of James II and William III* (Oxford, 1969)

Pincus, S., '"Coffee Politicians Does Create": Coffeehouses and Restoration Political Culture', *Journal of Modern History*, 67 (1995)

Pincus, S., '"To Protect English Liberties", The English Nationalist Revolution of 1688–9, in *Protestantism and National Identity*, eds. T. Claydon and I. McBride (Cambridge, 1999)

Quintilla, M. S., 'Late Seventeenth-Century Indentured Servants in Barbados', *The Journal of Caribbean History*, 27 (1993)

Ransome, Mrs Cyril, *Elementary History of England* (London,1897)

Rose, C., 'Providence, Protestant Union and the Godly Reformation in the 1690s', *Transactions of the Royal Historical Society*, 3 (1993)

Rose, C., *England in the 1690s* (Oxford, 1999)

Ross, R., *Outlines of English History for Junior Classes in Schools* (London, 1860)

Rubini, D., *Court and Country 1688–1702* (London, 1967)

Rupp, E. G., *Religion in England 1688–1971* (Oxford, 1986)

Sachse, W. K., 'The Mob and the Revolution of 1688', *Journal of British Studies*, 4 (1964)

Schwoerer, L., 'Propaganda in the Revolution of 1688–9', *American Historical Review*, 82 (1977)

Schwoerer, L., 'Press and Parliament in the Revolution of 1689', *Historical Journal*, 20, no. 3 (1977)

Schwoerer, L., 'The Glorious Revolution as Spectacle: A New

Perspective', in *England's Rise to Greatness, 1660–1763*, ed. S. B. Baxter (Los Angeles, 1984)

Schwoerer, L., 'Images of Queen Mary II, 1689–95', *Renaissance Quarterly*, 42 (1989)

Sharp, B., 'Popular Political Opinion in England 1660–1685', *History of European Ideas*, 10, no. 1 (1989)

Shoemaker, R. B., *Prosecution and Punishment: Petty Crime and the law in London and Rural Middlesex, c. 1660–1725* (Cambridge, 1991)

Short, M., 'The Corporation of Hull and the Government of James II, 1687–8', *Historical Research*, 71 (1998)

Slaughter, T. P., ' "Abdicate" and "Contract" in the Glorious Revolution', *Historical Journal*, 24 (1981)

Slaughter, T. P., '"Abdicate" and "Contract" restored', *Historical Journal*, 28 (1985)

Sosin, J. M., *English America and the Revolution of 1688* (Lincoln, Nebr., 1982)

Speck, W. A., *The Butcher: The Duke of Cumberland and the Suppression of the '45* (Oxford, 1981)

Speck, W. A., 'The Orangist Conspiracy Against James II', *Historical Journal*, 30 (1987)

Speck, W. A., *Reluctant Revolutionaries; Englishmen and the Revolution of 1688* (Oxford, 1988)

Speck, W. A., 'The Revolution of 1688 in the North', *Northern History*, 25 (1989)

Speck, W. A., *James II* (Basingstoke, 2002)

Spurr, J., 'The Church, the societies and moral revolution in England, 1688', in J. Walsh, C. Haydon and S. Taylor (eds.), *The Church of England c. 1688–c.1833: from Toleration to Tractarianism* (Cambridge, 1992)

Spurr, J., *England in the 1670s: 'This Masquerading Age'* (Oxford, 2000)

Steele, I. K., 'Communicating an English Revolution to the Colonies, 1688–1689', *Journal of British Studies*, 24 (1985)

Szechi, D., 'Mythistory versus History: The Fading of the Revolution of 1688', *Historical Journal*, 33 (1990)

Szechi, D., 'The Jacobite Revolution Settlement, 1689–1696', *English Historical Review*, 108 (1993)

Taillemaite, E., 'Un Conflict Vauban-Louvois', *Histoire, Economie et Société*, 15 (1996)

Thompson, E. P., *Whigs and Hunters: the origins of the black act* (London, 1976)

Thornton, N., 'Guarding the Glorious Revolution', *Quarterly Journal of Military History*, 13 (2001)

Timmons, S. A., 'Executions following Monmouth's Rebellion: A Missing Link', *Historical Research*, 76 (2003)

Trevelyan, G. M., *The History of England* (3rd edn., London, 1945)

Twigg, J., *The University of Cambridge and the English Revolution* (Woodbridge, 1990)

Vallance, E., 'The Decline of Conscience as a Political Guide: William Higden's *View of the English Constitution* (1709)' in H. E. Braun and E. Vallance (eds.), *Contexts of Conscience in Early Modern Europe, 1500–1700* (2004)

Villiers, P., 'Victoire de Barfleur ou Défaite de la Hougue: 29 Mai–2 Juin 1692', *Revue du Nord*, 74 (1992)

Waller, M., *Ungrateful Daughters: The Stuart Princesses Who Stole Their Father's Crown* (London, 2002)

Warner G. T., and Marten, C. H. K., *The Groundwork of British History* (London, 1936)

Watson, J. N. P., *Captain-General and Rebel Chief, the Life of James, Duke of Monmouth* (London, 1979)

Webb, S. S., *Lord Churchill's Coup: The Anglo-American Empire and the Glorious Revolution Reconsidered* (New York, 1995)

Weil, R., *Political Passions, Gender, the Family and Political Argument: 1680–1714* (Manchester, 1999)

Wigfield, W. MacDonald, *The Monmouth Rebellion: A Social History* (Bradford-on-Avon, 1980)

Williams, E., *Capitalism and Slavery* (Chapel Hill, 1944)

Zaller, R., 'Breaking the Vessels: the Desacralization of Monarchy in Early Modern England', *Sixteenth Century Journal*, 29 (1998)

Zee, Henri and Barbara Van der, *1688 Revolution in the Family* (Harmondsworth, 1988)

Zook, M., '"The Bloody Assizes" Whig Martyrdom and Memory after the Glorious Revolution', *Albion*, 27 (1995)

ON-LINE RESOURCES AND UNPUBLISHED WORK

Barclay, Andrew, review of Louis G. Schwoerer, *The Ingenious Mr Henry Care, Restoration Publicist*, H-Albion, H-Net Reviews, April 2004

Barclay, Andrew, 'The impact of James II on the departments of the royal household' (Cambridge University PhD thesis, 1994)

Findon, J. C., 'The Non-Jurors and the Church of England 1689–1716' (Oxford University D.Phil thesis 1978)

Norton, R., sourcebook on homosexuality in eighteenth-century England http://www.infopt.demon.co.uk/eighteen.htm

Oxford Dictionary of National Biography: from the earliest times to the year 2000 eds. H. C. G. Matthew and Brian Harrison (Oxford, 2004) http://www.oxforddnb.com

INDEX